Taste

DENISE GIGANTE

Taste

A LITERARY HISTORY

Yale University Press
New Haven &
London

Designed by Sonia L. Shannon
Set in Postscript Sabon type by Keystone Typesetting, Inc.
Printed in the United States of America.

Library of Congress Cataloging-in-Publication Data
Gigante, Denise, 1965–
    Taste : a literary history / Denise Gigante.
        p.   cm.
    Includes bibliographical references and index.
    ISBN 978-0-300-17224-9
    1. English literature — History and criticism. 2. Taste in literature. 3. Food habits in literature. 4. Gastronomy in literature. 5. Aesthetics, British. 6. Food in literature. I. Title.
PR408.T37G54 2005
820.9′3559 — dc22
2004058452

A catalogue record for this book is available from the British Library.

The paper in this book meets the guidelines for permanence and durability of the Committee on Production Guidelines for Book Longevity of the Council on Library Resources.

Contents

Acknowledgments

Like most books, this one is hardly the product of one mind. My deepest debts of gratitude are to Harold Bloom for inspiring and supporting my life as a scholar; to Jay Fliegelman for his keen insight into this project and other matters; and to Christopher Rovee for uncompromising companionship throughout the writing of this book.

Thanks to generous, meticulous comments by James Engell on an earlier version of the manuscript, *Taste* has become what it is. And I am very grateful to Starry Schor and Michael Wood, both of Princeton University, for wading through early drafts and allowing me to brush up against their original minds.

I wish to acknowledge a number of scholars for their perspicacity and helpful commentary at various points along the way, particularly Ian Balfour, John Bender, Terry Castle, David L. Clark, Ian Duncan, Diana Fuss, Erik Gray, Mark Hansen, Andrea Henderson, Gavin Jones, Rob Kaufman, Jonathan Lamb, Seth Lerer, Herbie Lindenberger, Anne Mellor, Timothy Morton, Joanna Picciotto, Robert Polhemus, Tilottama Rajan, Christopher Ricks, Hollis Robbins, Chuck Rzepka, Nigel Smith, Abraham Stoll, David Wagenknecht, Joseph Wittreich, and Susan Wolfson. I am grateful to my editors, John Kulka and Nancy Moore of Yale University Press, and to Otto Bohlmann and Tim Blackburn for copyeditorial interventions. Three Stanford undergraduates, Mark Ganek, Jenny Kim, and Elizabeth Ridgeway, provided valuable research assistance.

I have accrued debts to several institutions, organizations, and programs for financial support of this project, including the Keats-Shelley Association of America, Princeton University's Center for Human Values and Dean's Fund for Scholarly Travel, the Stanford Humanities Center, and the School of Humanities and Sciences at Stanford. In addition, the International Conference on Romanticism, the North American Society for the Study of Romanticism, and the Nineteenth-Century British Cultural Studies Working Group at the University of California at Berkeley offered critical opportunities to work through parts of the book. I thank the Trustees of Boston University for permission to reprint "Keats's Nausea," an earlier version of which appeared in *Studies in Romanticism* (2001), and Johns Hopkins University Press for permission to reprint "Milton's Aesthetics of Eating" from *Diacritics* (2000) in chapter 2.

My immeasurable debts to my parents, David and Frances Gigante, and in-laws, Carolyn and George Collier, as well as to Yvonne Toepfer, who among other things helped to raise our beautiful boy Julian Rovee during the first three years of his life, should go without saying but will not go unrecorded here.

Abbreviations

AN   Immanuel Kant, *Anthropology from a Pragmatic Point of View,*
       trans. Victor Lyle Dowdell (Carbondale: Southern Illinois
       University Press, 1978).

BLJ   George Gordon, Lord Byron, *Byron's Letters and Journals,* ed.
       Leslie A. Marchand. 13 vols. (Cambridge, Mass.: Harvard
       University Press, 1976).

C   Anthony Ashley Cooper, third earl of Shaftesbury, *Characteristics
       of Men, Manners, Opinions, Times,* ed. Lawrence E. Klein
       (Cambridge: Cambridge University Press, 1999).

CCL   Samuel Taylor Coleridge, *Collected Letters,* ed. Earl Leslie Griggs.
       6 vols. (Oxford: Clarendon Press, 1956–71).

CCW   Samuel Taylor Coleridge, *The Collected Works of Samuel Taylor
       Coleridge,* gen. ed. Kathleen Coburn. 14 vols. (Princeton: Princeton
       University Press, 1969–98).

CDP   Plato. *The Collected Dialogues of Plato; including the Letters,* ed.
       Edith Hamilton and Huntington Cairns (Princeton: Princeton
       University Press, 1961).

CJ   Immanuel Kant, *The Critique of Judgement,* trans. James Creed
       Meredith (Oxford: Clarendon Press, 1952).

CN   Samuel Taylor Coleridge, *The Notebooks of Samuel Taylor Coleridge,* ed. Kathleen Coburn. 5 vols.; each in 2 vols.: 1 text, 2 notes (London: Routledge, 2002).

CPB   William Blake, *The Complete Poetry and Prose of William Blake,* ed. David V. Erdman. 2d ed. (New York: Anchor, 1988).

DJ   George Gordon, Lord Byron, *Don Juan,* in *The Complete Poetical Works,* ed. Jerome J. McGann. 7 vols. (Oxford: Clarendon Press, 1991).

EMP   David Hume, *Essays: Moral, Political, and Literary,* ed. Eugene F. Miller. 2d ed. (Indianapolis: Liberty Fund, 1985).

FB   Bernard Mandeville, *The Fable of the Bees: or Private Vices, Publick Benefits,* ed. F. B. Kaye. 2 vols. (Oxford: Clarendon Press, 1924).

FBP   William Wordsworth, *The Fourteen-Book Prelude,* ed. W. J. B. Owen (Ithaca: Cornell University Press, 1985).

HCW   William Hazlitt, *The Complete Works of William Hazlitt,* ed. P. P. Howe. 21 vols. (London: J. M. Dent, 1930).

KC   Hyder Edward Rollins, ed. *The Keats Circle.* 2 vols. 2d ed. (Cambridge, Mass.: Harvard University Press, 1965).

KCP   John Keats, *Complete Poems,* ed. Jack Stillinger (Cambridge, Mass.: Harvard University Press, 1978); all poetry cited by line number is from this edition.

KL   John Keats, *The Letters of John Keats.* 2 vols. (Cambridge, Mass.: Harvard University Press, 1958).

KPL   John Keats, *Keats's Paradise Lost,* ed. Beth Lau (Gainseville: University Press of Florida, 1998).

LEY   William and Dorothy Wordsworth, *The Letters of William and Dorothy Wordsworth: The Early Years,* ed. Ernest De Selincourt. 2d ed., ed. Chester L. Shaver (Oxford: Clarendon Press, 1967).

LL   Charles and Mary Lamb, *The Letters of Charles Lamb, to which are added those of his sister, Mary Lamb,* ed. E. V. Lucas. 3 vols. (London: Methuen, 1935): the authoritative edition of letters from October 1817 through 1843.

LLY   William and Dorothy Wordsworth, *The Letters of William and Dorothy Wordsworth: The Later Years,* ed. Ernest De Selincourt, vols. 6–7. 2d ed., ed. Alan G. Hill (Oxford: Clarendon Press, 1988).

LM   Charles and Mary Lamb, *The Letters of Charles and Mary Anne Lamb,* ed. Edwin W. Marrs Jr. 3 vols. (Ithaca: Cornell University

Press, 1975): the authoritative, though incomplete, edition of
letters from May 27, 1796, through October 1817.

LMY   Ernest De Selincourt, ed., *The Letters of William and Dorothy
Wordsworth: The Middle Years,* 2nd edition Mary Moorman
(Oxford: Clarendon, 1970).

PE   Edmund Burke, *A Philosophical Enquiry into the Origin of Our
Ideas of the Sublime and Beautiful,* ed. James T. Boulton (Notre
Dame: University of Notre Dame Press, 1958).

PL/PR   John Milton, *Complete Poems and Major Prose,* ed. Merritt Y.
Hughes (New York: Odyssey, 1957); poetry is cited *PL* for *Paradise
Lost; PR* for *Paradise Regained;* and by line number for other
poems.

PN   Georg Wilhelm Friedrich Hegel, *Philosophy of Nature; Being Part
Two of the Encyclopaedia of the Philosophical Sciences* (1830),
trans. A. V. Miller (Oxford: Clarendon Press, 1970).

PRL   William Wordsworth, *The Prelude: 1799, 1805, 1850,* ed.
Jonathan Wordsworth, M. H. Abrams, and Stephen Gill (New
York: W. W. Norton, 1979).

PT   Jean Anthelme Brillat-Savarin, *The Physiology of Taste: Or,
Meditations on Transcendental Gastronomy,* trans. M. F. K. Fisher
(Washington, D.C.: Counterpoint Press, 1949).

PW   William Wordsworth, *The Prose Works of William Wordsworth,*
ed. W. J. B. Owen and Jane Worthington Smyser. 3 vols. (Oxford:
Clarendon Press, 1974).

R   Edmund Burke, *Reflections on the Revolution in France,* ed.
Thomas H. D. Mahoney (Indianapolis: Bobbs-Merrill, 1955).

SP   Percy Bysshe Shelley, *Shelley's Prose; or the Trumpet of a Prophecy,*
ed. David Lee Clark (London: Fourth Estate, 1988).

SPP   Percy Bysshe Shelley, *Shelley's Poetry and Prose,* ed. Donald H.
Reiman and Sharon B. Powers (New York: W. W. Norton, 1977).

SPT   Joseph Addison, *The Spectator,* ed. D. F. Bond. 5 vols. (Oxford:
Clarendon Press, 1965).

SPW   Jonathan Swift, *The Prose Works,* ed. Herbert Davis. 14 vols.
(Oxford: Basil Blackwell, 1939–68).

TBP   William Wordsworth, *The Thirteen-Book Prelude,* ed. Mark L.
Reed. 2 vols. (Ithaca: Cornell University Press, 1990).

THH   Bernard Mandeville, *A Treatise on the Hypochondriack and
Hysterick Passions* (1711 reprint; New York: Arno Press, 1976).

THN   David Hume, *A Treatise of Human Nature,* ed. L. A. Selby Bigge.
2d ed. (Oxford: Clarendon Press, 1978).

WCL   Charles and Mary Lamb, *The Works of Charles and Mary Lamb,*
        ed. E. V. Lucas. 8 vols. (London: Methuen, 1903).
WMP   William Makepeace Thackeray, *The Works of William Makepeace
        Thackeray.* 26 vols. (New York: C. L. Bowman, 1915).
WU   William Wordsworth, *The Five-Book Prelude,* ed. Duncan Wu
        (Oxford: Blackwell, 1997).
YP   John Milton, *Complete Prose Works of John Milton,* ed. Don M.
        Wolfe et al. 8 vols. (New Haven: Yale University Press, 1953–82).

Taste

Aesthetics and Appetite: An Introduction

As soon as an edible body has been put into the mouth, it is seized upon, gases, moisture, and all, without possibility of retreat.

Lips stop whatever might try to escape; the teeth bite and break it; saliva drenches it; the tongue mashes and churns it; a breathlike sucking pushes it toward the gullet; the tongue lifts up to make it slide and slip; the sense of smell appreciates it as it passes the nasal channel, and it is pulled down into the stomach to be submitted to sundry baser transformations without, in this whole metamorphosis, a single atom or drop or particle having been missed by the powers of appreciation of the taste sense.

—*Jean Anthelme Brillat-Savarin*, The Physiology of Taste *(1826)*

Romantic gastronomers, self-proclaimed professors of taste, considered the profoundly physical pleasures of the palate to be the pinnacle of aesthetic appreciation. Various "committees of taste" established in early nineteenth-century Britain elevated food to the status of the fine arts, adopting the same juridical language and concern with philosophical principles that defined the eighteenth-century discourse of aesthetics. Just as the Enlightenment Man of Taste worked hard to distinguish specific qualities of beauty and to pronounce exact judgments of taste, the Romantic gourmand worked with equal aesthetic imperative to distinguish among different flavors of food.[1] Yet food had never been far from the concept of mental discrimination, and from the earliest instantiations of British empiricist aesthetics at the outset of the eighteenth century its vocabulary was invoked in relation to the concept of taste. Taste, call it *gustus, gusto,* or *goût* (the Continent, after all, got there before the English), was an apt metaphor for a kind of pleasure that does not submit to objective laws: *de gustibus non est disputandum; chacun à son goût; sobre los gustos, no hai disputa;* or, there is no disputing about taste. While most accounts of aesthetic history avoid the gustatory aspect of taste, this book offers a literary history of taste in all its full-bodied flavor. What writers in this history discover is the creative power of taste as a trope for aesthetic judgment and its essential role in generating our very sense of self.

Unlike classical aesthetics, which were primarily linked to the higher senses of sight and hearing, modern aesthetics as evolved from the concept of taste involves pleasure, and pleasure is its own way of knowing. Genealogies that trace modern aesthetic theory back through British empiricism to the mid-seventeenth-century European concern with *goût* and *gusto* skip over a source much closer to home. For at roughly the same time that "taste" was gaining currency as a term for aesthetic experience, Milton was struggling to represent the gustatory metaphor in *Paradise Lost* and *Regained*. Satan conjures appetite, manipulating consumer desire and turning the fruit into more than a common apple, or dietary container of nutriments. Eve does not give into temptation to taste the fruit because she is hungry, any more than Christ resists the luscious feasts of *Paradise Regained* because he has no hunger. As these works suggest, the Miltonic fall involves more than epistemological or moral errors of judgment: it also involves a kind of judgment inextricable from pleasure. That taste involves pleasure is a lesson the Romantics learn from Milton and that we learn from Romanticism — and the literary history presented here reroutes aesthetic history from its origins in European neoclassicism, or British moral-sense philosophy, to the forgotten ground of its metaphorical genesis in Milton.[2]

As Percy Bysshe Shelley remarks in *A Defence of Poetry,* poetic "language is vitally metaphorical; that is, it marks the before unapprehended relations of things" (*SPP* 482), and most theorists of metaphor agree that rather than operating by reference to external reality or truth, it has a "world-generating" capacity.[3] Writers in the literary history of taste wield the gustatory metaphor of taste to project and reveal a number of worlds, from Milton's alimentary cosmology, to Wordsworth's transcendentally feeding (and digesting) mind, to Keats's experience of epic nausea. Confronting the metaphor of consumption in the field of representation, as this book will show, these writers perform their own critique of the Romantic ideology (conceived as a transcendence of history by aesthetics) in a manner that anticipates the kind of literary criticism that presumes to displace it. Other disciplinary communities, including historians, anthropologists, economists, and sociologists, have recognized that the enormous cultural changes that came into being during the Romantic era were the result not only of an Industrial Revolution, but of a Consumer Revolution as well. Unlike the social structures of production, consumption is considered a matter of individual choice, and the so-called Man of Taste had to navigate an increasing tide of consumables, seeking distinction through the exercise of discrimination.[4] An overdetermined, multivalenced concept, consumption is grounded in the power of metaphor, and it is time for literary history to examine rigorously its related subsets of taste and appetite. By the turn of the nineteenth century, the dialectical counterpart to taste was not only bodily appetite but also the wider sphere of material desires fed by consumer culture. Romantic writers deployed the gustatory metaphor of taste in the full awareness that by this point in the extended culture of taste, its subsets were not only taste and appetite but also a commingled version of the two in consumerism. When mapped against its philosophical and physiological background in the long eighteenth century, the literary history of taste described by the chapters of this book reveals the complex relations between aesthetic taste and the more substantial phenomena of appetite.

The Philosophy of Taste

Taste has always ranked low on the philosophical hierarchy of the senses as a means of ingress to the mind.[5] Whereas sight and hearing allow for a proper representative distance from the object of contemplation (hence for the regulating principles of consciousness and morality), taste, like its closest cousin smell, is bound up with the chemical physiology of the body. The two are thought to convey immediate pleasure or disgust, serving to mediate discrete individuals (if at all) based on bodily instinct without reference to shared ideals. Not only is taste bound up with the unruly flesh; traditionally, it is associated with *too* intense bodily pleasure and the consequent dangers of excess. While the exertion of the higher senses theoretically leads to more mind, the exercise of the lower senses of taste and smell can result in too much body and its various forms of sensuousness: to indulge the most basic human appetites is to risk becoming a glutton, a drunkard, or a voluptuary.[6] All the major Enlightenment philosophers of taste were involved in the civilizing process of sublimating the tasteful essence of selfhood from its own matter and motions, appetites and aversions, passions and physical sensibilities. Above all, what the culture of taste energetically resisted was the idea that human beings were propelled not by natural cravings for virtue, beauty, and truth but by appetites that could not be civilized or distinguished from those of brutes.

Human beings may be taxonomized as *Homo sapiens*, but in the eighteenth century the man of reason was really only half the story of the embodied Man of Taste, whose other half was the man of sensibility and feeling. John Locke's *Essay Concerning Human Understanding* (1690), a source for the many paradoxes of identity that centered on the concept of the self in this period, fused the related binaries of the man of sense and the man of sensibility, the private citizen and the civic individual, the self-made man and the passive product of circumstantial experience. By doing away with the concept of innate ideas, Locke made identity (no longer "identity" or assumed oneness) into a more complex social construct of selfhood dependent on how human beings process experience through the senses. Once the flesh was involved in the formation of selfhood, identity could not be explained away on Cartesian principles as a disembodied thinking spirit. As Hume and other British empiricist philosophers discovered, a gap had opened up between the mind and the world of sensory reality, mediated only by the senses, which were themselves highly unreliable. How could one tell, for instance, whether the sense impressions conveyed to the mind were an accurate representation of the world outside? The result was a highly unstable human subject whose doubts were epistemological bleeding into the ontological.

Locke himself did not worry too much about extrapolating a higher selfhood from human substance. While he did insist that something like a soul must exist (if only not to clash directly with scholastic Christian tradition), he never pinned down the exact relation of this soul to matter, or of the soul to mind, or to the thing he calls identity. Rather, the metaphysical question of what it means to be human — or more than an assemblage of animal anatomy — was a bone he tossed to the theologians or "those, who have better thought of that matter."[7] The empirical tradition that grew up in his wake of course had much more (if not better) thought on the matter. Ernst Cassirer argues that the central project of Enlightenment humanism was to characterize the essence of the human and that in devoting itself to this central problem philosophy extended past the limited terrain of metaphysics.[8] By this logic, ventures in political philosophy attempting to determine the social nature of humanity through the State of Nature were naturally consubstantial with efforts of comparative anatomists to distinguish the animal economy of humans from that of other organisms. This wide-ranging effort to sublimate the human from the physiological ground of its lived experience was simultaneously an effort to sublimate the social body into something more than the sum of its parts.

As one might expect, such an effort resulted in a proliferating set of definitions of what it meant to be human. If "man" was no longer a thinking animal, what kind of an animal was he? Benjamin Franklin proposed "a tool-making animal," to which James Boswell replied that he was rather "a Cooking Animal": "The beasts have memory, judgment, and all the faculties and passions of our mind, in a certain degree; but no beast is a cook," he claimed. "The trick of the monkey using the cat's paw to roast a chestnut, is only a piece of shrewd malice in that *turpissima bestia,* which humbles us so sadly by its similarity to us."[9] Boswell's definition of man as *homo culinarius,* the seeming offhand remark of an urban bon vivant, is offered here in conversation with Burke at a time when contending definitions of civic humanism (the condition of our existence in civil society) were jostling for cultural dominance.

Man was an industrious animal, a culinary animal, and, more broadly, "a social animal," as the philosopher William Godwin remarked in *An Enquiry Concerning Political Justice* (1793).[10] As a social animal, man doesn't just eat: he dines. Anthropologists today confirm that while human beings have much in common with beasts, only humans develop what are called cuisines: "Humans are virtually the only creatures in the world that observe rules about what is eaten, how it is prepared, and with whom it is to be eaten. The only other animals that do anything remotely approximate are the Japanese macaque monkeys, among which strong food preferences have developed."[11] Whether the Japanese macaque monkeys are to be identified with Boswell's *turpissima bestia* I am unqualified to determine, but the idea that symbolically regulated, discretionary dining is unique to human beings recurs throughout the Century of Taste.[12] Combined with an evolving etiquette and a social imperative for commensality, dining in civilized society involved a range of food preferences through which the individual could establish claims to distinction. Romantic epicureans and aesthetic philosophers alike stressed the importance of taste, which governed the cultural politics of food and commensality as well as the metaphysical implications of eating.

The emergent public sphere made possible through commercialism entailed a belief that people were held together volitionally through bonds of shared feeling, rather than squashed together through external authority into the shape of a political body. In a very real sense, the Enlightenment culture of taste was a reaction against Hobbes's "Leviathan," depicted in the 1651 frontispiece to the work of that title as a gigantic human torso crammed full of tiny anonymous citizens and presided over by a monarchical Stuart head. For Hobbes, society was a clash of individual appetites, and his political treatise defined all human activity as the result of appetite or aversion: a mental instinct toward or away from an object, regulated by external control. His portrait of the state as an aggregation of appetites only gained sway after Locke raised the stakes of bodily experience for human identity. Once the body itself could think, the Hobbesian image of the state was especially threatening.

Like other early modern theorists, Hobbes gave appetite the serious philosophical attention that taste would provoke in the eighteenth-century discourse of aesthetics. Contemporary physiology identified three distinct categories of appetite, including the "natural," the "animal," and the "voluntary" (or "intellective"). As J. B. Bamborough explains, natural appetite was "the tendency of things to move according to their nature," and "Sensitive or Animal Appetite was the power which controlled the vital functions common to man and beast, such as breathing, digestion and the circulation of the blood."[13] However, the appetites to which the most meaning could be ascribed—and with which philosophers like Hobbes were most concerned—were the voluntary appetites for pleasure and their counterpart, an aversion to pain. These voluntary appetites were further divided into "concupiscible" or "coveting" appetites, which perceived pleasure and pain apart from circumstance, and "irascible" or "invading" appetites, which were stimulated by obstruction.[14] In *Leviathan*, Hobbes defined these twin voluntary drives as a mental propulsion or endeavor that "when it is toward something which causes it, is called APPETITE, or DESIRE; the later, being the generall name; and the other, often-times restrayned to signifie the Desire of Food, namely *Hunger* and *Thirst*"; by contrast, "when the Endeavour is fromward something, it is generally called AVERSION." Of these mental cravings driving human behavior, the most powerful was an appetite for (or aversion to) food. Physical motion could be accounted for by means of nerves and muscles, but it was far more difficult to explain the mechanism of mental activity. Hobbes wrote that "the Schooles find in meere Appetite to go, or move, no actuall Motion at all: but because some Motion they must acknowledge, they call it Metaphoricall Motion; which is but an absurd speech: for though Words may be called metaphoricall; Bodies, and Motions cannot."[15] Appetite regulated a Hobbesian world in which life was nasty, brutish, and short with no room for metaphorical motion. The Enlightenment culture of taste, by contrast, would train this appetite into a metaphorical endeavor—a taste for this or that.

By the eighteenth century, physicality provided access to cognitive dimensions of human experience, such as epistemology, morality, aesthetic pleasures and pains; the umbrella term for this new mode of embodied cognition was taste. Anthony Ashley Cooper, third earl of Shaftesbury, was the prototype for the eighteenth-century Man of Taste, and the moral and intellectual struggle waged between him and his philosophical rival, Bernard Mandeville, highlights the tension between the conceptual spheres of taste and appetite in the early years of the eighteenth century. Mandeville shared with Shaftesbury certain fundamental assumptions of Whig philosophy regarding state, religious authority, and individual freedom, but the two differed radically over their view of human nature and its ability to be refined.[16] Mandeville's *Fable of the Bees,* published in 1714 and expanded in 1723 as a more direct response to Shaftesbury, shocked its readers as a consumerist legacy of Hobbes. Mandeville also viewed the state as an organization of clashing appetites in which the civic "bee" buzzes about its business, seeking to satisfy private desires (appetites and aversions) in a consuming, and increasingly consumerist, crowd. Such a vision ran counter to the ideal of the *sensus communis,* promoted by Shaftesbury and other taste philosophers as a community united in a tasteful harmony of feeling.

The philosophical project of sublimating the Man of Taste from his own matter and motions involved the parallel rhetorical project of sublimating taste from the conceptual apparatus of appetite. As Burke remarked in his 1759 "Introduction on Taste," "if Taste has no fixed principles, if the imagination is not affected according to some invariable and certain laws . . . it must be judged an useless, if not an absurd undertaking, to lay down rules for caprice, and to set up for a legislator of whims and fancies" (*PE* 12). Unlike appetite, aesthetic taste was at once instinctual *and* guided by certain fixed rules that taste philosophers set out to identify. Shaftesbury believed that an aesthetic taste for beauty was a mental compulsion amounting to law, or that it is "a taste which governs men" (*C* 413). Similarly, Hume defined the standard of taste as the "joint verdict" of all ideal critics, assured that beauties "maintain their authority over the minds of men" (*EMP* 241, 233). Reflecting the juridical language of the discourse, Terry Eagleton argues that taste was particularly suited to "refashioning the human subject from the inside, informing its subtlest affections and bodily responses with this law which is not a law," for if "there is a right and a wrong to taste quite as absolute as the death sentence — this is not at all the way it feels."[17] Garnering the authority left over from the divine, taste became the most vivid strand of a complex civilizing process in which individuals were taught to regulate themselves, and their motivating appetites, from within.[18]

Situated at the intersection of appetite and manners, taste was in many ways a middle-class affair targeted to producing "tasteful" subjects.[19] Economically, the middle ranks grew in importance from 1660 through 1760, as the largest market for consumer goods was among them.[20] Lance Bertelsen defines the eighteenth-century term *middling* as "that protean segment of society above peer and below the gentry and nobility; . . . the psychological and material arena in which the elections of what has been called the 'politics of signification' were contested."[21] Whereas the animal pleasures of eating demand appetite, the sociocultural "politics of signification" rule the table, where one sits down to eat without it, or at least with enough manners to know how to hide it. Thomas Newcomb's 1733 "The Woman of Taste" (a gendered differential to which we shall return) satirizes the social necessity of controlling one's appetite in public:

> When seated at the board you take your place,
> Invited by his honour, or his grace;
> Though hungry, when you view the fowl or fish,
> Seem nice, and only piddle o'er the dish.
> The rabbits carv'd, from wings and legs refrain,
> And though half starving, only beg the brain:
> The palate only choose, the choicest meat,
> When the whole carp with pleasure you cou'd eat.[22]

These lines express a precept still in effect today: one does not sit down in polite society with the brawny appetite of a barbarian. To display hunger at all on such occasions is to risk disqualifying oneself from tasteful society. "Hunger is the best sauce," as Kant writes in *The Critique of Judgment* (echoing Cervantes), "and people with a healthy appetite relish everything, so long as it is something they can eat. Such delight, consequently, gives no indication of taste having anything to say to the choice. Only when men have got all they want can we tell who among the crowd has taste or not" (*CJ* 49–50). Philosophically, the culture of taste involved elevating eating, the most basic of all human drives, into bourgeois commensality or dining; in practice, this meant civilizing appetite through the developing etiquette of manners.

Dr. Samuel Johnson, despite his own infamous table manners, recognized the symbolic power of the dinner table as a site of social communion. According to his biographer James Boswell, Johnson described it as a place "to eat and drink together, and to promote kindness."[23] Nineteenth-century British gastronomers would all look back to Johnson, whom Boswell described as "Jean Bull Philosophe," discoursing on the affairs of the stomach as an urgent philosophical matter. "Some people," declared Johnson in an oft-repeated flourish, "have a foolish way of not minding, or pretending not to mind, what they eat. For my part, I mind my belly very studiously, and very carefully; for I look upon it, that he who does not mind his belly will hardly mind anything else."[24] Mind, eat; mind, belly. The juxtapositions are fully self-conscious. Like his heirs in gastronomical tradition, Johnson was a self-made intellectual who acknowledged a necessity to work for his taste and who condemned the social necessity to avoid (or give a show of avoiding) all interest in food.[25]

In an issue of *The Rambler* (no. 206) that Boswell misreads as "a masterly essay against gulosity" (gluttony), Johnson fashions a fictional "philosophe" of food.[26] Venturing from table to table and pronouncing judgment upon the food he is served, "Gulosulus" (the title character) "by this practice . . . acquires at a feast a kind of dictatorial authority; his taste becomes the standard of pickles and seasoning."[27] Having a taste to distinguish between pickles and seasonings may seem a far cry from distinguishing among the finer shades of poetry or painting, but by the final quarter of the eighteenth century, the two were becoming pragmatically conflated. Johnson himself claimed that he "could write a better book of cookery than has ever yet been written . . . upon philosophical principles." Rather than leaving the body behind for the purposes of aesthetic contemplation, the connoisseur by the end of the eighteenth century worked for his taste, comparative shopping for comestibles and earning his reputation as a discerning consumer. "I," Johnson bragged, "who live at a variety of good tables, am a much better judge of cookery, than any person who has a very tolerable cook, but lives much at home; for his palate is gradually adapted to the taste of his cook; whereas . . . in trying by a wider range, I can more exquisitely judge."[28] As a public forum for exercising taste, Johnson preferred the tavern (the British forerunner of the restaurant), and Boswell informs us that he would complain if he were invited to dinner at a private establishment and given insufficient fare on which to practice his fine art of judgment.

For less belletristic taste philosophers as well, the meal was an occasion for social community that transcended physical gratification. Kant delivered his early thoughts on taste in a series of lectures from 1772 to 1773, later published as *Anthropology from a Pragmatic Point of View* (1798), in which he describes a dinner party of companions "aesthetically united" in pleasure:

> When I think of companions for a dinner party to be composed solely of men of taste (aesthetically united), who are not only interested in having a meal together but also in enjoying one another, then this little dinner party (since their number cannot amount to many more than the number of the Graces) must not only try to supply physical satisfaction — which everyone can find for himself — but also social enjoyment for which the dinner must appear only as a vehicle (*AN* 187).

In this Kantian vision of commensality, the social conventions of appetite bear a direct relation to aesthetics.[29] The meal is a materialized version of the *sensus communis*, further elaborated in *The Critique of Judgment* as an intersubjective community united in a shared ideal through the faculty of representation. Food (in Kant's words) "must appear only as a vehicle" for this more important event of social community. Kant's anthropological successors also read the meal as a symbolic system in which food is "a highly condensed social fact," its significance never purely nutritional.[30] The first task of the host is to exercise social discrimination (a term now freighted with pejorative significance) in the selection of guests, and Kant's recommended number of guests is in line with that of contemporary conduct books treating the bourgeois dinner party. As Daniel Pool explains, dinner parties were given inordinate attention in European "etiquette books for the upwardly anxious, perhaps with good reason, given the opportunities dinner parties offered for improving the acquaintance of those who could be helpful in one's way up the social ladder in a society whose middle class was increasingly upwardly mobile."[31] In the culture of taste, food and the etiquette surrounding it were laden with meaning.

The years at the end of the eighteenth century also witnessed, however, extremities of appetite — starvation and aristocratic feasting — that did not conduce to the kind of aesthetic community promoted through the bourgeois ideology of the dinner party.[32] In England as in France laborers could barely afford bread, while the corpulent Prince of Wales hosted extravagant feasts at Carlton House and the equally large Louis XVI was caricatured as eating his way toward the border on his flight from France, arrested in the act of eating pig's feet.[33] "Those so-called festive entertainments (feasting and gorging)," Kant says of aristocratic excess, are incommensurate with middle-class ideals of politeness and by the 1790s are "pretty much in bad taste" (*AN* 187). Writing to his patron and friend Thomas Poole on March 23, 1801, Coleridge complained: "I am oppressed at times with a true heart-gnawing melancholy when I contemplate the state of my poor oppressed Country. — God knows, it is as much as I can do to put meat and bread on my own table; & hourly some poor starving wretch comes to my door, to put in his claim for part of it."[34] Coleridge himself contemplated emigrating to America owing to "the difficulty of procuring sustenance in this Country" and leaving behind "England . . . a place where the laborious poor are dying with grass [in] their bellies" (*CCL* 2:389). Once middle-class ideals of tasteful moderation governed the ideology of consumption, neither the rich (whose palates were symbolically vitiated by overindulgence) nor the poor (whose objective was merely to eat) contributed representative members to tasteful society.

The Physiology of Taste

Philosophers since ancient times have recognized that taste is metaphorically tied to the "lower" somatic world of appetite. In *Timaeus* Plato attempts a solution by limiting aesthetic experience to the head and cordoning the body off from the mind through the thin isthmus of the neck, a partition precarious at best. The Platonic stomach was accordingly tied down in the lower regions "like a wild animal which was chained up with man, and must be nourished if man was to exist" (*CDP* 1194). In a later creation narrative, William Blake envisions the creation of the human form divine, following the philosophical hierarchy of the senses in the production of eyes, ears, nose, and then the more problematic organ of taste, reaching out from the belly: "A craving Hungry Cavern / Thence arose his channeld Throat, / And like a red flame a Tongue" (*CPB* 76). The tongue, commonly considered the organ of taste, was housed in the head but extended all the way down through the digestive tract to the anal orifice, an organ of unsignifying emission opposed to the expression of taste. As Stanley Cavell remarks in his insightful analysis of Shakespeare's fable of the belly in *Coriolanus*, "the body has (along with the senses) two openings, or two sites for openings, ones that are connected, made for each other. . . . I gather that no one is in a position to say what the right expression is of our knowledge that we are strung out on both sides of a belly."[35] How to express the knowledge that our material being mediates mouth and anus? For the civilizing discourse of taste, the effort was to repress, not to express, that knowledge.

Despite the fact that the latter part of the seventeenth century introduced new models of human digestion and nutrition by way of Jean Baptiste Van Helmont, Franciscus Sylvius, Thomas Willis, and other iatrochemists, eighteenth-century taste philosophers inherited the humoral model of human physiology descended from Galen: one that viewed mind and body as a psychosomatic system of four humors (blood, choler, phlegm, and bile) produced and distributed through the stomach.[36] The stomach cooked food by means of heat, sending it out through the alimentary avenues of the body, as if from a kitchen. According to Galen, fountainhead of early modern medicine, timing and environment were impor-tant, since if food were undercooked it could rot like raw meat, breeding worms and corrupting the system. Should it be overcooked, it could putrefy, causing foul vapors, crudities, and other bodily distempers. The humoral body was thus a delicately balanced system, constantly in need of "correction" through diet, since every food had its own delicate balance of the four fundamental fluids as well.[37] This idea of the animal economy as oriented around the stomach — and vulner-able to the slightest digestive malfunction — persisted in the Century of Taste when the human was conceived of as a *tasting* organism.

Taste is etymologically related to touch, and in the era of sensibility the skin became an expanded organ of assimilation, the subjective interface by which human beings touch and taste the world of sensory reality. A perhaps unex-pected analogy for the enlightened Man of Taste can be found in Milton's angels, who experience pleasure not only in localized bodily sites but also throughout their entire "intelligential" substance. As Raphael explains in book 8 of *Paradise Lost,* angels do not experience pleasure exclusively through the eye, any less than through the mouth. Rather, they take it in through every pore, a connection between sensibility and taste that includes the entire organism in aesthetic experience.[38] As Hegel writes in his *Philosophy of Nature* (1830), "the stomach and intestinal canal are themselves nothing else but the outer skin, only reversed and developed and shaped into a peculiar form (*PN* 2:400). At a time when the physical assimilation of the outside world was a leading concern of natural philosophy, sensibility was conceptually involved in the extended economy of digestion.

Yet, like the philosophical mystery of what it means to be human, the manner in which the sentient being processes the physical world was far from clear. In 1786 the British physiologist John Hunter noted that digestion is "one of the most important operations of the animal oeconomy, and most obvious in its effects . . . yet little has been hitherto made out towards investigating the various circumstances under which it is performed."[39] Following Hunter, the German physiologist J. F. Blumenbach wrote in 1817 that "the organ of digestion . . . exists, what cannot be affirmed of any other viscus, in perhaps all animals without exception; and, if the importance of parts may be estimated in this way, evidently holds the first rank among our organs."[40] As subjectivity hinged on sensory experience, the physiology of taste came to play a central role in determining human identity. According to Coleridge, the "lower" faculties, such as the "Olfactories, Gustatories, and organ of the Skin," carried on the work of touch in order to "assimilate or transform the external into the personal, or combine them thus assimilated" (*CN* 1:1822). No longer banished to the world beyond philosophy, the senses of taste, smell, and touch in the Romantic period presided over the production of tasteful subjects.

Before modern medicine made probing beyond the subjective border of skin a less problematic venture, physicians relied on what was evacuated or expelled from the organism to determine its internal condition. A popular scientific spectacle of the eighteenth century was Jacques de Vaucanson's mechanical duck, which demonstrated the process of digestion by ingesting corn and converting it into excrement. This duck began its European tour in 1742 and was viewed by William Hogarth, Goethe, and other prominent figures, though by 1781 it was revealed that the duck excreted premanufactured feces. Vaucanson instructed audiences that in the digestive system of the duck, food was "dissolved, and not by trituration as some physicians claim. . . . The digested matter in the stomach is conducted by pipes, as by the bowels of the animal, to the anus, where there is a sphincter that allows it to exit."[41] Those physicians who judged humans by their physiological evacuations found a counterpart in eighteenth-century taste philosophers who judged the person of taste by what he or she expressed in the form of discourse or poetry.

Even Kant, who dismissed the tradition of British empiricism as philosophically unsound, began his lectures on taste with a rumination on its physicality: "How might it have happened," he asks in his *Anthropology*, "that the modern languages particularly have chosen to name the aesthetic faculty of judgement with an expression (*gustus, sapor*) which merely refers to a certain sense-organ (the inside of the mouth), and that the discrimination as well as the choice of palatable things is determined by it?" (*AN* 144). What Kant faced was the difficulty of proceeding philosophically (according to a priori logic) when aesthetic taste experience was stubbornly rooted in physical sensation. His *Critique of Judgment* continues to worry the analogy as a stumbling block to a coherent aesthetics. At one point, he resorts to a culinary analogy to explain how the subjective quality of taste resists abstract speculation: "a man may recount to me all the ingredients of a dish, and observe of each and every one of them that it is just what I like, and, in addition, rightly commend the wholesomeness of food; yet I am deaf to all these arguments. I try the dish with *my own* tongue and palate, and I pass judgement according to their verdict (not according to universal principles)" (*CJ* 140). There may be no disputing a gustatory taste for food, but the extensive amount of disputation about taste in the philosophical arena suggests that the maxim "De gustibus non est disputandum" did not apply to aesthetics.

Bodily taste may be tied to the fleshy organ of the tongue, its sensory "tentacles" or "papillae," but mental taste conceived of as a feeling or sentiment of beauty entailed more than physical sensation. It had to involve an element of cognition, or there could be no meaning ascribed to it — no standard, no principles, nothing beyond physical instinct. In his "Preface to *Lyrical Ballads*," Wordsworth disapproved of those "who will converse with us gravely about a taste for poetry, as they express it, as if it were a thing as indifferent as a taste for rope-dancing, or Frontiniac or Sherry" (*PW* 1:139). The analogy to food or drink could only go so far, and in his *Philosophical Lectures* of 1819, Coleridge complained that it had gone too far: "One man may say I delight in Milton and Shakespeare more than Turtle or Venison another man that is not my case for myself I think a good dish of turtle and a good bottle of port afterwards give me much more delight than I receive from Milton and Shakespeare you must not dispute about tastes" (*CCW* 8.2:668–70). The problem with the gustatory trope is that it made room for pleasure in aesthetic experience only at the risk of reducing Milton to soup, as it were, mixing his sublimities in the unmediated stew of sensual gratification.

By the nineteenth century, the fine arts were no longer the exclusive domain of males, just as the kitchen was no longer strictly the province of women (particularly with the influx of French chefs after the Revolution who approached food professionally as a fine art).[42] Nevertheless, the association of mind with male and body with female continued. As Carolyn Korsmeyer points out, the denigration of taste in the hierarchy of the physical senses, which "accords with the elevation of mind over body: of reason over sense; of man over beast and culture over nature . . . also lines up with another ranked pair of concepts not yet mentioned; the elevation of male over female and with 'masculine' traits over those designated 'feminine.' "[43] To gain knowledge and transcend the senses was to make (or keep) oneself embodied male, while to give in to the dangerous pleasures of appetite was to edge oneself closer to the cultural construction of effeminacy.

Although the British Man of Taste was gendered male, he asserted himself (in practice at least) as a consumer, navigating the middle-class divide between aesthetic taste and material desires. David Garrick's prologue to Samuel Foote's 1752 comedy *Taste* suggests how the civilizing progress from necessity to luxury was also conceived of as a trajectory away from instinctual desire, whether coded as "natural diet" or "natural" (hetero)sexuality:

> Why laugh at *TASTE?* It is a harmless Fashion,
> And quite subdues each detrimental Passion;
> The Fair ones Hearts will ne'er incline to Man,
> While thus they rage for — China and Japan.[44]

This speaker views a contemporary taste for commodities, such as china, with their uneasy proximity to the feminized cultural sphere of Orientalism, as a challenge to the virility of the European Man of Taste balanced on the border between aesthetics and consumerism. He differed from the Restoration fop, an aristocratic and French-influenced phenomenon, as he did from the Regency figurehead, George IV, who was caricatured as an effete, appetitive voluptuary (both qualities that swerved from the staunch paternity of the Hanoverian dynasty). As a result, his crisis of sexuality was an issue of cultural centrality.[45] One anonymous verse satire, "The Connoisseur; or a Satire on Men of Taste" (1735), also suggests the danger that the taming of appetite into taste simultaneously tames men into something "less" than men:

> And what the girls were deem'd in Ages past,
> Are our top *Beaux*, and modern Men of Taste.
> But now so lessen'd is the Progeny,
> That the next Race will only Women be;
> And tir'd Nature, having lost its Force,
> Stop Propagation, and so end its Course.[46]

Lacking the bullish appetites of John Bull, "modern Men of Taste" offer a critical lens on the eighteenth-century culture of taste and its defining fiction: the Man of Taste as a universal symbol for the self in society.

Following the philosophical hierarchy of the senses was the hierarchy of the arts, identified by a similar dichotomy, namely, high versus low, philosophical versus physiological, aesthetic versus bodily.[47] While the higher arts of sight and hearing were thought to promote reflective pleasure, the "lower" experiential arts appealing directly to the senses promoted pleasure, which Aristotle for one claimed is "not the product of art." In classical aesthetics, smell and taste produce no mental activity, and for Aristotle, therefore, "the arts of the perfumer and cook are the arts of pleasure."[48] His hierarchy ranked visual arts, music, and poetry at the top; cookery and other feminized crafts, such as floristry, perfumery, and fashion, at the bottom. The male-gendered mechanical arts were also ranked with the "lower" arts as appealing to "the judgment of sense and experience," but in this case class exerted a feminizing influence.[49]

In the complex arena of the modern arts, the popular genre of the novel was feminized as a sensational form of escapism from serious mental labor. Its constitutive feature — the marriage plot — narrated the commodification and consumption of women, along with the shopping, exhibition, and other types of female consumerism that fed into the story. To top it off, the novel contained frequent scenes with food, and writers as diverse as Mary Wollstonecraft and Wordsworth expressed frustration with its seeming capacity to stimulate the passions. Wollstonecraft complained of the irrationality of female novel readers in *A Vindication of the Rights of Woman* and *Maria, or the Wrongs of Woman,* while Wordsworth railed against indiscriminate readers, who were unable to distinguish spiritual food from "Frontiniac" and were forever in quest of "food for fickle tastes, and fickle appetites" (*PW* 1:124).[50] Poets and novelists alike acknowledged that an increasing demand for "ephemera," such as newspapers, memoirs, and novels, posed a serious challenge to the poet who held himself responsible for creating (not catering to) the taste of the public.

The danger was always the potentially "bad" taste of the economically empowered consumer. In his "Bill of Fare to the Feast" in *Tom Jones* (1749), Henry Fielding observed that the novelist "ought to consider himself, not as a gentleman who gives a private or eleemosynary treat, but rather as one who keeps a public ordinary, at which all persons are welcome for their money." In the former case, "good-breeding forces them to approve and to commend whatever is set before them," since their job is to learn taste from their betters. On the contrary, "Men who pay for what they eat, will insist on gratifying their palates, however nice and even whimsical these may prove; and if everything is not agreeable to their taste, will challenge a right to censure, to abuse, and to d——n their dinner without controul."[51] Coleridge similarly grumbled in 1816 of the "vulgar" indiscretions of those who "dieted at the two public *ordinaries* of Literature, the circulating libraries and the periodical press" (CCW 6:38). Catering to what Wordsworth called an unthinking "craving for extraordinary incident," such fare was accused of blunting the "discriminating powers of the mind" (PW 1:128). The following literary history of taste, which unfolds as a drama of metaphor mainly in poetry and nonnovelistic prose, should also make these critical issues in the history of the novel accessible through writers who have typically been considered outside it.

The Metaphor of Taste

The aesthetic field of vision and hearing may yield a vaguely ideal-immaterial subjectivity, but the senses of touch, taste, and smell demand an actual self engaged in the world of material presence. Coleridge for one stressed the role of "all *tangible* ideas & sensations" in forming the *"real Self,"* for to create one's "own self in a field of Vision & Hearing, at a distance, by [one's] own ears & eyes" was to renounce one's *"real Self"* altogether (CN 1:979).[52] Rather than abstract intellectual pleasure, taste understood as a gustatory phenomenon connoted a totality of aesthetic sense experience whereby, as Hazlitt put it in "On Gusto" (1816), "the impression made on one sense excites by affinity those of another" (HCW 4:78). David Bromwich points out that gusto is "a word for taste, but one picked out for a few special implications which remove it as far as possible from the idea of taste as a passive and inculcated knowledge."[53] A term imported from the Continent at the outset of the British discourse of taste (itself the early form of modern aesthetics), "gusto" had been used in English in the seventeenth century in a culinary context and became a staple term of Romantic aesthetics by way of Hazlitt.[54] In experiencing gusto, as James Engell writes, the "senses work together like fingers on a hand and grasp the object in its totality."[55] Taste, understood in its fullest sense as a gustatory mode of aesthetic experience, is a way out of abstraction and into a robust sensibility that flourished in the period known as Romanticism.

Precisely when taste was first used as a metaphor for aesthetic discernment is open to debate. According to Raymond Williams, " 'Good taast' in the sense of good understanding is recorded from 1425 and 'no spiritual tast' from 1502"; Dabney Townsend reports in the *Oxford Encyclopedia of Aesthetics* that "Among the first to use the metaphor of taste in connection with judgment was Leon Battista Alberti (1404–72)."[56] Other aesthetic histories trace the metaphorical usage of taste as a mental capacity to the seventeenth-century Spanish author Baltasar Gracián y Morales, who maintained that "just as large morsels are suited to big mouths, so are high matters to high minds."[57] The cue for this critical approach occurs in the opening sentence of Joseph Addison's 1712 *Spectator* essay "On Taste": "Gratian very often recommends the fine Taste, as the utmost Perfection of an accomplished Man" (*SPT* 3:527). The importance of the reference is that, already for Gracián, as Hans-Georg Gadamer writes, "the sensuous differentiation of taste . . . is in fact not merely an instinct, but strikes the balance between sensory instinct and intellectual freedom."[58] The tasting self hangs in the balance between subjective response and objective principles, prompting Voltaire to observe in his entry on taste for Diderot and d'Alembert's *Encyclopedia* that "this capacity for discriminating between different foods, has given rise, in all known languages, to the metaphorical use of the word 'taste' to designate the discernment of beauty and flaws in all the arts."[59] More recently, Remy G. Saisselin claims that in mid seventeenth-century France, the *je ne sais quoi* came to stand for the inexplicability of aesthetic experience in the field of the fine arts; Luc Ferry, extending this genealogy to Italy and Spain, proposes that at this point "the term acquires pertinence in the designation of a new faculty, capable of distinguishing the beautiful from the ugly and of apprehending through immediate sentiment."[60] The application of gustatory language (*gusto, goût, Geschmack*) to the faculty of aesthetic judgment at the very least suggests the degree to which sensory pleasure had begun to define aesthetic experience.

Just as the *virtuosi* of seventeenth-century Europe sought virtue and knowledge through empirical testing, Milton's Eve paves the way for the aesthetic virtuoso, or connoisseur seeking pleasure through the empirical experience of taste.[61] As opposed to the neoclassical concern with canons of correctness and aesthetic *justesse,* Milton made room for *gusto* in aesthetic experience. The twelve-book *Paradise Lost* appeared in the same year as Boileau's French translation of *Peri Hypsous,* marking the beginning of the sublime tradition in England, and as W. J. Bate observes: "The neo-classic 'School of Taste' in England both facilitated and in turn drew encouragement from the rising popularity of the famous Greek treatise, attributed to Longinus, *On the Sublime.*"[62] On the verge of the eighteenth-century effort to repress, sublimate, or otherwise discipline appetite into aesthetics, Milton described an embodied mode of taste with serious consequences for human subjectivity. Taste philosophers beginning with the third earl of Shaftesbury, and continuing through Addison, Hume, and Burke, all engage Milton as the prime example of rhetorical sublimity in English.[63] His epic representations of gustatory taste, the following chapter of this book argues, describe a fictional world that anticipates and renders visible the philosophical construction of taste as a symbolic economy of consumption.

As *Paradise Lost* and *Regained* make clear, the discrimination of taste can lead to higher things, such as expression, or (if misused) to the nether world of dregs and purgation. In the Century of Taste, Enlightenment philosophers take up the Miltonic model to represent the Man of Taste as a consumer — and digester — of beauty whose tasteful self remains vulnerable to its own abject dimension. Just as Milton's God purges all evil "dregs" as morally corrupted waste, Enlightenment taste theorists purge all defects and dregs (the term is used here too) from the philosophical ideal of tasteful selfhood — or to cite Shaftesbury, they adopt a "method of evacuation" (*C* 74). Sir Joshua Reynolds instructed audiences in the 1770s that the "refinement of taste . . . by disentangling the mind from appetite" results in virtuous and "exalted" persons of taste, and chapter 3 focuses on the specific means by which aesthetic taste philosophers attempted to disentangle the concept of taste from the discursive trappings of appetite.[64] Here, stylistically "miscellaneous" authors like Shaftesbury, rational empiricists like Hume, and political rhetoricians like Burke join the metaphorical trajectory constituting literary history.

The following four chapters highlight Romantic authors who establish themselves as pivotal nodes in the metaphorical trajectory of taste by the intensity of their concentration on, and degree of self-reflexiveness built into, their use of the gustatory trope. Wordsworth looks back to Milton as a divine feeding source in the literary history of taste for confirmation of its ontological power, while Lamb deploys the cultural politics of flesh-eating to describe a masochistic countervision of low-urban taste. Byron uses cannibalism to critique the vampiric forces of nineteenth-century capitalism, and his contemporary Keats portrays an epic scene of consumption with side effects of hunger and existential longing. The final chapter opens up more broadly into nineteenth-century British cultural history, where the traditionally feminine arts of food and fashion are the real material markers of taste. No longer to be confused with gluttons, gourmands at the turn of the century had become respectable members of civil society and even leaders in public taste under the appellation of the gastronome. In these years gastronomy emerged as a distinct literary genre — witty, eclectic as table talk, treating food with philosophical consequence — and the dandyish gourmand as a distinct cultural figure, an up-to-date Man of Taste in a public scene of conspicuous, discretionary consumption.

For Milton's digesting God, as for the ruminating Spirit of German Romanticism and Wordsworth's creatively feeding mind, creation entails more than the airy intake of inspiration. Chapter 4 shows how Wordsworth's lifelong preoccupation with the concept of aesthetic taste manifests itself in one of the most enduring emblems of the Romantic period: the mind that "feeds upon infinity" in the climactic scene of *The Prelude*. His mid-career essays on taste, including the 1810 *Essays upon Epitaphs* and *Guide to the Lakes* (begun in 1810, published in 1835), map the feeding mind directly onto the material ecology of the Lakes. Later, his two letters addressed to the *Morning Post* in December 1844 protest the "rash assault" of the English railway into the Lake District and encourage "all persons of taste" to join him in denouncing the threat (*PW* 3:339). Together, these writings suggest the degree to which the poet's extraordinary ambitions for taste (whereby "the taste, intellectual Power, and morals of a Country are inseparably linked in mutual dependence") come face to face with contending forces of consumerism (*PW* 2:85). To see how Wordsworth resists — but finally participates in — rendering the feeding mind as one more consumable commodity, chapter 4 examines his extensive editorial revisions to the Mount Snowdon passage of *The Prelude*. Behind its numerous textual layers one discovers an embodied mind that feeds according to the bodily logic of ingestion, digestion, and excretion.

While Wordsworth and Coleridge supported an ideal of natural taste against the "fickle tastes and fickle appetites" promoted through urban commercial commotion, Charles Lamb was employed by a major importer of colonial foodstuffs, such as tea and sugar, and hence was involved in an enterprise of British commercial expansion. What the Lake poets shared with a second generation of high Romanticism, defined by Shelley and his circle through "natural" or "pure" diet, was an ideal of subjectivity free from the pollutants and cultural corruptions of the city. Lamb found himself positioned on the "wrong" side of the politics of food that informed the concept of taste in the Romantic period, and the fifth chapter of this book examines how he manipulated contemporary dietary politics to develop his literary persona as a gastronomically sophisticated Londoner. Unlike the middle-class Man of Taste or Romantic gourmand, however, whose tasteful status hinged on moderation, Lamb figured forth an avid eater who swings between the alternate extremes of savage carnivore and sickly-delicate connoisseur. Essays like "Edax on Appetite," "Hospita on the Immoderate Pleasures of the Palate," and "Confessions of a Drunkard" develop this persona as a flesh-loving gourmand, but "A Dissertation Upon Roast Pig" reveals the degree to which Lamb's unique style of comic melancholy is physiologically seated in the stomach.

In a similar but opposite manner to Lamb, Byron responds to a world in which taste means knowing the limits of consumption, whether of food, of the beautiful (in nature, art, sexual objects), or of commodities. In a culture that puts all appetite, gastrointestinal as well as sexual, to work within a symbolic economy of consumption, there can be no room for nonproductive expenditure: all pleasures that do not lead directly to the propagation of the species (more workers to perform more work) are labeled perversions. Chapter 6 shows how Byron brings taboo appetites to light not from some barbaric, transgressive exterior but from the heart of European society in which institutionalized heterosexuality is just one more form of restraint.[65] Viewed against other journalistic, pictorial, and theatrical representations of contemporaneous shipwrecks (and their horrific tales of survival by cannibalism), Byron's comic representation of cannibalism in canto 2 of *Don Juan* performs a critique of British middle-class taste that rewrites cannibalism as vampirism: a distinctively nineteenth-century mode of consuming the other. Both cannibal and vampire represent figures of social critique, but the vampire undermines any self-validating stance against the uncivilized other. The Byronic narrator of *Don Juan* appears as a creature driven by desperate physical compulsion to eat but who nevertheless maintains a claim to taste and distinction. As such, he unites appetite and aesthetic discernment, two modes of processing the external world that had always been conceptually at odds in the literary history of taste.

Despite (or perhaps owing to) their social positioning outside the commercial mainstream—Byron notwithstanding the commercial popularity of his work holding himself ideologically above the "middling" and Keats struggling to survive beneath it in the "literary lower empire" (*DJ* 11.62.1)—both poets experienced physical hunger and fantasies of aversion that extend their shadows past Romanticism.[66] One high, the other low; one striking readers as world-weary, the other striking them as wide-eyed: Byron and Keats shared more than the sense that love in a hut with a crust of bread is cold. The seventh chapter of this book examines how Keats's similar (indeed, far worse) problems with the physiology of taste prompted an enduring aesthetic critique that takes the form of an epic nausea we would now identify as existentialist. While his starving speaker in *The Fall of Hyperion* fails to relish the stale food he encounters in the poem's opening banquet, the eponymous hero of *Hyperion* suffers a repugnance or bad aftertaste from the repulsive smells he attempts to consume: both are residues of a barefaced existence that will not be idealized away. In order to explain how Keats's effort to relish the world with gusto results in his existentialist vision in the *Hyperion* poems, the chapter shows how he develops a theory of aesthetic experience as an *allegory* of taste, based on Milton.

From the heights of transcendental poetry, chapter 8 descends to the set piece of the Victorian novel, the middle-class dinner party and its concomitant aesthetic of snobbery. Once the meal was packaged as a consumer commodity (and an extremely complex one at that), a public of educated diners began to emerge, guided by gastronomical writers in English and French during the British Regency. The chapter traces representations of George IV from Romantic-era visual satire into the fictionalized space of the Victorian novel. William Makepeace Thackeray satirizes him in *Vanity Fair* (1847–48) in the form of the great Jos Sedley, whose aesthetic disinterestedness reduces to a snobbish display of material self-interest (as defined by Thackeray's 1848 *Book of Snobs*). Charles Dickens also capitalized on the frenzy of conspicuous consumption characterizing mid-nineteenth-century Britain; the ostentatious dinner parties of *Our Mutual Friend* (1865) reveal the latter-day aesthetic of snobbery as one legacy of the culture of taste. The book thus concludes where aesthetic taste philosophy found itself stuck in analogy: at the middle-class dinner party whose participants are ideologically if not "aesthetically united" in pleasure.

The literary history of taste described above incorporates the major concerns that have preoccupied Romantic critics for the past half-century. As an evolution of a presecular ontology of eating based on the edible Word of Christianity, for instance, the phenomenological subject of high Romanticism has been revitalized through recent interest in the life sciences and the organic processes of digestion. The expansion of the field through gender studies has revealed how the virile *homo aestheticus* was constructed against such feminized concerns as food and diet, as well as such historically feminized genres as the novel. Questions of empire have become inextricable from the politics of colonial foodstuffs, such as sugar, spice, and tea, and cultural studies have revealed the ways in which the social landscapes of Romantic-period fiction took shape against all-too-real panoramas of crop shortages, bread riots, and Corn Laws. Revisiting central moments of British literary history through the metaphorical lens of consumption may help to initiate a dialogue among these diverse fields of research and recall the power of literary history as a methodology for grounding such disciplinary diversity within literary studies.

2

Mortal Taste: Milton

It is not a little curious that, with the exception of Ben Jonson (and he did not speak gravely about it so often), the poet in our own country who has written with the greatest gusto on the subject of eating is Milton. He omits none of the pleasures of the palate, great or small. In his Latin poems, when young, he speaks of the pears and chestnuts which he used to roast at the fire with his friend Diodati. Junkets and other "country-messes" are not forgotten in his "Allegro." The simple Temptation in the Wilderness, "Command that these stones be made bread" (which was quite sufficient for a hunger that had fasted "forty days"), is turned, in Paradise Regained, *with more poetry than propriety, into the set out of a great feast, containing every delicacy in and out of season. The very "names" of the viands, he says, were "exquisite." And in* Paradise Lost, *Eve is not only described as being skilful in paradisaical cookery ("tempering dulcet creams"), but the angel Raphael is invited to dinner, and helped by his entertainers to a series of tid-bits and contrasted relishes —*

> *Taste after taste, upheld with kindliest change.*
>
> *— Leigh Hunt, "Eating-Songs" (1854)*

The title of an old play gives us a direct taste and surmise of its inwards, as the first lines of the Paradise Lost *smack of the great Poem.*

— John Keats, "On Retribution, Or, The Chieftain's Daughter*" (1818)*

That Milton's Romantic readers should invoke the "taste" of his epic poetry suggests an awareness beyond the anecdotal. For Milton complicates the category of physiological taste in such a way as to set the terms for the emergence of aesthetic taste theory in the early years of the eighteenth century. Milton was not the first to use the term *taste* in its metaphorical capacity to indicate mental discrimination, but he narrates the tale of "mortal taste" announced in the second line of *Paradise Lost,* and such critics as Christopher Ricks have noticed his "ruthless and relentless pressure on 'taste,' " the fact that the word and its variants appear thirty times in book 9 alone.[1] One might ask precisely how, prior to the interventions of Shaftesbury, Hutcheson, Hume, Burke, Alison, Gerard, and the entire tradition of post-Miltonic philosophers of taste, is one to read Adam's darkly sardonic postlapsarian remark: "*Eve,* now I see thou art exact of taste . . . / And Palate call judicious" (*PL* 9.1017–20)? One of the most overdetermined moments of literary history, if not of Western tradition itself, this taste is more than a physical sensation or appetite (though that is critically implicated too): it is a highly freighted philosophical concept with serious consequences for the creation of selves in society.

Miltonic taste involves a moral as well as an epistemological component whereby to partake of God is to know God, and thereby to know oneself. Throughout *Paradise Lost* and *Paradise Regained* Milton plays on the semantic implications of taste, the fact that the Latin *sapere* means "to taste" and "to know." The fruit whose "mortal taste" was the source of all our woe did, after all, grow on the tree of knowledge, knowingly described by Satan as "precious of all Trees / In Paradise, of operation blest / To Sapience" (*PL* 1.2, 9.795–97). It contains "sciential sap," and when Adam calls Eve "exact of taste," he adds, "of Sapience no small part" (*PL* 9.838, 1018). Elsewhere Milton evokes the epistemological connotation of taste, as in the 1671 companion to *Paradise Regained* when Samson Agonistes declares, "The way to know were not to see but taste" (*Samson Agonistes* 1091). For Milton, as for aesthetic philosophers in the Century of Taste, the beautiful, the true, and the good were all bound up together in the philosophical complexity of taste, which as a gustatory metaphor now expanded to include pleasure in aesthetic experience.[2]

The following pages posit Milton as a foundational theorist for aesthetic taste through his epic wrangle with the metaphor; or perhaps it is better to say that he posits himself at the origin of its literary genealogy. Were it solely a matter of representations of gustatory taste finding their way into aesthetic philosophy, Milton's fictional cosmology would seem a more arbitrary place to begin. The robust world of Renaissance literature offered numerous representations of appetite, from Shakespeare to Jonson to Rabelais.[3] But the pleasures of the palate described by these authors predate the sociopolitical

conscription of those pleasures into the civilizing process. The past few decades of Milton scholarship have been increasingly attuned to Milton's role as
a protothinker of republicanism and the bourgeois public sphere, and this
chapter suggests that his metaphorical investment in taste is also foundational
to the eighteenth-century culture of taste as a particular manifestation of that
public sphere.[4] Taste, after Milton, includes the sublime, the beautiful, and all
the other pleasing illusions that were to shape and sustain individual and
communal identity in civil society. In a brilliant fictional cosmology of eating,
Milton's God, or the divine Word of Christianity, becomes a thing that can be
tasted, which is to say, consumed and sublimated into spirit — or expressed.
Somewhere in the gap between *De Doctrina Christiana* and his epic poetry,
Milton confronts the ontopoetic power of taste as more than a matter of
subjective discernment: it becomes constitutive of subjectivity.

Economies of Consumption

Milton's portrayal of gustatory taste asks us to take seriously the ontological power of eating and the proposition that paradise was lost (and
society made) because Eve, and then Adam, ate. Within *Paradise Lost* Milton
reduces the fall to four highly charged words: "She pluck'd, she eat" (*PL*
9.781). The 1611 King James translation of Genesis (3:11–13) provides Milton with his past-tense "eat," and though later translations of the bible use
"ate," its grammatical placement remains the same. When Milton's Son descends to pronounce judgment on the transgressors, he demands: "hast thou
eaten of the Tree / Whereof I gave thee charge thou shouldst not eat?" (*PL*
10.122–23). After floundering eloquently enough for a while, Adam admits:
"Shee gave me of the Tree, and I did eat" (10.143). Also deflecting blame, Eve
responds: "The Serpent me beguil'd and I did eat" (10.162). In Milton's text,
as in Genesis 3, the question and the two responses it generates are punctuated
with the word *eat*. Visually, it dangles from the end of each line like the
forbidden fruit itself, suggesting something sinful about eating. Yet when Eve
foresees her own transgressive eating in a dream influenced by Satan, she
reflects, "He pluckt, he tasted" (*PL* 5.65). This ambiguity between eating and
tasting signals the tension between physiological and philosophical taste
bound up in Milton's gustatory trope.

The objection will be raised that Adam and Eve did not simply eat, they ate
unlawfully in disobedience of the Word. "The poem centers on the distinction
between forbidden and permitted food," Regina M. Schwartz remarks: "An
ur-dietary law governs Paradise."[5] But disobedience is only one of the moral
transgressions in the catalogue of sins that Milton associates in *De Doctrina*

Christiana (hereafter *Christian Doctrine*) with that "mortal taste."[6] To be sure, diet dictates our moral condition in the poem, and critics have found much to chew over in the dietetics of the fruit. In the original Hebrew this fruit is *tappach,* which the Vulgate translates as *malum,* or apple, with a pun on the short-a variant meaning bad. Some argue that "apple" can stand for any fleshy fruit, since only Satan calls it an apple, thereby reducing it to its lowest common denominator.[7] Karen L. Edwards suggests that in the context of contemporary experimental science the naming of botanical species is important, because to misname is to falsify natural phenomena.[8] Robert Applebaum insists more specifically on the importance of the apple as such, claiming that to ignore it "is to neglect the meaning of sensuality of Milton's paradise; it is to avoid the sensuality that Milton is at such pains to represent."[9] Whether or not the fruit was an apple, its status as a dietary symbol is clear, and from a dietary perspective the familiar narrative — "To pluck and eat" (*PL* 8.309); "ye shall not eat" (9.657); "she pluck'd, she eat" (9.781) — constitutes what William Kerrigan calls "the great myth of the evil meal."[10]

Byron jokes in *Don Juan* that "all human history attests / That happiness for man, the hungry sinner, / Since Eve ate apples, much depends on dinner" (13.101), and his friend Shelley more seriously attributes all the ills of society to the corruptions of diet: "The allegory of Adam and Eve eating of the tree of evil, and entailing upon their posterity the wrath of God and the loss of everlasting life, admits of no other explanation than the disease and crime that have flowed from unnatural diet" (*SP* 82). Like English vegetarians in the seventeenth century, Shelley believed that flesh-eating was an "unnatural" postlapsarian practice, though the more common view in Milton's day was that raw, uncooked fruit was unnatural. Dietary authors of the time often resorted to metaphors of physical economy in discussing what was "natural" to humans. Arkady Plotnitsky, who attempts to unravel the various symbolic economies of taste operative in aesthetic philosophy and poststructuralist theory, observes that "the history of theory from Kant to Hegel, Marx, Nietzsche, Freud, Bataille, and many others demonstrates that the metaphors of economy have proved to be as theoretically *productive* as they are unavoidable."[11] In the seventeenth century as today, theories of economy suggest that nutrients like wealth must be processed efficiently in order for the individual or social body to thrive.[12]

Milton himself recognized a distinction between what Georges Bataille calls a *restricted* economy of waste-free circulation and a more *general* economy, which produces excesses that cannot be tastefully reincorporated.[13] While in a restricted economy everything circulates, a general economy allows for excesses that cannot be utilized or conscripted back into a closed cycle of consumption and symbolic circulation. There can be no "un-productive expenditure" in a restricted economy, since the "circle of power" (which for Bataille also means the cycle of pleasure) is closed. In the commercial economy underwriting the culture of taste, luxury becomes conceived of as nonproductive excess, a filthy lucre imagined in bodily terms: "When in a dream a diamond signifies excrement, it is not only a question of association by contrast; in the unconscious, jewels, like excrement, are," writes Bataille, "a part of oneself destined for open sacrifice."[14] Interpreting Bataille, Michele Richman adds that "vomit or excrement, for example, overflows any project of containment or circumscription, and such excess is responsible for defying the restricted economy of mimetic representation."[15] This is also true of aesthetic consumption where the aesthetic consumer processes the world according to an economic logic, a cycle of return that takes in through the mouth and gives back in the form of expression. The place of consumption as well as expression is the mouth, a feature "no longer . . . situated *in* a typology of the body," as Jacques Derrida writes (also interpreting Bataille), but one that organizes all sites and systems unto itself.[16] Taste, for Milton, is a restricted economy in which things circulate smoothly, so that what the consuming organism ingests it sublimates back into expression.

Because Milton's world is a Christian world, subjects find their being by partaking of God, "not only he *by* whom, but also he *from* whom, *in* whom, *through* whom, and *on account of* whom all things are" (*YP* 6:302). Christianity is founded on sacrifice, which in a postlapsarian world means Christ, the Word made flesh. The problem for Milton in portraying this metaphorically is that (if we follow the process of ingestion through to digestion), the symbolically consuming—or tasting—subject must inhabit a world prepurged of all digestive excess, of everything that will not cleanly pass through the mouth, in order to avoid a cycle of coprophagy. Like other Protestants, Milton takes the sacrament of communion to be a symbolic act, since if flesh is actually consumed, one is transported out of the sacramental and into the superstitious sphere of idolatry. This denial of the literal interpretation of the mandate to accept sacrifice and eat flesh was part of the Reformation phenomenon that, as Deborah Shuger explains, "not only abolished the pageantry of the Roman rite but rejected the sacrificial character of the Eucharist altogether. . . . The moral inwardness of Protestantism—its ethical rationalism, which drives its antipathy to the spectacular 'magic' of the Mass—also problematizes sacrifice."[17] But what does it mean to "problematize sacrifice," or to call into question what is, etymologically, sacred making?

Milton writes that in the Mass "Christ is sacrificed each day by the priest . . . [his body] is supposed to be made out of bread at the moment when the priest murmurs the four words, *this is my body,* and to be broken as soon as it is made" (*YP* 6:559). But if God is to operate as mere sign, if he is to circulate economically rather than to remain in his original unity as the Un-exchangeable divine presence sustaining this cycle of consumption, does that not destabilize the traditional view that God (in Derrida's words) "gives more than he promises, [that] he submits to no exchange contract, his overabundance generously breaks the circular economy"?[18] Does the Protestant rejection of the sacrificial character of the Eucharist, in other words, not set in motion a chain of deferral whereby the Christian subject is always at least one step removed, not only from God as the master signifier of this economy but from his or her own presence as well? If the Christian self is dependent for subsistence (indeed, existence) on flesh, what happens when one instead ingests a vacuity, which installs itself at the constitutive center of self like a gap perpetually craving the presence of real flesh?

Such questions can best be approached from within Milton's own *Christian Doctrine* as a theoretical framework for the metaphoric use of taste in his epic poetry. Scholars never seriously credited William B. Hunter's thesis that this lengthy theological treatise in Latin was spurious, but the critical debate it provoked in the 1990s should remind us that the John Milton of *De Doctrina Christiana* is not always, if ever, the John Milton of *Paradise Lost* and *Regained,* and in the crack between the two arise tensions that can productively complicate his fictional ontology of eating.[19] One thing both treatise and poetry make abundantly clear is that Milton was at all times anti-Catholic. At the bottom of his lifelong abhorrence of "Popery" was the doctrine of transubstantiation.[20] While he agrees with Paul that Christians must *"partake of that one bread,"* he denies the "monstrous doctrines" responsible for "turning the Lord's Supper into a cannibal feast" (*YP* 6:554). For Milton, "Consubstantiation and particularly transubstantiation . . . or cannibalism are utterly alien to reason, common sense and human behavior" (*YP* 6:554). Of course, as Maggie Kilgour has demonstrated in her wide-ranging study of metaphors of incorporation, there has always been a fine line between communion and cannibalism.[21]

In a key moment of Milton's discussion of the Eucharist in *Christian Doctrine,* he insists that "not teeth but faith is needed to eat his flesh": "The Papists hold that it is Christ's actual flesh which is eaten by all in the Mass. But if this were so, even the most wicked of the communicants, not to mention the mice and worms which often eat the eucharist, would attain eternal life by virtue of that heavenly bread. That living bread which, Christ says, is his flesh, and the true drink which, he says, is his blood, can only be the doctrine which teaches us that Christ was made man in order to pour out his blood for us. . . . Whereas if we eat his flesh it will not remain in us, but, to speak candidly, after being digested in the stomach, it will be at length exuded" (*YP* 6:553–54). This nightmare fantasy of "Christ's actual flesh" passing through the Christian subject in so literal a fashion arrives at its logical (though horrible) conclusion: "after being digested in the stomach, it will be at length exuded." The unspiritual, uncivilized possibility that God can be physically digested, and then "exuded," results in the Protestant doctrine of excluding him from the Host — extruding him, so to speak, from the extrusion. *Yet, such exclusion conflicts with Milton's own monist worldview, whereby God is present in all matter.*

There has been ongoing debate about the precise nature of Miltonic matter, and whether Milton's monism is to be understood as materialism, but such debate is only relevant here insofar as it exposes a rift between the cosmology of his theological treatise (which is not always consistent in itself) and that of his epic fiction.[22] Whereas the author of *Christian Doctrine* denies the possibility that God can be literally tasted, hence digested and exuded, the archangel Raphael explains in great detail in *Paradise Lost* how angels concoct, digest, and assimilate real food as part of one divine substance, a fictional world described as "one first matter all, / Indu'd with various forms, various degrees / Of substance" (5.472–74). His discussion of the Eucharist above suggests that Milton is unable to visualize the possibilities entailed by this "one first matter." To represent the sacred meal of communion in these terms would be to turn Christian sacrifice into scatology: "Materialized in the Host, God becomes a digested excrementum that is nonetheless indigestible and inedible; the universe of spirit becomes mouse droppings, its eschatology a scatology."[23]

Yet, is there not a certain sublime pleasure to be discerned as Milton describes the process of exclusion? The experience of sublimity involves a "negative pleasure" in which, as Kant writes, "the mind is not simply attracted by the object but is also alternately repelled thereby" (*CJ* 91). Milton does not let the matter go with a simple extrusion, but upon further reflection describes an even more graphic evacuation: "the Mass brings down Christ's holy body from its supreme exaltation at the right hand of God. It drags it back to the earth, though it has suffered every pain and hardship already, to a state of humiliation even more wretched and degrading than before: to be broken once more and crushed and ground, even by the fangs of brutes. Then, when it has been driven through all the stomach's filthy channels, it shoots it out — one shudders even to mention it — into the latrine" (*YP* 6:560). Milton's disgust for any doctrine that would allow even "brutes" access to the corporal body of Christ is metonymic for a more general horror at the literalization of the sign. The "fangs of brutes" are signatures for their capacity to enter a symbolic system in which they have no place, in which they do not figure, since they lack access to the *logos,* or the ability to speak what they eat. Milton's restricted economy coheres in itself as a precariously balanced system in which all eating signifies and from which all exclusion is precluded. From Milton's monist perspective, all of creation participates directly in a single divine substance — the feeding source of all virtue, beauty, and truth — and in his fiction extrusion is converted into expression through the symbolic economy of taste. As we shall see, this Miltonic possibility of tasting and expressing (rather than tasting and excreting) paves the way for eighteenth-century taste theory.

In book 7 of *Paradise Lost,* Milton depicts a sublime, primordial expulsion as the founding gesture of creation. In this act the "dregs" of creation are forever purged from the symbolic world of tasteful circulation:

> the Spirit of God outspread,
> And vital virtue infus'd, and vital warmth
> Throughout the fluid Mass, but downward purg'd
> The black tartareous cold Infernal dregs
> Adverse to life. . . . (*PL* 7.235–39)

Here Raphael describes creation as the dark obverse of everyday logocentric creation, whereby "his word all things produc'd" (*PR* 3.122): a divine expulsion or cosmic purgation of waste. This newly made, symbolic world of creation may entail no loss, but it is founded on an originary loss, or expulsion, which once made can never be reclaimed. What Milton discovers in his effort to render divine consumption metaphorically, in other words, is a surplus that, unable to pass through the mouth, must therefore be consigned to a more general economy beyond the symbolic cycle of signification.

It has long been acknowledged that one of the central "heresies" of Milton's *Christian Doctrine* is its rejection of *creatio ex nihilo* in favor of a more material creation. Unlike *ex nihilo* creation, introduced into Christian theology by the neoplatonist Philo and converted into dogma by the Christian Fathers Origin and Augustine, *ex deo* creation theory originates with Plotinus and was Christianized through a trajectory of esoteric monism that includes pseudo-Dionysus, Erigena, Eckhart, Boehme, and Nicolas of Cusa.[24] Whether or not we situate Milton within this esoteric tradition (and there has been considerable resistance to doing so), he himself writes "that the world was made out of some sort of matter," which "must either have always existed, independently of God" (as in the Platonic creation narrative) "or else originated from God at some point in time," as in *ex deo* creation (*YP* 6:307). Milton's "God creates *ex se,* drawing out of himself the forms to be imposed on an already teeming universe," as John Guillory observes. "This matter too must ultimately be *ex se.*"[25] The nature of that matter remains a topic of ongoing debate, but Milton scholars have been surprisingly silent about the astounding fact that in book 7 of *Paradise Lost,* some of that matter is abjected. In the heat and fury of creation, we find, Milton's God shoots out his dregs (one shudders even to mention it) into the deep, Milton's cosmic latrine.[26]

Half a century ago, A. S. P. Woodhouse speculated (in a footnote) that this primordial purgation might be "a relic of some anxious consideration of the problem of evil."[27] Yet any suggestion of an evil creative act, even despite Milton's heterodoxy, is distinctively un-Miltonic. In a more recent footnote, John P. Rumrich proposes that because these dregs materialize "does not mean that evil is latent in chaos, any more than evil is latent in the deity who establishes hell . . . God's material potency must include the possibility of matter with which to create such a place as hell."[28] Milton in fact claims that "this original matter was not an evil thing, nor to be thought of as worthless: it was good, and it contained the seeds of all subsequent good. . . . It was in a confused and disordered state at first, but afterwards God made it ordered and beautiful" (*YP* 6:308). His Latin reads, "Substantia erat . . . indigesta modo et incomposita, quam Deus postea digessit et ornavit," which Charles Sumner in the original translation of 1825 rendered: "It was a substance . . . though at first confused and formless, being afterwards adorned and digested into order by the hand of God."[29] Although John Carey departs from the digestive metaphor in his revised translation for the Yale edition of Milton's *Complete Prose Works,* Milton was attuned to the English resonances of Latin words, as he was to the reverse, and it would not be far-fetched to conjecture that the idea of God's "digesting" the cosmos into order is implied in his theological treatise.

Recently, John Rogers has contextualized Milton's primordial "dregs" within seventeenth-century medical discourse, in which "dregs" and "tartar" stood for inassimilable elements of food that had been consumed.[30] According to humoral theory, ill-digested food could breed corrupt (burnt or putrefied) humors that, instead of being conveyed by the normal means through the veins to the brain, could ascend directly from the stomach. These foul or corrupted humors (called vapors), unless quickly dispersed, could obstruct the operations of the mind, including the perception of physical sensation. Milton speaks physiologically of "the lees and settlings of a melancholy blood" in *A Masque Presented at Ludlow Castle* (published in 1637) before magnifying these dregs to macrocosmic dimensions in *Paradise Lost.* What would be endlessly suggestive, though perhaps futile to dispute, is whether Milton viewed his own digestion as responsible for his creation as a poet. In a letter to Leonard Philaras, he records: "It is ten years, I think, more or less, since I noticed my sight becoming weak and growing dim, and at the same time my spleen and all my viscera burdened and shaken with flatulence" (*YP* 4:2, 869). Kerrigan has argued convincingly that Milton believed his blindness to have been caused by indigestion.[31] From this perspective, the paradigm of "blindness and insight" becomes in the invocation to book 3 of *Paradise Lost* one of "blindness and indigestion," as the poet asks divine aid to "Purge and disperse" all inward mist so that he may create.

This primordial purgation of book 7 sets Milton apart from other *ex deo* models of creation in which, rather than being expelled or "downward purged," the dregs form part of a single divine substance extending from the innermost essence of God. The Neoplatonist Macrobius, for instance, writes that "from the Supreme God even to the bottommost dregs of the universe there is one tie, binding at every link and never broken."[32] The Miltonic dregs, on the other hand, are consigned to a general-economic sphere beyond time and space, past the outer shell of the universe that divides the "inferior Orbs, enclos'd / From *Chaos* and th' inroad of Darkness old" (*PL* 3.420–21). In the argument to book 1, Milton makes clear that these dregs were expelled *before* the existence of heaven or earth, cast into "a place of utter darkness, fitliest called Chaos." This subtle confusion between "utter darkness" (or hell) and Chaos in what is otherwise a highly articulated universe suggests that the place (if such a term may be used where no space exists) of the cosmological waste is itself "Abject and lost" (1.312).

Unable to face the metaphor of taste at its gustatory extreme, Milton manages a primordial expulsion that is the founding gesture of creation as a symbolic world of clean, waste-free circulation in which tasteful subjects can exist. Sigmund Freud thinks in psychoanalytic terms about the devil as "an agent of economic discharge," and Satan himself recognizes that within the cosmology of *Paradise Lost* he represents inassimilable waste, or the black cosmic matter called dregs: "myself am Hell" (*PL* 4.75).[33] Similarly, when Adam aligns himself with the excluded dregs by eating badly, he too must be purged as God commands: "Eject him tainted now, and purge him off / As a distemper, gross to air" (*PL* 11.52–53). Later in *Paradise Regained*, Milton portrays the hellish dregs circling the earth in "midair," inhabiting the outer regions of the restricted world, "roving still / About the world. . . . Within thick Clouds and dark tenfold involv'd" (*PR* 1.33–41). These atmospheric terms suit the macrocosm of Milton's fictional universe as they do the microcosm of human physiology, conceived by humoral theory in terms of mists and vapors. Having been purged in the constitutive act of creation, Satan remains in circulation within a more "general" cosmology that includes God at his radical limits: God and the "Infernal dregs" he has had to repress (in his view, reject) in order to establish a symbolic world of tasteful, waste-free circulation.

Taste Deceived: Paradise Lost

While in *Christian Doctrine* a gap must exist between God and the kind
of bready matter that can be consumed, digested, and exuded in his name, in
Paradise Lost Raphael describes a symbolic economy of consumption in
which all of creation participates. In a luncheon colloquy with Adam, having
been invited to "sit and taste" (5.369), he explicates this monist world in
which all eating leads back up to God:

> food alike those pure
> Intelligential substances require
> As doth your Rational; and both contain
> Within them every lower faculty
> Of sense, whereby they hear, see, smell, touch, taste,
> Tasting concoct, digest, assimilate,
> And corporeal to incorporeal turn.
> For know, whatever was created, needs
> To be sustain'd and fed. . . . (*PL* 5.407–15)

Scholars have studied this meal as a symbolic event: John E. Parish compares it
to other biblical scenes of eating and to classical meals shared between gods
and mortals; John F. Huntley finds reference to the meal Sin prepares for Death
in *Paradise Lost* and the one Satan offers Christ in *Paradise Regained;* Marshall Grossman interprets it as a prelapsarian communion associated with a
Protestant understanding of the sacrament; Anthony Low focuses on the vegetarian nature of the meal as a typological prefiguration for the Puritan communion service; and Jack Goldman, also reading the meal for its sacramental
significance, questions the distinction between prelapsarian vegetarianism and
postlapsarian carnivorousness.[34]

Seventeenth-century authorities on health assumed that while fruit may
have been fine food for a prelapsarian meal, God sanctioned flesh-eating with
the Fall as a food closer to our substance than vegetables, hence easier of
digestion and more nutritious.[35] But vegetarianism was also part of the re-
formist energies of these years when health guides disseminated an ideal of
"pure diet," supposed to result in a purification of perception. Such guides, as
Nigel Smith explains, "look very much like the account of 'higher appetite' in
Milton's *Paradise Lost* book 5, where enhanced purification for unfallen mankind is explained in terms of a rarefying of digestion."[36] Liberated from all
dregs or waste, the symbolic economy of consumption described by Raphael
produces similarly refined persons of taste. Excretion becomes aspiration in
this world, evacuation a form of expression. His *scala naturae* is circular in
shape: a looped food chain from which all excremental dregs have already

been excluded. Because the dregs have been *pre*purged in the constitutive act of creation, everything under the sun can partake, or find its being, through eating; more precisely, a kind of symbolic eating that stops at the head, better known as taste.

Raphael's description of angelic eating in *Paradise Lost* thus invests all meals — all eating whatsoever — with new significance. One no longer need limit oneself to bread, for the Word opens up to include a world of edible matter that is all part of one divine substance. In this sense, the Protestant problem of ingesting a vacuity in a purely symbolic version of communion is solved, since now one can really eat God, displayed in a manifest world of unified taste objects. Raphael makes clear that in addition to virtue and knowledge, such eating provides *pleasure*. He explains that angels (here simply a higher form of humans) enjoy eating with all five senses, "whereby they hear, see, smell, touch, taste, / Tasting concoct, digest, assimilate" (5.411–12), a pleasurable process that knowingly controverts a scholastic tradition accustomed to viewing angels as purely spiritual, "the common gloss / Of Theologians" (*PL* 5.435–36). But Raphael challenges tradition not only in asserting *that* angels eat: he also describes *how* they eat in a manner certain readers have found discomforting. C. S. Lewis, for instance, protests that the physiological detail was poetically necessary because *true* (emphasis his): "It is inconceivable that Milton should have so emphasized the reality of angelic nourishment (and even angelic excretion) if the bodies he attributed to his angels were merely a poetical device . . . Milton put it there simply because he thought it *true*."[37] Despite Lewis's insistence on the veracity of the scene, Milton has nothing specific to say about how or what angels eat in *Christian Doctrine*, and one might conclude against him that Milton's silence on this matter in his lengthy theological treatise suggests he had no particular investment in the "truth" of angelic eating. But it is important not to miss the accent of Lewis's defense: his readerly distaste with the passage stems from the *gust* of it, the fact that having been invited to "sit and taste," Raphael does not hesitate to indulge in epicurean pleasure.

Milton's relatives inform us that the poet was a bit of an epicure himself and that "what he had, he always loved to have of the best."[38] The picture of the poet that emerges is one of a temperate but fine connoisseur, not afraid of sensual delight. (Temperance is stressed by all modern gastronomers as a means to prolong and heighten the pleasures of the palate.) Shortly before his death, Milton recalled his marriage vows to his third wife, Elizabeth, in culinary terms: "God have mercy, Betty, I see thou wilt perform according to thy promise in providing me such dishes as I think fit whilst I live; and, when I die, thou knowest that I have left thee all."[39] When Raphael falls to his food in

Paradise Lost "with keen dispatch / Of real hunger, and concoctive heat / To transubstantiate," his lower faculties are put to work tasting, concocting, digesting, assimilating, and corporeal to incorporeal turning in a systematic process whose ultimate end is the Almighty, but whose immediate end is pleasure (5.436–38): "O *Adam*," exclaims the happily feasting angel, "one Almighty is, from whom / All things proceed, and up to him return" (5.469–70). Of course, Raphael intends "transubstantiate" in a sense opposite from that of the author of *Christian Doctrine,* since here it means turning the corporeal into the incorporeal.

In *Paradise Lost* God's substance is not "downward purged" so much as sublimated upward as spirit in a symbolic economy of circulation that comes to define aesthetic taste. Leigh Hunt, one of the poem's most acute Romantic critics, was quick to recognize the importance of the pleasures of eating to Milton: "the great poet shewed so deep a sense of the attention worth bestowing upon his diet, and of the possible dignity, nay, divineness of the pleasure of feeding, that, during the above blissful dinners in the fifth book of *Paradise Lost,* he enters into an elaborate argument to shew the probability of there being eating and drinking in heaven itself; which is what few persons, we suspect, ever cared to think about, when they hoped to go there."[40] By calling attention to the divine "pleasure of feeding," Hunt emphasizes that Raphael joins a symbolic economy *of pleasure.* It is certainly pleasure that is at stake later in the poem when the archangel Michael warns Adam: "Judge not what is best / By pleasure" (*PL* 11.603–04). He might have stepped in several books earlier, and he might have said, "judge not what is best by pleasure *alone,*" for in Milton's world pleasure is tied to knowledge, as it is to virtue, and Raphael does not attempt to disguise his pleasure when he judges it best to accept Adam's invitation to "sit and taste." Raphael's consumption is bodily yet restricted, the pleasures of taste sublimed from grosser appetite.

The cosmic dregs, on the other hand, are excluded from the cycle of pleasurable consumption and mimic the condition of subjective possibility by attempting, hopelessly, to eat. In book 10 an illusory tree springs up amidst the fallen angels who are gathered to celebrate Satan's victory in paradise. Immediately, "parcht with scalding thirst and hunger fierce . . . greedily they pluck'd / The Fruitage fair to sight" (*PL* 10.556–61). The fruit may be pleasurable to the more objective, distal sense of sight, but as the devils discover, it is not pleasurable to taste:

> not the touch, but taste
> Deceiv'd; they fondly thinking to allay
> Thir appetite with gust, instead of Fruit

Chew'd bitter Ashes, which th' offended taste
With spattering noise rejected: oft they assay'd,
Hunger and thirst constraining, drugg'd as oft,
With hatefullest disrelish writh'd thir jaws
With soot and cinders fill'd. . . . (*PL* 10.563–70)

Writhing their jaws full of soot and cinders, the devils are blocked at the point of expression, and Wordsworth for one found these lines in bad taste: "The '*spattering noise*' &c. are images which can ⟨only⟩ excite disgust. The representation of the fallen Angels wreathing [*sic*] their jaws filled with soot and cinders with hatefullest disrelish contains in it nothing that can afford pleasure."[41] The creative power they *would* gain from eating the deceptive fruit is contrary to that of the procreative Word, and rather than becoming incorporate unto truth and sustaining themselves via a pleasing "gust," they instead become incorporate unto their own hollow lies, which do not signify in a symbolic economy of logocentric consumption.

This self-consuming cycle of destruction is graphically embodied by Sin, who cannibalizes herself in a grotesquerie of satanic fabrication. In book 2 she bemoans "mine own brood, that on my bowels feed," the "yelling Monsters" who "gnaw / My Bowels, thir repast" (*PL* 2.863, 795, 799–800). The portrait has its precursor in Spenser's description of Errour, who "bred / A thousand yong ones, which she dayly fed, / Sucking upon her poisonous dugs. . . . Into her mouth they crept, and suddain all were gone" (*Fairie Queene* 1.1.15).[42] Both derive from the Horatian portrait of false fabrication: "Turpiter atrum desinit in piscem mulier formosa superne [The woman, well shaped on top, ends below ugly in a black fish]" (*AN* 150n.).[43] In his *Anthropology,* Kant relates fabrication to metaphor as its own darker half by way of this Horatian portrait: "To fabricate is consciously representing the false as true. . . . Fiction propagated as truth, however, is a lie" (*AN* 150n.). Like her satanic father, "compos'd of lies" (*PR* 1.407), Sin does not creatively fabricate in the sense of *fabricare* (to make) but destructively fabricates in the sense of "to lie." As an evolution of Horatian fabrication, Milton's Sin "seem'd Woman to the waist, and fair, / But ended foul in many a scaly fold" (*PL* 2.650–51), resembling Dagon, "upward Man / And downward Fish" (1.462–63), or any of the other false, "monstrous shapes" (1.479) represented in various forms of fleshly disfigurement. For what those who swerve from the divine, procreative Word to their own false fabrications discover is that lies do not conform to a symbolic economy of tasteful expression, but instead must be spewed forth in a compulsive tautology deprived of all signification.

Milton's rhetorical strategy elsewhere suggests that an effective way to demonize another is to show that person not expressing her words but vomit-ing or spewing them forth. The antagonist of Milton's *Second Defence of the English People* (1654), for instance, referred to as "unmixed filth," "a defiler of holy things," and "a veritable devil," "vomits up . . . all the filthy language of slaves and scoundrels that can be found anywhere . . . croaking like a frog from the hellish swamps in which he swims" and "belch[ing] forth utter nonsense" (*YP* 4:1.637, 594, 633). Vomit, as Seth Lerer puts it, is "a form of oral perfor-mance that undermines the expectations of a public utterance, a form of anti-rhetoric that does not so much bring listeners into an audience of civilized communion as . . . shatters them into a clutch of horribly offended individ-uals."[44] The emetic, satanic lie represents false fabrication, parodic of the Word, and vomiters cohere as no *sensus communis*. They belong instead to a general economy of dysfunctional consumption in which waste clogs the sys-tem, obstructing tasteful expression. One need only recall Linda Blair's perfor-mance in *The Exorcist* to realize how this paradigm of satanic spewing forth, as a parody of logocentric expression, continues.[45]

Raphael provides another parodic version (or perversion) of the symbolic economy of consumption in *Paradise Lost* when he explains to Adam that

> Knowledge is as food, and needs no less
> Her Temperance over Appetite, to know
> In measure what the mind may well contain,
> Oppresses else with Surfeit, and soon turns
> Wisdom to Folly, as Nourishment to Wind. (*PL* 7.126–30)

Raphael's epistemology of eating is based on an understanding of taste as *sapere*, dating back to classical times. Plato, for instance, explains that there are "two desires natural to man — one of food for the sake of the body, and one of wisdom for the sake of the diviner part of us" (*CDP* 1207). Yet, in the final line above, turning "Nourishment to Wind" can be read in a number of ways: it can mean (1) tossing knowledge to the wind (that is, turning it into nothing rather than spirit); (2) turning it into spirit, or the proper expressive end product of food; or (3) turning it into the kind of "subterranean wind" that means flatulence (e.g., *PL* 1.231). Describing hell as the topos of waste, Milton follows early modern medical theory in putting the four elements to work for physiological ends: hell's "fuell'd entrails thence conceiving Fire . . . aid the Winds, / And leave a singed bottom all involv'd / With stench and smoke" (1.234–37). According to this scatological pun, the intemperate eater becomes aligned with the same expressive impotence displayed by the devils in book 10. Such a reading again posits the mouth (now of "fools," as earlier of "slaves and scoundrels" and "veritable devils") as the Ur-site of emetic expression — a parody of logocentric expression and hence not really expression at all. Such representations of satanic "expression" invert, indeed pervert, the divine logocentric model, suggesting that those who follow Sin in all her varieties, rather than becoming incorporate unto the Word, become incorporate unto Wind, which is to say nothing.

In "Lycidas" (1637) Milton directs this demonizing strategy against prelates, or "Blind Mouths!" whose unfortunate flock

> are not fed,
> But swoln with wind, and the rank mist they draw,
> Rot inwardly, and foul contagion spread:
> Besides what the grim Wolf with privy paw
> Daily devours apace, and nothing said. . . . (125–29)

The "grim Wolf" here is the Roman Catholic Church, whom Milton renders elsewhere as a band of "ravenous and savage wolves threatning inrodes and bloody incursions upon the flock of Christ, which they took upon them to feed, but now clame to devour as their prey" (*YP* 1:856–57). The idea recurs in *Paradise Lost,* when Michael predicts that "Wolves shall succeed for teachers, grievous wolves" (12.5089) and where Satan appears as "a prowling Wolf" (4.183). As these prelatical "Blind Mouths" spew forth "wind" and "rank mist" into the mouths of their "hungry Sheep" (125–26), expression transfigures into a rank wind that fails to signify.[46] Satanically, they devour their own progeny, who rather than drawing sustenance from the parental feeding source, are bloated with the rank and corrosive wind of meaningless expression. Instead of piping the traditional pastoral pipe, they inharmoniously "Grate on their scrannel Pipes of wretched straw" (124), an act more vomitive than expressive, since (as his contemporary John Aubrey tells us) Milton in his more satirical moods pronounced the letter *R* very hard: "wretched" becomes "retched."[47]

Because Satan's self-devouring egotism will not allow him to eat outward, to partake of the Word expressed as a monist world, he becomes an unincorporable lump, a dyspeptic "blocking agent" who must be forever repressed from the otherwise integrated system at large.[48] In such a system, one becomes incorporate unto what one eats. Milton writes in his *Apology for Smectymnuus* (1642), "I conceav'd my selfe to be now not as mine own person, but as a member incorporate into that truth whereof I was perswaded, and whereof I had declar'd openly to be a partaker" (*YP* 1:871). To partake of the "truth" is to partake of God, since, according to Milton, the primary attribute of God is truth (*YP* 6:140). As one partakes of truth in the original sense of "taking part" in that truth, one becomes "a member incorporate" unto the thing consumed. Not only is it true that as one eats one is eaten, therefore; we may even venture to assert, on the authority of Milton, that one eats *in order to* be eaten — to become part of a wider cycle of signification.

Taste Redeemed: Paradise Regained

Maintaining himself in the chaos of waste that surrounds creation, Satan offers an alternative (albeit emetic) discourse, a supplemental fecundity in the form of lies. Chaos may be "always available to substantiate alternatives to the established order,"[49] but in *Paradise Regained* Satan's words constitute a compulsive tautology deprived of signification sustaining the four books of the poem. Its narrative structure "presents one of the most difficult problems in the entire field of Milton interpretation," as Hunter observes: "There is no agreement, for instance, about how many temptations Satan offers Jesus (to say nothing of what they mean)."[50] Some consider the overall structure to be one of intensification, building toward the final temptation on the "pinnacle" of book 4, while others claim that there can be no structure to the temptations.[51] Still others (such as Hunter himself) see the structure as simply "botched."[52] The following pages depart from this schematic by suggesting that, after his initial defeat in getting the Son of God to eat, Satan knows he stands no chance in tempting him with the less bodily temptations of wealth and glory. Nevertheless, he stubbornly persists, haranguing the Son in a parody of logocentric expression that constitutes an anticlimactic, interminable structure of decline.

Readers dispute whether the first temptation in book 1 represents a temptation to gluttony or to "distrust" in God's provenance (*PR* 1.355). Whatever his motives, Satan's first words to the Son challenge him to eat, to "save" himself with food, specifically bread, in order to avoid dropping like a "Carcass, pin'd with hunger and with drought":

> But if thou be the Son of God, Command
> That out of these hard stones be made thee bread;
> So shalt thou save thyself and us relieve
> With Food, whereof we wretched seldom taste. (*PR* 1.325, 342–45)

With some irony, the Son responds:

> Think'st thou such force in Bread? is it not written
> (For I discern thee other than thou seem'st)
> Man lives not by Bread only, but each Word
> Proceeding from the mouth of God, who fed
> Our Fathers here with Manna? (*PR* 1.347–51)

As if to a negligent or unwilling pupil, Jesus recites what is at once a basic formula of Christianity and a virtual Protestant mantra that converts food into spirituality: "one does not live by bread alone, but by every word that comes from the mouth of the Lord."[53] As the embodied voice of this doctrine, the Son appears as something less and yet something more than human — a symbolic castrato or sacrifice to an economy of consumption in which he circulates as "that living Bread which, Christ says, is his flesh" (*YP* 6:553). For Milton, both Satan and Son are created, and both play a role in creation.[54] The crucial distinction is that the Son recognizes his status as part of the made world ("first of created things" and "firstborn of all creation"), while Satan regards himself as "self-begot" (*YP* 6:206, 419). This fatal self-delusion on the part of the false (or fabricated) son necessitates his exclusion from the world of logocentric circulation.

Milton believed that the fallacy of interpreting Jewish law in Christian terms, and thereby translating the material bread of Deuteronomy into the "living bread" of the Gospel ("I am the bread of life" [John 6:35]), was responsible for the Catholic doctrine of transubstantiation, which he calls a "cannibal feast" (*YP* 6:554).[55] After his first rebuff, Satan returns to the other dregs, who are still circulating in the "middle region of thick air," and reports that he has "found him, view'd him, tasted him, but find[s] / Far other labor to be undergone" (*PR* 2.117, 131–32). The Son has certainly been "tested" in the Latinate sense of taste (*tastare*), but it is worth considering that he has also literally been tasted by an antagonist who finds him to be something he cannot digest. Satan is Satan, after all, by virtue of his refusal to partake of the "living bread," and in a symbolic economy centered on the Son, his meaningless, nonproductive expression makes no sense. Unable to recognize what Satan in his deepest heart knows, and what his words indicate here (the futility of "other labor"), the devils propose tempting the Son next through his sexual appetite: "Set women in his eye and in his walk" (2.153). Satan rejects the idea out of hand and proclaims that "with manlier objects we must try / His constancy" (2.225–26). The possibility remains, however, that these "manlier objects" are figured homoerotically in the banquet scene of book 2, indicating that Satan does ultimately take their suggestion despite his knowledge of its futility.[56] Against all odds and his own better judgment, Satan feels that he still "must try."

Not until the second book of the poem does the Son admit any appetite, and some have taken him to mean that he "does not actually experience hunger until book 2."[57] Although he has been fasting for forty days, he claims that he is "Now hung'ring first":

> But now I feel I hunger, which declares
> Nature hath need of what she asks; yet God
> Can satisfy that need some other way,

> Though hunger still remain: so it remain
> Without this body's wasting, I content me,
> And from the sting of Famine fear no harm,
> Nor mind it, fed with better thoughts that feed
> Mee hung'ring more to do my Father's will. (*PR* 2.244, 252–59)

Note that Jesus does not say "I" hunger. Instead, he assumes a critical distance from the "I" who hungers and observes (somewhat abstractly for a starving person), "I *feel* I hunger," separating himself from the hungering "I" as he does from bodily need. It is not Jesus himself who needs, we are led to believe, but the more abstracted Nature who "hath need of what she asks." But if hunger is, as Satan calls it, "life's enemy" (*PR* 2.372), can there really be hunger without bodily need, or the visceral fear of death? Here the Son's "hunger" appears one step removed, allegorically deferred from a more primal hunger that can be heard in the sound of the word: *Hunger,* a cry reverberating back through the Old English *hungor,* Old Saxon *hungar,* Germanic *hunger,* Old Teutonic *huhru,* meaning to ache (*OED*). Yet there is very little torment or aching in this highly rational, seemingly disinterested soliloquy on the Son of God's hunger. Even when he dreams of food in biblical tradition, he himself does not dream but appetite dreams "as appetite is wont to dream, / Of meats and drinks, Nature's refreshment sweet" (*PR* 2.264–65). In the face of gnawing hunger, his position is the impossible one of tasteful disinterestedness.

If Nature needs and appetite dreams, however, where is the "I" who says, "I feel"? Satan wonders too, as he provides scriptural precedent for giving in to one's hunger and receives the following rebuff: "What conclud'st thou hence? / They all had need, I as thou seest have none" (*PR* 2.317–18). Quite naturally wondering how, if Jesus has no need, it can be possible for him to hunger, Satan demands: "How hast thou hunger then?" (2.319). Unfortunately, he does not pursue this question or even pause for an answer. Rather, in his self-destructive dash to perform the impossible, to get Jesus to eat or partake of his food (words, emetic lies), he quickly continues: "Tell me, if Food were now before thee set, / Would'st thou not eat? Thereafter as I like / The giver, answer'd Jesus" (*PR* 2.320–22). Jesus' answer has been interpreted to mean that he will eat inasmuch as he *likes* the giver, as in Paul's letter to the Corinthians: "Ye cannot drink the cup of the Lord, and the cup of devils: ye cannot be partakers of the Lord's Table, and of the table of devils" (1 Cor. 10:21).[58] Milton employs the same idea in his *Masque* when the Lady refuses the food offered her by the shady epicure, Comus: "I would not taste thy treasonous offer; none / But such as are good men can give good things" (702–03). Like the Son's response to Satan in *Paradise Regained,* her lines imply that if one eats, one will become like the giver, or a part of what one partakes of. Satan seems to intuit this same meaning, for his effort to get the Son to partake (to *like/be like* him, or in plain terms to "sit and eat") becomes increasingly desperate. His courteous invitation, "only deign to sit and eat," transforms into the more testy, "What doubts the Son of God to sit and eat?" (*PR* 2.336, 368). Finally, he loses all patience and commands: "What doubt'st thou Son of God? sit down and eat" (2.377). This repeated overture to "sit and eat" perverts Adam's invitation to Raphael to "sit and taste" in book 5 of *Paradise Lost,* the crucial difference being that Satan's offerings are not part of the divine substance (the difference between eat and taste).

By the final quarter of the seventeenth century, insatiable luxury, gluttony, and perverse gourmandizing had come to be seen as sins opposed to the ideology of healthful living. In this context, the banquet Satan presents to the Son in book 2 of *Paradise Lost* appeals to a courtly ethic of immoral indulgence.[59] Charles Lamb interprets it as the "severest satire upon full tables and surfeits," observing that "The mighty artillery of sauces which the cook-fiend conjures up is out of proportion to the simple wants and plain hunger of the guest. He that disturbed him in his dreams, from his dreams might have been taught better. To the temperate fantasies of the famished Son of God, what sort of feasts presented themselves?" (*WCL* 2:93–94). Opposed to the temperate, discretionary pleasures of tasteful refinement, Satan offers a

> Table richly spread, in regal mode,
> With dishes pil'd, and meats of noblest sort
> And savor, Beasts of chase, or Fowl of game,
> In pastry built, or from the spit, or boil'd,
> Grisamber stream'd; all Fish from Sea or Shore. . . .
> Alas how simple, to these Cates compar'd,
> Was the crude Apple that diverted *Eve!* (*PR* 2.340–49)

Readers have wondered why, given the ill success of his first attempt to get the Son to eat, Satan tries again, conjuring this elaborate feast in the desert. Ought one to agree with Hunter that "having failed in the former, Satan is a simpleton to propose the latter"?[60] Is he a fool, a proverbial dog returning to his vomit? We know from book 10 of *Paradise Lost* that devils do repeat their folly in mock-creative gestures that are as tautological as they are self-destructive. However, like most things in this problematic poem, it is not entirely clear that Satan does repeat himself here. Critics divide over whether the feast is part of a second temptation (to worldly wealth and glory) or an awkward repetition of the first temptation (to eat). Whether the banquet is intended to appeal to Jesus' hunger for the first or the second time, it is excessive and discordant with the kind of wants one would expect of the self-sacrificing Son, a tasteful consumer.

In the King James version of Genesis, when Satan is referred to as "subtil," the term besides clever means ethereal or refined, both senses included in the idea of the subtle palate. When Satan introduces the illusory nymphs and stripling youths who cater to his feast, he proclaims them "Spirits of Air, and Woods, and Springs" (*PR* 2.374) in words that seem to come directly from the mouth of Shakespeare's Prospero. Indeed, to discern the Shakespearean resonances in Satan's speech is to discover something that the Son already knows, namely, that the banquet is an elaborate fabrication. In *The Tempest* Prospero observes to his spellbound guests, "You do yet taste / Some subtleties o' th' isle, that will [not] let you / Believe things certain."[61] Fabrication, as we have seen, can mean both metaphor making and lying, and Prospero's light, fanciful confections resemble Satan's "subtleties," an early modern term for those highly ornate, architectural desserts that adorned courtly banquet tables.[62] In fact a singular feature of the condemnation of court cuisine that took place at the end of the seventeenth century was the ostracization of sweets. By 1699, as the diarist John Evelyn reports, sugar was "almost wholly banish'd from all, except the most effeminate Palates."[63] Ironically, at the very moment that sugar was becoming more widely available through colonial importation, subtleties were becoming improper fare for the morally substantial Man of Taste. When the Son refuses to taste Satan's subtleties in *Paradise Regained,* "Both Table and Provision vanish'd quite / With sound of Harpies' wings and Talons heard," just as they do in act 3 of *The Tempest*.[64]

Although Satan seems to have tried every means, and failed, to get Jesus to "sit and eat," he does not cease in his effort to get him to swallow what he has to say, sweetening his words to the best of his abilities. There is a scriptural tradition of seeing text as food and textual consumption as a means to cognitive nutrition as well. The prophet Ezekiel is told, "eat this scroll," which to him tasted as sweet as honey (Ezek. 3:1–3); in the book of Revelation, John is similarly given a little scroll by an angel, who commands: "Take it, and eat; it will be better to your stomach, but sweet as honey in your mouth" (Rev. 10:9–10). After the Restoration, the scriptural word was being confounded with other (literary) forms of text as fodder for those seeking self-improvement, and Milton supported the uncensored proliferation of printed matter in *Areopagitica* (1644), urging consumers to practice discrimination: "books are as meats and viands are; some of good, some of evil substance (*YP* 2:512). That the "good" book is a means to taste, as well as to virtue, is an idea that reverberates through the Century of Taste. Christopher Smart's hymn on "Taste," for instance, describes the practice of reading the Bible in these terms: "How greatly sweet, how sweetly grand / Who reads the most, is most refin'd."[65] For such textual consumption to qualify as aesthetic, of course, pleasure must be involved. Otherwise, despite its other qualities, it merely constitutes what Shaftesbury calls "a sort of task-reading, in which a taste is not permitted" (*C* 153).

Admittedly, Satan spends the remainder of the poem tempting Jesus not with the pleasures of text per se (*that* delectation is left to the reader) but with a seemingly endless stream of spoken verbiage. Readers complain that *Paradise Regained* is devoid of action and almost wholly composed of speeches, but these post-banquet harangues are precisely Milton's point. They are manifestations of Satan's general-economic nature and his corresponding capacity for nonproductive expenditure. As Alan Fisher points out, Milton had many years' experience with a style of prose oration that conflates text with speech: "Milton did not think his readers would be detached listeners. Speechmaking implies the same attention he described as the 'ingesting' of books — indeed, a book, for Milton, is an oration in print."[66] That spoken words may be consumed as food we know from *Paradise Lost,* where Adam says to Raphael, "sweeter thy discourse is to my ear / Than Fruits of Palm-tree pleasantest to thirst" (*PL* 8.211–12). The temptations following the banquet of book 2 of *Paradise Regained* offer food in the form of speech-text, or Satan's own honeyed words. As the Son tells him in book 1, "[It] was thy chosen task, / To be a liar in four hundred mouths; / For lying is thy sustenance, thy food" (*PR* 1.427–29). The history of readerly distaste with his speech only testifies to his efficacy as blocking agent, his tartarlike indigestibility. The Son, for his part, yields to an impulse to taunt Satan by mocking his manner of speech. Once the long-winded fiend has done his best to arouse his appetite for all the wealth and glory of Rome, the Son instructs him: "thou should'st add to tell / Thir sumptuous gluttonies, and gorgeous feasts / On *Citron* tables or *Atlantic* stone" (4.113–15). Joining in the rhetorical game, he demystifies it, stripping his antagonist of all power of illusion. He sees through his subtleties, as it were, which soon melt into air. Nevertheless, it is in Satan's nature to persist, and though "desperate of success," he continues to heap sugary fabrications on his temperate foe (*PR* 4.23).

Finally, after nearly two thousand lines of Satanic frustration, of failing to get Jesus to "sit and eat" either literally or figuratively, Satan sets him on the highest pinnacle of Jerusalem and demands: "There stand, if thou wilt stand" (*PR* 4.551). This pinnacle scene has a literature of its own, but the two critical points at issue remain, as Stanley Fish states them, "(1) whether or not this scene is a part of the temptation proper or is a 'climactic epilogue' to an action already complete, and (2) whether this confrontation is decisive in a way that its predecessors were not."[67] Unlike the previous temptations in which the *via negativa* of resistance was simply the best way to proceed, it is impossible now for the Son to resist. Should he choose to save himself by resorting to divine intervention, he would give up his human status and so give in to Satan. If, on the other hand, he allows himself to fall, he gives in to presumption, self-destruction, and, consequently, Sin and Satan. One might agree with Fisher that "The situation is Satan's masterpiece."[68] Indeed, if we set his command to "stand" against his repeated challenge to "sit and eat," this final act is an even cleverer maneuver on the part of the "subtle Fiend" to undermine his opponent's *via negativa* of resistance, his stance of refusing to sit. Since Satan cannot get him voluntarily to sit and eat, in other words, he ingeniously takes away the possibility that he can remain standing.

Yet as literary history tells us, the Son "said and stood" (*PR* 4.561). Presumably, through some force of will or muscular agility, he stands his ground and proclaims: "Tempt not the Lord thy God; he said and stood. / But Satan smitten with amazement fell" (4.561–62). The consecutive line endings "stood" and "fell" are meant to contrast one another as alternate modes of conduct, but it is crucial to this meaning that the latter line is enjambed. Satan does not merely fall: he falls like Antaeus, as we learn in the following line, and this mythic figure famously gains renewed strength with every fall. Satan is perpetually falling, perpetually eating his own words, perpetually being rejected. As Raphael makes clear, "whatever was created, needs / To be sustained and fed," and eating one's own words as a created thing is lying and self-consuming. Within the confines of the poem, therefore, Satan self-destructs in fulfillment of Milton's prophetic words, "evil on itself shall back recoil": "Gather'd like scum, and settl'd to itself, / It shall be in eternal restless change / Self-fed and self-consum'd" (*A Masque* 593–97). Excluded from the symbolic economy of productive expression, Satan's end product is waste and emission.

As the Satanic school of Milton's Romantic readers attest, however, this supplemental Son has a dangerously seductive appeal. Such appeal prompts us to take seriously the proposition that

> The Son of God . . . bears no single sense;
> The Son of God I also am, or was,
> And if I was, I am; relation stands;
> All men are Sons of God. . . . (*PR* 4.517–20)

Satan is supplemental to the Son, if we define the term as "a surplus, a plenitude enriching another plenitude, the *fullest measure* of presence," in Derrida's words; "the supplement supplements. It adds only to replace. It intervenes or insinuates itself *in-the-place-of;* if it fills, it is as if one fills a void."[69] Satan supplements by filling in the potentiality of what the Son could be by extending him to his radical limits. Yet in doing so, he insinuates himself "*in-the-*

place-of." James Nohrnberg argues that the Son's "filial identity is the birth-right Satan as twin has deeded over to his other," and Kilgour observes that these "antithetical brothers stand together on the temple of their father — giving Milton a choice opportunity to knock one down." [70] Who is Milton's Savior-hero? The one whose sacrifice places him at the center of a symbolic economy of consumption founded on the "living bread," or the one who by becoming a sacrifice (an ejected, rejected member) enables that economy in the first place?

Milton ingeniously averts this moral dilemma by proscribing his supplementary Son to an outside that prohibits true supplementarity. As the abjected dregs of creation, Satan is an indigestible, inassimilable irritant within the system at large. Yet where he and the (legitimate) Son ultimately do converge is the ground of their mutual resistance, Jesus refusing to eat the false fabrications (food, speeches, lies) of Satan, and Satan refusing to swallow the Word that is Christ. Humans may have been seasoned by Sin, but the divine Son has not, and in him Satan finds something he can or will not consume — the Word incarnate. Despite the biblical portrait of Satan as stalking the earth, indiscriminately "looking for someone to devour" (1 Peter 5:8), Satan's taste is as discriminating as it is bad and flies in the face of the good, because correct, taste of the Son.[71] Both Satan and Son are, ironically, "exact of taste," and in the obstinacy of their resistance they define themselves as what they will not eat, what they will not be, their not-to-consume forming the condition of possibility for taste.

Corporeality necessitates particularity, and one is finally led to suspect that the discrimination of Miltonic taste resounds in the depths of despair, the bottomless sarcasm of Adam's "*Eve*, now I see thou art exact of taste. . . . And Palate call judicious." Perhaps a more poignant claim for the ontopoetic power of taste, its ability to delimit and hence define the self, may not anywhere be found. As Louis Althusser remarks, "the category of the subject is only constitutive of all ideology insofar as all ideology has the function (which defines it) of 'constituting' concrete individuals as subjects."[72] Orthodox Marxism notoriously draws its representational devices from Christianity, and Milton's symbolic economy of consumption prefigures the economy that is at once consumerism and the ideology of taste responsible for constituting people as subjects. As consumers turned from the Word that is Christ to its multiplicity in literary form, a plurality of consumable printed words began to shape and sustain the culture of taste. As one aspect of the multidimensional process of secularization, Milton's own work trumped the Bible as the edible core of a symbolic economy based on taste.

All the major eighteenth-century taste theorists turn to Milton, and in particular *Paradise Lost,* as the definitive word on taste. Shaftesbury uses Milton as proof that poets "may easily, with the help of their genius and a right use of art, command their audience and establish a good taste" (C 124); Hume turns to him as a kind of aesthetic gold standard in his 1757 essay "Of the Standard of Taste" to overturn the view that all sentiment is right, or *de gustibus non est disputandum* (EMP 230–31); Addison finds that "in the greatness of his Sentiments . . . [Milton] triumphs over all the Poets both Modern and Ancient, *Homer* only excepted" (SPT 2:587), a view echoed by others, including Hugh Blair in his 1783 lecture on taste: "Paradise Lost is a poem that abounds with beauties of every kind; and that justly entitles its author to a degree of fame not inferior to any poet."[73] Milton is proof that even ugliness can be aesthetically represented as beauty, which for philosophers like Kant is the only true province of taste: "Even the portrayal of the evil or ugly (for example, in the figure of the personified Death in Milton) can and must be beautiful whenever an object is to be aesthetically imagined" (AN 144). As the ontic Word of Christianity crumbles into a proliferation of words in the literary print culture of the eighteenth century, Milton's metaphorical display of gustatory taste sets the terms for aesthetic taste theory as a symbolic economy of consumption.

The Century of Taste: Shaftesbury, Hume, Burke

TASTE *is at present the darling idol of the polite world, and the world of letters; and, indeed, seems to be considered as the quintessence of almost all the arts and sciences. The fine ladies and gentlemen dress with Taste; the architects, whether* Gothic *or* Chinese, *build with Taste; the painters paint with Taste; the poets write with Taste; critics read with Taste; and in short, fidlers [sic], players, singers, dancers, and mechanics themselves, are all the sons and daughters of Taste. Yet in this amazing superabundancy of Taste, few can say what it really is, or what the word itself signifies.*

— Mr. Town, *Critic and Censor-General,* The Connoisseur
(May 13, 1756)

By the middle of the eighteenth century taste encompassed the fields of art, architecture, landscape, furniture, dress, manners, and eventually gastronomy. As George Colman and Bonnell Thornton remark in *The Connoisseur,* a mock-Addisonian journal published from 1754 to 1756, "in this amazing superabundancy of Taste, few can say what it really is, or what the word itself signifies."[1] Standard histories of the development of the bourgeois public sphere recognize that the political and economic restructurings that took place in the latter part of the seventeenth century realigned civil society as a culture of consumption. "Taste became the vogue" at this time, as Lance Bertelsen writes, "a code word for knowing how and what to consume, and for judging how and what one's neighbor consumed."[2] Historians, sociologists, and anthropologists have begun to explicate the many ways in which British culture was contested and shaped at this time through the processes of consumption, but these accounts do not reveal just how important the *metaphor* of consumption, with its internal dialectic of taste and appetite, was to the civilizing process. This chapter in the literary history of taste shows how several key Enlightenment philosophers take up the gustatory metaphor from Milton to dispose of all rudeness (the phrase is Kant's, as we shall see) from the paradigm of the tasteful self.

Although by the early years of the eighteenth century newer iatrochemical models of digestion had loosened Galen's powerful hold on the study of physiology, the idea of poorly concocted vapors and putrefied spirits that needed to be purged from the animal economy persisted in literary, philosophical, and medical discourse of the era. As Roy Porter writes, "putrefying *excrementa* and indurated faeces would, many feared, produce gastric ferments, flatulence and bile, leading to auto-poisoning . . . popular physiology attended to evacuations no less than to appetites."[3] The contemporary medical obsession with bodily evacuation informing physiological practice of the time also served as a powerful image for identity formation. Philosophically, the system-clogging dregs came to stand for all manner of rudeness that needed to be purged from the aspirant Man of Taste. Against the civilizing discourse of taste, begun by Shaftesbury and Addison at the start of the century, the physician and philosopher Bernard Mandeville, whose specialty was stomach and nerve disorders, promoted a counterdiscourse of appetite that plagued aesthetic taste theory throughout the century of its unfolding. Through the windows of Shaftesbury, Hume, and Burke, this chapter will examine gustatory moments of eighteenth-century taste theory, fleshing them out and returning them to the metaphorical trajectory constituting literary history. To understand how individual and communal identities were metaphorically shaped through the Enlightenment discourse of taste, canonical moments of aesthetic taste theory combine in the final pages of the chapter with visual satires from the 1790s as critical confrontations with the gustatory trope of consumption.

Disposing of Rudeness

Shaftesbury's *Characteristics of Men, Manners, Opinions, Times* (1711), together with Addison's "Pleasures of the Imagination," published in *The Spectator* in 1711 and 1712, are foundational texts of eighteenth-century aesthetics, replacing the immanence of the divine Word with the aesthetic ideal of Beauty. Addison's "Pleasures of the Imagination" are based largely on a discussion of *Paradise Lost,* and when considered against Milton, Shaftesbury seems to have instantiated the philosophical discourse of taste upon the same metaphorical framework as his literary forebear. Like other Cambridge school Platonists, Shaftesbury believed that human beings were naturally tasteful, rather than naturally pathological, or full of moral, epistemological, and phenomenological "dregs." To get back to that original condition of purity, he argued, one need simply evacuate (Shaftesbury's image) the corruptions accrued through lived existence in society. Backing this philosophical idealism was a political idealism: the Whiggish faith, inherited from his grandfather the first earl, that all citizens are relatively equal, interdependent members of the body politic. Applied to aesthetics, this logic dictates that to judge correctly is to judge without interest, from a condition of subjective transparency, from which all idiosyncrasies of birth, habit, or circumstance have been purged. The requisite for aesthetic experience, then, personal disinterestedness, has its sociopolitical dimension in the ideal of universality.

The third treatise of *Characteristics* was originally published in 1710 as "Soliloquy: or, Advice to an Author," and in it Shaftesbury elucidates a theory of tasteful self-making, described as a "method of evacuation" (*C* 74). As he conceived it, this was a technique by which the aspiring author, orator, or expresser could dispose of all culturally accrued rudeness to emerge in his "natural" purity as a polite Man of Taste. Shaftesbury maintained that human beings were inclined to virtue and that virtuous action was naturally reinforced through pleasure, but his notebooks reveal a darker side to this purported idealism: "This is life," he writes some time around the turn of the century, "recruiting, repairing, feeding, cleansing, purging; aliments, rags, excrements, dregs."[4] In "Soliloquy," he positions himself as a physician to others such as himself and promotes his "method of evacuation" as a technique to be practiced by individuals in private: "one should have but an ill time to be present at these bodily operations" (*C* 74). Just as Milton's symbolic economy of consumption is founded on the abjected dregs of Creation, the self-making Man of Taste (in theory, at least) must purge himself in order to become a microcosm of clean, waste-free circulation.

What Shaftesbury adapted to the higher philosophical concern of human subjectivity, his philosophical rival, Bernard Mandeville, treated as a direct physiological problem. Mandeville was an actual physician with specific training in digestive disorders, and in the same year that Shaftesbury's major collected work appeared, he published *A Treatise on the Hypochondriack and Hysterick Diseases* (1711), offering a countervision of humanity as founded on the perpetually craving (and largely dysfunctional) stomach.[5] Mandeville's second dialogue between Philopirio, a physician, and his patient Misomedon describes the spleen as the depository for all the "dregs," "faeculencies," and "muddy parts" of the body; normally, these are volatized through the culinary concept of a "ferment" and sent forth into the blood, but if the spleen should become diseased, and refuse to perform its functions, "then what becomes of the Dregs of the Blood? Which way does the Blood get rid of them?" (*THH* 97). The implied response is that it cannot, and this is where the "method of evacuation," philosophically as well as physiologically, comes into play.[6]

Shaftesbury warns that if one does not administer privately to one's own bodily operations and instead "discharge[s] frequently and vehemently in public," then "there is great danger lest the party, through this habit, should suffer much by crudities, indigestions, choler, bile, and particularly by a certain tumour or flatulency, which renders him of all men the least able to apply the wholesome regimen of self-practice" (C 75–76). According to him, poets are used to raving in private and thereby evacuating the mind of its crudities, but prose authors, "being denied an equal benefit of discharge, and withheld from the wholesome manner of relief in private, it is no wonder if they appear with so much froth and scum in public . . . writers of memoirs and essays are chiefly subject to this frothy distemper" (C 74). Above all, Shaftesbury wished to avoid the scatological indecency of novelists, memoir writers, Grub Street hacks, and others who offered their mental evacuations in printed form for public consumption.

Shaftesbury claimed that it is "very indecent for any one to publish his meditations, occasional reflections, solitary thoughts or other such exercises as come under the notion of this self-discoursing practice. And the modestest title I can conceive for such works would be that of a certain author who called them his crudities" (C 74). The reference is to Thomas Coryate's popular seventeenth-century travel narrative, *Coryats Crudities: Hastily Gobled vp in Five Moneths Trauells in France, Sauoy, Italy . . . Newly Digested in the Hungry aire of Odcombe in the County of Somerset, & now dispersed to the nourishment of the trauelling members of this kindgome* (1611). Hastily consumed landscape, art, and other taste matter function like those residual obstructions left over from digestion called crudities, which can block the functions of the mind and forestall tasteful expression. However indecent it may be to gobble greedily (and attend to other digestive operations in public), Shaftesbury claimed that it is worse to cough up ill-digested matter, discursive dregs or crudities, and offer them for public consumption.

Crudity was a term covering all forms of digestive derangement that could produce corrupted humors and influence the mind. As Ken Albala writes, early modern "pedagogues took careful consideration of the time, order, quality, and substance of the books offered to young students in exactly the same way as dietaries dealt with these issues regarding food."[7] Milton instructs young men in *Of Education* (1644) that printed crudities are "odious to be read, yet not to be avoided without a well continu'd and judicious conversing among pure Authors digested, which they scarce taste" (*YP* 2:373). His imperative to know how to "manage a crudity" (*YP* 1:392–93), like Shaftesbury's concern with the management of all bodily "indecencies," extended past the physical into the more culturally resonant arena of mental taste. According to Shaftesbury, readers turned to authors not to be fed "from hand to mouth" like undiscriminating beasts, but to find material for the exercise of mental discernment or taste (*C* 1:119). In this, he follows a venerable tradition of treating text as food, as I discussed briefly in the previous chapter. As Francis Bacon instructs, "Some Bookes are to be Tasted, Others to be Swallowed, and Some Few to be Chewed and Digested: That is, some *Bookes* are to be read onely in Parts; Others to be read but not Curiously; And some Few to be read wholly, and with Diligence and Attention."[8] The eighteenth-century editorial fashion for collecting and publishing "Beauties" was in line with this notion that the tasteful consumer should cull the choice bits from text, discarding the rest if not up to his or her discriminating standards. Shaftesbury's Man of Taste was an expresser as well as consumer, and he bore a hefty responsibility not only to *be* tasteful, to exercise taste in the form of critical discernment, but to express himself tastefully and make his taste available in positive printed form for a public of consumers.

Evacuating defects was only half the story, therefore, of tasteful self-making. From his earliest origins, the Enlightenment Man of Taste was both an active creator, who could express taste rhetorically, in positive discursive form, and a consumer.[9] The higher objective was self-expression, which Kant describes in his *Anthropology* as the positive manifestation of taste: "To be well-mannered, proper, polite, and polished (*by disposing of rudeness*) is, nevertheless, only the negative condition of taste. The representation of these qualities in the imagination can be a tasteful, externally intuitive way of imagining an object, or one's own person, but for two senses only, hearing and sight. . . . On the other hand, the discursive way of imagining through the spoken or written word embraces two arts wherein taste can manifest itself: rhetoric and poetry" (*AN* 147; my emphasis). Never merely a passive consumer of beauty, the Man of Taste exercised more than his faculty of critical discernment. He had as much to do with production as consumption. And when the concept of taste left the world of reception and entered the realm of production, its cultural and political stakes were only increased. Reviewing Alison's *Essays on the Nature and*

Principles of Taste in 1811, the Romantic critic Francis Jeffrey observed: "If we aspire . . . to be creators, as well as observers of beauty, and place any part of our happiness in ministering to the gratification of others — as artists or poets, or authors of any sort — then, indeed, a new distinction of tastes, and a far more laborious system of cultivation, will be necessary."[10] A division of the category of taste is proposed: one for play or private enjoyment, which need not adhere to wider social standards, and one that must obey rules and go to work in the public sphere of production. Rather than catering to his audiences' "first relish and appetite" (C 118), Shaftesbury's author had an implied moral duty to *create* the taste of his readers, an idea later adopted as an imperative for the poet by Wordsworth and Coleridge.

In *The Connoisseur*, Colman and Thornton recognized the two ways in which taste could become manifest. "The Man of Taste may be considered as a *Bon Vivant*," they state in the persona of Mr. Town, "who is fond of the dishes before him, and distinguishes nicely what is savoury and delicious, or flat and insipid, in the ingredients of each"; but, at the same time, "he may be regarded as the Cook, who from knowing what things will mix well together, and distinguishing by a nice taste when he has arrived at that very happy mixture, is able to compose such exquisite dishes."[11] In his dual capacity of *Bon Vivant* (equivalent later to epicure or gastronomer) as well as chef, the Man of Taste participated in a larger economy of consumption. James Engell has elaborated the multiple ways in which "eighteenth-century critics eventually turned the principles of criticism into the principles of the imagination itself. Critics begin to equate — or, depending on one's point of view, to confuse — imagination with taste, so that the two become nearly inseparable."[12] Taste, in short, was a guide to creation and the eighteenth-century Man of Taste a provider of food (whether discursive or culinary) for others.

In his 1726 *Letter to a Young Poet*, Swift parodied Shaftesbury's "Soliloquy; or, Advice to an Author" by proposing a similar "method of evacuation" to be used by Grub Street poets and hacks.[13] Suggesting that city administrators cordon off a quarter of the town for such scribblers to dispose of their mental rudeness, he writes:

> Every one knows, *Grub-street* is a Market for *Small-Ware* in WIT, and as necessary considering the usual Purgings of a *Human Brain*, as the *Nose* is upon a Man's *Face* . . . and yet those whose Province it is, have not yet thought fit to appoint a place for *Evacuations* of it, which is a very hard Case . . . I am of opinion we suffer in our Health by it: I believe our corrupted *Air*, and frequent thick Fogs are in a great measure owing to the common exposal of our *Wit*, and that with good Management, our Poetical *Vapours* might be carried off in a *common Drain*, and fall into one Quarter of the Town, with-

out Infecting the whole, as the Case is at present, to the great Offence of our *Nobility,* and *Gentry,* and *Others* of nice *Noses.* When writers of all sizes, like Freemen of the City, are at liberty to throw out their *Filth* and *Excrementatious Productions* in every Street as they please, what can the Consequence be, but that the Town must be *Poyson'd.* (*SW* 9:341–42)

The idea, again, is that printed works that have not been properly purged of rudeness provide bad and even nauseating fare to a consuming public. Whereas beauty was an ethereal sensation perceived through the higher sense of sight, smell was conceptually tied to disgust from the time of classical aesthetics, and in the passage above Swift knowingly appeals to people "of nice *Noses.*"[14] Between 1760 and 1780 smell was confirmed as the most appropriate sense for studying the phenomena of putrefaction, and Alain Corbin reports that from the 1770s, "translation of olfactory vigilance into scientific language . . . had manifold aims: to detect irrespirable gases and particularly 'airs,' and to discern and describe hitherto imperceptible viruses, miasmas, and poisons."[15] Swift already alludes to the rapid rise of waste-disposal systems in eighteenth-century European metropolises (of which, by this point, London was the largest) in his *Proposal for erecting and maintaining publick offices of ease within the cities and suburbs of London and Westminster* (1726).[16] Philosophically, such waste had to be disposed of in private in order for one to appear in public as a purified person of taste. Swift and Shaftesbury were both concerned with the dangers that could result from an audience disposed, through lack of taste, to consuming unpredigested material as readily as tasteful rhetoric. The difference is that Shaftesbury believed his concept of "evacuation" could have social efficacy, while it was mainly a topic of satire for Swift. Having less hope for human nature, he also had less faith in taste, the consuming activity by which the self raises itself out of its own appetitive nature into a moral, and hence social, being.

Normally, one does not associate Shaftesbury and Swift by similarity of style or thinking, but the former initiates the philosophical discourse of taste in a prose laden with the same rhetoric of appetite that Swift, from a differing perspective, uses to mock British pretensions to civility.[17] In *The Mechanical Operation of the Spirit* (1704), Swift satirizes an undiscriminating populace ready to consume crudities, dregs, and anything else that flows (so to speak) from the pen of a famous author: "A Master Work-man shall *blow his Nose so powerfully,* as to pierce the Hearts of his People, who are disposed to receive the *Excrements* of his Brain with the same Reverence, as the *Issue* of it. Hawking, Spitting, and Belching, the Defects of other Mens Rhetorick, are the Flowers, and Figures, and Ornaments, of his" (*SPW* 1:183). Like Milton, who could (or would) not imagine a coprophagic universe in *Paradise Lost,* and so produced a fictional cosmology in which God could be tasted and expressed, Enlightenment taste philosophers imagined the tasteful self against a background of excluded rudeness. Swift was far more skeptical than Shaftesbury about the possibility of purging rudeness from the self and society, but one nevertheless detects a half-bitter, half-wistful attachment to the tasteful ideal.

Mandeville, by contrast, flatly declared that there could be no "disposing of rudeness" from the individual or social body. Even more of an outsider to English society than the Irish Swift, the Dutch Mandeville sought to reveal the appetite motivating Shaftesbury's ideal Man of Taste. As Ronald Paulson writes, his purpose was "to expose the desire, economic and sexual, under the supposed disinterestedness of Shaftesbury's civic humanist."[18] Paulson's study of eighteenth-century aesthetics and heterodoxy focuses on Hogarth, who "instead of turning upward with Shaftesbury to a moral sense of benevolent virtue, turned downward with Mandeville to discover beneath Shaftesbury's idealism the sensations aroused by the human body."[19] Such renegade propagandists for appetite maintained that modern commercial society developing in England should find a way to live with its rudeness, since "every Moment must produce new Filth; and . . . what Cost and Care soever be bestow'd to remove the Nastiness almost as fast as 'tis made, it is impossible *London* should be more cleanly before it is less flourishing" (*FB* 1:11–12). This is Mandeville's statement from the preface to the second edition of *The Fable of the Bees,* which was more pointedly in dialogue with Shaftesbury. When it first appeared on the heels of *Characteristics* in 1714, it prompted critics to adapt Mandeville's own physiological language against him. They accused him of being a quack physician, performing a faulty evacuation on the social body: "The best Physician in the World did never labour more to purge the *Natural* Body of *bad* Qualities, than this Bumble-Bee has done to purge the Body *Politick* of *good* ones" (quoted in *FB* 1:397). While Mandeville offered to "physick" private bodies comprising consumer society in a literal manner, Shaftesbury offered to minister to the minds of all persons of taste. For him, the social body was not past cure, and to treat the problems caused by poorly concocted mental food, authors needed simply to practice his "method of evacuation." Consumers, in turn, were to cultivate discernment, for texts as well as for the panoply of food and other consumables made available through British commercial imperialism.

Purging Mist

As we have seen by way of Shaftesbury and Mandeville, humoral medicine still provided conceptual imagery for the Enlightenment discourse of taste. The humoral body was one in which the least imperfection (crudity or other digestive defect) could corrupt or distemper the whole system, and Hume like another good physician directs his famous essay "Of the Standard of Taste" (1757) to all *potential* Men of Taste, all who "either labour under some defect, or are vitiated by some disorder; and by that means, excite a sentiment, which may be pronounced erroneous" (*EMP* 241). His tone is prescriptive, for the main impediments to a correct judgment of taste are defects that cloud or confuse the organs. Similarly, Alexander Gerard claims in his mid-century *Essay on Taste* (1759) that "a man may be sensible, that his not receiving pleasure or disgust in the fine arts, does proceed, in particular instances, from an imperfection in the organs."[20] For Hume and many of his contemporaries, qualities that excite a sentiment of aesthetic pleasure (or disgust) exist "out there" somewhere in the object waiting to be perceived *correctly*. Hume also writes that when "men vary in their judgments, some defect or perversion in the faculties may commonly be remarked" (*EMP* 243). In addition to being "cleared of all prejudice," his ideal critic must achieve a "perfect serenity of mind" (*EMP* 243, 232). Such a condition, besides meaning calm or disinterested, can also mean clear, as in a "serene" and cloudless sky (another atmospheric term used to describe to the holistic humoral body).

Just as he applies the term *serene* to the mind, Hume applies "mist" to the corrupted organs of the Man of Taste. When defects are removed from the perceptive (tasting) organs, he says, "The mist dissipates which seemed formerly to hang over the object: The organ acquires greater perfection in its operations" (*EMP* 237). Mists and vapors clouded the humoral body when food, having passed through the stomach into the liver, was not converted properly into humors and spirits.[21] Normally, these proceeded through the blood to the brain, but under abnormal circumstances "they may ascend straight from the stomach or other abdominal organ to the brain in a vapour, like vapour ascending from the earth to the air, to be distilled into rain."[22] Should the vapor putrefy, or become burnt or corrupt, it could fail to distill into rain and instead linger, like a black cloud or mist, obstructing the operations of the mind. Hume's mist at first glance seems to hang over the object, but when this mist dissipates, the critic finds that his "organ acquires greater perfection in its operations." Hume's own analysis of the sound and defective state of the organ(s) also prompts us to consider his mist physiologically as well as atmospherically.

Hume relies heavily upon Milton in the essay, particularly *Paradise Lost,* a poem in which Milton asks divine aid to "Purge and disperse" all inward "mist from thence" so that he may create (3.53–54).[23] These lines are a meditation on Milton's blindness, which the poet attributed to foul digestive vapors that had failed to evacuate his system. The immediate cause of the obstruction to his eyesight, he thought, was a corrupted vapor produced during the digestion of food that had hardened into opacity on his visual nerve. These same mind-clouding mists, which supposedly blinded Milton, afflict Adam after the "mortal taste" of the fruit. Milton writes in book 11 that the "false fruit that promised clearer sight / Had bred" instead a misted vision, until the archangel Michael "purged with euphrasy and rue / The visual nerve" (11.413–15). Like Milton, Adam was a man (in Kerrigan's words) "whose food had solidified into an impenetrable barrier between his mind and the world."[24] This humoral concept of unpurged bodily vapors that could cloud and "mistify" the brain extended past Milton into philosophical and literary texts of the eighteenth century.

Kant, for instance, a philosopher obsessed with his health, complained one year after Hume's death: "I have such a difficult and usually insufficient evacuation every morning that the remaining feces that accumulate become the cause, as far as I can tell, not only of that gas I mentioned but also of my clouded brain."[25] Similarly, Coleridge reported "the most distressing stomach-attacks," all too often accompanied by indigestion, painful evacuations, and "*breezes* of Terror blowing from the Stomach up thro' the Brain," elsewhere "winds & breezes, gusts from the bowels of the Volcano upward to the Crater of the Brain, rushings & brain-horrors" (*CCL* 2:739, 976; *CN* 1:1822).[26] As late as 1819, sixteen-year-old Fanny Keats would have understood the reference to foul digestive vapors in a letter from her brother not long before his death: "I have left off animal food that my brains may never henceforth be in a greater mist than is theirs by nature" (*KL* 2:225). Hume's mist can be read in these same terms as a metaphoric remainder of poor aesthetic consumption. A gross vapor hanging between self and object, clouding the organs and obstructing judgment, it is an endogenous source of corruption for the tasting subject. Hugh Blair recurs to this Humean mist in his 1783 *Lectures on Rhetoric and Belles Lettres:* "When one is only beginning his acquaintance with works of genius, the sentiment which attends them is obscure and confused. . . . But allow him more experience in works of this kind, and his taste becomes by degrees more exact and enlightened"; as a result, "The mist dissipates which seemed formerly to hang over the object."[27] One must work hard to achieve this serenity, since it does not take much for the human tasting machine to malfunction and produce an erroneous judgment of taste.

Newtonian experimental science had had its effect on the study of the human, and Mandeville, for instance, employed a mechanistic model of human physiology when he wrote that "the chief Organs and nicest Springs more immediately required to continue the Motion of our Machine, are not hard Bones, strong Muscles and Nerves, nor the smooth white Skin that so beautifully covers them, but small trifling Films and little Pipes that are either overlook'd, or else seem inconsiderable to Vulgar Eyes" (*FB* 1:3). A decade before Hume's essay on taste, Julien de la Mettrie in *L'homme machine* (1748) did away with any lingering ghost in this machine by doing away with the concept of the human soul.[28] Hume also adopts the rhetoric of mechanical physiology when he warns, "The least exterior hindrance to such small springs, or the least internal disorder, disturbs their motion, and confounds the operations of the whole machine" (*EMP* 232). Such mechanistic vocabulary formulates the tasting subject as a highly delicate living mechanism.

The Enlightenment Man of Taste was particularly vulnerable, therefore, to physical conditions and internal phenomena that could influence his taste. Hume draws on contemporary medical knowledge that fevers take away the physical sensitivity of taste when he asserts: "A man in a fever would not insist on his palate as able to decide concerning flavours; nor would one, affected with the jaundice, pretend to give a verdict with regard to colours. In each creature, there is a sound and a defective state; and the former alone can be supposed to afford us a true standard of taste and sentiment" (*EMP* 233–34).[29] To judge correctly "with regard to colours," one must remain oneself uncolored — unfevered and unjaundiced. Critics find that Hume took the analogy between "bodily" and "mental" taste to be more than a vague comparison. Korsmeyer remarks that he "went as far as anyone in attempting to establish a standard of Taste upon the fact that human beings are morphologically and psychologically similar to one another."[30]

To be sure, the most famous analogy between "mental" and "bodily" taste in eighteenth-century aesthetics occurs in Hume's essay, "Of the Standard of Taste." In order to make the point that "A good palate is not tried by strong flavours; but by a mixture of small ingredients" (*EMP* 236), Hume retells the wine-tasting episode of Sancho Panza's kinsmen from *Don Quixote*. Two of Sancho's kinsmen (whose last name appropriately means belly) demonstrate an ability to distinguish nicely between different flavors in wine. As Hume describes it, they attempt what might be considered an empiricist "experiment" of taste: "One of them tastes it; considers it; and after mature reflection pronounces the wine to be good, were it not for a small taste of leather, which he perceived in it. The other, after using the same precautions, gives also his verdict in favour of the wine; but with the reserve of a taste of iron, which he could easily distinguish. You cannot imagine how much they were both ridiculed for their judgment. But who laughed in the end? On emptying the hogshead, there was found at the bottom an old key with a leathern thong tied to it" (*EMP* 234–35). In the original story by Cervantes, the kinsmen do not determine whether the wine tastes good or not. One simply says that it tastes of iron, the other of leather. The two judgments are not necessarily opposed, and they do not add up to a definitive judgment of taste. But Hume alters the original version of the story as an analogy for critical discernment: pronouncing the wine to be good, these critics pronounce aesthetic judgment.[31]

Hume's analogy has its literary precedent in Cervantes, but philosophically it descends from a much closer analogy between "bodily" and "mental" taste in Addison's 1712 essay "On Taste." Addison opens his discussion of "The Pleasures of the Imagination" by acknowledging the confusion that stems from the gustatory metaphor and the "great Conformity between that Mental Taste, which is the Subject of this Paper, and that Sensitive Taste which gives us a Relish of every different Flavour that affects the Palate" (*SPT* 3:527). Like Hume's wine tasters, Addison's ideal critic is a connoisseur, this time with an expertise in tea: "having tasted ten different Kinds of Tea, he would distinguish, without seeing the Colour of it, the particular Sort which was offered him; and not only so, but any two sorts of them that were mixt together in an equal Proportion" (*SPT* 3:527). In working up this analogy to "Sensitive Taste," Addison does not stop at two flavors but proceeds to three and more (read: aesthetic qualities of beauty) that can be discerned by the critic.[32] The problem for all Enlightenment taste theorists was that while there may be empirical evidence for gustatory taste, there is no comparable key "with a leathern thong tied to it" that can be produced to refute or confirm judgments of mental taste.

Delicacy of physical taste sensation can be measured by the number of taste buds per papilla on the tongue, and Hume's analogy hinges on the idea that the organ(s) of mental taste — whatever those are (and there was considerable disputation, to be sure) — could also be cultivated to a similar degree of delicacy. He claims that delicacy of feeling is something "every one pretends to: Every one talks of it; and would reduce every kind of taste or sentiment to its standard" (*EMP* 234). The relation between delicacy and taste traces back to Dominique Bouhours' 1687 use of "la délicatesse" in *La manière de bien penser dans les ouvrages de l'espirit,* a key text for shifting aesthetic theory from neoclassical principles of correctness to feeling as a foundation for aesthetics.[33] For Hume, a "delicacy of taste is as much to be desired and cultivated as delicacy of passion is to be lamented" (*EMP* 5). Yet while the organs of gustatory taste can be readily identified (papillae, tongue, hard palate), exactly what Hume means by the "internal organs" (*EMP* 234, 237) that are to distinguish delicately among qualities of beauty is far from clear. He does not rank among those who *would* identify an internal organ of aesthetic perception. Francis Hutcheson, Alexander Gerard, and Thomas Reid, to name three prominent examples, all speculated that just as there was an external bodily sense of taste to perceive sapid particles, there must be a corresponding internal (or mental) sense fitted to the perception of beauty.[34] But taste was by no means thought of uniformly as a distinct faculty, and even when it was, the question of where it resides (or where *they* reside, since there were often several internal aesthetic senses or faculties) was difficult to determine.

Thomas Reid pronounced in his 1785 essay "Of Taste" that "the internal power of taste bears a great analogy ... to the external," but he did not specify this "internal power" in terms of human anatomy.[35] John Gilbert Cooper went into slightly more detail in his *Letters Concerning Taste* (1757), describing "that *internal Sense* we call Taste (which is a Herald for the whole human System, in it's three different Parts, the refined Faculties of Perception, the gross Organs of Sense, and the intermediate Powers of Imagination)."[36] For Archibald Alison, taste was a "faculty of the human mind" that produced a particular emotion, delight: "We are *pleased,* we say with the gratification of any appetite or affection — with food when hungry, and with rest when tired. ... But we say we are *delighted* with the prospect of a beautiful landscape."[37] Gerard multiplies this idea of an "internal power," "*internal Sense,*" or "faculty of the human mind" into seven discrete mental faculties, as defined in his 1759 *Essay on Taste*. However mystified, these thinkers were all explicit about the existence of an internal organ — or organs — of taste analogous to the external five senses.

Traditionally, the tongue had been considered the chief organ of taste, but eighteenth-century physiologists also had trouble narrowing external taste sensation down to this.[38] They found that the tongue was not the organ of taste for all animals, just as the nose was not uniformly the organ of smell. "We are not justified in considering the tongue as an organ of taste in all animals, because it is subservient to that function in the human subject," wrote Blumenbach in *A Manual of Comparative Anatomy;* "this organ, in many cases, merely serves for taking in the food."[39] The seventeenth-century anatomist Nehemiah Grew argued that for certain ruminating animals the stomach was the organ of taste: "The pointed Knots, like little *Papillae,* in the Stomachs of divers Ruminating Beasts, are also of great use, *viz.* for the Tasting of the Meat."[40] Accordingly, the application of physiological concepts and language to the organ(s) of mental taste in Enlightenment taste philosophy is perhaps necessarily vague.

Careful analysis shows Hume also struggling with the idea of an internal power along the lines of the external sense organs, but in the end no organ (or morphologically complete organism) of taste emerges. As Jeffrey Wieand suggests, Hume may be thinking of "the judging subject itself as an organ — an organ of judgment, as it were — but this will not explain his use of the expression 'internal organs.' "[41] One might conclude that what Hume means by the organ(s) of mental taste is nothing other than the fleshed-out substance of the Man of Taste himself, a holistic tasting organ. Whereas Shaftesbury rejects the empiricist model that provides the substance for his Man of Taste, Hume's empiricism yields a collection of tasteful attributes that do not cohere into an actual person of taste. Nevertheless, the essay holds out the hope that if one expends enough effort to clear oneself of "mists" and other physiological "defects," one might occasionally perform accurate judgments of taste.

Grumbling Swine

Against the "serene" and "evacuated" Enlightenment Man of Taste, imagined in differing ways by Shaftesbury and Hume, Burke's aesthetic subject was from its very origins a creature of appetite. Like Mandeville, Burke believed that we can never purge the "defects of our naked, shivering nature" (R 87). Rather, we can only hope to cloak them in "the wardrobe of a moral imagination," a phrase that reworks Mandeville's claim (*pace* Shaftesbury) that "all Men endeavour to hide themselves, their Ugly Nakedness, from each other, and wrapping up the true Motives of their Hearts in the Specious Cloke of Sociableness, and their Concern for the publick Good, they are in hopes of concealing their filthy Appetites and the Deformity of their Desires" (*FB* 1:234–35). The symbolic economy of tasteful consumption described by Milton and later aesthetic taste philosophers is one that evacuates all organic "dregs" and "defects," but Burke maintained with Mandeville that we can only hide the "defects of our naked, shivering nature" from each other out of politeness. His "wardrobe of a moral imagination," like Mandeville's "Specious Cloke of Sociableness," was intended to conceal all the passions and unsociable appetites that humans have in common with brutes.

In *A Philosophical Enquiry into the Origin of our Ideas of the Sublime and Beautiful* (1757), Burke anchored the tasteful subject firmly within his own physiology, drawing on popular sensation science to track taste down in its intimate hiding places in the body: the operatic vibrations of the papillae of the tongue, the nervous convulsions of the eardrums, the dilation of the iris or "sphincter" of the eye — a term that turns the proverbial window of the soul into a window into the digestive tract of the tasting subject (*PE* 146). Qualities of beauty provided physical pleasure by "removing swellings and obstructions" and "relaxing the solids of the whole system" (*PE* 149–51).[42] Attending to the physiology of taste even more meticulously than the taste philosophers preceding him, Burke came to realize more fully than they the possibility that if we all share the same basic anatomy we are all capable of the same asocial appetites. The pleasures of taste went hand-in-hand with the gratification of appetite, and an aesthetic taste for beauty thus helped to "direct and heighten the appetite which [mankind] has in common with all other animals" (*PE* 42). Burke is referring specifically to sexual appetite, which some (such as Coleridge in his more religious moods) wished to elevate above bodily desire: "Are Lust & Hunger both alike Passions of physical Necessity, and the one equally with the other independent of Reason, & the Will? — Shame upon our Race, that there lives the Individual who does even ask the Question!" (*CCW* 12.3: 806).[43] Burke's later writings on the revolutionary war in France suggest that sexual desire is not only instinctual: it is another form of the most taboo of all appetites, an appetite for human flesh. As Leo Damrosch writes, Burke's "whole career embodies the belief that in a time of turbulent historical change, philosophy must be acted out in the arena of political power."[44] A comparison of his *Reflections on the Revolution in France* (1790) and *Letters on a Regicide Peace* (1795–97) with his aesthetic philosophy of three decades earlier suggests that it is less the rapacious lower orders of France than the civic ideal of the British Man of Taste that haunts Burke in the 1790s.[45]

Far from the disinterested *homo aestheticus,* Burke's Man of Taste treads dangerously close to Mandeville's view that "Man (besides Skin, Flesh, Bones, &c. that are obvious to the eye) [is] a compound of various Passions, that all of them, as they are provoked and come uppermost, govern him by turns, whether he will or no" (*FB* 1:39). Unlike spirits and humors, passions were mental as well as physical phenomena and constituted the most powerful of the six "Non-Natural" things regulating life, namely, emptiness and repletion, air, sleep, exercise, rest, and the passions or perturbations of the mind.[46] As Bamborough observes, "passion could therefore be spoken of as a disease, without undue straining after metaphor."[47] Mandeville's revised 1730 title, *A Treatise on the Hypochondriack and Hysterick Diseases,* originally *A Treatise on the Hypochondriack and Hysterick Passions,* demonstrates this fact. Pope wrote in his *Essay on Man* (1733–34) that "diff'rent Passions more or less inflame, / As strong or weak, the organs of the frame," but Burke resembled Mandeville in his belief that the passions themselves made the man.[48] Despite his investment in sensation science, he invoked the humoral notion that "the passions . . . are the organs of the mind" (*PE* 52). His Man of Taste, as a compound of passions, was thus somewhat at odds with the Enlightenment *homo aestheticus,* by definition disinterested and dispassionate.

Ostensibly the title of Burke's *Philosophical Enquiry* situates it within the Enlightenment discourse of taste in anti-Mandevillean tradition, echoing as it does Francis Hutcheson's *An Inquiry into the Original of our Ideas of Beauty and Virtue* (1725). This latter work was written as a direct rebuttal to Mandeville's "An Enquiry into the Origin of Moral Virtues" in *The Fable of the Bees,* itself (partly) a response to Shaftesbury.[49] Nevertheless, Burke's *Enquiry* falls back on Mandeville's central tenet that "a Man need not conquer his Passions, it is sufficient that he conceals them . . . good Breeding only requires we should hide our Appetites" (*FB* 1:72). As a creature pursuing his own appetites and aversions in a crowd of like-minded creatures, the Burkean citizen resembles Mandeville's bee in *The Fable of the Bees.* Originally this work began as a verse satire entitled *The Grumbling Hive: or Knaves Turn'd Honest* (1705), and the bee was originally a "grumbling" bee, consciously punning on the idea of digestion. When Mandeville's patient complains in *A Treatise on the Hypochondriack and Hysterick Diseases* of that "Old Distemper, the Grumbling in my Bowels" (*THH* 14), he refers to a condition that also plagues the social body in *The Fable of the Bees,* figured as a "Grumbling Hive." Francis Patrick McKee has argued that the mechanics of digestion are at the core of Mandeville's philosophy: "Mandeville's patients, reveling in the profits of the rising British Empire, are suffering from various forms of indigestion, having consumed too many texts, too many consumer goods and too many exotic foods that are new to the British diet."[50] As an Enlightenment legacy of Hobbes, Mandeville prepares the way for Burke, whose Man of Taste is basically a knave turned honest, seeking to gratify his appetites and consumer desires in a lawful, well-behaved manner.

When in his *Philosophical Enquiry* Burke treats of aesthetic qualities that are *not* the cause of beauty, he invokes the figure of the swine, whose physiognomy is fit for the purposes of survival but who has nothing to do with beauty, above all a "social quality" pertaining to taste.[51] If fitness *were* a cause of beauty, he argues, then "the wedge-like snout of a swine, with its tough cartilage at the end, the little sunk eyes, and the whole make of the head, so well adapted to its offices of digging, and rooting, would be extremely beautiful" (*PE* 105). When applied to swine, the term *rooting* means to dig with the snout in search of food, though it can also mean to pull, dig, or take out by the roots, hence to extirpate or destroy. Burke's swine may be fit for the animal functions of self-maintenance (foremost among them feeding), but he is incapable of rousing the social affections. The implications of this figure are latent in the *Enquiry,* but they become explicit in the 1790s as Burke's "swinish multitude" threatens to uproot all the civic ideals he had wished to defend (*R* 89).

In Burke's *Reflections on the Revolution in France,* the rebellious French mob, disregarding all the "pleasing illusions" that embellish society, exhibit the worst kind of appetites. At one point in the book he describes the "tragic farce" of ecclesiastical executions enacted before the people of France in order "to stimulate their cannibal appetites (which one would think had been gorged sufficiently) by variety and seasoning" (*R* 164). At times, Burke seems to want to confine such criminal appetites to a vulgar few: "I knew, indeed, that the sufferings of monarchs make a delicious repast to some sort of palates" (*R* 83). But the majority of the population appears to him an uncouth collection "of gross, stupid, ferocious, and, at the same time, poor and sordid barbarians" (*R* 90). He is invoking savagery as well as cannibalism to describe this moment in European history, and in his first *Letter on a Regicide Peace* he makes clear that he intends these "cannibal appetites" quite literally: "By cannibalism, I mean their devouring as a nutriment of their ferocity, some part of the bodies of those they have murdered; their drinking the blood of their victims, and forcing the victims themselves to drink the blood of their kindred slaughtered before their faces."[52] Burke's passionate, embodied Man of Taste was in tension with the ideal of universal human nature underwriting Enlightenment aesthetics, and by the 1790s he had multiplied into a radical multitude, indecently exhibiting its "filthy Appetites."

Naturally at home in Mandeville's "grumbling hive," as they are in Burke's "swinish multitude," Burke's swine embody the triumph of brute appetite over spirit. Both are perversely appetitive versions of the *sensus communis* in the tradition of Hobbes's *Leviathan*. The 1651 frontispiece to *Leviathan* featured a crowd of little men crammed into the outline of a human torso, an image that once seen is hard to forget. Swift recognized a relation between Mandeville's vision of civil society and Hobbes's when he described the human mind as "a Crowd of little Animals, but with Teeth and Claws extremely sharp . . . [which] cling together in the Contexture we behold, like the Picture of *Hobbes's Leviathan*, or like Bees in perpendicular swarm upon a Tree, or like a Carrion corrupted into Vermin, still preserving the Shape and Figure of the Mother Animal" (*SPW* 1:181). Swift plays on the humoral notion of "animal spirits" (from *anima*, soul) as an early modern version of neural impulses, or forces motivating the human mind, literalizing these *animae* as hungry "little animals." His comparison evokes Mandeville's, and by extension Burke's, portrait of the human as a greedy conglomeration of passions and appetites. Neither Mandeville's grumbling hive nor Burke's swinish multitude enables the sublimation necessary to convert appetite into taste, or the human animal — grumbling for food, printed matter, and the growing supply of consumable goods — into a tasteful individual.

Burke capitalized on the shameless appetite of the food-grubbing swine as a symbol for those who threatened the aestheticized ideal of national community. Indiscriminately feeding on refuse and dung, this voracious animal was originally associated with the rural exterior of the civil world, though its increased presence in cities by the end of the century became an uncomfortable mirror of human potentiality, as Peter Stalleybrass and Allon White have argued.[53] Burke's use of this powerful image perhaps not surprisingly produced an explosion of printed opposition. His opponents complained that "A feast of Words" was insufficient to satisfy physical craving. Daniel Isaac Eaton, for example, added an epigraph to the fifth edition of his twopenny publication, *Politics for the People; or, A Salmagundy for Swine*, pronouncing:

> Since Times are bad, and solid food is rare,
> The Swinish Herd should learn to live on air:
> Acorns and Pease, alas! no more abound,
> A feast of Words, is in the *Hog Trough* found.[54]

Burke's swinish multitude rapidly became a powerful emblem for radicals like Eaton who took up the cause of a starving multitude. In 1792 Richard Porson reminded readers of the relation between Burke's aesthetic philosophy and those unable to sublimate their appetites into taste, who were abjected from his tasteful community: "Q. What is your name? — A. *Hog* or *Swine*. Q. Did God make you a hog? — No! God made me a Man in his own image; the *Right Honourable* SUBLIME and BEAUTIFUL made me a Swine."[55] Burke's swine represented, as early as the *Enquiry*, every citizen stripped of his Mandevillean "Cloke of Sociableness."

James Gillray also took up the case of the civil swine in response to Burke in his visual satire of the 1790s. His *Substitutes for Bread; or Right Honourables Saving the Loaves and Dividing the Fishes* (1795) was "dedicated" to the writers of the Corn Laws, who were widely considered responsible for the scarcity of bread: "To the Charitable Committee, for reducing the high price of Corn, by providing substitutes for bread in their own Families, this representation of the Hard shifts made by the Framers and Signers of the Philanthropic agreement is most respectfully dedicated" (figure 1). This image dripping with irony depicts the British ministers William Wyndham, Henry Dundas, Baron Loughborough, Pepper Arden, and William Pitt dining on enormous platters of fish with scales in the shape of gold coins. A menu on the wall lists outrageously priced substitutes for bread, such as venison, roast beef, poultry, turtle soup, and fish boiled in wine, along with ragouts, jellies, burgundy, champagne, and the imperial drink Tokay. Lurking phantasmagorically in the background to the right, waiters with extended arms convey steaming platters of beef and pork toward the table where gravies and other accoutrements, similarly comprised of coins, await them. Heaped on the table are more haute cuisine substitutes for bread, including royal turtle soup, oysters, scallops, and snails, all composed of the same gold coins. While these ministers feast, their "Proclamation for a General Fast in order to avert the impending Famine" (posted on the wall) clearly yields different interpretations of fasting — as well as of substitutes for bread.[56]

The year 1795 in particular presided over extremities of appetite that could not be aestheticized away. English weather was unusually cold, devastating crops, doubling the death rate, and causing bread riots throughout the country. Outside the window in Gillray's *Substitutes for Bread* a "swinish multitude" petitions with signs identifying their bearers as "Starving Swine" and begging, "Grant us the Crumbs which drop from your Table."[57] Such satire points the finger at the ministerial diners as the real hogs. Forefront and center, Gillray features a basket of "Potatoe Bread to be given in charity" at a time when the white loaf was regarded jealously as a staple of the worker's diet.[58] In these years, as E. P. Thompson explains, "landowners, farmers, parsons, manufacturers, and the Government itself sought to drive labourers from a wheaten to a potato diet," though the majority of the population saw the substitution of potatoes for bread as a degradation.[59] For those "Right Honourables Saving the Loaves and Dividing the Fishes," white bread may have been a wasteful extravagance, but for many of the "Starving Swine," potatoes were ironically "fit only for pigs and Irish."[60]

Middle-class reformers added to the rising tide of rhetoric in the 1790s that urged the hungry to regulate their supposedly wasteful habits of consumption. Hannah More's *Cheap Repository Tracts,* including "The Way to Plenty" (1795) and "The Cottage Cook" (1796), for instance, offered specific recipes for cheap dishes and a general message to practice more moderate (tasteful) dietary habits. In order to counteract what she and others felt were unduly sophisticated working-class tastes for urban commodities, such as white bread and tea, she suggests: "A halfpenny worth of oatmeal or groats with a leek or onion, out of your own garden which costs nothing, a bit of salt, and a little coarse bread, will breakfast your whole family."[61] Against this tidy, home-grown vision, the harsher reality that one encounters in historical chronicles of the time led the starving poor to improvise tea by pouring boiling water over burnt crusts of bread, an "indication of the need for stimulants caused by excessive hours of labour on an inadequate diet."[62] Middle-class crusaders against waste, however, saw tea as an ill-judged, tasteless extravagance: "I dare not say how much of this [eight shilling per week income] goes for tea in the afternoon," More scolds, "now sugar and butter are so dear, because I should have you all upon me, but I will say that too much of this little goes even for bread, from a notion that it is the hardest fare. This at all times, but particularly just now, is bad management."[63] Management as a humoral concept applied to the body had become, by the mid-1790s, a way to regulate consumption through an ever more complex sign system in which certain foods (and therefore consumers) were coded morally corrupt.

In eighteenth-century visual iconography John Bull often appeared as a stalwart symbol of Britishness, an eater of beefsteak or plain cooked fare against the ornate fricassees of the extravagant French. Gillray's print of July 6, 1795, *The British-Butcher; Supplying John-Bull with a Substitute for Bread* (figure 2), gives Billy the Butcher's advice to John Bull in the form of a doggerel lyric, based on Marie Antoinette's proverbial "Let them eat cake":

> Since Bread is so dear, (and you say you must Eat,)
> For to save the Expence, you must live upon Meat;
> And as twelve Pence the Quartern you can't pay for Bread
> Get a Crown's worth of Meat, — it will serve in its stead.

The anapestic tetrameter of this quatrain contributes to its make-believe effect, and like most nursery rhymes it unfolds a gruesome tale: extremes of hunger and excessive consumption threatening civil order throughout Europe. As the Corn Laws combined with natural disasters contributed to the spread of starvation, the temperate middle road of taste sublimed from the material extremities of appetite seemed the only ideological path on which to proceed.

Coleridge lectured copiously in these years as Burke was composing his *Letters on a Regicide Peace* and *Thoughts and Details on Scarcity* (1795), which oppose government action to ameliorate food scarcity. In a biting "Letter from Liberty to her Dear Friend Famine" (December 1795), he criticized government manipulation of food for political ends from a perspective opposite to Burke's: "Over a recruiting place in this city I have seen pieces of Beef hung up to attract the half-famished Mechanic" (*CCW* 1:69). Intoxicated by drink, Coleridge himself had volunteered for an army regiment in a comic, sad, and complicated story of personal debt, disappointment and despair, and he too recognized the intoxicating lure of flesh (beef, mutton, lamb, veal) to the famished. The British substitute for bread was naturally enough beef (celebrated by Hogarth, Fielding, and others as the Roast Beef of Old England), but for the poorer — and larger — segment of the population meat eating was a rarely obtainable luxury.[64] Gillray's print portrays Prime Minister William Pitt (a "Butcher" insofar as his war policies were concerned), holding out a slab of meat with the demand: "A Crown, take it, or leav't." His list of meat prices, juxtaposed with his list of working-class salaries ("Journeymens Wages"), provides quantitative evidence (not too far from the truth) that these so-called "substitutes for bread" were beyond the grasp of the "swinish multitude."[65]

Anthropologists claim that consumption, while it may be influenced or incited, is not to be compelled, though as Burke's political intervention in the empiricist discourse of taste suggests, personal expression through consumption has upon it numerous restraints.[66] During the Century of Taste, as the consumptive unit shrunk from the larger group or family to the individual, the opportunity opened up for the expression of personal style through the discretionary consumption of food, words, and other consumables. On the other hand, this was tempered by the lived realities of hunger and dietary politics. An analogy can be found in the evolution of the dinner table itself: as the common trencher, accessed by means of knives, fingers, and communal spoons gave way to individual flatware settings — dishes and eventually (to avoid unnecessary contact with food) forks — the larger communal meal broke down into discrete units or samplings, allowing individuals to exercise taste preference.[67] Ultimately, with the development of the restaurant and a new public sphere of dining after the French Revolution, the individual found that judgment, call it taste or *gustus,* mediated what one consumed in a physical form of self expression.[68] In this transitional society, refocusing its energies on individual pleasure and preference, there was no extricating taste from appetite or its metaphorical cousin, consumerism. The following chapter takes up the problem of how Wordsworth's effort to shape the taste of the nation left him standing in a precarious position between these two cultural economies of consumption, aesthetic taste and consumerism. For Wordsworth, the two were in competition, with the former in decline and the latter on the rise in the shape of consumers unable to distinguish spiritual food from frontignac — or other material desires.

4

Digesting Wordsworth

TASME . . . *is a word which has been forced to extend its services far beyond the point to which philosophy would have confined [it]. It is a metaphor, taken from a passive sense of the human body, and transferred to things which are in their essence* not *passive, — to intellectual* acts *and operations.*
— *Wordsworth, "Essay, Supplementary to the Preface" (1815)*

In "Preface to *Lyrical Ballads,*" Wordsworth links taste to feeding when he refers to the faculty of aesthetic discernment as "the great spring of the activity of our minds, and their chief feeder"; on the degree of refinement of this faculty, he claims, "depend our taste and our moral feelings" (*PW* 1:148). For Wordsworth, taste refers to the positive intellectual acts of the imagination, but he prefers the metaphor *feed* as a way to revitalize a term whitewashed with too much abstraction.[1] Wordsworth's most memorable depiction of the feeding mind occurs at the climax of *The Prelude* (at once the climax of his poetic career) as his speaker perceives "The perfect image of a mighty mind, / Of one that feeds upon infinity," when climbing to the top of Mount Snowdon (1805 *PRL* 13.69–70). One need only consider the key revision, whereby the "moving soul" of the 1805 *Prelude* (13.193) becomes the "feeding source" of the 1850 *Prelude* (14.193), to recognize the work this particular

68

metaphor performed for the poet. As Geoffrey Hartman remarks, "Words-worth's metaphor is as serious as Milton's larger machinery bearing on the theme of angelic diet."[2] While not all Wordsworthian feeding bears the philo-sophical burden of Snowdon (sometimes sheep simply feed in his poems, and one would do well to leave the matter at that), the metaphor defines the concept of subjectivity as depicted by Wordsworth.

As a figure for the Wordsworthian "egotistical sublime," a consciousness assimilating everything into itself in a subjective expansiveness that knows no bounds, Wordsworth's feeding mind assumes new godly dimensions as a feed-ing source for tasteful subjects.[3] The metaphor of feeding in his poetry is exalted above the more mundane physical activity of processing the world through sensory perception, and it is perhaps no irony that, as Robert Southey tells us, the poet whose lifetime was preoccupied with taste was physically deprived of its sensory pleasures: "Wordsworth has no sense of smell. . . . He has often expressed to me his regret for this privation."[4] Smell is essential to the ability to discriminate through external taste sensation, and without the "sense of smell there would be no gourmets, only consumers of nutriments"; as one contempo-rary wrote in the *Edinburgh Review,* smell is "that sense from which every viand, solid and liquid, derives what is emphatically called its *flavour.*"[5] A careful examination of Wordsworth's textual obsession with the feeding mind of Snowdon reveals a poet in direct confrontation with this gustatory metaphor — and its ineluctable, unsublimable remainders.

This chapter will pull successive textual overlays away from the transcen-dently feeding mind of Snowdon in order to perform a literary archaeology on that prime emblem of Wordsworthian egotistical sublimity.[6] Early nineteenth-century stratigraphic investigations into the Lakes offered Wordsworth a model by which to understand aesthetic experience as an uneasy tension be-tween depths and surfaces, as Theresa Kelley has shown: one need not have made the trek to the Lake District of England to recognize the degree to which topographical and survey maps can influence the way we view nature. Pursued to its depths, the mind, like nature, can be seen as a series of stratified surfaces, layer upon layer of intellectual growth, and the "aesthetic conflict between poetic surfaces and depths often makes it difficult to pull one layer back and distinguish it from another or several others beneath it."[7] An archaeology of the mind reveals aspects of consciousness and "underconsciousness" (to use Wordsworth's term) existing side by side, shaping present behavior through their buried structures. Wordsworth's poetic description of the feeding mind also involves previous layers of text that retain unconscious power. The trans-parent overlays of the stratigraphic map that the visitor to Wordsworth coun-try uses to view nature find a textual equivalent in the infrared facsimiles of

Wordsworth's manuscripts, made available through the Cornell edition of *The Prelude*. These, together with his later essays on taste (which gloss this figure), expose an inassimilable element built into the poet's central symbol of auto-poiesis.[8]

The Mind That Feeds (and Digests)

Wordsworth had attempted to render his experience of climbing Mount Snowdon in poetry as early as 1793, in *Descriptive Sketches* (lines 492–511). Although this experience is absent from the two-book *Prelude* of 1798, it returns in the five-book *Prelude* of 1804 that scholars have reconstructed from Wordsworth's manuscripts.[9] In the expanded thirteen-book *Prelude* of 1805, it becomes a climax, a moment of divine self-consciousness rendered meta-phorically as a scene of consumption: a feeding mind. As the poet approaches his own spiritual pinnacle (along with the mountain's) in the final book of the poem, he upon the sudden envisions

> The perfect image of a mighty mind,
> Of one that feeds upon infinity,
> That is exalted by an under-presence,
> The sense of God, or whatso'er is dim
> Or vast in its own being— (13.69–73)

These lines have been subject to a degree of editorial revision remarkable even for Wordsworth. In manuscript A of the 1805 *Prelude,* from which the above lines are taken, the mind is "exalted by an under-presence"; in a subsequent A-stage revision made sometime between 1805 and 1818, it is "exalted by an underconsciousness" (*TBP* 2:967). In the fourteen-book *Prelude* of 1850, it is no longer exalted by anything: the poet now perceives "the emblem of a mind / That feeds upon infinity, that broods / Over the dark abyss" (14.70–72). This progression from a mind that is "exalted by an under-presence" to one that is exalted "over the dark abyss" renders Wordsworthian creation as distinctively Miltonic. The Norton edition of *The Prelude* notes the Miltonic nature of the 1850 mind that "broods / Over the dark abyss," and its editor Jonathan Wordsworth elsewhere remarks that there are certain "affinities between Wordsworth's 'mighty mind,' feeding upon the infinity of its own inner tur-moil, and Milton's Holy Spirit, brooding dove-like over an external abyss."[10] Wordsworth (the scholar) traces this brooding, creative act back not only to the opening lines of *Paradise Lost,* in which the divine spirit "Dove-like satst brooding on the vast Abyss" (1.21), but to the more fully developed account of creation in book 7, described as a cosmic purgation of waste. Wordsworth's feeding mind, by 1850, bears relation to Milton's God who digests — and excretes — the cosmos into order.[11]

As we have seen, in *Paradise Lost* the divine Spirit spreads its "brooding wings," breathing life into the matter of Chaos in an oviparous act depicted as purgative: "downward purg'd / The black tartareous cold Infernal dregs / Adverse to life" (*PL* 7.235–39). Brooding is an anglicized version of the Latinate term *rumination,* and Wordsworth's association of the brooding mind with a ruminating, or self-reflecting, mind also occurs in the five-book *Prelude:* "The meditative mind (best pleased perhaps / While she, as duteous as the mother dove, / Sits brooding)" (*WU* 1.148–50). Hazlitt recalls this as an appropriate image for Wordsworthian creation when he describes the poet as "a mind forever brooding over itself" (*HCW* 8:44). In his review of *The Excursion* (1814), he adds that Wordsworth "may be said to create his own materials. . . . His understanding broods over that which is 'without form and void' and 'makes it pregnant'" (*HCW* 4:112). Ostensibly, Hazlitt is referring to the divine Spirit who "satst brooding on the vast abyss / And mad'st it pregnant" in book 1 of *Paradise Lost* (1.21–22). But his claim that Wordsworth "may be said to create his own materials" derives from the brooding Spirit of book 7, who creates *ex se,* producing the very materials from which to create.

Milton is rewriting Genesis in *Paradise Lost,* just as Wordsworth is rewriting Milton. When Milton describes the creation of the earth, he writes that "the Mountains huge appear / Emergent, and thir broad bare backs upheave" (*PL* 7.285–86), and this line appears in all manuscript versions of the Snowdon passage: "A hundred hills their dusky backs upheaved / All over this still ocean" (*WU* 5.45–46; *TBP* 13.45; *FBP* 14.43). In the argument to book 1, Milton explains that the "dregs" have been purged into the Deep, a place of "utter darkness," and this deep, utterly dark realm of primordial purgation is specifically labeled a "dark Abyss" in the poem (*PL* 2.1027; 10.371). Wordsworth's "dark abyss," which evolves out of the obscure "under-presence" of 1805, evokes not only the "vast abyss" of the opening lines of *Paradise Lost* but also this obscure realm of creative purgation in which the dregs are "Abject and lost" (1.312). Milton is invoked by name following the Snowdon passage (*Prelude* 13.225) and, after several decades of brooding over this climactic scene of the poem, Wordsworth refers to Milton himself as "that mighty mind" (*LLY* 7:24). Just as Milton's digesting God expels its "dregs" in the founding gesture of creation — matter which never fully disappears — the feeding mind exists in tension with "whatsoe'er is dim / Or vast in its own being" (1805 *PRL;* 13.72–73). Herbert Lindenberger observes that through this darkly exalted figure Wordsworth "retreats from the problem of what it *is* or *does* and he tells us instead what it is 'exalted by,' what lurks behind it, what it is related to."[12] If this mind is seen as "reason in her most exalted mood" (1805 *PRL*; 13.170), that reason is "exalted by an under-presence" that may well be *under* consciousness; the "dark abyss" exalting the feeding mind of Snowdon is never fully brought to light in the Wordsworthian egotistical sublime.

If we approach Wordsworth's concept of feeding through the mechanics of assimilation, as described in Romantic *Naturphilosophie*, we find that the feeding mind naturally exists in a precarious state of tension with its own abjected matter. Werner Hamacher, who has studied Romantic-era digestion at length in Hegel's work, explains that for the idealist subject, there "remains a relationship to what has been expelled, to that repetition of itself which is already no longer or is not yet entirely true, in which therefore spirit can see itself only as deformed, rather than knowing and recognizing its own truth."[13] The nature of this relationship challenges the traditional critical view of the Mount Snowdon passage as a moment of subjective totalization and untroubled assimilation. In *Wordsworth's Poetry*, for instance, Hartman studies the poet's dialectic between an apocalyptic transcendence over nature and an absorption into organic materiality, with the feeding mind of Snowdon as his poetic correlative to Hegel's Absolute Knowledge in *The Phenomenology of Spirit* (1807). From this perspective, the Snowdon passage constitutes a climactic resolution of the dialectic between matter and spirit, dooming all further poetry to the status of anticlimax since (as Alan Liu writes) "post-self-consciousness is unimaginable in the Hegelian method."[14] Yet despite its use as a model for self-totalizing assimilation in *The Prelude*, Hegel's phenomenological subject involves its own material remainders.

Hegel's detailed analysis of the chemical composition of excrement in his *Philosophy of Nature* reveals that the philosophical subject consists of the same material as its own waste matter. In a manner of thinking common to German *Naturphilosophie*, he asserts that "the constructive instinct, too, like excretion, is a self-externalization," however, "this is only one side of the constructive instinct. The other side is that the animal excretes products of its own activity, but not out of disgust, not to get rid of them; on the contrary, the externalized excrement is fashioned by the creature to satisfy its need" (*PN* 2:406–07). In applying the organic process of assimilation to his philosophical system of self-creation or *Bildung*, Hegel implies that far from being a rejected *excrementum* the abjected aspect of the self constitutes nutriment, matter for assimilation. As mental food, it remains under consciousness, informing that consciousness and satisfying its "subjective need." Similarly, the creatively feeding mind of Snowdon, when viewed through the overlays of Wordsworth's ever-shifting text, contains an inassimilable element that will not be absorbed or subjectivized into the "egotistical sublime."

Insofar as excrement forms part of a more general economy externalized as an aspect of the self-dialectical, the biological Spirit of Romantic philosophy mimics the operations of Milton's self-abjecting God. Hegel in *The Phenomenology of Spirit* describes what Tilottama Rajan calls a "psychosomatics of Spirit," whereby the organism purposively forms itself by abjecting part of that self.[15] As it ruminates, it metaphorically digests itself into being. "Spirit [is] emptied out into Time; but this externalization, this kenosis, is equally an externalization of itself; the negative is the negative of itself," writes Hegel; "the Self has to penetrate and digest this entire wealth of its substance."[16] To feed upon infinity is the work of self-digestion, and excretion is the end product of digestion. Hegel's model of self-creation "requires that the subject digest and excrete not a foreign substance, but 'itself.' "[17] When read in the light of Naturphilosophie, the self-totalizing subject of Romantic idealist philosophy, as the philosophical correlative to the feeding mind of Snowdon, starts to look less like a creature of idealizing internalization and more like a self-digester.

Hegel arrives at his philosophical system through natural philosophy, and the second part of his *Encyclopaedia of the Philosophical Sciences (The Philosophy of Nature)* originates the idealist subject of *The Phenomenology of Spirit* at the level of physiology. In a section devoted to animal assimilation Hegel concludes, "the whole process of digestion consists in this, that the organism in angrily opposing itself to the outer world is divided within itself . . . in animals with a developed organization, digestion consists in the organism relating to itself" (*PN* 2:402). He therefore, as Rajan observes, "describes reflection as digestion and digestion as the 'organism's reflection into itself.' "[18] The notion of mental reflection as "rumination" was important to German Romanticism, as it would later be to Nietzsche, who announced that one must almost "be a cow" and ruminate (chew the cud, endlessly digest) in order to comprehend his works.[19] For Hegel, digestion as a physical form of self-reflection does not continue indefinitely; rather, the organism ultimately abjects part of itself: "The animal's abstract repulsion of itself by which it makes itself external to itself is excretion, the conclusion of the process of assimilation" (*PN* 2:402–04). To interpret the feeding mind of *The Prelude* as the disembodied activity of autopoiesis (along the lines of psychoanalytic internalization) is to interpret it as Wordsworth probably intended it to be read. But Romantic Naturphilosophie and its material rendering of digestion inform the psychoanalytic concepts of assimilation and internalization.

The philosopher F. W. J. Schelling was Hegel's rival and an important formative influence on Coleridge, and he too swerved from the high idealism of their teacher J. G. Fichte, who *did* believe in totalizing subjective assimilation. At the same time as Wordsworth was brooding over the nature of the "under-presence" or "underconsciousness" that exalts the feeding mind of Snowdon, Schelling imagined the creation (again in similar terms to Milton) as a primordial abjection.[20] His *Stuttgart Seminars* (1810) begin to work through the creation mythology that comes to fruition in *The Ages of the World* (1811–15); in them he writes, "What is superior in God expels, so to speak, the inferior [dimension] to which it previously related with indifference or in a mixed state . . . which also constitutes the *beginning* of consciousness and of personality both in man and in God."[21] As early as the five-book *Prelude,* Wordsworth had intuited that "that breach / Through which the homeless voice of waters rose, / That dark deep thoroughfare" was one in which "lodged / The soul, the imagination of the whole" (5:62–65). In 1805, the "dark deep thoroughfare" of the external landscape becomes internalized as an "under-presence," and then "underconsciousness." For Wordsworth's philosophical contemporary Schelling, the "development of self-consciousness involves man's *exclusion of the dark and unconscious* [dimension] within himself"; moreover, "this subordinate, dark, and unconscious dimension that God, as essence, continually *seeks* to expel and exclude from His proper self is *matter* (although not yet formed matter); thus matter is nothing but the unconscious aspect of God."[22] Schelling here lays the foundation for the psychoanalytic model of identity founded on an unconsciousness that must be abjected for consciousness to be achieved and the self to come into being.

Wordsworth's Subject of Taste assumes a moral responsibility not to abandon its own rejected matter, but to reassimilate it back into the domain of exalted feeding. Like the Miltonic poet who implores, "What in me is dark, / Illumine, what is low, raise and support" (*PL* 1.22–23), the Wordsworthian mind in its "most exalted mood" shows (in Schelling's words) "an impulse not to abandon the rejected and excluded nature in this state of rejection, but to transfigure it again back into the divine and to realign the entire universe in one vast creation of love."[23] The highest condition of such minds is "the consciousness / Of whom they are" (1805 *PRL* 13.108–09). Creation is an evolving process of coming into self-consciousness, and "the process of self-creation [*Selbstbildung*] always involves our raising to consciousness what exists in us in unconscious form, to turn our innate darkness into light."[24] When read as a narrative of *Selbstbildung,* Wordsworth's major poem reveals a poet attempting to realize a divine state of self-consciousness and, in so doing, expressing an intellectual love that "proceeds . . . from the brooding soul, and is divine" (1805 *PRL;* 13.164–65). The title page of the 1850 *Prelude* called it, after Coleridge, a poem on "Growth of a Poet's Mind," and

Coleridge writes in his 1816 *Theory of Life* that assimilation is a specific kind of feeding, or nutrition "for the purposes of reproduction and growth" (*CCW* 11.1, 490).

Julia Kristeva develops this Romantic notion whereby the subject processes the world by digesting itself in her Lacanian revision of Freud. In this rendering of the process, a loathing for food (particularly mother's milk, the "drinking in" so important to Wordsworth) is a developmental step on the road to identity: " 'I' want none of that element ... 'I' expel it. But since the food is not an 'other' for 'me,' who am only in their desire, I expel *myself,* I spit *myself* out, I abject *myself* within the same motion through which 'I' claim to establish *myself.*"[25] Rejecting the food of the mother, nurse, or feeder (in Wordsworth's case, nature), the self abjects itself as a loathsome mess. What remains after this formative abjection is an ego perpetually plagued by its abjected "underconsciousness." Throughout his poetry, Wordsworth addresses nature as his nurse and feeder, the one who "hast fed / My lofty speculations" (*Prelude* 2.462–63). Memories too serve as feeders, or places where the poet "would drink / As at a fountain" (11.382–83) and where his mind is "nourished and invisibly repaired" (11.263). In a typical maneuver, the hungry poet, having crossed the Alps in book 6, sublimates his desire for bread into a desire for more ethereal nutrition: "The cry of unknown birds, / The mountains. ... These were our food" (1805 *PRL;* 6.644–54). He describes the mind's "feeding pleasures," its "hidden appetites" for such edibles as "innocent milk," "innocent food," and books, "devoured, / Tasted or skimmed" (4.278; 5.530; 5.273–75; 6.28–29). The poet "drink[s] in / A pure organic pleasure" from nature (1.590–91) and feeds in such a rarified fashion that it too might be considered drinking — pure nutrition, mother's milk. Elsewhere in *The Excursion* the poet finds himself "daily thirsting" and "deeply drinking-in the soul of things" (1.69; 262) as his mind "draws its nourishment" from nature in a manner that "innocently satisfies / The humbler cravings of the heart" (3.581, 353–54).[26] Joshua Wilner has examined feeding in psychoanalytic terms in Wordsworth's poetry as a process of internalization, which keeps feeding in the ethereal realm of psychic incorporation.[27] Yet self-abjection is a feature of the consuming subject of Romantic *Naturphilosophie,* and its logic of ingestion — and digestion — can help us better understand the nature of the Wordsworthian "egotistical sublime" as an ego involving an id, or something buried under consciousness, giving shape to the self.

At one point in the revisionary process, Wordsworth considers transforming the "mind that feeds" into a mind that *sees* and *hears.* A C-stage recension to manuscript A of *The Prelude* (not an entirely authoritative document) reveals in the palimpsest of the Snowdon passage

A shadowy image of a mighty Mind,
That while it copes with visible shapes hears also
Through rents and openings in the ideal world
The astounding chorus of infinity. . . . (*TBP* 2:223)[28]

Because of their metaphoric distance from the body, sight and hearing have always been the most exalted form of sensory perception. Aesthetic taste philosophers prioritized vision, devoting most of their attention to it. Just as Hazlitt speaks of "the mind and eye of Taste," Coleridge insists that perception of the object through "mental taste" must proceed exclusively through "the eye and ear; which alone are true organs of sense" (*HCW*, 8:31; *CCW*, 11:1, 375–77). When Wordsworth describes a mind that "copes with visible shapes" and "hears also" in the C-stage revision above, he gives form to an intellectual operation at the furthest remove from the bodily organism. The *mind* takes in, appreciates, or aesthetically swallows infinity. However, he finds himself dissatisfied with this sensory means of perception and returns to a mind that feeds, albeit a form of feeding that can also take place through eyes and ears.[29] In "Tintern Abbey" Wordsworth commits himself to pursuing "all the mighty world / Of eye and ear" (105–6) and, true to his task many years later, he writes to his daughter, "You cannot guess how hard I work to see and hear all I can" (*LMY* 5:145). Despite the privileged hermeneutic status of seeing and hearing, however, Wordsworth's favored metaphor of feeding persists, dominating the final published version of the Snowdon passage. When the poet remarks that "even the grossest minds must see and hear, / And cannot chuse but feel," in fact, one wonders whether the slippage from "feel" to "feed" is the product of one's own imagining (1805 *PRL;* 13.83–84).

Mental taste may depend mainly on eye and ear, but Wordsworth does not relinquish the gustatory metaphor of feeding in his lifelong effort to render his moment of spiritual illumination. Feeding through the eye for Wordsworth breaks down into opposite modes of visual consumption, tasteful and appetitive, and the "mature" poet of "Tintern Abbey" considers it nature's task to "feed" the poet's heart and mind, "with lofty thoughts" (127–28). When "The picture of the mind revives again," he finds that "in this moment there is life and food / For future years" (61–66). Feeding here is purposely distinguished from the "appetite" that the younger, less philosophic Wordsworth felt for nature (80).[30] In the 1805 *Prelude,* his description of the eye as "The most despotic of our senses" (11.173) is meant to criticize a mode of seeing that privileges external objects over the mind that perceives them, attempting "absolute dominion" over the more privileged mental work of poetic vision (11.173–75). This passage, originally part of the Snowdon passage in the

1804 five-book poem, compares the poet's sublime experience to an earlier, more debased one that "fell / Beneath the dominion of a taste / Less elevated" (*WU* 5.180–82). For Wordsworth, taste depends on an individual's "imagination, and his understanding — that is, upon his recipient, upon his creative or active and upon his judging powers, and upon the accuracy and compass of his knowledge — in fine, upon all that makes up the moral and intellectual Man" (*PW* 2:98). Throughout his poetry seeing and hearing are subsumed into feeding as subsets of aesthetic taste experience. Yet, what (or who) is abjected from Wordsworth's "feeding source," not only of individual but also of communal identities, is a question raised by the substrata of the appetitive feeding mind to which we now turn.

Aesthetic Ecology

Wordsworth's mid-career essays on taste reveal the several ways in which his revision from a "moving soul" in the 1805 *Prelude* to a "feeding source" in the 1850 *Prelude* grounds the poem more emphatically within the materiality of his feeding mind-in-nature. His three *Essays upon Epitaphs* offer an analysis of the discursive principles of taste regarding a form of writing literally carved into stone. The first of these, published anonymously in Coleridge's briefly lived journal *The Friend* in February 1810 (later revised as a note to *The Excursion*), superimposes the figure of the feeding mind onto the material ecology of the Lake District as the forty-year-old, meditative poet observes: "Never did a child stand by the side of a running stream, pondering within himself *what power was the feeder* of the perpetual current, from what never-wearied sources the body of water was supplied, but he must have been inevitably propelled to follow this question by another: 'Towards what abyss is it in progress? what receptacle can contain the mighty influx?' And the spirit of the answer must have been, though the word might be sea or ocean . . . a receptacle without bounds or dimensions; — nothing less than infinity" (*PW* 2:51; emphasis mine). In this poetic rumination on Lakeland ecology, the feeding mind is absorbed into the materiality of nature. The "feeder" and "receptacle without bounds" participate in the same symbolic economy of consumption illustrated in the Snowdon passage. Here, that economy is conceived as what we might call an *aesthetic ecology*, a larger system, like the rivers and streams of the Lakes, which ultimately all connect and feed back into each other.

In this, Wordsworthian creation resembles the macrocosmic worldview, translated into humoral physiology, where the "blood, which disperseth itself by the branches of veins through all the body, may be resembled to those waters which are carried by brooks and rivers all over the earth."[31] These veins form part of an economic system, whether animal or ecological, originating in a central feeder that feeds as it is fed: feeding as a verb can be both transitive and intransitive. Immediately prior to the reflection above, in December 1809, Wordsworth made his first recorded reference to the work of Plato, specifically Thomas Taylor's translation of *The Cratylus, Phaedo, Parmenides and Timaeus of Plato* (1793). In the Platonic creation myth of *Timaeus* (which for Plato was no myth but a probable version of creation), Timaeus describes a third dimension of the created world beyond both visible materiality and the abstracted, intellectual world of forms, "the receptacle, and in a manner the nurse, of all generation" (*CDP* 1176).[32] The Platonic "receptacle" (*chora*) is the cause or "feeder," a kind of wet "nurse of all generation": "the mother and receptacle of all created and visible and in any way sensible things . . . is an invisible and formless being which receives all things and in some mysterious way partakes of the intelligible, and is most incomprehensible" (*CDP* 1178). Plato's feeder-receptacle, however, does not ingest, digest, or expel otherness, and in this sense Wordsworth's divine "feeder" does not qualify as Neoplatonic. Like Milton's self-digesting God, Hegel's self-digesting Spirit, and Schelling's excreting Absolute, the Wordsworthian "mind that feeds" remains in tension with its own abject dimension.

In the secondary climax of *The Prelude,* the Simplon Pass episode of book 6, the poet experiences a sublime reverie in which "whate'er / I saw, or heard, or felt, was but a stream / That flowed into a kindred stream" (1805 *PRL;* 6.672–74). In the 1850 revision, this image of transitively and intransitively feeding streams, which enter the poet through eyes, ears, and the all-sensitive skin of selfhood, is figured as creative expression: the feeding mind becomes "intent to hear / Its voices issuing forth to silent light / In one continuous stream" (1850 *PRL;* 14.72–74). The image again dates back to *Timaeus,* where "the river of speech, which flows out of a man and ministers to the intelligence, is the fairest and noblest of all streams" (*CDP* 1198). The ambiguous pronoun in "intent to hear / *Its* voices issuing forth" can refer either to the meditative mind or to the external chasm as the receptacle of material generation. Wordsworth employs the same idea of the mind (qua nature) as feeder-receptacle in Sonnets 22 and 23 of his *River Duddon* (1820) sonnet sequence. In Sonnet 22, the Wanderer (at once river and poet, natural and poetic streams of expression) broods on "the Deep / Where mightiest rivers into powerless sleep / Sink, and forget their nature" (22.4–6); in Sonnet 23 he "seeks that receptacle vast / Where all his unambitious functions fail" (7–8). The poet's "unambitious functions" are his physical functions, distinguished from "intellectual *acts* and *operations,*" which are *not* passive and which define the creative activity that Wordsworth associates with aesthetic experience. Like the organic rivers and streams of the Lakes, the feeding mind partakes of a greater infinitude that systematizes mind and nature, banishing all inassimilable matter from a symbolic economy of consumption conceived as an aesthetic ecology.

As Wordsworth was working out his metaphor of feeding through the material ecology of the Lakes in his 1810 *Essays upon Epitaphs,* he was simultaneously working on the first draft of what became *A Guide through the District of the Lakes in the North of England, with a Description of the Scenery, &c. for the Use of Tourists and Residents* (1835). This *Guide* addresses "the *Minds* of Persons of taste," since according to Wordsworth "it is upon the *mind* which a traveller brings along with him that his acquisitions, whether of pleasure or profit, must principally depend" (*PW* 2:155; 2:230). In a bitter retraction, he wrote in March 1842 that he "undertook about a twelvemonth since to furnish some new Matter in the way of a more minute Guide for the *Body* of the Tourist, as I found that the Guide Books which attended mainly to this were preferred much, by the generality of Tourists, to mine" (*LLY* 7:310.) Notwithstanding his complaint, his 1835 *Guide* addressed to "the *Minds* of Persons of taste" outsold all of Wordsworth's other work published during his lifetime, and it was a guide to viewing, or intellectually feeding upon, nature.

The opening section, "View of the Country as Formed by Nature," again maps the aesthetically feeding mind onto the material ecology of the Lake District. After a detailed topographical description, Wordsworth observes that "from the multitude of brooks and torrents that fall into these lakes, and of internal springs by which they are fed, and which circulate through them like veins, they are truly living lakes, '*vivi lacus*' " (*PW* 2:185). Wordsworth had read Lamb's copy of *The Anatomy of Melancholy* in 1810 as he was working on the original version of the *Guide,* and Robert Burton also refers to the humoral mind as containing "the receptacles of the spirits, brought hither by the arteries from the heart, and are there more refined to a more heavenly nature, to perform the actions of the soul."[33] In Wordsworth's *Guide,* the Lakes themselves, receptacles of the eternal "feeding source," acquire the same brooding capacity as the meditative mind of Snowdon: "Vapours exhaling from the lakes . . . brooding upon the heights, or descending towards the valleys with inaudible motion, give a visionary character to everything around them" (*PW* 2:190–91). The internal complexities of Wordsworth's feeding mind are reflected in a natural ecology whose changes are frequent and whose "every brook is vocal." His *Guide* addresses those who can discern in these streams the natural expression of their own finely nuanced minds.

Three decades later, Wordsworth heightened his rhetoric in a final, impassioned plea addressed to the minds of "all persons of taste" in the *Morning*

Post of December 1844, urging readers to join him in protesting the projected extension of the Kendal–Windermere railway line into the Lake District (*PW* 3:340).[34] While the letters are addressed to "all persons of taste," one need only consider the venue in which they first appeared to realize that he was hardly appealing to *all* persons of taste. In a letter to his publisher Edward Moxon, he wrote on January 23, 1845: "You observe that the Morning Post nobody reads — this is not correct. Its circulation among the Aristocracy, is very considerable; all the Ladies look at it and that puts it in the way of the Gentlemen" (*LLY* 7:650). The conservative *Morning Post* (known as the "Fawning Post") was "as devoted to dinners as was *The Times* to politics," and a contemporary dubbed it "the pet of the petticoats, the darling of the boudoir, the oracle of the drawing-room, and the soft recorder of ballroom beauties and drawing-room presentations."[35] The letters Wordsworth published in it constitute a bolder statement on taste than any he had published before, and they resent the imminent influx of urban persons who "labour daily with their hands [not heads] for bread" (*PW* 3:344). For Wordsworth, this category includes the lowliest Liverpool laborer as well as the wider circle of commercial classes who labor for and consume their bread but do not take time to cultivate the higher pleasures of aesthetic taste. Such consumers are unable to feed disinterestedly (their taste for nature too is unspirited, consumerist) and so feed into his symbolic economy of consumption: an aesthetic ecology whose feeding source has shifted from the Eucharistic meal to the poet's expression.

Wordsworth's *Essay, Supplementary to the Preface* of 1815 describes an aesthetic ideal of uninterrupted visual consumption in a natural world where all streams feed into each other and "everything is distinct, yet nothing defined into absolute independent singleness" (*PW* 3:77). Anything that blocks or disrupts the cycle of sublime visual feeding through the eye must be avoided, and thus artificial promontories and whitewashed houses are a particular source of lament in Wordsworth's *Guide to the Lakes*. He complains that such objects are "discordant," "gross transgressions" (*PW* 2:210), alternately referred to as "disagreeable speck[s]," "harsh *additions*," and "puny efforts of elegance . . . obtruded in rivalship with the sublimities of Nature" (*PW* 2:213–22). The sensibility of the poet, and consequently the health of the nation, require that such distasteful blots be removed, since "Bad taste, whatever shape it may put on, is injurious to the heart and the understanding" (*PW* 2:97). Throughout his *Guide* Wordsworth bemoans that "spiky tree, the larch," which is indigenous to Continental Europe but out of place in the natural ecology of Cumberland (*PW* 3:221). The distasteful larch comes to stand for all those discordant objects that, refusing to harmonize into the natural landscape, cannot be subsumed into the sublime feeding source, or mind that feeds in egotistical sublimity. "Add thousands to tens of thousands, and the appearance is still the same," he laments, "a collection of separate individual trees, obstinately presenting themselves as such" (*PW* 2:221). The imported larch insists on its own particularity and thereby appears as a bold and impudent blotch on an otherwise integrated aesthetic ecology.

Like the masses of trees "obstinately presenting themselves as such," masses of larchlike humans, invaders from a commercial outside, now threaten an even worse intrusion into the Lakes. If Wordsworth's *Guide to the Lakes* was concerned with the "intrusion of bad taste," by 1844 that intrusion had become an "inundation," or pouring in of "droves" and "large bodies" of "persons who must labour daily with their hands for bread in large towns" (*PW* 3:344–50). Peter T. Newby remarks that by the time Wordsworth wrote these letters in 1844, he "clearly drew a distinction between the tourist, a person of taste, and the railway visitor who would be unable to appreciate the landscape."[36] As the railway penetrates the aesthetic ecology of the Lakes — its feeding source and network of streams — it disrupts his symbolic economy of consumption, expelling its multitudes at designated stations. With a petulance we cannot ascribe to age (for we have seen it before in work from his mid-thirties), Wordsworth protests: "Go to a pantomime, a farce, or a puppet-show, if you want noisy pleasure — the crowd of spectators who partake your enjoyment will, by their presence and acclamations, enhance it; but may those who have given proof that they prefer other gratifications continue to be safe from the molestation of cheap trains pouring out their hundreds at a time along the margin of Windermere" (*PW* 3:345–46). These phantasmatic masses due to be disgorged at Windermere make explicit a latent political dimension of the poet's earlier aesthetics. Read as a gloss on the feeding mind, or sublime Wordsworthian Subject of Taste, they reveal the degree to which its procreative power is founded on a dark "under-presence" of "real men," whose real hunger and consumerist appetites disqualify them from the poet's dominion of elevated taste. Tim Fulford offers an analogy for reading Wordsworth's politics of landscape in the figure of his friend and contemporary, Uvedale Price. Price's influential *Essay on the Picturesque* (1794) was ostensibly apolitical in its delineation of the principles of this fashionable aesthetic, but when read in the context of a later pamphlet written in fear of a French invasion in 1797, it appears in a different light. In this pamphlet Price calls on landowners to make common cause against the unpropertied poor should they show any signs of rebellion, for as Fulford remarks, the concept of "taste had to be defended against groups whose increasingly organized self-representations — as well as their social inferiority — made them too threatening to be aestheticized."[37]

Throughout *The Prelude* Wordsworth similarly distinguishes his "feeding pleasures" from the "heinous appetites" of the barbarous mob (4.278; 10.339). The undiscriminating masses at the theatrical spectacles of London, for instance, seem as ready to devour a plump, yearling child as fruits and wine (7.382–84). Against the unruly (even cannibal) appetites of the city, where "the human heart is sick / And the eye feeds it not, and cannot feed," aesthetic feeding takes place naturally in the Lakes (12.204–05). Now the demonic railway intruder, with "its scarifications, its intersections, its smoke, and swarms of pleasure-hunters" (*PW* 3:353), comes straight from the depths of an urban "hell / For eyes and ears" (*Prelude* 1805; 7.659–60). Unlike the pastoral fair at the start of book 8, in which "Booths are there none . . . so gaiety prevails / Which all partake of, young and old" (8.25–46), the booths at St. Bartholomew Fair are portrayed as "vomiting, receiving, on all sides, / Men, women, three-years' children, babes in arms" (1805 *PRL;* 7.694–95). Wordsworth seems to have learned from Milton that a powerful way to demonize someone is to portray him or her not in the act of logocentric expression but in a parodic version of unsignifying emission. The vomiting, disgorging, or "pouring out" of hundreds of offensive railway travelers is a similar type of eruction. The "cheap trains" are demonized intruders into the poet's paradisiacal world of pure feeding, and the urban masses poured forth by these demons, like the rudely disgorged masses of Bartholomew Fair, represent an abject dimension of the tasteful world he had spent a lifetime trying to create.

Thirty years later, John Ruskin echoed Wordsworth's demonizing rhetoric, evoking the vomiting encampments in book 7 of *The Prelude* to accuse railway companies of trying to raise "Old Bartholomew Fair under Helvellyn."[38] Like the elder Wordsworth, Ruskin complained of those who "have been taught that nothing is virtuous but care for their bellies, and nothing useful but what goes into them" — a category that includes the hungry lower orders as well as the consumerist masses who view landscape as a commodity. Just as Wordsworth had predicted that "wrestling matches, horse and boat races without number, and pot-houses and beer-shops" (*PW* 3:346) would result from the railway's extension into the Lakes, Ruskin claimed that extending the railway into the heart of the Lake District would be "to open taverns and skittle grounds round Grasmere, which will soon, then, be nothing but a pool of drainage."[39] The receptacles that participated in Wordsworth's transcendental feeding economy were to become literally clogged with waste: the "dark abyss" over which the feeding mind broods was to be materialized as a dark, Tartarean lake.

Figure 1. James Gillray, *Substitutes for Bread; or Right Honourables Saving the Loaves and Dividing the Fishes.* To the Charitable Committee for reducing the high price of Corn, by providing Substitutes for Bread in their own Families, this representation of the Hard shifts made by the Framers & Signers of the Philanthropic Agreement is most respectfully dedicated. (London, 1795). Copyright the British Museum, London.

Figure 2. James Gillray, *The British Butcher; Supplying John-Bull with a Substitute for Bread* (London, 1795). Copyright the British Museum, London.

Figure 3. Théodore Géricault, *Despair and Cannibalism on the Raft*. Sketch (1819). Louvre, Paris. Réunion des Musées Nationaux/Art Resource, New York.

Figure 4. Théodore Géricault, *The Raft of the Medusa* (1819). Louvre, Paris. Réunion des Musées Nationaux/Art Resource, New York.

A VOLUPTUARY under the horrors of Digestion.

Figure 5. James Gillray, *A Voluptuary under the Horrors of Digestion* (London, 1792). Copyright the British Museum, London.

Figure 6. James Gillray, *Temperance Enjoying a Frugal Meal* (London 1792). Copyright the British Museum, London.

Séance d'un Jury de Gourmands dégustateurs.

Figure 7. Grimod de la Reynière, *Séance d'un Jury de Gourmands dégustateurs* (1806). Courtesy of Department of Special Collections, Stanford University Libraries.

Figure 8. James Gillray, *A Pair of Polished Gentlemen* (1801). Copyright the British Museum, London.

Guide to the Feeding Mind

Taste was threatened, Wordsworth claimed in the "Preface to *Lyrical Ballads*," by consumers who could not distinguish food from poetry, or physical from spiritual nutrition. Such consumers were now ready to purchase a railway ticket to the Lakes and obtrude themselves into the egotistical sublimity of his feeding economy as its inassimilable material remains. Wordsworth's enraged letters to the *Morning Post* refer to the railways as "pests, as they are likely too often to prove," conflating them with the urban crowds who represented a plaguelike, indiscriminate devastation of nature (*PW* 3:352). As early as June 1812 he had complained that "the lower orders have been for upwards of thirty years accumulating in pestilential masses of ignorant population" (*LMY* 3:21). Later, in his anxious reaction to the Reform Bill, he darkly predicted that should the bill pass, "every thing in the world of Taste will sink accordingly" (*LMY* 5:503). Wordsworth may have been afraid of the intrusion of bad taste and unbridled consumerism into the Lakes, but when the railway letters first appeared on the heels of the fifth (1842) edition of his *Guide to the Lakes,* the paradox of two such seemingly opposed works addressed to "all persons of taste" did not go unremarked.

Baron Field's reaction in a letter to Henry Crabb Robinson (both men presumably sympathetic readers, since they were both friends of the poet) lays bare the contradiction built into Wordsworth's major pronouncements on taste: "Has he not even published, besides his poems which have made the district classic ground, an actual prose 'Guide?' And now he complains that the decent clerks and manufacturers of Liverpool and Manchester should presume to flock of a holiday to see the scene of 'The Excursion,' and to buy his own 'Guide-book!' "[40] When transposed onto the material substance of the Lakes, Wordsworth's transcendentally feeding mind reflects a taste for landscape that had become irretrievably confused — and largely by Wordsworth himself, as Baron Field suggests, with consumerism. Raymond Williams remarks in his dictionary of cultural key words that "the idea of taste cannot now be separated from the idea of THE CONSUMER . . . the assumption that the viewer, spectator or reader is a *consumer,* exercising and subsequently showing his taste."[41] Wordsworth comes down to us today as a poet self-consciously caught between these two cultural modes of consumption, taste and consumerism, which Wordsworth would separate and which the "masses" tend to conflate.

The irreconcilability of his two works addressed to all persons of taste, namely, the letters voicing opposition to the railway scheme and the *Guide to the Lakes,* was soon swallowed up by an even more pressing concern: How should the author of the polemical letters protesting the entrance of the railway into the Lakes have it enter his head to compose "a Rail-way Guide" (*LLY* 7:607) for the convenience of picturesque consumers? Writing to his publisher, Edward Moxon, just two weeks before the publication of his first railway sonnet (at the head of the first railway essay), he writes that such a guide "ought to express by small drawings the object signified, a Church, a Castle, a Gentleman's Seat, a conspicuous hill, brook or river, or any other prominent object, marking its distance from the line" (*LLY* 7:607). The paradox is readily apparent: the very author who had complained of the illustrations ("drawings, or Etchings, or whatever they may be called") as a material reduction of his poetic descriptions in the original *Guide to the Lakes* ("Select Views in Cumberland, Westmorland, and Lancashire" [*LMY* 2:404]) now proposes a book of small drawings for which he himself will provide the text, illustrating this scenery for the railway traveler as it passes.[42] The type of picturesque guide Wordsworth has in mind described not just what but *how* to see, and in so doing so rendered a unique experience reproducible and exchangeable; in Matthew Brennan's words, a commodified "point of view repeatable by any tourist standing in the right place at the right time."[43] How can we reconcile Wordsworth's proposed "Rail-way Guide" with the ridicule intended in his poem "On Seeing Some Tourists of the Lakes Pass by Reading; a Practice Very Common"? Or with "The Brothers" (1799), whose opening line exclaims: "These Tourists, heaven preserve us!" How does such a guide square with his satire in the railway letters themselves, written shortly after his proposal to Moxon, of "pilgrims of fashion hurried along in their carriages . . . poring over their Guide-books" (*PW* 3:354)? In theory, Wordsworth's conception of aesthetic experience as sublime feeding through the eye cannot be reduced to the packaged viewing of picturesque travel, with its reproducible, regularly timed stations.

Technically, Snowdon is a mountain in Wales, but we are speaking of an aesthetic ecology crafted over a lifetime of writing that transcends geographical distinction, and the proposed railway guide makes it possible to ask whether Wordsworth's feeding mind *itself* can be packaged as one more picturesque item among many. When his friend Price established the picturesque aesthetic as a station midway between the sublime and the beautiful in 1794, he stated that "the effect of the picturesque is curiosity."[44] But as Burke had already established, curiosity "has an appetite which is very sharp" and so can have little to do with taste (*PE* 31). Far from promoting a "recollection of thought" or "a due attention to the object," which Hume, like Wordsworth, deemed necessary for the taste experience (*EMP* 232), the picturesque entailed a constant rushing after new combinations of forms — a forward drive from "station" to "station," rather than a solitary brooding over what the mind had perceived. Wordsworth's *Guide to the Lakes* addressed to "persons of pure taste" was, in effect, trying to have it both ways (*PW* 2:225). The picturesque genre in which he was writing militated against his effort to instruct "persons of pure taste" to participate in an aesthetic ecology through an elevated mode of consumption, figured as feeding.

The "feeder" and "receptacle" of the sonorous streams of the Lakes (metaphoric for the poet's stream of expression) may be "nothing less than infinity," but textual strata of the feeding mind suggest that Wordsworth's aesthetic consumer does, momentarily, succumb to this consumerist mode of viewing. The D-stage revision to manuscript A of *The Prelude* contains the following line (subsequently struck out) in italics:

> A meditation rose in me that night
> Upon the lonely Mountain when the scene
> Had pass'd away, and to my thoughts it showed
> *Embodied in material portraiture*
> The perfect image of a mighty Mind,
> Of one that feeds upon infinity. . . . (*TBP* 2:967; my emphasis)

Landscape "portraits" were a feature of picturesque guides as examples of how to see, snapshots for the consumerist eye. William Gilpin, who took the picturesque aesthetic on tour in the 1780s, apologized in the preface to his *Observations on the Mountains, and Lakes of Cumberland, and Westmoreland* (1786) for having printed several drawings "under the character of *portraits*," as he was "sensible, that sketches taken in that hasty manner in which those were taken, could not pretend to the accuracy necessary in portrait."[45] In the hierarchy of the visual arts, portraiture traditionally ranked very low since, more than any individual artistic *vision* it might express, it was held accountable to the visible world and truth of representation.

Gilpin, however, revised the meaning of portraiture to suit the picturesque aesthetic, criticizing those who "are determined to call nothing a *portrait,* but what is *exactly* copied from nature." The picturesque painter (consumer-expresser) may have "no right to add a magnificent castle — an impending rock — or a river, to adorn his fore-ground," but "he may certainly break an ill-formed hillock; and shovel the earth about him as he pleases, without offense. . . . These trivial alterations may greatly add to the beauty of his composition; and yet they interfere not with the truth of *portrait*."[46] Gilpin's picturesque aesthetic allowed the aesthetic consumer to manipulate nature in order to satisfy any particular "craving for prospect" (*PW* 2:211). Whether by breaking "an ill-formed hillock" and shoveling the earth, or by inserting different backing foils to his landscape glass to alter the tone of the landscape, the picturesque tourist could adapt nature to his or her particular palate and consume it in limited portions, or sight-bites.⁴⁷

With consumers scrambling to accumulate as many views or prospects as possible, landscape was converted into "portable property" (to borrow Wemmick's phrase from *Great Expectations*).⁴⁸ When Thomas Gray toured the Lakes in 1769, he went so far as to estimate the price of the "delicious views" he described: "I got to the *Parsonage* a little before sunset, and saw in my glass a picture, that if I could transmit to you, and fix it in all the softness of its living colours, would fairly sell for a thousand pounds."⁴⁹ Picturesque theory and practical guides offered "material portraits" that were comparable and exchangeable as commodities. Wordsworth's proposed railway guide, based on this same model of consumerist viewing, would accelerate the number of views available through the frame of the railway window, raising the question of whether his own "feeding source" could be reduced to the dimensions of "material portraiture." Any guide that would make personal immersion in nature unnecessary posed a challenge to his aesthetic ecology conceived as a symbolic economy of consumption. The feeder no longer needed to "feed" intransitively into the system, and excesses could be produced that need not be tastefully reincorporated (foul drainage among other things). The railway guide, in theory, threatened to drag Wordsworth's feeding mind from its transcendental position on high into the dark Tartarean lake that Grasmere verged on becoming.

Reducing the feeding mind to the dimensions of "material portraiture" would destroy the infinity upon which that mind depends for its sublimity. "Infinity is one of the most efficient causes of the sublime," wrote Price; "to give it picturesqueness, you must destroy that cause of its sublimity; for it is on the shape, and disposition of its boundaries, that the picturesque must, in great measure, depend."⁵⁰ To think of landscape in terms of portraiture is to delimit the infinite and give form to the undefinable feeding source of aesthetic experience. A picturesque Snowdon may seem unthinkable to us today, but from Wordsworth's perspective in the D-stage revision that embodies the feeding mind "in material portraiture," this very emblem of egotistical sublimity can be made to satisfy a consumerist "craving for prospect." Although the revision remains buried beneath layers of text, the 1850 *Prelude* retains a trace of it in the "*emblem* of a Mind / That feeds upon infinity" (14.70–71), the emblem being an early modern version of the etchings, drawings, or picturesque portraits that accompanied picturesque guides. For a fleeting moment in the poet's sublime state of self-consciousness, in other words, the feeding mind becomes, like other emblems scattered throughout the expressive stream of *The Prelude*, one more narrative station.

It would seem unlikely that the poet should destroy the cause of the feeding mind's sublimity by imposing boundaries upon it. But reducing the sublime experience atop Mount Snowdon to an "emblem" keeps the speaker from falling into the infinitude of "that receptacle vast / Where all his unambitious functions fail" (as described in *River Duddon*). Neil Hertz has argued that blockage is a necessary feature of any account of sublime experience, proposing that for Wordsworth "The power of the emblem is that it reestablishes boundaries between representer and represented and, while minimizing the differences between them, keeps the poet-impresario from tumbling into his text."[51] Wordsworth's own essay on the sublime and beautiful, which remained unfinished in manuscript, distinguishes between two different modes of sublimity: the first, a *positive* sublime, which is empowering and which calls on the mind to expand in an effort to "grasp at something towards which it can make approaches but which it is incapable of attaining" (*PW* 2:354); the second, a *negative* sublime, which overwhelms and "produc[es] a humiliation or prostration of the mind before some external agency" (*PW* 2:354). While the Simplon Pass episode in book 6 of *The Prelude* contains both positive and negative modes of sublimity, the Snowdon passage remains, as Brennan argues, "Wordsworth's greatest example of the Positive Sublime."[52] The stratigraphic overlay of the feeding mind that embodies it in "material portraiture" allows the consumer to continue tasting nature in an aesthetically integrated cycle of feeding without being overwhelmed. At the same time, as we have seen, it makes room for a consumerist taste that gobbles up landscape as portraits — "portable property," or commodified objects to hang on the wall.

Wordsworth's railway letters tend to be read as a radical reversal of his earlier aesthetics, according to which the essentialism of the "Preface" (everyone is potentially a person of taste) transfigures into a conservative ideal of learned or cultivated taste. But it is in the nature of taste to waver between immediate sensation and learned sensibility, and Wordsworth's major statements on taste partake of this same ambivalence.[53] The 1800 "Preface" does not adhere to a strictly essentialist account of taste any more than the 1844 railway letters adhere to a strictly acquired one. While the "Preface" agrees with Sir Joshua Reynolds, for instance, that "an *accurate* taste in Poetry and in all the other arts . . . is an *acquired* talent, which can only be produced by thought and a long continued intercourse with the best models of composition" (*PW* 1:156), the railway letters, despite their emphasis on educating taste, claim to be speaking on behalf of "every one, however humble his condition, who coming hither shall bring with him an eye to perceive, and a heart to feel and worthily enjoy" (*PW* 3:355). In the *Guide to the Lakes*, Wordsworth announced his wish to "be joined by persons of pure taste throughout the whole island, who . . . deem the district a sort of national property" (*PW* 2:225). He had then hoped that poetry (or his own stream of expression) would become the center of an aesthetic economy of consumption based on taste.

One year before the railway letters, Wordsworth had become poet laureate and a national emblem — or egotistical figure — for England, with a consequently intensified mission to "purify and strengthen" or else "corrupt and impair" the taste of the nation. When Keats made his walking tour of the Lake District in 1818, he found that "Lord Wordsworth, instead of being in retirement, has himself and his house full in the thick of fashionable visitors quite convenient to be pointed at all the summer long" (*KL* 1:299). The visitors' book at Rydal Mount (by no means a complete record) contains 2,500 names for the years 1830 through 1837, and it is probable that by the 1840s the poet was receiving more than five hundred visitors per year.[54] In 1845, Baron Field remarked that "Mr. Wordsworth . . . and Rydal can no more pretend to 'retirement' than the Queen. They have both bartered it for fame."[55] Despite the railway's triumphal advancement into the Lakes (the Windermere station opened on April 21, 1847), the service Wordsworth rendered in saving the Lakes from further commercial development is real.[56] But as his image was sympathetically projected onto the land as the materialized economy of the egotistical sublime, the poet found himself reduced to the consumerist constraints of "material portraiture."[57]

5

Lamb's Low-Urban Taste

The influence of the Stomach on the Eye and of the Eye (as in sea-sickness) on the Stomach is known and admitted — but are not Tears analogous (however ludicrous it may appear at the first thought) to the watering of the Mouth? Is there not some connection between the Stomach & the lachrymal Ducts? One or the other must be true, as the copious weeping and intense passion of Grief during Sleep, which on waking proves to be heart-burn or a pain at the pit of the Stomach.
— Coleridge, "On the Passions" (1828)

Unlike the transcendental food of Wordsworthian infinity or the inspirational breezes drifting through Coleridge's "Eolian Harp," the air that Charles Lamb breathes acquires a "substantial and satisfying" meatiness; his London fog "is also meat and drink at the same time: something between egg-flip and *omelette soufflée*, but much more digestible than either" (*WCL* 1:351). Taking refuge from the pure diet of high Romanticism, Lamb participates in an urban, early nineteenth-century genre of gastronomical writing in which the literary writer poses as an expert in the "art of eating," leading public opinion in matters of taste (a topic to which we return in further detail in chapter 8).[1] However extreme in his passion for fine dining, the gastronome stakes his claim to taste in moderation and his capacity for self-restraint amid the cornucopian pleasures of the table. Lamb's fictional essays challenge the generic borders of such writing, however, by describing the indulgence of the *immoderate* pleasures of the palate. While many of his epicurean predilections are perfectly in keeping with contemporary French theory of *gourmandise,* Lamb wields the witty, table-talky genre of gastronomical discourse in a sophisticated — and deeply melancholy — critique of Romantic dietetics.

A careful study of his letters from 1796 through 1800 reveals that Lamb gave up his poetic ambitions in response to the "day of horrors" on September 22, 1796, when his sister Mary in a fit of madness murdered their mother with a kitchen knife and wounded their father in the head with a fork, and that his identity as well as metaphoric preoccupation with taste was forever marked by the event.[2] Whether or not he was familiar with his friend Coleridge's view (in the epigraph above) that grief was physiologically based in the stomach, his work suggests a direct line from the stomach to the lachrymal ducts. Macabre and melancholy, Mary Lamb's tragic misappropriation of kitchen utensils left him no choice but to keep his job at the British East India Company in London, necessitating his permanent employment if he wished to keep his shattered household together. His "Dissertation Upon Roast Pig" is in many ways the finest fictional critique of taste in the Romantic era, and in it a masochistic fascination with the arts of carving, cookery, and culinary animal tortures reveal an epicurean cruelty as the condition of possibility for what Lamb labels "low-Urban Taste" (*LM* 1:271). Schiller would remind us that satire is never far from elegy, and this is especially so in the case of Lamb's melancholy aesthetics.[3] The following pages will demonstrate how his "judicious epicure," Elia, develops his taste against Romantic ideals of pure diet — and the virile ideal of pure aesthetic subjectivity that Lamb chose to forgo (*WCL* 1:124).

Romantic Dietetics

Coleridge's early conversation poem "This Lime-tree Bower My Prison: A Poem Addressed to Charles Lamb, of the India House, London" (1800) posed a personal, aesthetic, and ideological challenge to Lamb, who styled his literary identity largely in response. The headnote to the poem explains how the speaker was prevented by "an accident" (Sara Coleridge had spilled a pot of hot milk on her husband's foot) from joining his friends (the Wordsworths and Lamb) on a walk through Nether Stowey in the West Country. Secluded in his lime-tree bower, he accompanies them in spirit, imagining the joy and intellectual nourishment that "gentle-hearted Charles" would receive from nature. When the poem first appeared in Southey's *Annual Anthology* of 1800, Lamb immediately wrote to Coleridge, demanding that in the next printing of the poem (which he prays God forbid) he show more "delicacy" in referring to himself: "please to blot out *gentle hearted,* and substitute drunken dog, ragged-head, seld-shaven, odd-ey'd, stuttering, or any other epithet which truly and properly belongs to the Gentleman in question. And for Charles read Tom, or Bob, or Richard, *for more delicacy.* — Damn you, I was beginning to forgive you, & believe in earnest that the lugging in of my Proper name was purely unintentional on your part, when looking back for further conviction, stares me in the face Charles Lamb of the *India House*" (*LM* 1:224). This repudiation of "gentle-hearted Charles" is usually read in a comic vein as a spirited response to the poem's overt sentimentalism. But it is important not to be misled by Lamb's self-deprecating humor: the statement represents a foundational gesture of his literary personality.[4]

The phrase *gentle-hearted* became a signature term for Lamb in the nineteenth century, damning him to the critically irrelevant world of the benign. Wordsworth's "Extempore Effusion upon the Death of James Hogg"(1835) eulogizes "Lamb, the frolic and the gentle," and when Swinburne claimed that no good criticism could ever be written about him "because nobody can do justice to his work who does not love it too well to feel himself capable of giving judgement on it," he added that it is because Lamb's "gentle name" disarms the critic: "we find a homely magic in the name of Lamb, a special fragrance in the fame of it, such as hardly seems to hang about the statelier sound of Coleridge's or Wordsworth's or Shelley's."[5] The perfume of Lamb's "gentle name," domesticating and feminizing "gentle-hearted Charles," occurs twice within Coleridge's poem, a repetition whose significance is strengthened by the fact that Coleridge's manuscript originally contained a different apostrophe to "My sister & my Friends!" (*CCW* 16.2.1:484). Coleridge then crossed out "My sister & my Friends!" (perhaps owing to the overtly Wordsworthian nature of the address, which even adopts Dorothy for his sister) and substituted "My Sara" (tellingly with no exclamation point). This solution remained unsatisfactory, however, and in the final version of line 69 he replaced it with "gentle-hearted CHARLES!"[6] Sensing condescension, Lamb reacted by asserting his own low-urban taste, defining and elaborating it against Lake-school aesthetics.

From 1792 Lamb had worked as an accounting clerk for the British East India Company, which monopolized the tea trade until 1834 and was a major factor in providing domestic consumers with those international "luxuries" that the "natural" taste of Romantic poets like Coleridge, Wordsworth, and Shelley opposed.[7] While colonial food products, such as tea and sugar, had been around since the seventeenth century in Britain (when the East India house was founded), between 1794 and 1800 the East India Company imported vast quantities of sugar to England, and Coleridge's "Poem Addressed to Charles Lamb, of the India House, London" pegs his friend as a functionary of an urban institution synonymous with British commercial imperialism.[8] Like other radicals of the 1790s, Coleridge was active in opposing the importation of such colonial foodstuffs as East and West Indian sugar at a time when diet — and the commercial mechanisms supporting it — was highly politicized. The opening stanzas of "On Sugar," a poem printed anonymously in the *Manchester Herald* in 1792, prefigure Coleridge's 1795 *Lecture on the Slave-Trade* and Southey's "Poems on the Slave Trade" (1797) in the kind of rhetoric they use to protest the importation of East Indian sugar:

> Go, guilty, sweet seducing food,
> Tainted by streams of human blood!
> Emblem of woe, and fruitless moans,
> Of mangled limbs, and dying groans!
> To me, thy tempting white appears
> Steeped in a thousand Negroes' tears! . . .
>
> No! — I abhor the luscious food
> Purchas'd by many a *Brother*[']s blood!
> I'll wage with habit, virtuous strife,
> To save a fellow-creature's life;
> And bless the day I scorn'd the food
> Produc'd by *torments, groans,* and *blood!*[9]

Half of the lines above conclude with slant rhymes on "food" and "blood," an alliance that dietary reformers emphasized to the consuming public.[10] William Fox's *An Address to the People of Great Britain on the Propriety of Abstaining from West African Sugar and Rum* (1791) typically equated the eating of sugar with the eating of human flesh and the drinking of sugared tea with the drinking of human slave blood. According to such pamphlets as this, consumerism created the condition of possibility for cannibalism, or the economic consumption of people in the form of labor. Colonial food products like sugar and tea, after all, were commodities, which Marx defines as "the material integuments of homogenous human labor."[11] Coleridge's association of Lamb with the British East India Company, an importer of personified foods like these, also associated him with the rapacious commercial expansion and "bad" politics articulating themselves through the symbolic code of food at the turn of the nineteenth century.[12]

In Romantic dietary discourse, imported foods like sugar and tea were thought to dull one's sensibility, vitiate the palate, and destroy the delicacy needed to exercise the mental faculty of taste. In *A Vindication of Natural Diet*

(1813), Shelley claimed that "On a natural system of diet, we should require no spices from India; no wines from Portugal, Spain, France, or Madeira; none of those multitudinous articles of luxury for which every corner of the globe is rifled" (*SP* 87–88).[13] Timothy Morton has shown how the combined factors of urbanization, industrialization, and revolution prompted a return to nature that went hand-in-hand with the growth of vegetarianism among the Shelley circle in these years; London, he says, "exemplified these factors, and it is not surprising that many of the writers on vegetarianism in the period . . . articulated their support of the diet with the scourges of the city in mind."[14] Lamb, by contrast, devoted the major part of his day to tabulating the spread of these so-called scourges as an accountant for the East India Company.

Three months after his annoyed "Damn you" to Coleridge, he accepted a dinner invitation from his friend and colleague from the East India Company, Thomas Manning, in another letter "damning" the Lake poets. Manning invited Lamb to a feast of snipes ("The Snipes shall present themselves to you, ready roasted; *you* shall take the *digestible* parts, & *I'll* take the long bills"), and Lamb responded that he had already promised to spend his vacation with Wordsworth and Coleridge in the Lakes: "I need not describe to you the expectations which such an one as myself, pent up all my life in a dirty city, have formed of a tour to the *Lakes*. Consider, Grassmere! [*sic*] Ambleside! Wordsworth! Coleridge! I hope you will."[15] His self-ironizing reference, "pent up all my life in a dirty city," echoes Coleridge's description of him as an unfortunate city dweller who has "hunger'd after Nature many a year, / In the great City pent" in "This Lime-tree Bower" (29–30). Both allude to Milton's serpent who like one "long in populous city pent" found himself longing after Edenic nature (*PL* 9.445).[16] Although Lamb's irony is palpable, it is only when one turns over the page of the letter that his true sentiments become clear: "*Hills, woods, Lakes and mountains, to the Eternal Devil*. I will eat snipes with thee, Thomas Manning" (*LM* 1:247–48). Faced with the desire of Coleridge's speaker that he may "gaze till all doth seem / Less gross than bodily" ("Lime-tree Bower" 40–41), Lamb latches on to the digestible snipes to assert a more vigorous because carnivorous identity as an urban gastronome ("judicious epicure," gastronomer, gastronomist, gourmand, the terms were synonymous).

Shortly after the epistolary episode of the snipes (February 7, 1801), Lamb wrote to Robert Lloyd, defining more precisely the nature of his low-urban taste. Charles Lloyd (Robert's elder brother) had published poetry in Coleridge's *Poems To Which Are Now Added Poems by Charles Lamb, and Charles Lloyd* (1797), and Robert himself was living with Coleridge in the Lakes. Under the circumstances, Lamb's assertion of low-urban taste seems directed more to Coleridge than the Lloyds: "I dont know if you quite comprehend my low Urban Taste; — but depend upon it that a man of any feeling will have given his heart and his love in childhood & in boyhood to any scenes where he has been bred, as we[l]l to dirty streets (& smoky walls as they are called) as to green Lanes 'where live nibbling sheep' & to the everlasting hills and the Lakes" (*LM* 1:271). Lamb's local attachments to "dirty streets" and "smoky walls," elements of an urban environment marked by labor and industry, can rival any Wordsworthian attachment to the "everlasting hills and the Lakes." The pastoral lambs may feed (or "nibble") on the green stuff of the Lakes, but Lamb's urban dweller longs for more substantial fare. "Like the *Town* Mouse, that had tasted a little of urbane manners, I long to be nibbling my own cheese," he tells Manning, a type of food he "would not exchange for Skiddaw, Helvellyin [*sic*], James, Walter, and the Parson in the bargain" (*LM* 1:277). Choosing urban food over the central figures of Wordsworth's 1800 poem "The Brothers," he rejects the attitude encapsulated in its opening line: "These Tourists, heaven preserve us!" — and knowingly takes his place among the same urban consumers whom Wordsworth abjects from his aesthetic ecology.

"The Londoner" (1802) was Lamb's first published essay of note and the Ur-text for *The Essays of Elia,* and it is a rewriting of the above letter to Manning that repudiates Lakeland nutrition as too ethereal. Signed "A Londoner," this essay introduces his literary personality on a day of universal feasting: "The same day which gave me to the world, saw London happy in the celebration of her great annual feast" (*WCL* 1:39). The Lord Mayor's Feast was an occasion for gastronomical excess, a throwback to early modern forms of feasting and aristocratic festivity.[17] A traditional feature of the feast was the roasting of pigs, to which Swift refers in "A Modest Proposal" when he satirically recommends a human substitute for swine, who are in "no way comparable in Taste, or Magnificence, to a well-grown fat yearling Child; which, roasted whole, will make a considerable Figure at a *Lord Mayor's Feast*" (*SPW* 12:116).[18] Born in the midst of this annual return to courtly extravagance, Lamb's "Londoner" knows little of radical ideals of "pure diet," and perhaps even less of middle-class moderation. Shelley describes the feast as an occasion for extravagant, unnatural consumption, denouncing "the hypocritical sensualist at a lord mayor's feast, who declaims against the pleasures of the table" (*SP* 89), but Lamb was no hypocrite and worked hard not only to cultivate but also to demonstrate expertise in this area.

Lamb's fictional personae, particularly Edax and Elia, serve up a critique of aesthetic visions transcending the grosser experiential realms of human history, so often tragic in their sober reality. As Fred V. Randel observes, "it is one thing to refer, as Wordsworth does, to drinking the visionary power and feeding upon infinity, or as Coleridge does, to eating honey-dew, imbibing the milk of Paradise — but it is another thing to speak, as Lamb does, of a taste for roast pig's crackling or bread and cheese with an onion."[19] When Barry Cornwall (pseudonym for Bryan Walter Procter, literary man-about-town) asked Lamb how he felt among the lakes and mountains of Cumberland, he replied that "he was obliged to think of the Ham and Beef shop near Saint Martin's Lane; this was in order to bring down his thoughts from their almost too painful elevation to the sober regions of every-day life."[20] His comment can slice more than one way. The transcendental experience of feeding, or "gaz[ing] till all doth seem / Less gross than bodily," is painful either for its unpleasantness *or* its antithetical extreme: a pleasure too rich to be appreciated or mentally assimilated by the man of low-urban taste.

One year before "The Londoner," Lamb wrote to Wordsworth that the urban "crowds, the very dirt & mud, the Sun shining upon houses and pavements, the print shops, the old Book stalls, parsons cheap'ning books, coffee houses, steams of soups from kitchens, the pantomimes . . . work themselves into my mind *and feed me without a power of satiating me*" (*LM* 1:267; emphasis added). Lucy Newlyn has noticed that "Lamb makes use of his affection for London to challenge Wordsworthian values, but he uses Wordsworth to strengthen and enrich his affirmation of city life"; indeed, despite protestations to the contrary, one senses at the core of his work a speaker who longs to "feed" in a manner that provides more than material pleasure.[21] After one visit to the Lakes, Lamb complained to Coleridge of the "dead wood of the desk instead of your living trees!" and "how it weighs the spirit of a gentleman down!" (*LL* 2:247). Later, to Wordsworth he lamented "the very firs of the forest that look so romantic alive, and die into desks," a sentiment he also versified in a sonnet on the "dry drudgery of the desk's dead wood" (*LM* 3:149, *LL* 2:433). There is great deal of pathos in this reduction of romantic trees into office furniture, fitted to the performance of alienated labor. In another letter of September 8, 1802, written shortly after his return from the Lakes, Lamb admits: "very awkward I feel and strange at Business. I forget the name of Books, and feel myself not half so great a man as when I [was] a scrambler among mountains" (*LM* 2:66).

As a "scrambler among mountains," Lamb resembles the younger Wordsworth of "Tintern Abbey," who finds "life and food / For future years" in the nature surrounding him (64–65). But whereas Wordsworth relinquishes his "coarser pleasures" (73) for a more philosophical mode of feeding, Lamb finds it difficult to resign himself to a taste that is socially as well as geographically "low," or flat. The same year in which he published *The Essays of Elia* (1822), he confessed to Sir Walter Scott: "My disparagement of heaths and highlands — if I said any such thing in half earnest, — you must put down as a piece of old

Vulpine policy. I must make the most of the spot I am chained to, and console myself for my flat destiny as well as I am able" (*LL* 2:344). The fox, a natural enemy of the sheep, sees in his fellow creature nothing but food. Lamb's vulpine view of the sheep-bedecked lakes and mountains, heaths and highlands, like his imaginary trip to the ham and beef shop on Saint Martin's Lane, is at once a consolation for his "flat destiny" and a source of creative nutrition for this mock-gastronomical professor.

Edax on Flesh Eating

In the early nineteenth century, the campaign against flesh-eating was tied to the temperance movement. By pairing his carnivorous "Greater Eater" (Edax) with his Drunkard (or "Great Drinker"), Lamb exults in a taste calculated to oppose both the "natural" dietetics of Romantic aesthetics and the moderation of the middle-class ideology of taste. His early confessional personae are often misread as caricatures of tasteless gluttons, but they come closer to the Romantic figure of the gourmand insofar as they are carefully executed figures who consciously position themselves against the Romantic ideology of "natural diet."[22] According to Shelley, flesh-eating and drinking anything but distilled water were a violation of the "natural" diet of humans (*SP* 90); Benjamin Haydon, meeting him for the first time at a dinner party hosted by Leigh Hunt, records his surprise at "what a hectic, spare, weakly yet intellectual-looking creature it was, carving a bit of brocoli [*sic*] or cabbage on his plate, as if it had been the substantial wing of a chicken."[23] The myths that grew out of Shelley's food practices may have contributed to the idea of the poet as a thin, consumptive being, imaginatively assimilating the world through the mind but unable to digest reality. Lamb, by contrast, ultimately identifies with Elia as an urban gourmand, or "judicious epicure," based on these earlier, overeager consumers.

While Coleridge would have Lamb "hung'ring after Nature," Lamb's "Great Eater" boasts an anatomy designed to digest enormous quantities of flesh. Against the view supported by early nineteenth-century physiologists and comparative anatomists alike that the human body was naturally frugivorous (fruit eating), Edax insists that he is *naturally* driven to eat meat: "What work will they make with their acids and alkalines, their serums and coagulums," he wonders, to identify the "original peculiarity of constitution" that makes him crave flesh (*WCL* 1:124). His peculiar constitution contradicts the vegetarian view, extending back to Plutarch's essays against flesh-eating, that "man's frame is in no way similar to those creatures who were made for flesh-eating: he has no hooked beak or sharp nails or jagged teeth, no strong stomach or warmth of vital fluids able to digest and assimilate a heavy diet of flesh."[24] Shelley, like other Romantic-era vegetarians, relies upon Plutarch as an authority for his claim that "man resembles frugivorous animals in everything, and carnivorous in nothing; he has neither claws wherewith to seize his prey, nor distinct and pointed teeth to tear the living fibre. A Mandarin of the first class, with nails two inches long, would probably find them alone inefficient to hold even a hare" (*SP* 83).[25] By contrast, Lamb's Chinese carnivores in "A Dissertation Upon Roast Pig" "for the first seventy thousand ages ate their meat raw, clawing or biting it from the living animal" (*WCL* 2:120). Their constitution posed no challenge to a flesh diet, which, in Lamb's fictional prehistory, was entirely natural.

Unable to deny the "frugivorous" nature of the human constitution or to offer authoritative evidence of his own carnivorous one, Edax appeals to the sympathy of his reader by identifying with Mandeville's lion from Remark P of *The Fable of the Bees*. This is the same text that converted the antiquarian and vegetarian Joseph Ritson, whose *Essay on the Abstinence from Animal Flesh* (1802) was a source for both Shelley and Lamb, to a vegetable diet. Edax, however, reappropriates it in defense of flesh-eating: "The Lion has a ferment within him, that consumes the toughest Skin and hardest Bones, as well as the Flesh of all Animals without exception. . . . Oft have I tried with Roots and Herbs to allay the violence of [this appetite], but in vain; nothing but large quantities of Flesh can any ways appease it" (*WCL* 1:121–22).[26] Mandeville's lion speaks these words to a European merchant, or commercial imperialist much like the traders from the British East India Company who "rifle" the world (Shelley's word) for consumables. Starting in 1800, the London offices of the East India Company in fact featured a mechanical tiger eating an English merchant complete with the roars of the tiger and the cries of the man, presumably gaining the sympathy of crowds for the merchant.[27] Recognizing the moral savagery associated with his carnivorous diet, Edax exclaims, "Miserable man! *I am that Lion.* 'Oft have I tried with roots and herbs to allay that violence, but in vain; nothing but—'" (*WCL* 1:122). The italics stress the similarity of his physiology with that of the brute, but his emotions seem all-too-human and his sentence breaks off before he can give voice to the violence of his appetite. Deflecting his brute impulses onto the brute is a shrewd technique to gain the sympathy of an audience predisposed to sympathizing not with the carnivore but with the mangled victim of his carnivorous appetite.

Vegetarian writers regularly called on remote examples of comparative anatomy to argue against flesh-eating, and Edax follows this tradition in aligning himself next with a snake, or "reptile in Africa, whose venom is of that hot, destructive quality, that wheresoever it fastens its tooth, the whole substance of the animal that has been bitten in a few seconds is reduced to dust, crumbles away, and absolutely disappears: it is called from this quality, the Annihilator" (*WCL* 1:123). Given the confessional style of the essay, the flesh-eating snake, drawn from the phantasmatic bowels of Africa, also suggests an ongoing identification with the low-urban, unparadisiacal creature "long in populous city pent." Lamb was highly sensitive to the power of names, as his frequent punning on his own name attests, and traditionally the lion "slays the lamb that looks him in the face, / And horribly devours his mangled flesh" (in Shelley's words), while the lamb "crops the flow'ry food, / And licks the hand just rais'd to shed his blood" (as in Pope's *Essay on Man*).[28] Blake, who contrasts the "Tyger" and the "Lamb" in his *Songs of Innocence and Experience*, similarly remarks: "The Lamb misusd breeds Public strife / And yet forgives the Butchers Knife."[29] Lamb's identification, through Edax, with the flesh-eating lion nominally distances him further from the "gentle-hearted" lamb depicted by Coleridge.

Edax's schoolfellows also lampoon (or "Lamb-pun," to borrow Lamb's pun) the vegetarian reliance on comparative anatomy and its desire to taxonomize all life by inventing their own names for Edax: *Ventri natus* (stomach born); *Ventri deditus* (addicted to the stomach); *Vesana gula* (greedy gullet); *Escarum gurges* (sink of eatables); *Dapibus indulgens* (feast lover); *Non dans froena gulae* (not curbing the gullet); *Sectans lautae fercula mensae* (dainty hunting) (*LM* 3:325; *WCL* 1:120; Lucas's translations). The first couple of these Latin binomials resemble *frugi deditus,* a phrase that the vegetarian physician John Frank Newton (Shelley's mentor) defined as "inclined to subsist on the fruits of the earth," consequently in "the possession of almost every good quality which could grace our nature."[30] Lamb's mock-confessional identity as *Ventri deditus* (rather than *frugi deditus*) again indicates a taste more in line with the ham and beef shop of St. Martin's Lane than the paradisiacal, lime-tree bower.

Whereas advocates against consumer culture argued that society's many distempers were a result of luxury and overindulgence, especially in the wrong kinds of consumables made available through commercial imperialism, Edax insists that *his* food can never be "superfluous" (*WCL* 1:120). He is physically opposed to the "natural taste" of those who feed upon air, words, nature, and other emblems of divine infinitude. While Mandeville proposed "physick" for the intemperate consumer in his *Treatise on the Hypochondriack and Hysterick Diseases*, others, such as the physician George Cheyne, maintained that the best remedy for the civilized stomach was "a *total Abstinence* from Animal Foods of all Kinds, and all Sorts of strong and fermented Liquors, keeping only to Milk, with seeds or Grains, and the different Kinds of Vegetable food, according to the Nature of the Distemper."[31] When Edax quotes Mandeville in support of his carnivorous diet, he knowingly invokes a paradigm of selfhood anchored in the craving stomach of the British consumer.

Hospita does not name Edax directly in "Hospita, on the Immoderate Indulgence of the Pleasures of the Palate," but she protests the tasteless behavior of an "obnoxious visitor," whom Mr. Reflector (a.k.a. Lamb) notes "can be no other than my inordinate friend EDAX, whose misfortunes are detailed, ore rotondo, in the preceding article" (*WCL* 1:422n.). This essay followed "Edax on Appetite" in *The Reflector,* satirizing Edax's misguided attempt to enter a world in which the tasteful attitude is the disinterested attitude that he admittedly lacks. The typical conduct book instructed that "The Man of Manners picks not the best, but rather takes the worst out of the Dish, and gets of every thing, unless it be forced upon him, always the most indifferent Share."[32] Yet Edax displays an "Immoderate Indulgence" that is, even from a gastronomical perspective, distasteful. Unlike Elia, who calls himself a "judicious epicure" and enjoys his own ability to descant philosophically on his culinary preferences, Edax flouts the cultural politics of food *and* the code of manners surrounding it.

When Hospita protests the inordinate and conspicuous appetite of Edax, she complains that her guest "makes no scruple of keeping a joint of meat on the table, after the cheese and fruit are brought in, till he has what he calls *done with it*" (*WCL* 1:125), associating him with a meat item that had been effaced from the tasteful sphere of public dining. Norbert Elias has shown how people in the course of the "civilizing process" sought to suppress all characteristics considered "animal" in themselves, and accordingly all such qualities in their food.[33] Animality was gradually removed from the animal by carving and preparing it before it arrived at table, consigning culinary activities, such as cooking, roasting, boiling, and dressing animal flesh, to behind closed doors of the kitchen. The *Habits of Good Society* (1859) therefore recommended "ostracising that unwieldy barbarism—the joint . . . a huge joint especially is calculated to disgust the epicure. If joints are eaten at all, they should be placed on the sidetable, where they will be out of sight."[34] George Colman (Mr. Town) observed already in 1755 that large pieces of flesh have been "utterly banished from our tables," implying similarly to Lamb that such civilizing taboos had had their costs: "May we not live to see a leg of pork detested as carrion? and a shoulder of mutton avoided as if it were horse-flesh?"[35] In circles cultivating an ideal of "pure diet" as well as in tasteful gastronomical circles, Edax's treasured joint of meat had become a cultural code for barbarity.

In Romantic dietary discourse that evolved out of an era of sensibility, moreover, children were thought to be more "natural" than adults and to find flesh eating naturally repugnant. Following Rousseau, Newton writes, "Of all the children whom I have known or heard of, none has disliked fruit, but several have refused to eat meat."[36] Hospita's children ("perfect little Pythagoreans") also cannot comprehend the logic of flesh eating (*WCL* 1:125). They find Edax's appetite for flesh particularly offensive and are unable to conceive "how the substance of a creature that ever had life can become food for another creature. A beef-steak is an absurdity to them; a mutton-chop, a solecism in terms; a cutlet, a word absolutely without any meaning; a butcher is nonsense, except so far as it is taken for a man who delights in blood, or a hero" (*WCL* 1:126). Far from being thought of as heroes, butchers were traditionally held to be morally corrupt; rumor had it that their daily immersion in blood and guts hardened their natures.[37] While Lamb may be thinking metaphorically here (war heroes have always been called butchers by their enemies and heroes at home), he may also be thinking literally from Edax's point of view: the butcher is the hero of the ham and beef shop that maintains the Man of Low-Urban Taste. As always, Lamb's irony is complex, and if Hospita finds Edax's behavior unnatural, there is another distinct possibility at work, namely, that she and her family have cultivated a taste that seems highly unnatural to the author.

To be a carnivore in Romantic-era vegetarian discourse was merely one step away from being a cannibal. Reviewing Ritson's *Essay on the Abstinence of Animal Flesh* for the *Edinburgh Review* in 1803 (the same issue that reviewed Lamb's tragedy *John Woodvil*), Henry Brougham objected that " 'Eater of beef and mutton,' is here used as synonymous with cannibal."[38] When Edax eats the socially distasteful joint, his behavior veers from flesh-eating toward the even more savage realm of man eating. Vegetarians argued that in order to guard against cannibalism, society must make any kind of flesh-eating unthinkable, since the natural telos of flesh-eating is cannibalism. Ritson wrote that "those accustom'd to eat the brute, should not long abstain from the man: more especially as, when toasted or broil'd on the altar, the appearance, favour, and taste of both would be nearly, if not entirely, the same."[39] The oldest taboo is cannibalism, and the most taboo subject in the discourse of cannibalism is exactly what human flesh tastes like.[40] The fear is the very possibility voiced by Ritson that when roasted, broiled, or otherwise transformed by fire, human flesh is indistinguishable from the taste of other animals.

To Hospita's family, Edax is a "Tartar" unable to distinguish human joints from animal. At least since Gibbon, the term *Tartar* had stood for a savage creature of uncivilizable, uncoded appetite.[41] (Our haute-cuisine designation "steak tartare" is a relic of this tradition.) When Manning left for China on business for the East India Company, Lamb wrote to his friend to beware of the "nasty, unconversable, horse-belching, Tartar people! Some say, they are Cannibals; and then conceive a Tartar-fellow *eating* my friend, and adding the *cool malignity* of mustard and vinegar!"[42] Lamb is joking, but Hospita's daughter cannot conceptualize flesh-eating apart from cannibalism: "The first hint I gave her upon the subject, I could see her recoil from it with the same horror with which we listen to a tale of Anthropophagism" (*WCL* 1:126). This daughter does not speak for herself, however, and the possibility remains that it is the politically correct mother, rather than her "natural" daughter, who confounds flesh-eating with cannibalism.

According to vegetarians, human anatomy was not designed to process animal flesh, and those who violated a morally "pure diet" turned instinctively to alcohol to help them through the horrors of digestion (*SP* 89). William Lambe, the physician who put Keats on a vegetable diet, claimed that the consumption of "fermented liquors is, in some measure, a necessary concomitant and appendage to the use of animal food."[43] Lamb considered his "Great Drinker" a counterpart to his "Great Eater," and from the perspective of the radical dietary discourse against which he was writing, flesh-eating and the use of fermented liquors were twin corruptions of the same evil root.[44] Shelley spoke of the "narcotic effects of ordinary diet," and the physician Lambe found that fermented liquors operate upon "the brain in a manner analogous to animal food."[45] Alcohol was considered an alternate form of flesh, and Thomas Trotter tells us in *An Essay, Medical, Philosophical, and Chemical, on Drunkenness* (1804) that Erasmus Darwin "made amends for the want of vinous stimulus, by consuming large quantities of animal food."[46] Shelley makes this connection between flesh eating and the use of intoxicating liquors explicit in his *Vindication of Natural Diet*: "Animal flesh in its effects on the human stomach is analogous to a dram. It is similar in the kind though differing in the degree of operation" (*SP* 89). Having had their sensibilities dulled by excessive consumption, Lamb's Drunkard and his companion Edax both require enormous amounts of alcohol and flesh, respectively.[47] It is no surprise, perhaps, that Romantic gastronomers would downplay the use of fermented liquor, for physical sensibility is crucial to the delicacy of gustatory taste. Edax and the Drunkard both forfeit their capacity for the disinterested attitude necessary for aesthetic judgment.

In theory, Shelley wished to avoid any activity based on unthinking instinct, and he concludes his vegetarian manifesto with the twin prescriptions NEVER TAKE ANY SUBSTANCE INTO THE STOMACH THAT ONCE HAD LIFE and DRINK NO LIQUID BUT WATER RESTORED TO ITS ORIGINAL PURITY BY DISTILLATION (*SP* 90). Proponents of "natural diet" like Shelley believed that most of the diseases (moral as well as physical) that plagued society would disappear if humans would eat only uncooked fruits and vegetables. Such a diet would obviate the need for drink of any sort, vegetarians believed, for given contemporary conditions in London, even the supposedly pure drink of water had its defects.[48] Lamb's Drunkard is not merely driven to drink; he requires large quantities of the forbidden liquor. "In my dreams I can sometimes fancy thy cool refreshment purling over my burning tongue," he says. "But my waking stomach rejects it" (*WCL* 1:137). Just as Edax declines "to sup upon what may emphatically be called *nothing*" (light collations or delicacies), the Drunkard's "waking stomach" rejects the morally superior "pure element." Complementary men of low-urban taste, both flout the dietary principles of transcendental aesthetics.

The tidal wave of gastronomical intake defining the Great Eater and his spirituous twin leaves little room for refinement, but Elia is a self-proclaimed "judicious epicure" who steps out of the reactive *Reflector* mode and into a more sophisticated assertion of low-urban taste. For Elia, pig "is no less provocative of the appetite, than he is satisfactory to the criticalness of the censorious palate" (*WCL* 2:124). Roast pig satisfies both his private palate and the social performance of his taste, while more transcendent food, such as pineapple (a colonial version of the paradisiacal fruit), leaves him unsatisfied. "Pine-apple is great," Elia claims, but "She is indeed almost too transcendent . . . she stoppeth at the palate—she meddleth not with the appetite—and the coarsest hunger might barter her consistently for a mutton chop" (*WCL* 2:124). Unlike flesh, the pineapple has "Celestial energy," and like the lakes and mountains of Cumberland, it is "too ravishing for mortal taste" (*WCL* 2:124).[49] Elia may disavow "pure diet," but he has the mental volition necessary for tasteful discernment, and as a social being with a palate he knows his appetites to be subservient to his taste. The masochistic pleasure he receives from culinary methods used to culture—or torture—animal flesh into ever finer degrees of refinement is therefore all the more effective for Lamb's fictional critique of taste.

The Delicacy of Pig

Elia's language is saturated with references to gustatory taste.[50] But of all the "delicacies in the whole *mundus edibilis*," roast pig is by far "the most delicate—*princeps obsoniorum*" (*WCL* 2:123). Elia knows that his favorite delicacy is produced through culinary methods that many would find distasteful. Ritson, for instance, describes in graphic detail the kind of torments traditionally responsible for producing the delicate taste of pig: "some run red hot spits through the bodys of swine, that by the tincture of the quench'd iron the blood may be to that degree mortify'd, that it may sweeten and soften the flesh in its circulation: and others jump and stamp upon the udders of sows that are ready to pig, . . . and so eat the most inflame'd and disease'd part of the animal."[51] Elia's "delicate" taste involves the inteneration and acculturation of flesh, which is rendered so painfully when rendered material. Anthropological categories, such as the natural and the cultural, the raw and the cooked, may be highly fraught fields in their own right (rather than universal cultural givens), but they are the very binaries upon which Lamb's critique of taste in "Roast Pig" depends.[52]

At the outset of the essay, we are told that humans "for the first seventy thousand ages ate their meat raw, clawing or biting it from the living animal, just as they do in Abyssinia to this day" (2:120). Elia's statement openly contradicts the vegetarian belief that human beings, as opposed to other carnivores, require their flesh to be burnt or otherwise disfigured in order to be consumed. According to Shelley, the fact "that man cannot swallow a piece of raw flesh would be sufficient to prove that the natural diet of the human species did not consist in the carcasses of butchered animals."[53] Cookbooks of the eighteenth century acknowledged a need for cooks to be "knowledgeable about meat and how to disguise it in various ways."[54] And William Kitchiner, author of the best-selling *Apicius Redivivus; or, the Cook's Oracle* (1817) that Lamb knew well, assures us in an essay on health that "Our Food must be done — either *by our Cook,* — or by *our Stomachs* — before Digestion can take place . . . surely no man in his senses, would willingly be so wanting in consideration of the comfort, &c. of his Stomach, as to give it the needless trouble of Cooking and Digesting also — and waste its valuable energies in work which a Spirit or Stewpan can do better."[55] Elia admits that humans in a state of nature may have eaten their food raw, but for him it was not fruit and other vegetable foods that were eaten raw but flesh.

The narrative itself is extremely bizarre, and no allegory holds fast. Most readers, however, will find in it some version of a fall, broadly defined from "nature" into "culture." The story begins in a small Chinese village, where a young boy named "Bo-bo" (perhaps a linguistic stutter towards barbarian) sets fire to his father's hut, making the accidental "discovery, that the flesh of swine, or indeed of any other animal, might be cooked (*burnt,* as they called it)" (WCL 2:123). Having destroyed the hut and the nine pigs in it, he stoops down to feel for signs of life in a charred pig carcass and the following discovery takes place: "He burnt his fingers, and to cool them he applied them in his Booby fashion to his mouth. Some of the crumbs of the scorched skin had come away with his fingers, and for the first time in his life (in the world's life indeed, for before him no man had known it) he tasted — *crackling!*" (WCL

2:121). Surrendering himself to the pleasure, he begins to tear up handfuls of the scorched flesh, stuffing it down his mouth until his father, who had gone to collect mast for the hogs, appears "armed with retributory cudgel" (*WCL* 2:121). Far from diverting his son from the pig, the father's blows provoke the inarticulate plea, " 'Eat, eat, eat the burnt pig, father, only taste — O Lord,' with such-like barbarous ejaculations, cramming all the while as if he would choke" (*WCL* 2:122). The father curses his son, then curses himself for begetting such a son, grasps the abominable food, and stands debating what to do until he too burns his fingers. Bringing them to his mouth for relief, he tastes the tabooed flesh. Father and son thereby reconciled sit down to a banquet of pig, a meal repeated secretly at frequent intervals until their neighbors discover their practice and bring them to trial in Peking. At court, "the obnoxious food itself produced . . . the foreman of the jury begged that some of the burnt pig, of which the culprits stood accused, might be handed into the box" (*WCL* 2:122). Burning their own fingers on the pig, the jury pronounces a verdict of "not guilty," and from that time forth, we are told, the practice of roasting pigs caught fire (as it were) and spread throughout the civilized world.

A number of sources have been proposed for this strange story, though its most obvious antecedent, Porphyry's *Essay on the Abstinence of Animal Food,* has not been discussed, presumably because it was not translated into English until the year after Lamb's essay appeared. Yet the anecdote from Porphyry was available to Lamb through Ritson's *Essay on the Abstinence from Animal Flesh,* which excerpts a section of it in a chapter entitled "Animal Food the Cause of Human Sacrifices." Here is Porphyry's story, by way of Ritson, on the origin of flesh-eating:

> At first indeed no animal was sacrifice'd to the gods, neither was there any law upon this subject, because it was prohibited by the law of nature. But a certain occasion requiring life for life, the first sacrifice was made of animateëd beings, and thence, they say, a whole victim was consumed by fire. But, afterward, as the sacrifice was burning a small part of the flesh fel upon the ground, which the priest took up, and being burn'd in touching it, he unadvise'dly put his fingers to his mouth, in order to mitigate the pain proceeding from the burn. But when he had tasteëd the fat, he was enflame'd with the desire thereof, nor could he abstain, but allso gave part of it to his wife. . . . The thing, however, proceeding further, and men using the same sacrifice, and not abstaining through gluttony from tasteing flesh, the punishment has cease'd.[56]

The idea is that animal flesh intoxicates and inflames the passions of the eater, who loses control over his or her actions, devolving from polite into instinctual behavior. Unlike Porphyry, however, Lamb represents flesh-eating as an advance in civilization rather than a fall. Porphyry's priest becomes

Lamb's swineherd, who challenges the meaning of the natural by way of the raw.

Elia, like the Chinese pig-eaters in his culinary creation myth, displays no sympathetic disgust, only mouth-watering desire for the young pig while it is roasting. "Behold him, while he is doing," rhapsodizes Elia in the manner of the gastronomical connoisseur, "it seemeth rather a refreshing warmth, than a scorching heat, that he is so passive to. How equably he twirleth round the string! — Now he is just done. To see the extreme sensibility of that tender age, he hath wept out his pretty eyes — radiant jellies — shooting stars" (*WCL* 2:124). To him, the jellies pouring from the young pig's eyes are aesthetically "radiant" as opposed to vile. Normally, such tears of sensibility would provoke sympathetic tears in the viewer, as in so much poetry of sensibility (for example, Wordsworth's 1787 sonnet "On Seeing Miss Helen Maria Williams Weep at a Tale of Distress"). By nature, the sympathetic Man of Feeling would find the sight of a pig weeping from pain as he is roasted alive on the spit distasteful. But Elia savors the process of fleshly disfiguration as an appetizing event. "To gain the praise of Epicurean Pig-Eaters," Kitchiner instructs cooks sounding much like Elia, "the CRACKLING must be *nicely crisped* and delicately *lightly browned,* without being either blistered or burnt."[57] In his letters Lamb boasts of his ability "Doctor Kitchiner-like to examine the good things at table" (*LL* 3:97), and his fictional gourmand also applies the aesthetic discourse of delicacy to food as a matter of philosophical consequence. His low-urban relish for the fleshly mutilations underwriting his taste for roast pig testifies to his fine delicacy of discernment.

In a letter to Coleridge of March 9, 1822, another acknowledged source for "Roast Pig," the "gentle-hearted" writer describes with gusto the carnal realities of roasting: "You all had some of the crackling — and brain sauce," he asks, "did you remember to rub it with butter, and gently dredge it a little, just before the crisis? Did the eyes come away kindly with no Oedipean avulsion? Was the crackling the colour of the ripe pomegranate?" (*LL* 2:317). The pleasure with which he transforms pomegranate (an Edenic fruit in Renaissance iconography) into the purplish hue of the roast pig's flesh is tangible. Hallucinatory images like these — melting eyes, crackling skin, scrambled "brain sauce" — can rival any opium-induced visions on the part of the poet in "Kubla Khan" (1816). But whereas the transcendental food of "honey-dew" and "milk of Paradise" inspires the "Abyssinian maid" in Coleridge's poem, Elia imagines a savage world in which human beings ate their flesh raw "just as they do in Abyssinia to this day." His fictional Abyssinia, I am trying to suggest, critiques Romantic transcendental aesthetics from the colonialist perspective of "Charles Lamb, of the India House, London."

Lamb's friend Manning wrote to him from China in May 1819 as he was composing "Roast Pig," using rhetoric similar to Elia's to dwell with pleasure upon what otherwise ought to incite disgust: "Take my word for it, to those that know how many yards of Chitterling go to a Dozen Sausages . . . no music like the cry of a killing pig. What does your Brother John say to it? He's a man of taste, he loves sausages? For my part I know no better eating, except it be eel-pye."[58] Manning's equation of the "man of taste" with the man who "loves sausages" suits Elia, who relishes his memory of the annual sausage banquet hosted for the local chimney sweepers at Bartholomew Fair by his friend Jem White, who "would fit the tit bits to the puny mouths, reserving the lengthier links for the seniors . . . he would intercept a morsel even in the jaws of some young desperado, declaring it 'must to the pan again to be browned, for it was not fit for a gentleman's eating'" (WCL 2:113).[59] Lamb collaborated with White on the parodic *Falstaff's Letters* (1796) whose preface relates how one "Mistress Quickly" of the Boar Tavern found Falstaff's unpublished letters in a drawer of his desk and bequeathed them to her illiterate maiden sister, who used them in the preparation of pig. "A curse on her Epicurean guts, that could not be contented with plain mutton, like the rest of her ancestors!" exclaims the outraged "editor"; she "absolutely made use of several, no doubt invaluable letters to shade the jutting protuberances of that animal from disproportionate excoriation in its circuitous approaches to the fire."[60] Unlike the plain mutton chop, roast pig is calculated to appeal to the epicurean "man of taste" distin-guished by a taste not for poetry but for sausages, and from his gastronomical perspective, the maiden aunt made excellent use of Falstaff's letters.

Lamb was aware that Elia's taste for pig was implicated in a matrix of cruelties extending past the roasting of pigs live on the spit, to the boiling of lobsters and other shellfish to death by slow degrees, and as Shelley put it, "a certain horrible process of torture [that] furnishes brawn for the gluttonous repasts with which Christians celebrate the anniversary of their Savior's birth" (SP 94). One sympathetic writer in 1819 explained this "horrible process" as "Keeping a poor animal upright for many weeks, to communicate a peculiar hardness to his flesh."[61] Whereas Shelley lamented the "process of torture" that produces brawn (pickled boar) "for the gluttonous repasts" of Christians, Lamb preferred its hidden "gusto" to "the eyes of martyr'd Pigs," the "tender ef-fusions of laxative woodcocks," and "the red spawn of lobsters" (LM 2: 155).[62] Writing in a mischievous mood to Southey on March 20, 1799, he proposed a sequence of poems on the various abuses to which animals are subjected for the sake of human pleasure: "A series of such poems, suppose them accompanied with plates descriptive of animal torments, cooks roasting lobsters, fishmongers crimping skates, &c., &c., would take excessively" (LM 1:165).

Such urbane satire was directed against a culture of sensibility that articulated itself against urban commercial rapaciousness. As in the case of human rights, the so-called "rights of brutes" were promoted through such pamphlets and print publications as John Oswald's *Cry of Nature; or, An Appeal to Mercy and to Justice on Behalf of the Persecuted Animals* (1791). Shelley's friend Taylor, who translated Porphyry's vegetarian essays in 1823, published a parodic *Vindication of the Rights of Brutes* (1792), suggesting that when taken to its logical extreme the rhetoric of human rights must extend to animals, and even minerals: "whatever is here asserted of brutes, is no less applicable to vegetables, and even minerals themselves; for it is an ancient opinion, that all things are endued with sense."[63] Romantic ideals of "natural diet," promulgated through such works to which Taylor refers, protested the abuse and destruction of animals for the sake of the more "civilized" pleasures of the palate.

Lamb's own brother John had penned "A Letter to William Windham, on his opposition to Lord Erskine's Bill for the Prevention of Cruelty to Animals" (1810), adopting a tone of moral outrage to object (from the animal's point of view) to unnecessary culinary cruelties:

> If an eel had the wisdom of Solomon, he could not help himself in the ill-usage that befalls him; but if he had, and were told, that it was necessary for our subsistence that he should be eaten, that he must be skinned first, and then broiled; if ignorant of man's usual practice, he would conclude that the cook would so far use her reason as to cut off his head first, which is not fit for food, as then he might be skinned and broiled without harm; for however the other parts of his body might be convulsed during the culinary operations, there could be no feeling of consciousness therein, the communication with the brain being cut off; but if the woman were immediately to stick a fork into his eye, skin him alive, coil him up in a skewer, head and all, so that in the extremest agony he could not move, and forthwith broil him to death: then were the same Almighty Power that formed man from the dust, and breathed into his nostrils the breath of life, to call the eel into a new existence, with a knowledge of the treatment he had undergone, and he found that the instinctive disposition which man has in common with other carnivorous animals, which inclines him to cruelty, was not the sole cause of his torments; but that men did not attend to consider whether the sufferings of such insignificant creatures could be lessened: that eels were not the only sufferers; that lobsters and other shell fish were put into cold water and boiled to death by slow degrees in many parts of the sea coast; that these, and many other such wanton atrocities, were the consequence of carelessness occasioned by the pride of mankind despising their low estate, and of the general opinion that there is no punishable sin in the ill-treatment of animals designed for our use ... (*LM* 3:41)[64]

Whereas Elia relishes such carnal mutilations as "radiant jellies" melting out of roasting pigs' eyes, the indignant speaker of John Lamb's pamphlet makes it morally impossible not to take the side of the suffering animal. The magnificent sentence exerpted only partly (!) above sweeps the reader's sympathies clearly into the field of the tragic, Gloucester-like eel, blinded in an act of needless human cruelty. It situates itself within a tradition of vegetarian discourse dating back to Plutarch. "You call serpents and panthers and lions savage," he too complained in the voice of the animal, "but you yourselves, by your own foul slaughters, leave them no room to outdo you in cruelty; for their slaughter is their living, yours is a mere appetizer . . . 'Kill me to eat, but not to please your palate!' "[65] Lamb was conscious that Elia's connoisseurship of pig involves the kind of culinary "atrocities" described by his brother, which were intended to make food more tasty. When he wrote to Henry Crabb Robinson for help in getting the pamphlet reviewed, he joked: "dont shew it Mrs. Collier, for I remember she makes excellent Eel soup, and the leading points of the Book are directed against that very process" (*LM* 3:41). Mrs. Collier was Crabb Robinson's landlady and a leading supplier of pig to the Lamb household following the publication of "Roast Pig." His facetious desire to protect her from the harsh depiction of her culinary practice suggests the irony with which he must treat any cause so opposed to his rhetorical pose as low-urban gastronome, or Man of Taste who "loves sausages."

Within "Roast Pig," Elia celebrates the gustatory joys of acculturated flesh produced through culinary animal tortures, such as those described by John Lamb. At one point, he considers the abusive practice of whipping pigs to death in order to tenderize their flesh:

> The age of discipline is gone by, or it would be curious to inquire (in a philosophical light merely) what effect this process might have toward intenerating and dulcifying a substance, naturally so mild and dulcet as the flesh of young pigs . . . we should be cautious, while we condemn the inhumanity, how we censure the wisdom of the practice. It might impart a gusto —
>
> I remember an hypothesis, argued upon by the young students, when I was at St. Omer's, and maintained with much learning and pleasantry on both sides, "Whether, supposing that the flavour of a pig who obtained his death by whipping (*per flagellationem extremam*) superadded a pleasure upon the palate of a man more intense than any possible suffering we can conceive in the animal, is man justified in using that method of putting the animal to death?" I forget the decision. (*WCL* 2:125–26)

Just as "dulcifying" can mean both sweetening and making proper, "intenerating" can mean both softening and making polite, as in "refined and intenerated society" (1822; *OED*). As an extension of the broader cultural project of civilizing flesh, intenerating animals for finer delectation through such methods as bull baiting, electrification, and whipping pigs to death was not antithetical to taste so much as *distastefully tasteful*. A better phrase perhaps might be "sickly delicacy," which Mary Wollstonecraft associated with the false refinement of Burke, one that "turns away from simple unadorned truth" in favor of rhetorical ornamentation.[66] From Elia's sense that the "age of discipline" has gone by, to his spirit of inquiry "in a philosophical light merely," to his quest for "superadded . . . pleasure upon the palate," his rhetoric reflects the "sickly delicacy" of Burkean aesthetics. Flagellation was part of the visual iconography of abolitionist literature in which the contested issue of human rights was fought and which bled also into the "rights of brutes."[67] In considering these rights, Elia slips into a calculating, Benthamite morality of the greatest good for the greatest number, aesthetically revised as the greatest *pleasure* for the greatest number. In coyly forgetting the decision of his classmates, who debated the issue with "pleasantry," as he says, he lets the emphasis fall on the noncommittal hint, "It might impart a gusto —." Followed by Lamb's typical dash to avoid painful expression, this "gusto" is a floating signifier for a kind of cruel, yet tasteful desire.

Elia is no Edax, but he is no John Bull either, consuming large portions of beef and arrack punch in unthinking conformity to a British ideal of civic masculinity. His final words in "Roast Pig" are devoted to the philosophical principles of sauce: "Decidedly, a few bread crums [sic], done up with his liver and brains, and a dash of mild sage," instructs Elia: "But, banish, dear Mrs. Cook, I beseech you, the whole onion tribe" (*WCL* 2:126). From the seventeenth century, when the courtly meal was going out of style, the British had prided themselves as a symbolic nation of beefeaters on their indifference to culinary ornamentation, such as sauces.[68] Like British food in general, British recipes for sauce were plain in relation to more extravagant French recipes addressed to aristocratic male chefs. French sauces were the signature feature of a cuisine identified with courtly extravagance, and one nineteenth-century British cookbook accused the French of refining even plain onion sauce "until its fine gusto is lost in a weak civilisation."[69] But the relative simplicity of Elia's recipe does not conceal his ongoing concern with sauce, nor compromise his stance as "judicious epicure." In the last paragraph of his last publication "Table Talk by the Late Elia" (1834), he seeks a "rationale of sauces, or theory of mixed flavours," in order to understand "why the French bean sympathizes with the flesh of deer" or why loin of pork "abhorreth" butter (*WCL* 1:349–50). His concern is comically "philosophical," concerned with "principles" and the "reason of the relish that is in us" (*WCL* 1:350). Applying rhetoric from the Enlightenment discourse of taste to the material preferences of the body, Lamb invokes (and helps to invent) the gastronomical mode of writing as a nineteenth-century literary genre treating food with philosophical consequence. His sophisticated deployment of low-urban taste, wavering between the savage excesses of Edax and the effete epicureanism of Elia, always just misses the ideological middle mark of the middle-class, British Man of Taste.

Elegiac Roasting

Ultimately, Elia's tragicomical play with the metaphor of taste turns back on him in a grand display of elegiac "roasting" — a term that in addition to cooking also meant, as it does today, to satirize or to ridicule. Lamb himself used the term in this sense in a letter to Thomas Hood, remarking that what "by our milder manners is merely ridiculed, on the ruder banks of the Ganges is literally *roasted*" (*LL* 3:184). His unique literary mode of satiric, gastronomical roasting exposes him as a version of his own suckling pig, a symbolically overdetermined figure who is so cruelly and beautifully "roasted" in the best-known of the *Elia* essays.[70] The final section of this chapter will examine how Lamb enacts a literary form of masochism that qualifies his low-urban aesthetic and sets him apart from other gastronomical writers as leaders of middle-class taste.

In the same letter to Coleridge that provides the working draft for "Roast Pig," Lamb admits: "pigs are pigs, and I myself therein am nearest to myself" (*LL* 2:317). Literally, if not metaphorically, pigs have extremely thin skin and must protect themselves from the sun by fashioning an extegument of mud.[71] Preferring human scraps to grass, pigs are threshold creatures, mixing animal and human, overlapping with and confusingly debasing human habitat and diet.[72] In this sense, they were an appropriate symbol for the "swinish multitude," kept alive in periodicals and pamphlets, such as *Hog's Wash; Mast and Acorns;* and Thomas Spence's *Pig's Meat, or Lessons for the Swinish Multitude* (1794–95). Radicals poured forth poems, such as Spence's "Edmund Burke's Address to the Swinish Multitude," in an effort to "promote among the Labouring Part of Mankind proper Ideas of their Situation, of their Importance, and of their Rights."[73] Eaton's *Politics for the People; or A Salmagundy for Swine* (1793–95) offered a salmagundy (all-meat banquet) to "the Labouring Part of Mankind" and opened its fifth issue with a "Remonstrance of the Swinish Multitude," complaining that "our swineherds do not permit us to enjoy the produce of our hard labour: when we have chafed our snouts to the bare stumps of bone, by turning up the earth to procure a few roots, they send their deputies to take a great part of it to feed themselves." When Lamb reappropriates the disenfranchised pig as an emblem for himself, he symbolically situates himself among the urban masses as a swinish laborer against high-Romantic ideals of taste.

Pigs were known as unclean beasts, and the title character of Lamb's farce "*Mr. H——*" (Hogsflesh) was a "*marked*" man like Lamb himself from his fatal "day of horrors."[74] In the play, Mr. H—— is ostracized from society because of his unsavory cognomen, and the plot can be reduced to a pun on this name. As Lamb recounts the story, Mr. H—— visits a fashionable resort and finds "all the Ladies dying for him—all bursting to know who he is" until "his true name comes out, *Hogsflesh,* [and] all the women shun him" (*LM* 2:246). Lamb prided himself as "a Chef d'oeuvre" on the manner in which this name was revealed, but when it *was* revealed during the play's single performance in December 1806, the audience hissed, and Lamb (a good sport) joined them (*LM* 2:247).[75] Although Lamb intended to have the play end happily with Hogsflesh changing his name to Bacon, unfortunately "no one in the audience who had stayed at Worthing, the new fashionable watering-place, can have been amused" since, as E. V. Lucas explains, "Hogsflesh was the name of one of the two inn-keepers there, the other being, by an odd chance, Bacon."[76] Whether or not he recognized its biographical significance, Lamb's identification with Hogsflesh is evident and commences early.

In a letter of January 6, 1823, to Mr. and Mrs. John Dyer Collier, thanking them for their gift of pig, Lamb makes the connection between himself and the hog explicit:

> How do you make your pigs so little?
> They are vastly engaging at the age:
>   I was so myself.
> Now I am a disagreeable old hog,
> A middle-aged gentleman-and-a-half. (*LL* 2:361)

Gerald Monsman proposes, rightly I believe, that Lamb is "hinting, since a hog is a gelded pig, at . . . his celibate, incomplete sexual identity."[77] Lamb's one marriage proposal failed in July 1819 because the actress, Fanny Kelly, would not take up residence in an atmosphere of mental instability with "an old bachelor and maid" (*LL* 2:256n.). Elia set the terms for this reception of Lamb in "Mackery End, in Hertfordshire," where he remarked: "We house together, old bachelor and maid, in a sort of double singleness" (*WCL* 2:75). As one writer summed up the Victorian view, Mary's "heart and her intellect have been through life the counterpart of his own. The two have lived as one, in double singleness together. She has been, indeed, the supplement and completion of his existence."[78] Elia's humor is underwritten by Lamb's infamous "day of horrors," which prompted him to take up permanent residence with his sister Mary. Like his reputation as "gentle-hearted," his life of "double singleness" castrated him symbolically. Freud associates castration with masochism, observing that in "masochistic phantasies a feeling of guilt comes to expression, it being assumed that the subject has committed some crime (the nature of which is left uncertain) which is to be expiated by his undergoing the pain and torture."[79] Given Lamb's identification with pig, the roasting that his *Elia* essays effect serves to expose the pathology of his low-urban taste.

Above all, Elia celebrates roasting in "Roast Pig" for its ability to make the pig's flesh yield up its crispy outer layer: "I am not ignorant that our ancestors ate [pigs] seethed, or boiled," he says, "but what a sacrifice of the exterior tegument!" (*WCL* 2:123). The most "delicate" part of the pig is its "crackling," a term emphasized twice in the essay—the only italics besides its Latinisms and Elia's insistence that pig *must be roasted* (*WCL* 2:123). "There is no flavour comparable," he contends, "to that of the crisp, tawny, well-watched, not over-roasted, *crackling,* as it is well called" (*WCL* 2:123). The poet John Kenyon, a friend of Wordsworth, Coleridge, Southey, and Lamb, once published some lines in honor of Elia, which he sent to Lamb along with a tributary pig: "Elia! Thro' irony of hearts the mender, / May this pig prove like thine own pathos—tender; . . . And quaintly cackle, like the crackling jest . . . dry without—rich inly—as thy wit" (*LL* 3:403n.). Kenyon's verse intuits the relation between "crackling" and "the crackling jest" of Elia in a fictional essay where the pig is both literally and figuratively roasted.

Recently, Seamus Perry has proposed that we "see the *Elia* essays as themselves written in a kind of equivocal mode: not the brilliantly familiar essay-style of Hazlitt, yet not the mind-baring mode of the personal lyric . . . for the poetic mode they invoke but decline in the courage of their whimsy is elegy."[80] If Lamb's satire works as a mode of elegy, such elegy is self-consciously satiric. Coleridge describes him "winning [his] way / With sad yet patient soul, through evil and pain / And strange calamity!" in "This Lime-tree Bower" (30–32); Leigh Hunt echoes these lines when he recalls in his autobiography that "Lamb had seen strange faces of calamity."[81] In a heartfelt letter to Sara Hutchinson of October 1815, after one of his sister's recurrent bouts of insanity, Lamb echoed them too: "My own calamities press about me & involve me in a thick integument not [to] be reached at by other folks misfortunes" (*LM* 3:203). Such calamity seems to recur with each return of Mary's illness, pressing about him as a "thick integument."

In "A Dissertation upon Roast Pig," however, this extegument lifts off the Elian pig in the delightful form of "crackling": "O call it not fat—but an indefinable sweetness growing up to it—the tender blossoming of fat—fat cropped in the bud—taken in the shoot—in the first innocence—the cream and quintessence of the child-pig's yet pure food— —the lean, no lean [*sic*], but a kind of animal manna—or, rather, fat and lean (if it must be so) so blended and running into each other, that both together make but one ambrosian result, or common substance" (*WCL* 2:123–24). Here the flesh of the young pig "taken in the shoot" becomes a type of vegetable flesh, "budding" and "blossoming" into a fine "exterior tegument" (a term that can refer to the outer layer of either a plant or an animal). Crackling is the "cream and quintessence" of his favorite food, the latter a technical term for the substance so essential to the edifice of French haute cuisine. (The gastronomer Brillat-Savarin tells of a French chef who boasted an ability to distill fifty hams to their "quintessence" in a "glass bottle no bigger than my thumb" [*PT* 54]). In Elia's version of "pure food," the paradoxical foodstuffs of vegetable-flesh and "animal manna" depend on a rather bloody reality: the tissues of the young pig's flesh melting into his fat, his bodily juices coursing through him as he suffers a culinary martyrdom.

Unlike mourning, melancholy is a pathological condition, according to Freud, one in which the process of psychically "devouring" the lost object turns back again on the subject. In psychoanalytic terms, the condition occurs when the object of desire has disappeared from consciousness. The melancholy subject responds to a loss, but it is not precisely clear what that loss is, for even if one knows the *who*, the *what* may still be unclear. The subject therefore attempts to disassociate itself from the object of loss by incorporating its own ego, and abusing it through the subconscious work of "disparaging it, denigrating it and even as it were killing it." While mourning constitutes a direct response to an external object of loss, in other words, melancholia involves a pathological conflict within the ego, one that substitutes for a psychic struggle with an external object an unconscious self-conflict, which Freud says "must act like a painful wound."[82] The masochistic obsession with the fleshly mutilations that enable Elia's low-urban taste is also an ongoing elegy for himself—and his own lost opportunities following the "day of horrors."

Elia intuits his role as elegist when he claims that the pig "hath a fair sepulchre in the grateful stomach of the judicious epicure—and for such a tomb might be content to die" (*WCL* 2:124). Originally, tomb or sepulcher meant "flesh-eater," a connotation that Pope evokes in *An Essay on Man* when he describes the human carnivore as "the butcher and the tomb" of the animals he consumes (3.163). Like the supposedly flesh-eating stones used for ancient Greek burial purposes, Plutarch's carnivore was "sarcophagus," derived from *sarko* (flesh) and *phagos* (eater). *Sarcophagus* (tomb) and *sarcophagous* (carnivorous) are phonetically equivalent in English, and a single letter of difference is all that stands between the man-eating stone (of Plutarch's tomb) and the human flesh-eater. Lamb's fictional carnivores are all in this respect living tombs, or sarcophagous memorials, to himself.

Long before Freud, Coleridge also recognized mourning as a form of oral desire. In his 1828 "Essay on the Passions," he traced this form of psychological craving directly to the stomach: "The Organ appropriate to or chief *residenz-stadt*, of Hunger I suppose to be the Stomach; but with regard to this and to the parts of the Body which are most obviously affected by Thirst, I must question. — Hunger is Fear, and ⟨as⟩ its principal Seat I have stated the hypogastric viscera. — Lastly, the analogous Passion is Grief; and its chief Organ like that of Hunger is the STOMACH — tho' whether in the same region exactly, I have yet to inquire. . . . The *wanting*, the *craving* of Grief . . . the characteristic wasting and marasmus of Grief — all these & there are many more, prove Grief to be a Hunger of the Soul" (CCW 11.2:1450–51). In Coleridge's anatomy of grief as a "Hunger of the Soul," the stomach is the chief organ of mourning and the alimentary system a materially realized site of psychic "*wanting*" and "*craving*." When applied to Lamb, this translates into an anatomy of melancholy, since (as his readers have always recognized), "A sort of melancholy was often the source of Mr. Lamb's humour," one that "used to throw out into still more delicate relief the subtleties of his wit and fancy, and which made his very jests 'scald like tears.' "[83] Elia's gastric juices produce acid tears and "delicate relief" for what Freud would call "the internal work which is consuming his ego."[84]

Despite Lamb's extensive identification with pig and Elia's belief that there is nothing in the whole *mundus edibilis* like the taste of roast pig, his final published essay, "Thoughts on Presents of Game, &c." (1833), renounces his signature taste for pig in favor of the hare, a creature medically and symbolically coded as melancholy. Myths about hares abounded, suggesting variously that this timid, panicky creature bound to leap or fly from the slightest fright changed its sex every year, that its male sex could also give birth, and that it was hermaphroditic. Given the sexual ambivalence of the hare (*Lepus europaeus*) as a creature metaphorically hard to pin down, it is appropriate that shortly after *The Last Essays of Elia* Lamb should publish "The Lepus Papers," dropping the signature "Elia" in favor of "Lepus."

This late pseudonym plays on the Latin *lepores*, which can mean either the plural of *lepus* (hares) with a short *o*, or "delicate" with a long. "The ancients must have loved hares," Elia observes, "Else why adopt the word *lepores* (obviously from *lepus*) but for some subtle analogy between the delicate flavour of the latter, and the finer relishes of wit in what we most poorly translate *pleasantries*" (WCL 1:343). Despite the mad-hatter jest of the hare and its sexually mad behavior, the hare was primarily a symbol of melancholy. Robert Burton (a favorite author of Lamb's) described hare as "a black meat, melancholy, and hard of digestion."[85] Animals were thought to pass on their dominant humors to the person who ate them. The hare, whose flesh was therefore categorized as cold and dry, was a source of the melancholy humor.[86] Humans were also thought to imbibe the characteristics of the animal they ate, and hares were thought to be "very sad and melancholy, supposing to hear the noise of dogs where there are none such stirring, then . . . fearing and trembling as if they were fallen mad."[87] Although Lamb returns to the pseudonym Elia in "Thoughts on Presents of Game," his late preoccupation with the figure of the hare continues: "The fine madnesses of the poet are the very decoction of his diet," he writes. "Thence is he hare-brained. Harum-scarum is a libellous unfounded phrase of modern usage" (*WCL* 1:343). Lamb's essays are "harebrained" insofar as they are a melancholy, poetical madness, the dietary decoction of a low-urban poet in prose.

Lamb remembers a time "when Elia was not arrived at his taste, that he preferred to all luxuries a roasted Pig. But he disclaims all such green-sickness appetites in future" (*WCL* 1:343). His editor, E. V. Lucas, reads "Presents of Game" as a postscript to "Roast Pig," and notes that it has even been printed as "A Recantation." In place of the "grossness" of pig, Elia now chooses the light celerity of the hare: "how light of digestion we feel after a hare! How tender its processes after swallowing! What chyle it promotes! How etherial! as if its living celerity were a type of its nimble coursing through the animal juices" (*WCL* 1:344). Only from a symbolic point of view, however, could the hare be seen as "etherial." Hare's meat was typically gamy, dark and pungent in taste and smell, and eighteenth-century recipes usually recommended dousing it in wines, thick seasonings, and other strong marinades.[88] Over one year old, the hare was reputed to be so tough that not even the dogs who hunted it would find it light of digestion: "after a day's hunting of the hare the animal's flesh should not be given to the dogs because it is indigestible," claimed one Game Master. "They should have only the tongue and the kidneys and some of the blood soaked in bread."[89] Given its gaminess, the hare was valued principally as a creature to be hunted — hounded, tortured, persecuted. For Lamb it had symbolic value.

In the decades following Lamb's death in 1834, *The Essays of Elia* were gobbled up in edition after edition, their great Victorian popularity to a large extent owing to the domesticated (and symbolically castrated) identity that had been melancholically consuming their author. Despite the fact that everyone loved Lamb, his relative eclipse within academic literary studies is a sad fact of disciplinary history. Jane Aaron traces it to two critical moments in British and

American scholarship: the Leavisite criticism of the 1930s, which dismissed Lamb from the literature of high seriousness, and the New Criticism, whose effort to establish a rigorous academic approach to literary studies could not countenance his "fine madnesses."[90] Lamb's unique mode of low-urban taste was at odds not only with high Romantic taste as defined (metonymically) by Wordsworth and Shelley; it was also out of sync with middle-class standards of taste practiced as conspicuous consumption and rendered so well by the Victorian realist novel. Long seen as a bridge between Romantic and Victorian literary-period designations, Lamb set the tone for a nineteenth-century poetics in which idealism was no longer an option and in which the note of melancholy forever resounds. He has since been eclipsed by the far more feminized — and paradoxically far more virile — creature of high-urban taste depicted by Byron.

6

Taste Outraged: Byron

*He would exist on biscuits and soda-water for days together, then, to
allay the eternal hunger gnawing at his vitals, he would make up a horrid
mess of cold potatoes, rice, fish, or greens, deluged in vinegar, and gobble it up like a famished dog. On either of these unsavoury dishes, with a
biscuit and a glass or two of Rhine wine, he cared not how sour, he called
feasting sumptuously. Upon my observing he might as well have fresh fish
and vegetables, instead of stale, he laughed and answered,*

    *"I have an advantage over you, I have no palate; one thing is as good
as another to me."*

    *The pangs of hunger which travellers and shipwrecked mariners have
described were nothing to what he suffered; their privations were temporary, his were for life, and more undendurable, as he was in the midst
of abundance.*

               — *Edward Trelawny,* Recollections of the Last Days of
                             Shelley and Byron *(1858)*

According to Byron's friend Edward Trelawny, Byron insisted he had no
palate, and if Trelawny exaggerates he nevertheless renders visible the extreme
to which the poet would go to maintain a studied indifference toward food.[1]
Unlike Keats, who supposedly "covered his tongue & throat as far as he could
reach with Cayenne pepper, in order as he said to have the 'delicious coolness

of claret in all its glory,' " Byron doused his stale food with vinegar to annihilate whatever taste it had left.[2] Most critics who have paid any attention to the topic of Byronic food and eating speculate that the driving energies of appetite in Byron's poetry are based on "his own abstemious habits," some even diagnosing particular eating disorders.[3] Trelawny suggests that a metabolic predilection to fatten, combined with a physical handicap (known at the time as a club foot) that restricted his exercise, left him only one solution to retain his tasteful appearance: the painful one of self-starvation.[4] Byron confided to his friend Thomas Moore that if he "was born, as the nurses say, 'with a silver spoon in my mouth,' it has stuck in my throat, and spoiled my palate, so that nothing put into it is swallowed with much relish; — unless it be cayenne" (*BLJ* 4:153). This self-induced hunger, caused by a lifelong endeavor to accommodate his figure to the cultural ideal of the Man of Taste, underwrites his metaphoric critique of taste in *Don Juan,* where the Byronic narrator emerges as a romantically revamped cannibal, a model fin-de-siècle Man of Taste.

While famous for its outrageous depiction of cannibalism, *Don Juan* rewrites cannibalism as vampirism, a paradoxically tasteful mode of consuming the other.[5] So long as the enemy to aesthetic community was simply precivil appetite, it was possible to locate bad taste *out there,* in the barbaric hinterland or dark abyss beyond the pale of tasteful society. But once appetite has been successfully repressed and made a driving force of society, to be aesthetically was to be extraordinary, or defined in ways other than commodity consumption. Putting the passions to work for commercial purposes was a principal task of the civilizing process, theorists as diverse as Freud and Foucault have shown; this process accelerated in the nineteenth century and involved disciplining the libido to serve the larger cultural apparatuses of production as well as channeling all "irrational" passions aroused by sexuality into the more socially, economically, and politically manageable form of marriage.[6] At the same time, it required the ostracization of all nonproductive desires.[7] This chapter argues that Byron's legacy is the oxymoronic paradox of the tasteful cannibal, whose taboo desires resist incorporation into the symbolic economy of consumer capitalism. In particular, it reads the cannibalism episode in canto 2 of *Don Juan* as a critical moment in the literary history of taste, one that launches a critique of the cultural ideology of taste with its nationalist claims to distinction.

Cannibalism Aboard the Medusa

Accounts of shipwrecks were all too familiar to the British reading public in the years that Byron was writing, but two contemporaneous wrecks — of the French frigate *La Méduse* (the *Medusa*) and the British *Alceste* — were ascribed enormous symbolic significance. To appreciate the shipwreck episode of *Don Juan* as the sophisticated critique of taste that it is, it needs to be read in the cultural context of survival cannibalism surrounding these events. Whereas the former caused an international scandal when its horrid consequences became known, the latter was portrayed by the British press as an occasion of tasteful decorum, avoiding the symbolic atrocities of cannibalism. As distinguished from the ancient concept of anthropophagism, the colonial discourse of cannibalism worked in concert with the civilizing discourse of taste to reinforce distinctions between "civil" and "savage." The term *cannibal* is itself a product of European colonialism, imported into English through Spanish explorations in the Caribbean, where some linguistic confusion between the letters *n* and *r* made possible by the Spanish language turned the "savage" *Carib* of a fierce West Indian tribe (said to be cannibals) into a *Canib,* and thence into a *cannibal.*

The politics defining taste in eighteenth and early nineteenth-century Britain relied on the concept of "savage" otherness, or the barbarity of non-Europeans. Even Montaigne's famous essay "On the Cannibals" (1580), which elevated the cannibal to the status of Noble Savage, found him savage nonetheless and, therefore, other. By the end of the eighteenth century, the dichotomy of "civil" and "savage" had been mapped onto Europe itself, as the Continental extremism associated with French aristocrats and their antithetical starving multitudes gave Burke his rhetoric of cannibal appetites.[8] Such cannibalism turned frightfully literal when Napoleon's army resorted to cannibalism in the disastrous retreat from Moscow, and among the survivors of the French *Medusa* in 1816 were the embattled remains of his colonial regiments. The wreck was immediately viewed as an emblem of foreign (specifically French) savagery, as opposed to British ideals of tasteful moderation.[9] Owing to the incompetence of the French royalist captain, the ship ran aground and the captain boarded himself, his family, and his friends aboard five lifeboats, abandoning one hundred and fifty passengers to an unprovisioned, half-submerged raft — and then cutting the cords that bound it to the lifeboats. Napoleon's desertions of his army had figured prominently in anti-Gallic propaganda, and this fiasco and its consequences gained political notoriety in a continent shaken by years of war.

Two of the *Medusa*'s survivors, J. B. Henri Savigny and Alexandre Corréard, published their account of the events following the wreck, including madness, mutiny, massacre, and cannibalism in the *Journal des débats* on September 13, 1816, which was immediately translated into English and printed in the London *Times* on September 17.[10] Only one in ten survived the fatal raft of the *Medusa*, and those who did resorted to the dreadful necessity of feeding on the flesh of their companions. Savigny and Corréard recall that after improvidently wasting their scant supply of wine and biscuit, and failing to catch any fish from the sea, the survivors "fell upon the dead bodies with which the raft was covered, and cut off pieces, which some instantly devoured."[11] Other stories of European survival cannibalism had been documented in Romantic-period publications, such as Sir J. G. Dalyell's *Shipwrecks and Disasters at Sea* (1812), but in these accounts cannibalism was stripped of cultural essentiality: it was simply portrayed as a desperate act of survival. Stories of survival cannibalism force the reader to imagine himself or herself in the same situation, while the "ritual" cannibalism associated with the *Medusa* affair is defined as a cultural phenomenon, and thus a far more symbolically freighted event.[12]

From a conservative perspective, the bloody flesh-strewn raft of the *Medusa* was no "necessary expedient" but further evidence of the ritual behavior of an unruly mob unable to civilize its immoderate appetites, instincts, and urges. From a republican perspective, however, the cannibalism following the wreck was an "extreme resource," necessary for survival against the forces of French imperial tyranny — the result of the same oppressive, monarchical rule against which the middle-class discourse of taste, with its attendant ideologies of sympathy and sensibility, had come into being. Savigny and Corréard consequently appeal to their reader through the eighteenth-century discourse of sympathy: "we beseech you, do not feel indignation towards men who are already too unfortunate; but have compassion on them, and shed some tears of pity on their unhappy fate."[13] By contrast, the contemporaneous wreck of the British *Alceste* was portrayed by its survivors as a civilized event in which all involved followed rules of tasteful decorum. The ship's surgeon John M'Leod published a narrative of the wreck in 1818, in which he recorded how the ship's provisions were dutifully saved (rather than greedily gorged) by the English captain, who rather than fleeing with his family and friends remained with his crew. Captain Maxwell shared the limited quantity of food left over from the wreck among all survivors equally: "The small stock of provisions saved from the wreck, and the uncertainty of our stay there, rendered economy in their distribution, as well as the preventing any waste or abuse, a most important duty."[14] Eliminating the extremities of appetite — an aristocratic self-indulgence on one hand, and a rapacious hunger veering toward cannibalism on the other — the ideal of tasteful moderation triumphs in the account of the *Alceste*.

Combining a middle-class ethos of economy with a Protestant ethic of duty, Captain Maxwell prevails over a democratic distribution of nutriments in which hierarchical distinction plays no role: "The mode adopted by Captain Maxwell, to make things go as far as possible, was to chop up the allowance for the day into small pieces, whether fowls, salt beef, pork, or flour, mixing the whole hotch-potch, boiling them together, and serving out a measure of this to each, publicly and openly, and without any distinction. By this means no nourishment was lost; it could be more equally divided than by any other way; and although, necessarily, a scanty, it was not an unsavoury, mess."[15] The author's use of the rhetorical device of litotes, or understatement, in the form of "it was not an unsavory mess," denotes the degree to which sensual enjoyment is here tempered by restraint. As the captain doles out the food "publicly and openly, and without any distinction," he creates an alimentary equivalent of moral and social community, a mess of ingredients in which individual flavors are submerged but not necessarily destroyed. The survivors find themselves reflected in a batch ("hotch-potch") of food valued for its alimentary value, to which they all have an equal right. An 1820 edition of M'Leod's account, printed together with Savigny and Corréard's narrative of the *Medusa* shipwreck, embellishes the above narrative by tacking on a moral: "No man received as much as to satisfy either hunger or thirst, yet every one was content and cheerful."[16] Avoiding the alternate extremes of hunger and self-engorgement, the *Alceste*'s survivors maintain not only a tasteful external decorum but also its internal equivalent.

W. T. Moncrieff's dramatic adaptation of the *Medusa* story, *Shipwreck of the Medusa; or, The Fatal Raft!* (1830), celebrates such decorous behavior as typically British. An anglicized Don Juan named Jack Gallant (with a side-wink to Byron) complains, "we're in a bad case truly — sailing without compass or provision — all our biscuit gone — our grog drank, and we left to strike our colours to starvation . . . I wish I only had that cowardly scoundrel, Master Adolphe, here! . . . when did he ever find a British officer desert his men in this way?"[17] Representations such as this one transform a culturally unsignifying account of "survival" cannibalism into the "ritual" behavior of an undisciplined, unconstitutional mob. The juxtaposition of the two shipwrecks in the British media served a didactic purpose, which the combined edition of the two narratives makes clear: "On the one side, we shall find discipline, moral feeling, and trust in Providence, producing, as their obvious reward, a deliverance from the most immanent dangers; whilst, on the other, it will be found, that the greatest misfortunes arise from the want of these good qualities."[18] This anonymous editor's use of the charged words *Providence* and *deliverance* signifies a particularly English form of Protestantism that involves both work and faith. (For Robinson Crusoe, they became a mantra.)

In his turn-of-the-century *Essay on Population* (1798), Thomas Malthus suggests that civil individuals, who have constantly to labor for their bread, are better able to maintain a middle road between feast and famine than "savages": no one receives as much as appetite and thirst might desire, yet everyone consumes and is content. By contrast, he argues, "savages are wonderfully improvident, and their means of subsistence always precarious, they often pass from the extreme of want to exuberant plenty, according to the vicissitudes of fortune in the chase, or to the variety in the produce of the seasons."[19] In a review of the *Medusa* and *Alceste* shipwreck narratives for the *Edinburgh Review,* Richard Chenevix translates this into a vision of cultural essentiality based on land and labor. Whereas the French are spoiled by sunshine and flowing vines, "happily for the moral character of England, we must labour, before we can enjoy, and the penury of nature has bound the inhabitants of Great Britain together, for their common interest, with a stronger chain, than any which her prodigality could forge."[20] The paradisiacal ideal of an always available, self-renewing food supply was a dangerous myth in a consumer society that channeled all appetite (sexual as well as oral) into expressions and practices that were productive of regulated consumption. Unlike the British survivors of the *Alceste,* who are content to work for their bread, which they share in a ritual moment of community, the *Medusa* survivors naturally descend into instinctive, taboo behavior when their flow of food is cut off. Bereft of provisions, they "were seen to rush upon their comrades with their sabres drawn, demanding the *wing of a chicken,* or *bread* to appease the hunger which devoured them."[21] From a sympathetic point of view, these were "unfortunate wretches," but to many contemporaries they were merely savages caught in the trap of their own indolence, unable to enter into the spirit of the symbolic economy of taste.

Malthus's savages are frequently reduced to gobbling up belts, shoes, and other leathern objects prior to resorting to "the dreadful extremity" of eating each other, and similar (even worse) food experiments are attempted on the raft of the *Medusa* prior to the "extreme resource" of cannibalism. "We tried to eat swordbelts and cartouch-boxes," write Savigny and Corréard. "We succeeded in swallowing some little morsels. Some eat linen. Others pieces of leather from the hats, on which there was a little grease, or rather dirt. . . . A sailor attempted to eat excrements, but he could not succeed."[22] Byron recasts this event in *Don Juan,* assuming an audience familiar with the topos of savage improvidence, as the shipwreck survivors share "leathern caps and what remained of shoes" (*DJ* 2.74). Improvidence was equated with uncivilized behavior, and Juan's companions purposely display a "savage" mentality. The Byronic narrator relates: "They ate up all they had and drank their wine / In spite of all remonstrances, and then / On what in fact next day were they to dine?" (2.69.4–6). From an account of survival cannibalism, the affair becomes again a symbolic, ritual event enacted by immoderate consumers, who in their inability to harness their appetites and respond dispassionately to the crisis, "fell all ravenously on their provision, / Instead of hoarding it with due precision" (*DJ* 2.68.7–8). One imagines that if only Captain Maxwell or Crusoe had been aboard, Juan's companions *would* have hoarded their provisions with due precision.

When the first two cantos of *Don Juan* appeared in the summer of 1819, one reviewer from *Blackwood's Magazine* found "the best and the worst part of the whole" to be Byron's description of the shipwreck as "a piece of terrible painting": he "paints it well, only to shew that he scorns it the more effectually."[23] In a letter to Byron of 26 May 1820, Shelley uses similar language, criticizing the moral tone of Byron's shipwreck, which is nevertheless "a masterpiece of portraiture."[24] A month earlier, the Romantic painter Jean Louis André Théodore Géricault had unveiled his notorious *Naufrage de la Méduse* (1819). This cultural event caused a *succès de scandale* at the Louvre and in London, where it appeared the next year. Géricault did not portray cannibalism directly, but his study *Despair and Cannibalism on the Raft* reveals what it *might* have looked like had he chosen to do so (figure 3). In the left forefront of the raft, one man's attempt to take a bite out of his neighbor's arm looks nothing if not ridiculous.[25] In the final version of Géricault's painting, *The Raft of the Medusa,* cannibalism is subsumed into a more abstract vision of sublime suffering, but this earlier study suggests that there can be nothing sublime about cannibalism, the most debased form of appetite. In Géricault's *Raft of the Medusa,* the cadaver trailing off the right forefront of the raft derives from the cannibalism sketch, and the father holding a dead son in his arms stands in for the inexpressible, unsublimable horror of cannibalism in its allusion to Dante's Ugolino (figure 4).[26] Géricault had sketched bloody limbs and heads directly from the *Medusa* survivors (the skin on the lower part of their bodies having been worn away by salt water), and he modeled other figures on guillotined heads, cadavers, and severed limbs. Presumably he did not go so far as to consume human flesh, but he fed his imagination with the nauseous smells of human decay, shaving his head and locking himself in his studio with the decomposing body parts, further feeding into the myth of "ritual" savagery shrouding the *Medusa* affair.

In *Don Juan* Byron applies the more culturally resonant form of ritual cannibalism not to the French but to the supposedly "civilized" British in a biting satire of taste. In his review of the poem for *The Examiner,* Leigh Hunt complains of Byron's "laughable description of Juan's dislike to feed on 'poor Pedrillo,'" and his preference for 'chewing a piece of bamboo and some lead'"—scruples sadly out of place in a genuine scene of survival cannibalism.[27] For Keats, the Byronic shipwreck was an explicit satire of taste: "Keats took up Ld

Byrons Don Juan," according to his friend Joseph Severn, "& singular enough he opened on the description of the Storm, which is evidently taken from the Medusa frigate & which the taste of Byron tryes to make a jest of" (*KC* 2:134).[28] Byron himself recognized the degree to which taste had become "the thermometer / by whose degrees all characters are classed" (*DJ* 16.48), and if we take his own cue in the preface to the poem, *Don Juan* is a calculated outrage to taste. His critique is directed not only at the transcendental taste that Wordsworth, Coleridge, and Southey were trying to create but also at the reigning consumer taste for food, women, and other commodities that characterized a society in which discretionary choice was enabled by the rejection of taboo desire.

Tasteful Don Juan

Harold Bloom remarks that in canto 2 of *Don Juan,* the shipwreck "survivors turn to a cannibalism that is rather nastily portrayed."[29] But what is perhaps most striking about this scene is its utter tastefulness. Byron's survivors observe impeccable table etiquette in carving up their victim, tossing the distasteful bits overboard and keeping the choice cuts of human flesh for themselves (*DJ* 2.77). Swift's "A Modest Proposal" may provide a useful analogy for Byron's satire in this scene. For just as Swift seems to satirize the tasteful pretensions of the supposedly civilized English, accustomed to cannibalizing colonial others, but ultimately targets the middle-class Proposer whose utilitarian spirit and calculating mentality conscript everything into a commercial economy of consumption, Byron's satire in *Don Juan* is deflected from the aristocratic Juans and poor Pedrillos to the more common rung of survivors, who pragmatically and diplomatically cannibalize their companions.[30]

A self-styled, cosmopolitan citizen of the world, Byron was less interested in ridiculing the extravagancies of Catholics and other confirmed cannibals than the beef-eating British, the commercial John Bulls who formed the substance of his own contemporary consumer-capitalist society.[31] In the fifth canto of *Don Juan* (a good place for a feast, as Byron knew from Milton), the narrator wonders "who / Would pique himself on intellects, whose use / Depends so much upon the gastric juice?" (*DJ* 5.32.6–8). Elsewhere he puns on the French term *goût,* relating aesthetic taste to physical craving: "Taste or the gout, pronounce it as inclines / Your stomach" (*DJ* 15.72.3–4). Writing to Murray on February 1, 1819, as he was copying out the fair copy of canto 2 of *Don Juan,* Byron confided: "Within this last fortnight I have been rather indisposed with a rebellion of the Stomach—which would retain nothing—(liver I suppose) and an inability or phantasy not to be able to eat of any thing with relish" (*BLJ* 6:99). His fantasy is of *not* eating with relish, of a stomach raging not with appetite but aversion — the fantasy of having no palate. Whereas the slender Charles Lamb identified with the hog, Byron found this symbol of appetite too close for comfort: "I remember one of his old friends saying, 'Byron, how well you are looking!'" Trelawny records: "If he had stopped there it had been well, but when he added, 'You are getting fat,' Byron's brow reddened, and his eyes flashed — 'Do you call getting fat looking well, as if I were a hog?'"[32] The hog mirrored his ever-threatening obesity, serving as a reminder that with a little less restraint he too might slip into the tasteless abyss of the "swinish multitude," who must have meals, at least one meal per day. The stomach thinks throughout much of *Don Juan*, but the Byronic narrator maintains his stance of tasteful disinterestedness. Aesthetic taste or the gout, pleasure or pain, take it or leave it.

Like Charles Lamb in *Elia*, Byron shapes the cultural politics of diet defining taste in the Romantic era into a metaphorical critique of taste that climaxes in cannibalism. Preparing for that event, the narrator of *Don Juan* challenges the vegetarian belief that humans are anatomically designed to digest vegetable food only:

> . . . man is a carnivorous production
>   And must have meals, at least one meal a day.
> He cannot live like woodcocks upon suction,
>   But like the shark and tiger must have prey.
> Although his anatomical construction
>   Bears vegetables in a grumbling way,
> Your labouring people think beyond all question,
> Beef, veal, and mutton better for digestion. (*DJ* 2.67)

The manipulation of dietary discourse in this stanza is complex. While one would expect that if "man" is carnivorous, he "must have meat" (in line 2 above), we are instead told that he "must have *meals,* at least one *meal* a day," a substitute repeated twice for emphasis. In line four, humans "must have prey," a second verbal substitute for meat that reads metaphorically as well as literally (sexual, financial, and other prey not necessarily found at the butcher's).[33] Byron's laborers think flesh better for digestion, but the narrator does not say "flesh" any more than "meat." Rather, the specific terms he uses are "Beef, veal, and mutton," which rhetorically process animals into food, flesh into edible commodities, and the raw appetite of "labouring people" into the consumer predilections identified by the British public with taste. Completing the formulaic "man is a — animal" with the adjective *carnivorous*, he essentializes humans as carnivores. At the same time, this tongue-in-cheek claim that man is a carnivorous animal denaturalizes carnivorousness by turning man into a "carnivorous *production*." The shipwreck survivors are corrupted through their expectation of flesh, and it is not merely the *fact* of animal flesh viewed as food but also a culture that disguises its appetite to itself that comes in for Byronic critique.

Like the dog shipwrecked with Robinson Crusoe and made his companion on the island, Juan's dog (who helps to stave off the cannibal feast of canto 2 for a few days) is a symbol of man's (particularly the Englishman's) property and propriety. Crusoe's dog guarded his property and was consequently a shield for his propriety, thereby avoiding the fate of Crusoe's pet lamb, pragmatically devoured when it refused to eat. Juan's dog is a spaniel, and as such he is linguistically typecast as Spanish — hence Catholic, a more appropriate object of sacrifice. Juan views this dog once belonging to his father as a brother in patrilinear descent, but to his companions he is simply a "meal." On the fifth day as "hunger's rage grew wild," therefore, "Juan's spaniel, spite of his entreating, / Was killed and portioned out for present eating" (*DJ* 2.70.6–8). Juan opts not to partake of his dog but on the sixth day gives in and accepts a paw, though whether this implies *eating* the paw is deliberately ambiguous:

> On the sixth day they fed upon his hide,
>   And Juan, who had still refused, because
> The creature was his father's dog that died,
>   Now feeling all the vulture in his jaws,
> With some remorse received (though first denied)
>   As a great favour one of the forepaws,
> Which he divided with Pedrillo, who
> Devoured it, longing for the other too. (2.71)

In the final lines above, we do not know whether Juan divides "the forepaws" (plural) with Pedrillo, keeping one for himself, potentially as a relic, or divides a single fore*paw*, which is thereby partly on the way to being food. The fact that Pedrillo longs "for the other too" after devouring his own suggests that it is still available for consumption. The syntax itself works to avoid saying that Juan eats his dog, allowing him to retain a sense of distinction in the midst of this taboo meal. Byron had a legendary fondness for his own dog Boatswain, whom he considered his "firmest friend," who rode beside his valet on his carriage, and with whom he desired to be buried.[34] Indeed, the most conspicuous memorial at his ancestral home at Newstead Abbey marks not the tomb of the poet but of his pet. Shadows of this dog as Byron's "firmest friend" appear in his poem "Darkness" (1816) and in Mary Shelley's fictional portrait of him at the siege of Constantinople in *The Last Man* (1823). Not only in a vegetarian but also in a Byronic context, then, eating one's dog is barely a step away from being a cannibal.

Byron's grandfather, the swashbuckling Admiral "Jack" Byron, also lived through a shipwreck by making a meal of his dog. His account of the wreck of the *Wager,* published in 1768 (a book owned by Byron), relates: "One day, when I was at home in my hut with my Indian dog, a party came to my door, and told me their necessities were such, that they must eat the creature or starve." Honor compels the elder Byron to plead for his dog, but once the responsibility for the creature's death is assumed by others and the creature is killed for food, he pragmatically takes part in the communal meal: "thinking that I had at least as good a right to a share as the rest, I sat down with them, and partook of their repast." The meal over, he was then "glad to make a meal of the dog's paws and skin," which he found decomposing in a pile of bodily remainders. In its tenor of description ("partook of their repast"), Jack Byron's meal veers away from survival cannibalism and the desperation of his companions, one of whom "having picked up the liver of one of the drowned men (whose carcase had been torn to pieces by the force with which the sea drove it among the rocks) was with difficulty withheld from making a meal of it."[35] Rather, the anecdote rings other associations, from Captain James Cook's narrative of a New Zealander eating a broiled human liver on the deck of his ship (prepared by his crew for this purpose), to Dr. Hannibal Lecter's dining on a haute cuisine preparation of human liver and fava beans in the film version of *The Silence of the Lambs*.[36] Turning his pet into a "meal," Jack Byron blurs the distinction between men and brutes in a manner that suggests more than an unthinking act of survival: in retrospect anyway, his account of his own behavior is layered over with a symbolic code of manners.

Byron names his doomed ship the *Trinidada,* simultaneously evoking the cannibalistic associations of the Spanish Caribbean and the Catholic doctrine of the Trinity as a "cannibal feast."[37] From a Protestant point of view, as we have seen by way of Milton, to take the Lord's Supper literally as Catholics do is to convert the sacred act at the heart of Western culture into its oldest taboo. Byron joked to his Catholic friend Moore in March 1822 that "those who swallow their Deity, really and truly, in transubstantiation, can hardly find anything else otherwise than easy of digestion" (*BLJ* 9:123). Turning the raw fact of eating human flesh into a "meal," Byron also sets the stage for cannibalism as a symbolic occasion of commensality. Savigny and Corréard record how the *Medusa*'s survivors dry out their dead companions' flesh in the sun to make it less repulsive, a deed of utility that one conservative reviewer from the *Quarterly* turns into an epicurean experiment to make the meal more tasty: "By means of a little gunpowder and linen, and by erecting an empty cask, they contrived to make a fire; and mixing with the fish the flesh of their deceased comrade, they all partook of a meal, which, by this means, was rendered less revolting."[38] The description of this human barbecue is pure fantasy; Savigny and Corréard merely report that since the "horrid nourishment had given strength to those who had made use of it, it was proposed to dry it, in order to render it less disgusting."[39] Their representation of cannibalism insists on its status as *survival* cannibalism, an instinctual, unsignifying means to satisfy hunger. By contrast, Byron's shipwreck survivors rank among themselves a few vegetarians "not quite so fond of animal food" (*DJ* 2.78.2), who insist on exercising their taste, declining to partake of the taboo meal, and maintaining an impossibly disinterested attitude to food and the primal enticements of appetite.

Whereas Savigny and Corréard record cannibalism on the third day after the *Medusa* shipwreck, Byron places his "meal" on the Sabbath or *seventh* day, a more symbolically loaded occasion. "The seventh day and no wind," the narrator reports. "The longings of the cannibal arise / (Although they spoke not) in their wolfish eyes" (*DJ* 2.72). Adopting Savigny and Corréard's method of relating the events following the shipwreck as they occurred day by day to build narrative tension toward the cannibal feast, Byron commences his stanzas with such lines as "The fourth day came, but not a breath of air"; "The fifth day, and their boat lay floating there"; "On the sixth day they fed upon his hide"; "The seventh day and no wind" (2.70–72). Yet his satire is directed less against Catholics and other Continental cannibals than against his own Protestant culture, whose cannibalism is tastefully made symbolic (through the Church of England, as through the logic of commercial capitalism that converts people into commodities whose consumption does the work of intersubjective relations).

Once Juan's dog disappears, the tutor Pedrillo becomes the first human sacrifice. Hunger represents the antithesis of the aesthetic attitude, canceling all capacity to exercise taste, but Juan again chooses to exercise discretion with regard to his food. In so doing, he chooses aesthetics over appetite, art over nature, or any of the other ways we conceptualize — and privilege — imaginary experience over the real. Of our romantic hero Juan, we are assured: " 'Twas not to be expected that he should, / Even in extremity of their disaster, / Dine with them on his pastor and his master" (*DJ* 2.78). Byron's use of the charged word "extremity" at once evokes Malthus's "dreadful extremity" and Savigny and Corréard's "extreme resource" as code phrases for cannibalism. Even those who do opt to "dine" on human flesh make the typically British decision to draw lots, reasonably and democratically, for their food: "Out they spoke of lots for flesh and blood, / And who should die to be his fellow's food" (2.73.7–8). Rather than procuring human flesh in the brutal and haphazard manner of the *Medusa* shipwreck's survivors, their behavior (under the circumstances) suggests an egalitarian and relatively civilized mode of proceeding. In this social contract between men, they are all given an equal chance for survival.

Freud narrates the origins of civilization as a primal contract between men, which begins when the brothers of the originary "primal horde" kill their father and devour him in order to satisfy their sexual appetites with their sisters; the social contract that results from this deed forbids literal as well as sexual cannibalism, or incest. In *Totem and Taboo,* he can find no rational explanation for why these mythic ancestors devoured their father after killing him. Rather, he simply states, "Cannibal savages as they were, it goes without saying that they devoured their victim as well as killing him."[40] Cannibalism seems gratuitous in this account, a subsidiary of the more culturally significant (for Freud) act of sexual cannibalism.[41] In Byron's poem, the cannibal pact is made from the material remainder of the love affair between Juan and Donna Julia. Her last love letter to him is torn up in the making of lots: "Having no paper, for the want of better, / They took by force from Juan Julia's letter" (2.74.7–8). Through this act, the material sign for a private heterosexual passion becomes a bond uniting the male survivors of the wreck. We are, after all, told that the situation is one in which "none were permitted to be neuter" (2.75.7), and the narrator's use of the charged word "neuter" for "neutral" in the "lots" stanza does more than enable the rhyme with tutor. It suggests that none were permitted to be *sexually neutral;* according to the *Oxford English Dictionary,* "Neither masculine nor feminine." In Byron's version of civilization based on cannibalism, in other words, the brothers do not destroy their father to sleep with his wives: they destroy the emblem of a wife who becomes a vanishing mediator between men.[42]

The sacrifice of Juan's tutor Pedrillo is symbolic, if not sacramental, and rather than drinking transubstantiated wine from a chalice, the survivors bleed him in a relatively polite and painless process in which the victim participates. The method had been used in actual shipwrecks, such as one chronicled by Sir J. G. Dalyell in which the survivors suck blood directly from their victim's veins.[43] But Byron merges it with the cultural reference of the *Medusa* to depict not survival but ritual cannibalism in which individual preference plays a role: his surgeon "being thirstiest at the moment . . . / Preferred a draught from the fast-flowing veins" (2.77.3–4). Jerome Christensen remarks that Pedrillo's willingness to participate in this ritual by holding out his jugular and wrist to be bled "smacks of the bizarre: it's the sort of thing a Catholic would do. . . . As his sacrifice takes on the pattern of Christ's, it invites a disagreeable reflection on the cannibal feast as a commemoration in letter and spirit of the Last Supper."[44] Originally in Byron's manuscript, however, Pedrillo does not give himself up voluntarily to be bled. Rather than holding "out his jugular and wrist" (2.76.8), he was transitively (and one imagines less politely) *bled:* "They bled him in the Jugular & wrist."[45] This line is subsequently crossed out and replaced with one in which Pedrillo is more complicit, as the redemptive wine of Eucharistic dietetics transforms into a somewhat vampiric exchange of blood between men.

What Freud describes as "culture" is a homosocial world instantiated by a social contract between men, one that puts all sexual appetite to work, confining its pleasures to the legalized sphere of the domestic. Once sexual energies are restricted to the monogamous institution of marriage, they can be legally, socially, and economically regulated. Society's aim is to channel these energies back into a cultural system of productivity, conscripting all private drives and desires into the socioeconomic purposes of production.[46] In his late work *Civilization and Its Discontents* (1930), Freud writes that what the individual "employs for cultural aims he to a great extent withdraws from women and sexual life"; moreover, "his constant association with men, and his dependence on his relations with them, even estrange him from his duties as a husband and father."[47] In the nineteenth-century discourse of vampirism, blood, like wine, offers a symbolic route out of the ideological structures of consumer capitalism.

Moncrieff's theatrical adaptation of the *Medusa* shipwreck emphasizes even more explicitly the homosociality of Byron's cannibal feast. When the captain announces, "we will cast lots—let fate decide it," Jack Gallant replies, "But what are we to do for paper?—I have it, here's the love letter that my Nan sent me the last time I left old England.—I've kept it next my heart ever since, but it must go now—poor Nan! It was as pretty a bit of penmanship—but no matter, I shall never see her again—poor Nan!"[48] The name Julia evokes high romance (after Shakespeare's famous Capulet), whereas the name Nan is a diminutive of Nanna, Nanny, or Granny, symbolically stripping its owner of sexual power (*OED*). By the time the melodrama was produced in 1830, the term also connoted "nancy-boy" or "nancy," meaning an effeminate male and, by the fin de siècle, a homosexual.[49] By renaming Byron's hero "Jack" and his Julia "poor Nan," Moncrieff brings into relief the gender dynamics latent in canto 2 of *Don Juan*: once the contractual, heterosexual love letter disappears, the exchange between men can commence. When the Romantic painter Eugène Delacroix returned to the theme of the *Medusa*, he did so through Byron, specifically his memorable scene of drawing lots.[50] Delacroix's sketches for *Le naufrage de Don Juan* (1841) portray the person holding the hat from which the lots were to be drawn as a turbaned Oriental (adhering to Savigny and

Corréard's original account of the demographics aboard the fatal raft). But in the final version of the painting he is European, capitalizing on the self-critical nature of Byron's shipwreck. The final section of this chapter will look more carefully at the nineteenth-century discourse of vampirism as it evolves out of Byronic cannibalism in the literary history of taste.

The Byronic Vampire

Unlike the cannibal, which is defined simply as "a man-eater," the vampire entails a moral component as a "person of malignant & loathsome character, esp. one who preys ruthlessly upon others; a vile and cruel exactor or extortioner" (*OED*). As we can see from this citation, the vampire from its earliest incarnations in the British cultural imaginary was conceived on an economic register as a sucker of capital or cash. One exemplary 1741 quotation refers to "vampires of the publick, and riflers of the kingdom" (*OED*). Marx also employs the vampire motif in *Capital* (1867), defining capital itself as "dead labour which, vampire-like, lives only by sucking living labour, and lives the more, the more labour it sucks."[51] Through the example of colonial food products like sugar and tea, we can see how the concept of physically cannibalizing another can be synonymous with sucking the living life out of another through a capitalist exploitation of labor. Charlotte Sussman remarks that "the British drinker of sugared tea never sees the slaves, but only consumes the alienated products of their labor" in an exchange that is commodified (insofar as subject relations are posited in object relations) and materialized through the act of consumption.[52] "The slave-dealer, the slave-holder, and the slave-driver are virtually the agents of the consumer," writes William Fox in 1791, "and may be considered as employed and hired by him to procure the commodity," using a term now associated with Marx to urge British consumers to resist the "forced feeding" of mercantile traders: "They may hold it to our lips, steeped in the blood of our fellow-creatures; but they cannot compel us to accept the loathsome portion."[53] To suck the "loathsome portion" directly from the veins of one's neighbor is to literalize the taboo appetites whose very suppression and redirection enables civilization to advance on the pattern of capitalism.

In *Don Juan* Byron redirects the taboo energies from an outrageous because comic representation of survival cannibalism, into a ritual cannibalism that is better classed as vampirism. Byron, like his onetime physician John Polidori, based his knowledge of vampires on Southey's extended note on Joseph de Tournefort in *Thalaba* (1801). Polidori rephrases this in his introduction to *The Vampyre* (1819), and Byron cites it in a footnote to *The Giaour* (1816), a poem containing an autobiographical portrait of a vampire (lines 755–86) that is also quoted by Polidori in the introduction to *The Vampyre*.[54] When Polidori's tale first appeared in the *New Monthly Magazine* on April 1, 1819, under the title *The Vampyre: a Tale by Lord Byron,* the false attribution of authorship was a source of frustration to Polidori and of embarrassment to Byron.[55] Polidori had named his vampire Lord Ruthven, after Colonel De Ruthven in Lady Caroline Lamb's transparently autobiographical 1816 novel based on her adulterous affair with Byron. This brooding figure romanticized by Polidori was visibly based on Byron: "a nobleman, more remarkable for his singularities, than his rank," who "gazed upon the mirth around him, as if he could not participate therein."[56] As Patricia L. Skarda observes, "Polidori fashioned a version of a vampire tale more remarkable for its echoes than for its originality."[57] Perhaps its loudest echo, one that continues to reverberate today, is the noble unquiet creature we have come to call the vampire. No longer a repulsive peasant of Eastern European folklore feeding on cows and commoners, the nineteenth-century literary vampire was occasionally male (albeit an effeminate male), occasionally female (a frightfully aggressive female), but certainly never neuter. The Romantic era transformed the vampire into a sexually appealing, homoerotic cult hero modeled on the celebrity persona of Byron.[58]

When discussing the Byronic narrator of *Don Juan*, contemporary reviews painted a proleptic likeness of Bram Stoker's Dracula. *Blackwood's* remarked that "this miserable man, having exhausted every species of sensual gratification — having drained the cup of sin even to its bitterest dregs, [seems] resolved to shew us that he is no longer a human being, even in his frailties; — but a cool unconcerned fiend."[59] The most common criticism of the poem was its narrator's seemingly inhuman attitude as "dead" to all pleasure and pain. When Keats deplored the cannibalism episode, he too lamented "that a man like Byron should have exhausted all the pleasures of the world so compleatly [*sic*] that there was nothing left for him but to laugh & gloat over the most solemn & heart rending [scenes] of human misery" (*KC* 2:134). For Keats, the representation of the shipwreck was "one of the most diabolical attempts ever made upon our sympathies," and *Blackwood's* was similarly disturbed by "the demoniacal laugh with which this unpitying brother exults over the contemplation of their despair."[60] Byron's narrator claims that "ennui is a growth of English root, / Though nameless in our language . . . / That awful yawn which sleep cannot abate" (*DJ* 13.101.5–8), and Hazlitt, as if remembering this remark, writes that his "only object seems to be to stimulate himself and his readers for the moment — to keep both alive, to drive away *ennui,* to substitute a feverish and irritable state of excitement for listless indolence or even calm enjoyment."[61] Described as "no longer a human being" and trying to keep himself "alive, to drive away *ennui*," the Byronic narrator of *Don Juan* is himself the prototype for the literary vampire.

Don Juan "could be most things to all women / Without the coxcombry of certain she-men" (*DJ* 14.31.7–8), and presumably he could be something as well to a narrator not directly identified as a she-man but who nevertheless admires his hero as a "pretty gentleman" with a "Half-girlish face" (1.170.8, 171.8). Jonathan Gross suggests that the Byronic "narrator makes Don Juan the subject of his erotic gaze and transforms him and the Don Juan legend in the process."[62] To the narrator, Juan is "almost man" (1.54.5), and as he weeps on his departure from Spain in canto 2, the narrator remarks, "Sweets to the sweet" (2.17.3). Even when he most closely resembles that typical British figure of masculine self-reliance, Robinson Crusoe tossed ashore after shipwreck on an unknown isle, Juan is highly feminized through the narrator's gaze: "And like a withered lily, on the land / His slender frame and pallid aspect lay, / As fair a thing as e'er was formed of clay" (2.110.6–8). He is portrayed as "a young flower snapped from the stalk, / Drooping and dewy" (2.176.5–6), and by the fifth canto he has been dressed as a woman, put in a seraglio, and treated as a "maid" and "new-bought virgin" made to "blush and shake" (5.84.7, 156.2).

As the poem progresses, he is repeatedly referred to as Juanna (6.57–73) and with a female pronoun: "I say her, because / The gender still was epicene," by definition grammatically androgynous (6.58.1–2). Juan stands out from Catherine's other lovers in the Russian court as "slight and slim, / Blushing and beardless" (9.47.1–2, 53.1); in the English cantos, "Juan with his virgin face" is "wont / To take some trouble with his toilet" (16.13.8, 29.1–2). Gary Dyer has recently argued that "Not all the secrets in Byron turn out to be sodomy, but even when a secret is something else, the supreme dangers of sodomy have helped shape the nature of secrecy."[63] In a poem where food, symbolized by Ceres, is tied to drink, symbolized by Bacchus ("Without whom Venus will not long attack us" [*DJ* 2.169–70]), the sensual enjoyment of appetite often traces back to this eroticized relationship between men. Indeed, when the second canto breaks off abruptly after "Two hundred and odd stanzas" (*DJ* 2.216.3), one senses that it as well as the poem could continue indefinitely with more wine, women, and food, the "rack of pleasures" upon which the Byronic narrator enjoys wracking Don Juan (14.79.2).[64]

Stoker brings the erotic tension between vampire and romantic hero to light in *Dracula,* where Count Dracula's fascination for the younger Jonathan Harker is evident from the start: "How dare you touch him, any of you? How dare you cast eyes on him when I had forbidden it? Back, I tell you all! This man belongs to me!" Harker narrates these events of his entrapment in Castle Dracula in his diary much like a sentimental heroine of gothic fiction: "Then the Count turned, after looking at my face attentively, and said in a soft whisper: — 'Yes, I too can love; you yourselves can tell it from the past. Is it not so? Well, I promise you that when I am done with him you shall kiss him at your will.' "[65] Christopher Craft was one of the first to discuss the relation between kissing and blood sucking in *Dracula,* which has since become a critical commonplace in scholarship on the literary vampire.[66] Just as Dracula's single-minded pursuit of Harker takes place by way of vanishing intermediary women, the Byronic narrator pursues Don Juan in a mad dash through Europe by way of a series of female mediators: female love interests who facilitate the central relationship between the narrator and his romantic hero.[67] The objects of Juan's taste seem exchangeable, and, to this reader at least, the real evidence of oral and libidinal appetite in the poem is expressed by the narrator whose driving energies complement Juan's own passivity, verging on indifference, toward women.

Byron challenges the heterosexual ideal of "constant love" in *Don Juan* in a critique that only increases with the amount of narrative digression, itself a formal reflection of male inconstancy. From its first appearance, the poem was considered a blatant attack on the heterosexual institution of marriage, experienced firsthand by Byron and Annabella Milbanke.[68] At one point, remembering his own inconstancy stimulated by the mysterious identity of a stranger encountered at masquerade, the narrator concludes himself a villain:

> I hate inconstancy; I loathe, detest,
> > Abhor, condemn, abjure the mortal made
> Of such quicksilver clay that in his breast
> > No permanent foundation can be laid.
> Love, constant love, has been my constant guest,
> > And yet last night, being at a masquerade,
> I saw the prettiest creature, fresh from Milan,
> Which gave me some sensations like a villain. (*DJ* 2.209)

His cynical attitude toward the ideal of "constant love," combined with an excessive sexual curiosity at the masquerade, prompt one to wonder whether the stranger is a she, a "she-man," or no she at all. The narrator pursues his villainy into the following stanza, where he recalls his thoughts of the previous night: "I'll just inquire if she be wife or maid / Or neither — out of curiosity" (2.210.5–6). As the poem becomes more digressive in the later cantos, it becomes more gothic, driving the narrator's fantasies into the nocturnal recesses of the English country house. Rewriting the discourse of cannibalism as vampirism, he sends it underground, symbolically beneath the structures (family, property) sustaining capitalist society.

One of the principal concerns as the poem proceeds is the alienation of its hero in capitalist society, a concern emphasized increasingly in the English cantos: "Alas, to them of ready cash bereft, / What hope remains?" (13.45.3–4). Christensen has suggested that the poem opposes the moral logic of capitalism with an older symbolic economy of extravagant expenditure and consumption in which "few things surpass old wine" (2.178.5). Other critics have noticed all the drinking in the poem, and one unsigned review in the *Edinburgh Review* compares Sir Walter Scott to Byron in these terms: "With the one, we seem to share a gay and gorgeous banquet — with the other, a wild and dangerous intoxication."⁶⁹ Against the asceticism of the Shelleyan "natural diet," which insisted that no liquid was fit to drink but distilled water, Byron claims that "Man being reasonable must get drunk; / The best of life is but intoxication" (*DJ* 2.179.1–2). Insofar as the shipwreck of canto 2 rewrites cannibalism as vampirism, it provides an intoxicating escape route out of consumer society and its legitimized, workaday sexuality.

An anonymous parody published in 1819 as canto 3 of *Don Juan* describes Byron's somewhat fictive, somewhat scrambled biography, culminating in a retirement to Lake Geneva, where *The Vampyre* was originally conceived:

> In rival conclave there and dark divan
>   He met and mingled with the Vampyre crew
> Who hate the virtues in and the form of man,
>   And strive to bring fresh monsters into view. . .⁷⁰

By borrowing the archaic-gothic spelling of "Vampyre," the verse reinforces Byron's status as monstrous protagonist of *The Vampyre*. The commodification of the "Byronic" began in earnest with the publication of *Don Juan,* in a process of feeding off Byron's literary corpus that Ghislaine McDayter for one reads as vampiric: "while promiscuously reproducing the original (Byron) in every detail, this process simultaneously drained the 'life blood' of the poet's legitimate progeny in order to reproduce hundreds of false replicas — replicas, all animated, with an uncanny life of their own."⁷¹ Byron once wrote to Murray regarding *The Giaour* (1813) that "the thing is tolerably *vamped* and will be *vendible*" (*BLJ* 3:51). In the nineteenth-century discourse of vampirism, to be "vamped" is to be "vendible," though Byron would likely have resented the above lines associating him with "the Vampyre crew" in the same year that *The Vampyre* was attributed to himself within the context ("canto 3") of *Don Juan*. By the time Polidori's vampire story appeared in print on April 24, 1819,

Byron had already sent off the second canto of *Don Juan* to his publisher John Murray, remarking in another letter around the same time: "Damn '*the Vampire*,' — what do I know of vampires" (*BLJ* 6:114). Despite this disavowal, Byron refers within his own comic epic to the necessary ability "to soothe and flatter / With the same feelings as you'd coax a vampire" (*DJ* 11.62.4–5).

Publicly, Byron denied all acquaintance with vampires, though he nevertheless tantalizes his reader with the implication that he could — if he would — "divulge their secrets" in a more competent manner: "the formality of a public advertisement of a book I never wrote — and a residence where I never resided — is a little too much. . . . I have besides a personal dislike to 'Vampires' and the little acquaintance I have with them would by no means induce me to divulge their secrets" (*BLJ* 6:119).[72] Byron admitted to his friend Thomas Medwin that "the foundation of [*The Vampyre*] *was* mine; but I was forced to disown the publication, lest the world should suppose that I had vanity enough, or was egotist enough, to write in that ridiculous manner about myself."[73] Polidori named his vampire Lord Ruthven after the scandalous society figure of Byron, but Byron chose the name August Darvell after his step-sister Augusta, suggesting at once taboo sexual relations (based on their rumored affair) and self-reflection in an opposite gender. At the heart of Byron's fragmentary vampire tale, begun at Villa Diodati on June 17, 1816, is a talented aristocrat who fascinates the narrator (a fictionalized Polidori) as "an object of attention of interest and even of regard."[74] On a deserted spot in Greece, he pressures him into a secret pact, swearing him to secrecy about his true nature, which is monstrous, illicit, and vampiric. Polidori's version of the story retains this secret pact, as the vampire chases his young male admirer back to London, provoking his psychological breakdown by keeping him to the secret.

The Romantic vampire originated in the East, specifically Greece, which as Louis Crompton has shown, played directly into the early nineteenth-century homophobia associated with Hellenism.[75] Byron's actual experience in Greece remains shadowed in mystery, since his friend John Cam Hobhouse destroyed all relevant journals and memoirs after his death. Hobhouse had traveled to Greece with Byron during the years 1809 to 1811, though Byron concluded the trip alone after Hobhouse returned to England under dubious circumstances. Of Byron's surviving materials, his friend Moore deleted further portions, some of which have been retrieved, revealing (in Crompton's words) "the code by which Byron communicated his homosexual adventures to Hobhouse in England."[76] What seemed to rankle Byron the most about the spurious "memoir" of his residence in Greece, published with *The Vampyre* in the *New Monthly Magazine* and in subsequent editions, was its portrayal of the protagonist as an eccentric character residing in privacy on one of the Greek islands. "With respect to his loves or pleasures," comments the mysterious memoir writer, "I do not assume a right to give an opinion."[77]

Juan's "nautical existence" is an experience that "unmans one quite" (*DJ* 2.12.3–8), and it detaches him not only from his nation but also from the institutions sustaining it, foremost among them marriage. To enter a "nautical existence" is to enter an overtly homosocial world in which "the bond of the sea" unites men, as Joseph Conrad puts it in his fin-de-siècle tale of savagery, horror, and cannibalism, *Heart of Darkness* (1899). The bond uniting this all-male community of capitalist traders, "holding [their] hearts together through long periods of separation" is glossed by no ideology of heterosexual romance.[78] Conrad's novella renders Kurtz, living with African "cannibals" and gratifying his "monstrous passions" in unspeakable ways, as the natural telos of the commercial European trader. "I saw him open his mouth wide," relates Marlow, "it gave him a weirdly voracious aspect, as though he had wanted to swallow all the air, all the earth, all the men before him." Conrad renders imperialism as a type of cannibalism that looks a lot like vampirism, for Kurtz is sexually alluring and physically phantasmatic: "unsteady, long, pale, indistinct, like a vapour exhaled by the earth."[79] The libidinal bond between men in this capitalist nightmare story of fin de siècle Britain has its forerunner in the cannibal pact of *Don Juan,* one that is reinforced each time the romantic hero leaves one of his female lovers to recommence his "nautical existence."

Another text that launches a critique of nineteenth-century capitalism through a fictional fantasy of cannibalism is H. G. Wells's *The Time Machine* (1895). This bizarre, futuristic monster narrative opens similarly in the "luxurious after-dinner atmosphere" of a club of male friends who lounge on chairs that "embraced and caressed us rather than submitted to be sat upon," prior to being transported imaginatively into a world in which gender is undefined and where sexuality flourishes among androgynous beings. "Where population is balanced and abundant, much child-bearing becomes an evil rather than a blessing to the State," the Time Traveller recounts, "there is less necessity — indeed there is no necessity — for an efficient family, and the specialisation of the sexes with reference to their children's needs disappears."[80] In this fin-de-siècle world of soft chairs and soft sexuality, pleasure is an end, not an economic means to something else — as it was for the "rival conclave" of Byron's "Vampyre crew." In the latter's mode of paradoxically tasteful cannibalism, taboo or transgressive appetites are transformed into a style of high-urban taste that sets the standard for fin-de-siècle aesthetics.

Byron recognized the degree to which appetite and taste were conceptually related in the figure of the vampire, whose most famous cultural counterpart was the title character of Robert Louis Stevenson's *The Strange Case of Dr.*

Jekyll and Mr. Hyde (1886). His uncontrollable appetites define the monstrous Hyde, though he inhabits a flat in the Soho quarter of London that is "furnished with luxury and good taste" in the style of his better half, Henry Jekyll, "who was much of a connoisseur." Jekyll is the quintessence of the unmarried, middle-class connoisseur living in London at the end of the nineteenth century whose closest companions are other unmarried bachelors, and Hyde is a monster by virtue of his lack of restraint, especially in "those appetites which [Jekyll] had long secretly indulged" and to which by the end of the novel he instinctively returns "with a greedy gusto."[81] He, like the Byronic speaker of *Don Juan* who drives the poem forward with his own powerful, sexualized appetites, finds a natural home in the drawing room of fin-de-siècle monster narratives like *The Time Machine* and *Dracula*.

Byron vindicates his urbane pleasures in a satiric critique of high Romantic taste, much as Charles Lamb had done from a similar but opposite ("low") perspective. But Keats, to whom we now turn, never ceased to long for more transcendental flavors. "Would we were a sort of ethereal Pigs, & turn'd loose to feed upon spiritual Mast & Acorns," he wrote to his friend John Reynolds, "which would be merely being a squirrel & feed[ing] upon filberts. [F]or what is a squirrel but an airy pig, or a filbert but a sort of archangelical acorn" (*KL* 1:223). Whereas the legendary figure of the chameleon feeds upon air (as Keats knew from *Hamlet*), he himself could not be sustained on the transcendental food of airy infinity any more than could Byron or Lamb. Keats shared the Cockney orientation of Lamb, labeled by Coleridge as a member of the urban masses, and by the time he wrote to Reynolds he too had been corralled into the "swinish multitude" by *Blackwood's*.[82] His poetic critique of taste came not in the form of a conscious satiric attack in the manner of Byron or Lamb; rather, his frustrated effort to exist in the ethereal world of airy pigs thrust him — and the idealism implicit in the cultural ideology of taste — into the modernist condition of nausea.

7

Keats's Nausea

Now no comfort avails any more; longing transcends a world after death, even the gods; existence is negated along with its glittering reflection in the gods, or in any immortal beyond. Conscious of the truth he has once seen, man now sees everywhere only the horror or absurdity of existence . . . he is nauseated.
— Friedrich Nietzsche, The Birth of Tragedy

Perhaps I eat to persuade myself I am somebody.
— John Keats, Letter to Richard Woodhouse, 21 September, 1819

Keats is known to have as perplexed a relation to the sensory — particularly the savory — as any poet. For Elizabeth Bishop, he was "almost everything a poet should have been in his day," except, that is, "for his unpleasant insistence on the *palate*."[1] For Carlyle, he was "a miserable creature, hungering after sweets which he can't get; going about saying, 'I am so hungry; I should so like something pleasant!'"[2] Yeats portrayed him as a schoolboy with face and nose pressed to a sweet-shop window.[3] Critics from the time of Lionel Trilling continue to read him as "possibly unique among poets in the extensiveness of his reference to eating and drinking and to its pleasurable or distasteful sensations."[4] References to gustatory taste inform not only his poetry but also much of his poetic theory. The chameleon poet famously "lives in gusto," a term derived from *gustus* (taste) and characterized by Hazlitt as an effect whereby the eye acquires "a taste or appetite for what it sees" (*HCW* 4:78). His "poetical character" is defined by its ability to "taste" and "relish" the world it perceives: "its relish of the dark side of things . . . its taste for the bright one" (*KL* 1:387). And on the eve of his *annus mirabilis* (December 31, 1818), Keats himself declared that he had "not one opinion upon any thing except in matters of taste" (*KL* 2:19). While it would be misguided to assume that Keats really did renounce everything except "matters of taste," the distinguishing mark of the Keatsian poet is his ability to experience the world through his "palate fine."[5]

As his own experience never let him forget, however, it is the body that tastes or perceives the world by way of sensory experience. In Keats's final year(s) that body was a consumptive one that wasted away, consuming itself as it literally starved to death. "The chief part of his disease," his physician James Clarke prognosticated, "seems seated in his Stomach," and the tragic account of his last days left by Joseph Severn shows Keats constantly raving that he would die from hunger. His stomach, rather than nourishing the rest of his body, became at last its devourer: "his Stomach — not a single thing will digest," writes Severn, "the torture he suffers all and every night — and the best part of the day — is dreadful in the extreme — the distended stomach keeps him in perpetual hunger or craving" (*KC* 1:172, 177). By the time he reached Rome (where he died), Keats had suffered "a ghastly wasting-away of his body and extremities" (*KC* 1:202). But for a poet devoted to acts of self-definition through "matters of taste," to be hungry, to be physically driven by appetite, cancels all pretensions to taste. This chapter will examine how Keats's effort to "taste" and "relish" the world through the reflective pleasures of the imagination sickens his eponymous hero in *Hyperion*. Nauseated from the mundane smells that force themselves through his "ample palate," he is a forerunner and epic magnification of the human speaker of *The Fall of Hyperion,* who also, from the first stale feast he encounters, struggles hard to escape from a condition of unpalatable and finally unallegorizable existence.

Keats's Allegory of Taste

Keats always acknowledged a debt to Hazlitt's "depth of Taste," which he proclaimed to be (along with Benjamin Haydon's paintings and Wordsworth's poetry) one of the three great things of the age in which to rejoice (*KL* 1:203, 205). Hazlitt thought of taste in terms of "gusto," and his 1816 essay "On Gusto" describes the creative process in aggressively gustatory terms based on Milton: "Milton has great gusto. He repeats his blows twice; grapples with and exhausts his subject. His imagination has a double relish of its objects" (*HCW* 4:79–80). Gusto was a critical term for Hazlitt to indicate a kind of full-bodied aesthetic experience, ripe with sensual enjoyment. In the aesthetic experience of gusto, as James Engell explains, the mind embraces the object "until the last iota of pleasure and pain is wrung from the embrace and its associations."[6] Whereas the neoclassical Joshua Reynolds claimed that the "*gusto grande* of the Italians . . . and the *great style, genius,* and *taste* among the English, are but different appellations of the same thing," Hazlitt distinguished "gusto" from "taste."[7] For him, gusto entailed a "double relish," including direct gustatory sensation and its secondary, reflective pleasures.

Sometime during his reading and annotation of *Paradise Lost,* Keats adapted Hazlitt's Miltonic paradigm of pouncing on, grappling with, and relishing the world of aesthetic pleasure to his own allegory of taste: "Milton in every instance pursues his imagination to the utmost — he is 'sagacious of his Quarry' . . . he sees Beauty on the wing, pounces upon it and gorges it to the producing his essential verse" (*KPL* 14).[8] Even more explicitly than Hazlitt, Keats puts into allegorical form the symbolic economy of consumption that defines taste: the consumer takes in beauty metaphorically through the mouth and processes it back into expression. What Keats shared with Hazlitt perhaps above all was an emphasis on *gusto* as central to the creative process, and both portray the poet as a ravener. For Keats, "A Man's life of any worth is a continual allegory," his foremost example being Shakespeare, who "led a life of Allegory; his works are the comments on it" (*KL* 2:67). To Keats, "a life of Allegory" meant "a life like the scriptures, figurative" in which existence is elevated above phenomenal reality (*KL* 2:67). He viewed allegory in much the same way that Coleridge viewed symbol, as a manner of projecting the self into vital-material, or "translucent," form.[9] The poet who pounces and gorges upon beauty, converting it into essential verse, elevates his existence over that of "The greater part of Men [who] make their way with the same instinctiveness, the same unwandering eye from their purposes, the same animal eagerness as the Hawk" (*KL* 2:79). Yet, as his comment makes clear, knowledge of a predatory food chain symbolically drives Keats's allegory of taste.

The marginalia in Keats's edition of *Paradise Lost* that contains his allegory of pouncing and gorging on beauty is scrawled around the margins enclosing a passage from the creation of book 7 in which Raphael describes a sea of hungry generation. Keats underscores lines that suggest a harmless, herbivorous world of "fry innumerable," who scavenge the waters for "Moist nutriment" (*PL* 7.401, 408; *KPL* 141). But these innocent appetites soon give way to a more savage cycle of feeding, as the epic perspective pulls back to reveal predatory birds who hover above these fish in the sea (*PL* 7.423–24; *KPL* 142). As he was nursing his brother Tom through the final stages of tuberculosis, Keats wrote to his sick friend John Reynolds of a "sea; where every maw / The greater on the less feeds evermore: / . . . the core / Of an eternal fierce destruction" (*KL* 1:262). W. J. Bate suggests that this image represents "the huge hungry diversity of life, for which the heart, with its simple presuppositions, is so unprepared," but Keats's heart has already been prepared (if his reading of *Paradise Lost* is any indication) to recognize a predatory hunger lurking beneath the very surface of creation.[10]

Shortly after his Miltonic marginalia above, Keats compared his own creative process to the pouncing (or swooping) activity of a predator bird. Writing again to Reynolds on May 3, 1818, he joked that "like the Gull I may *dip* [crosswise across the page] — I hope, not out of sight — and also, like a Gull, I hope to be lucky in a good sized fish" (*KL* 1:280). From this playful analogy, he turned to Wordsworth and the question of whether he "is an eagle in his nest, or on the wing" (*KL* 1:280). Presumably, the elder poet would be admired for his ability to take wing, to grapple with and exhaust his subject just as Keats does his "good fish." To his brother and sister-in-law, George and Georgiana Keats, he remarked that if each predatory creature were to halt its ravenous pursuit, "the Hawk would loose his Breakfast of Robins and the Robin his of Worms" (*KL* 2:79). There can be no escape from this eternal cycle of fierce destruction: "The shark at savage prey — the hawk at pounce, / The gentle Robin, like a pard or ounce, / Ravening a worm" (*KL* 1:262). While the predatory pursuit of most people merely extends their condition of embodiment, the kind of gorging that Keats describes in his allegory of taste allows the poet to sublimate his identity into that of the "poetical character."

However, what often goes unremarked in Keats's model of pouncing and gorging on beauty is that in *Paradise Lost* it is not Milton (nor his epic narrator) who is "sagacious of his Quarry" but the allegorical figure of Death. In his edition of the poem, Keats underscored the lines in which Death "Grinn'd horrible a ghastly smile, to hear / His famine should be fill'd, and blest his maw / Destin'd to that good hour" (*PL* 2.846–48; *KPL* 41). His fascination with the hungry creature comes to a peak later in book 10 when, again in lines Keats underlines, Death anticipates the mortal feast spreading out before him and "upturn'd / His nostril wide into the murky air / Sagacious of his quarry from so far" (*PL* 10.280–81; *KPL* 162). Sagacious was a hunting term for the pouncing creature's acute sense of smell. In Milton's analogy, therefore, Death is sagacious "As when a flock / Of ravenous fowl . . . come flying, lur'd / With scent of living Carcasses" (*PL* 10.273–77). Like the sense of taste, smell has always been tied to the physicality that keeps humans on a level with animals.

But since olfactory perception is essential to the discrimination of flavors, it can also elevate one above the animal pleasures of eating to the aesthetic level of the gastronome or gourmet. Complete gustatory taste involves smell, and Milton's Death is, in Byron's words, a "Gaunt gourmand" (*DJ* 15.9.5). Far from the indiscriminate, distasteful glutton, the "gourmand" by the time Byron used this term had come full circle to mean epicurean connoisseur, or gastronomical Man of Taste. Romantic gastronomers worked to "separate gourmandism from voracity and gluttony," as Brillat-Savarin writes, and "to separate from this social grace, once and for all, the gluttony and intemperance with which it has for so long and so unfortunately been linked" (*PT* 301, 343). In his *Culinary Chemistry* (1821), Frederick Accum outlines "a popular view of the philosophy of cookery" when he asserts "that there exists a material difference between a *gourmand,* or epicure, and a *glutton.* The first seeks for peculiar delicacy and distinct flavour in the various dishes presented to the judgment and enjoyment of his discerning palate; while the other . . . looks merely to quantity."[11] For Milton, Death is a glutton, or embodiment of indiscriminate hunger, though by the fifteenth canto of Byron's poem he has become a Romantic seeker of gusto, following his nose through the flavors surrounding him.

Also written in 1819, during the same fruitful spring as the Great Odes, "La Belle Dame sans Merci" is Keats's ballad on taste. The ballad is set in the same luscious, overripe world as the odes are, but with a difference. Compare Keats's "Ode on Melancholy," in the final two stanzas of which there is, in Leon Waldoff's words, "a richer concentration of gustatory and ingestive imagery . . . than in any of the other odes or, for that matter, in most of Keats's poems."[12] After being urged to "glut" his sorrow on "a morning rose" and to gorge deeply upon his beloved ("feed deep, deep upon her peerless eyes"), the reader is treated to a grand display of gusto by the poet, whose "strenuous tongue" in the climactic moment of the poem "burst[s] Joy's grape against his palate fine" (27–28). David Perkins remarks that this is a speaker who "would not sip but glut, and the phrase 'deep, deep' lengthens out the feeding."[13] For Helen Vendler, the poem represents Keats's "ode on the sense of taste," describing a "world of violently taken pleasure."[14] Marjorie Levinson, by contrast, finds the phrase "burst Joy's grape" metonymic for an unnaturally restricted gratification: whereas "the verbal joy of grapes is . . . the pleasure of fullness and plurality: clusters, bunches, all those engorged sounds," she claims. "The complete Keatsian pleasure (revealingly, a melancholic delight) consists of a single grape not swallowed."[15] Whether Keats's "Ode on Melancholy" illustrates a vigorous, successful taste experience à la Vendler, or a dysfunctional inability to consume à la Levinson, its memorable displays of gustatory taste are recognized as an analogue for aesthetic enjoyment. Just as the "Ode on Indolence" is "Ripe [with] the drowsy hour" and "To Autumn" is filled "with ripeness to the core," Keats's ballad on taste is ripely harvested too: "The squirrel's granary is full, / And the harvest's done" ("La Belle Dame"). But when viewed through the hungry eyes of his ailing knight in this poem, the world appears as a blighted "Autumn."

The knight is physically wasting away for no explained reason, though seemingly for lack of proper nutrition. He has been given "roots of relish sweet," "honey wild," and "manna dew" by the mysterious "Belle Dame," and although we never see him eat this food within the poem, we assume that he has consumed it and that he is suffering some form of terminal food poisoning as a result. For most readers, the knight "has become addicted to what he can never again taste," as Bloom writes. "The question next becomes, what has he eaten, and who gave him to eat that he might become accursed?"[16] Bate defends the Belle Dame's culinary intentions (if not the quality of the food itself) from her adverse critics: "The food she finds for him — roots, 'honey wild and manna dew' — is meant neither to delude him nor to starve him by preventing him from taking other food. However inadequate it is for him, it is appropriate enough to her, and the only food she is able to provide."[17] I would go further and suggest that her intentions are not only innocent; they are irrelevant to his condition.

Just as the knight reads into the Belle Dame's words (which he could not understand, since they were spoken "in language strange") the message, "I love thee true," we read into his words when we assume that he actually eats the food he has been given. One question we would do well to ask, but which seems so antithetical to the spirit of the poem that we have not bothered to ask it, is whether the knight could have been ailing *before* he encountered the fairy maid and the ethereal food she provides. Critics have noticed that Porphyro's elaborate meal in "The Eve of St. Agnes," for example, never gets consumed, but here we presume, although we never see this food eaten either, that the food is not only consumed but is also wreaking havoc upon the withered frame of the knight.[18] This knight differs from the pining lover of *Endymion* (1817), for instance, who prior to becoming "Gaunt, wither'd, sapless, feeble, cramp'd, and lame" (3:638) at least gluts himself on "juicy pears," "blooming plums," and "cream, / Deepening to richness from a snowy gleam" within the poem (2.444–51). While the ailing knight of "La Belle Dame sans Merci" may eat between the lines of the poem, one never knows for certain whether any food has been consumed.

We do know that he is in no position to taste, appreciate, or ravage with gusto any of the pleasures offered to him. Jack Stillinger, in his notes to the standard collected edition of this poem, suggests a relation between the starving knight of "La Belle Dame sans Merci" and the allegorical knight of Addison's "Pleasures of the Imagination" (1712), to my knowledge through this trenchant connection has never been pursued. Addison's *Spectator* papers (411–21) were foundational texts for the eighteenth-century discourse of taste, works that Keats read prior to writing the ballad. His journal letter of April 1819 that contains the only existing manuscript version of the poem refers indirectly to Addison through Hazlitt. Specifically, he quotes Hazlitt's reply to William Gifford in the *Quarterly Review* of January 1818: "Is this a new theory of the Pleasures of the imagination, which says that the pleasures of the imagination do not take rise soly [*sic*] in the calculations of the understanding?" (*KL* 2:75). This was Hazlitt's way of implying that aesthetic experience, as a mental response to bodily sensation, involves more than rational cognition. Describing gusto, Hazlitt claims that "the impression made on one sense excites by affinity those of another" (*HCW* 4:78), and in paper no. 412 of the *Spectator* Addison establishes the foundation for this aesthetic concept: "if there arises a Fragrancy of Smells or Perfumes, they heighten the Pleasures of the Imagination, and make even the Colours and Verdure of the Landskip appear more agreeable; for the Ideas of both Senses recommend each other, and are pleasanter together than when they enter the Mind separately" (*SPT* 544). To relate Addison's knightly quester after beauty, whose imagination fails him in the midst of essay no. 413, with Keats's aimless poetical character, unable to pounce on anything with gusto, is to shift critical focus on the ballad from the femme fatale and her supposedly evil appetizers to the nauseated condition of the knight.

In paper no. 413, which Stillinger cites as a potential source for the ballad, Addison wonders why the Creator should have furnished human beings with secondary, reflective pleasures that are not immediate incentives to appetite. The question is one he inherits from Hobbes, who distinguished the "Pleasures of Sense" from the "Pleasures of the Mind." The former included both the direct, "sensual" pleasures of appetite (emptying and filling the belly) and the intermediate pleasures of "sense," of which "kind are all Onerations and Exonerations of the body; as also all that is pleasant, in the *Sight, Hearing, Smell, Tast, or Touch.*"[19] The "Pleasures of the Mind" were superadded to such sensory experience by the imagination. Like other philosophers in the British empirical tradition following him, Hobbes found that "any thing that is pleasure in the sense, the same also is pleasure in the imagination."[20] Addison's "Pleasures of the Imagination" also offered a version of mental taste approaching gusto insofar as it was rooted in the bodily pleasures of sense.

These pleasures surpassed mere animal enjoyment and distinguished humans from beasts, through not reason but aesthetic capacity. Addison's "disconsolate Knight," who suddenly finds himself in a world stripped of beauty, is left "on a barren Heath, or in a solitary Desart" (*SPT* 3:546–47). He loses the "pleasing Shows and Apparitions," the "imaginary Glories in the Heavens, and in the Earth" that give the material world its color, flavor, and three-dimensionality. The aesthetic pleasures of the imagination have a real existence for Addison, who wonders "what a rough unsightly Sketch of Nature should we be entertained with, did all her Colouring disappear, and the several Distinctions of Light and Shade vanish?" (*SPT* 3:546–47). Keats similarly asks in a letter of March 19, 1819, "is not giving up, through goodnature, one's time to people who have no light and shade a capital crime?" (*KL* 2:77). Like Addison's knight, disconsolate in the loss of imaginative pleasure, the knight in Keats's ballad on taste suffers because he can no longer take in the beauty surrounding him. It is entirely possible that he may have entered the ballad in this condition, a fevered condition that Hume assures us is no condition for a correct experiment of taste. When viewed as an interloper from Addison's colorless field of no taste, his sickness can be seen as an inability to relish the world as the true "poetical character" should.

Keats himself frames the ballad as an allegory of taste. Its title alludes to a medieval ballad of the same name, but the signature that accompanied the poem in Hunt's *Indicator* on May 10, 1820, was "Caviare," a name for a dainty dish designed to satisfy a "palate fine." Keats recognized in September of 1819 that his "name with the literary fashionables is vulgar" (*KL* 2:186), and in this context, substituting "Caviare" for his own "vulgar" name is (as Levinson argues) a defense against the criticism leveled at him for "that sugar & butter sentiment, that cloys & disgusts," as even Keats's friend Richard Woodhouse remarked of *Endymion* (*KC* 1:91).[21] "Junkets" was Hunt's nickname for Keats, meaning sweetmeats, cakes, or confections that provide untutored enjoyment for the young child to enjoy. But caviar is a passport into the more cultured world of gastronomical connoisseurs and palates fine. Framing the poem as a delicacy that is more sophisticated than the "mawkishness" offered up for public consumption in the preface to *Endymion*, Keats distances it from what he called "the mass [who] are not of soul to conceive ⟨of themselves⟩ or even to apprehend when presented to them, the truly & simply beautiful ⟨in⟩ poetry," since theirs is "A taste vitiated by the sweetmeats & kickshaws" of the age (*KL* 1:381). By 1819, he had gained the critical distance necessary not only to parody "Junkets" with the more knowing "Caviare" but also to complain of "Men like Hunt who from a principle of taste [*only*, it is implied] would like to see things go on better" (*KL* 1:396). Hunt's aesthetic principles had worn thin on a poet for whom beauty was no mere superfluous gratification but a vital source of sustenance in a world growing bleak and barren of hope.

Hyperion's "Ample Palate"

The Keatsian "poetical character" wanders through his ballad on taste in a sickened condition, too hungry to wrestle a "double relish" from any of the objects he perceives, and in the epic world of *Hyperion,* his experience sours further into the philosophical condition of nausea. Readers often wonder why Keats should have entitled his epic *Hyperion* rather than, say, "Apollo," when it is the latter who is the ascendant god, the ostensible poet, and the figure who presumably transforms into the human speaker of *The Fall of Hyperion.* Stuart Sperry suggests that Keats "was in different ways committed to both deities at once, that they were projections of conflicting sides of his own poetic nature he could not as yet resolve."[22] True, neither Hyperion nor Apollo provides a viable paradigm of the poet for Keats, but I do not believe that the two fragments of the poem constitute a progression, or in Sperry's words, "the purgation of the unstable, tormented existence he in many ways detested and the birth of the secure, serene type of creator he desired to become."[23] The "unstable, tormented existence" of Keats's "poetical character" is embodied by *all* the gods in *Hyperion,* and in *The Fall of Hyperion* it struggles forward in human form. As the first-person speaker of Keats's final epic fragment drags himself forward through various agonies of the flesh — in order, we are told, to avoid encroaching starvation — he seems to be running from the nausea afflicting all the oversized gods of *Hyperion,* emblems of his own existence writ large.

In *Hyperion,* when we first encounter the epic hero, he is in the act of attempting to taste (or snuff, a synaesthesia we'll return to in a moment) the world as the "poetical character" should. As the central brooding figure of the poem's "mammoth-brood" (1.164), he recalls Milton's brooding Spirit of Creation (*PL* 7.235–39) and Wordsworth's revision of this figure as a feeding mind "that broods / Over the dark abyss" (*Prelude* 14.71–72). Likewise an epic emblem of creation for Keats, the brooding Hyperion sits crouched over, attempting to relish the smells drifting up to him from the world below:

> Blazing Hyperion on his orbed fire
> Still sat, still snuff'd the incense, teeming up
> From man to the sun's God; yet unsecure.... (1.166–68)

In this description of Hyperion, Andrew Bennett points out, the function of the repeated "still" ("Still sat, still snuff'd") is unclear; it "presupposes a former reference which is unavailable to the reader — an anterior disnarrated — so that the sense of stillness or silence is produced through narrative absence."[24] When referred back through the literary history of taste to the "Sagacious" creature of *Paradise Lost,* however, Hyperion is still sitting, still snuffing the smell of "mortal change" on earth like the ravenous figure inscribed as poet into Keats's allegory of taste. As we have seen, Keats allegorizes the poet as a ravenous pursuer of beauty, after Milton's figure of Death. In a line Keats marked in his copy of *Paradise Lost,* Death, sensing the mortal feast spreading out before him, "snuff'd the smell / Of mortal change on Earth" (*PL* 10.272–73; *KPL* 40).

Of course, as philosophers then as now have recognized, snuffing is a form of gustatory taste. Smell and taste are linked as the two most bodily hence primitive senses, and Keats notes the intimate connection between them in his anatomical and physiological notebook from his school years at Guy's Hospital in London: "The different sensations reside in peculiar structures as the toes & fingers which have papillae through which the sense of feeling — the papillae of the Tongue are different from those of the Toes & fingers & are larger — the papillae of the Membrane of the nose are very minute & sensitive."[25] The term *papillae* is still in use today, though not all of these small observable bumps are sense receptors. Taste buds, microscopic cells housed by the hundreds within a single papilla, were not discovered as the actual taste receptors until 1867. Of the four distinct kinds of papillae (fungiform, foliate, circumvallate, and filiform), all but the filiform contain taste buds.[26] In the early nineteenth century, as Keats records, physiologists considered the papillae to be the bodily receptors of taste, smell, and touch, observing that they were "very minute & sensitive" on the nose, and much larger and coarser on the tongue.

The English physiologist John Hunter (1728–93), whose lessons Keats imbibed, ranked smell above taste after the higher senses of sight and hearing: "This sense has a degree of refinement above taste; and . . . I am inclined to think that we can in some measure judge of the taste of a body from the smell, and *vice versa*."[27] The German Romantic physiologist J. G. Spurzheim reported that "some physiologists regard smell as a completion or a finer and higher degree of taste."[28] In his 1826 *Physiology of Taste*, Brillat-Savarin went so far as to assert that "smell and taste form a single sense, of which the mouth is the laboratory and the nose is the chimney; or, to speak more exactly, of which one serves for the tasting of actual bodies and the other for the savoring of their gases" (*PT* 39). In the Romantic era, snuffing was considered a version of tasting; Hegel in his *Philosophy of Nature* claimed that taste and smell "are very closely allied and in Swabia not distinguished, so that there one has only four senses. For one says, 'The flower tastes good,' instead of 'It smells good';

we Swabians therefore smell, as it were, with the tongue too, so that the nose is superfluous" (*PN* 2:217).

Eighteen lines after Hyperion snuffs the incense drifting up from the mortal world, the scene suddenly recurs in a manner that explicitly confuses taste with smell:

> Also, when he would taste the spicy wreaths
> Of incense, breath'd aloft from sacred hills,
> Instead of sweets, his ample palate took
> Savour of poisonous brass and metal sick. . . . (1.186–89)

If this passage is metonymic for the whole of the poem, as Bloom keenly suggests, then Hyperion's snuffing (or rather, his frustrated efforts to snuff) represents a sustained effort at creative self-expression that strains past the bounds of the first *Hyperion* and into the second, where the speaker's first task is to taste.[29] Whereas sight and hearing were oriented toward the external world and its objects of perception, the bodily senses were thought to say more about the perceiving subject. Kant stressed the physical intimacy of taste and smell in his *Anthropology,* both senses that he considered "chemical" (as opposed to "mechanical") and "subjective" rather "objective" (*AN* 44–45). In 1787 J. F. Blumenbach, an important influence on Kant and mediator between British and German physiology, also remarked that taste and smell "have been generally named chemical or subjective senses."[30]

Of the two "subjective senses," smell was thought to be more sensitive to negative tastes than to pleasure, hence the feeling of disgust. Scientists speculated that in order to be perceived, an odor must physically detach itself from the object and invade the perceptive organs of the subject. Plato had it right in *Timaeus* when he wrote that "smells are of a half-formed nature" and "always proceed from bodies that are damp, or putrefying, or liquefying, or evaporating, and are perceptible only in the intermediate state, when water is changing into air and air into water, and all of them are either vapor or mist" (*CDP* 1190).[31] Odors do generally proceed from organic rather than inorganic substances and are given off by a chemical change in a body. Natural philosophers like Spurzheim could, therefore, conclude that smell was the only unmediated sensation: "smell in its immediate functions perceives odorous particles emanating from external bodies, without any reference to the object."[32] By invoking smell as a means of tasting and relishing the world in *Hyperion,* Keats predisposes his epic hero to disgust far more than to pleasure.[33]

The experience of disgust involves agency and a sense of subjective violation. As Kant reasons, "when confronted with many dishes and bottles, one can choose that which suits his pleasure without forcing others to participate in that pleasure"; on the other hand, "Smell is, so to speak, taste at a distance, and other people are forced to share a scent whether they want to or not" (*AN* 45). The obtrusive nature of smell returns to disturb him in *The Critique of Judgment,* where he takes up the problem of the scented handkerchief. Even the sweet smell of perfume can be a source of disgust, especially in a crowd where it is forced, as it were, upon us: "the man who pulls out his perfumed handkerchief from his pocket gives a treat to all around whether they like it or not, and compels them, if they want to breathe at all, to be parties to the enjoyment, and so the habit has gone out of fashion" (*CJ* 196). Elsewhere, Kant speaks of that "strange sensation" that occurs when "the object is represented as insisting, as it were, upon our enjoying it, while we still set our face against it" (*CJ* 174). Derrida remarks of this insistent, repulsive aesthetic object: "By limitlessly violating our enjoyment, without granting it any determining limit, it abolishes representative distance. . . . It irresistibly forces one to consume, but without allowing any chance for idealisation."[34] Smell in its sensual invasiveness left little room for idealization. Given its acuteness of perception, the result was often not pleasure but nausea.

In *Hyperion* the point is precisely that when Hyperion "*would* taste" the incense sweet, the "Savour of poisonous brass and metal sick" forces itself upon his otherwise capacious palate, inducing a sense of sickness. As Kant explains, when pleasure "is forced upon us, the mind finds it repugnant and it ceases to be nutritive as food for the intellect. . . . Thus the natural instinct to be free of it is by analogy called nausea" (*AN* 45). By the same token, and to a far worse degree, objects calculated not to please but disgust "awaken nausea less through what is repulsive to eye and tongue than through the stench associated with it . . . *this sense can pick up more objects of aversion than of pleasure*" (*AN* 45–46; my emphasis). Snuffing the smells from the mortal world, Hyperion is particularly vulnerable not to pleasure so much as disgust. The only existing holograph of *Hyperion* reveals that the line "Savour of poisonous brass and metal sick" did not originally begin with "Savour," or taste proper, but instead with "A nausea."[35] As Jonathan Bate narrates Keats's process of revision, " 'A nausea,' he begins. 'A nauseous feel,' he then tries, but 'feel' is heavily crossed out, perhaps because it smacked of Leigh Huntism. 'Poison' then replaces 'nauseous' and 'feel' has to be reinstated: the line thus becomes 'A poison feel of brass and metals sick.' . . . But when the manuscript is adapted for *The Fall of Hyperion,* Keats again rejects 'feel,' so that in the new poem the line becomes 'Savour of poisonous brass and metals sick' " (2, 33).[36] Keats's revisions indicate that he struggled with the line describing Hyperion's response to the smell, but perhaps not "in an attempt to convey the sickly sweet smell of incense," as Bate suggests. The incense may be sweet, but there is nothing to indicate that it is excessively or "sickly" sweet. And according to the grammar, it is the metal — not the incense — that is sick.

The only other time the word *metal* appears in Keats's poetry is in the description of the other fallen gods of *Hyperion* — and here too it is productive of sickness. At the start of book 2, Hyperion's fellow Titans are introduced in a similar crouched position:

> Their clenched teeth still clench'd, and all their limbs
> Lock'd up like veins of metal, crampt and screw'd;
> Without a motion, save of their big hearts
> Heaving in pain, and horribly convuls'd
> With sanguine feverous boiling gurge of pulse. (2.24–27)

The grammatically dubious "still" makes another appearance in these lines, mediating between the adverbial perpetuity of the god's suffering and the adjectival stillness of the scene. Their "clenched teeth still clench'd" convey their sense of being cabined, cribbed, confined — or "clench'd," "crampt, and screw'd" in metal. As Hyperion sits and snuffs the metallic fumes from the world below, he too seems merely in an earlier stage of having all his limbs "Lock'd up like veins of metal." Indeed, as Keats was working on *Hyperion,* he was himself familiar with the poisonous taste of metal, for he was consuming it in prescribed portions of mercury.

Writing to Benjamin Bailey in October 1817, Keats records that as a result of having taken mercury he has "corrected the Poison and improved my Health" (*KL* 1:171). There is some debate among Keats's biographers about whether he took mercury during 1817 and 1818 as a remedy for syphilis (Aileen Ward), or gonorrhea (Robert Gittings), or a different ailment entirely (for example, Douglas Bush).[37] In the early decades of the nineteenth century, mercury was widely prescribed as a treatment for venereal disease, itself considered a morbid poison. Hunter explains that "The Venereal Disease arises from a poison, which, as it is produced by disease, and is capable of again producing a similar disease, I call a morbid poison, to distinguish it from the other poisons, animal, vegetable, and mineral."[38] The French physiologist M. J. B. Orfila lists six classes of animal and mineral poisons in *A General System of Toxicology* (1814), a text available to Keats at Guy's Hospital, as Hermione de Almeida points out, and two are relevant here: the corrosive poisons, such as copper, brass, tin, and zinc, which irritate and corrode the organs; and the narcotico-acrid poisons, such as mercury, which stupefy, paralyze, convulse, and cause a red or (as Keats writes above) "sanguine feverous" color.[39] When Keats writes to Bailey that he has "corrected the Poison" and improved his health by consuming mercury, he effectively substitutes a metallic for a morbid poison.

In addition to producing pains like those of rheumatism and locking up the veins like metal, this particular "metal sick" *blocked the ability to taste.* Hunter cautions that attention must be given to the patient's diet, for "the local effects of the medicine, in the mouth, preven[t] his taking many kinds of nourishment, especially such as are of a solid form, fluids must form his only nourishment." As a remedy for "Venereal Poison," mercury primarily afflicted the mouth but also the rest of the digestive tract. Hunter records that it "produces very disagreeable effects upon the stomach and intestines, causing sickness in the one, and griping and purging in the other."[40] As an antidote to the morbid poison of venereal disease, it caused hunger and a constant state of anxiety. Roughly a year after his letter to Bailey, Keats records: "I live now in a continual fever — it must be poisonous to life although I feel well . . . after all it may be a nervousness proceeding from the Mercury" (*KL* 1:369). When Hyperion snuffs the "metal sick," he too is "unsecure," his "horrors, portion'd to a giant nerve" (*Hyperion* 1.175). If his nervous, and possibly feverous, shudderings resemble the nervousness proceeding from mercury, as Keats speculates with regard to himself, then the poisonous metal he consumes turns taste into the "nauseous feel" of existence.

Anxious, nauseated, and "unsecure," Hyperion is one of the first philosophically "absurd" creatures in literature, a statement that can be made of the other fallen gods.[41] Saturn's behavior, for instance, is typical of one who has failed to allegorize his existing self through taste and so lapsed into "the horror or absurdity of existence" (to borrow Nietzsche's phrase). Faced with an existence that cannot be palated, an existentialist reasoning suggests that the best thing to do is to commit oneself to action in an arbitrary way. Accordingly, when Saturn wakes up from his cramped, stupefied condition in *The Fall of Hyperion,* he calls upon his fellow gods to lament. Then, for no apparent reason (and within the space of a single line), he calls on them to rebel. His extended Lear-like lament, "Moan, brethren, moan" (1.412), "Moan, brethren, moan" (1.418), "Moan, moan, / Moan, Cybele, moan" (1.424–25), "Moan, brethren, moan" (1.427), concludes:

> O, O, the pain, the pain of feebleness.
> Moan, moan; for still I thaw — or give me help:
> Throw down those imps and give me victory. (1.429–31)

After Saturn's extended moaning, the sudden shift in the middle line above indicates a quintessentially existentialist attitude. He senses that all action, whether moaning or fighting, is absurd in that it is meaningless. He seems to have experienced the same "metal sick" that nauseates Hyperion, for he too is clenched and "crampt." When de Almeida discusses the potential effects of mineral poisoning upon the gods of *Hyperion,* she tellingly assumes that it is Saturn, not Hyperion, who is doing the snuffing, for viewed in light of Keats's allegory of taste *all* the "metal-veined" gods are absurd.[42]

Keats's advice to Shelley of August 16, 1820, to "load every rift" of his subject with "ore" (metal, especially precious metal) may thus bear retrospectively upon a poem in which he seems to have taken his own advice literally. "A modern work it is said must have a purpose," Keats complains, "which may be the God — *an artist* must serve Mammon — he must have 'self-concentration' selfishness perhaps. You I am sure will forgive me for sincerely remarking that you might curb your magnanimity and be more of an artist, and 'load every rift' of your subject with ore" (*KL* 2:322–23). In the episode of *The Faerie Queene* to which Keats refers, Spenser describes the Cave of Mammon where "rich metall loaded every rifte" (2.7.28). There is a degree of bitterness in his tone (Shelley, he believed, condescended to him as Coleridge had done to Lamb), but his statement acknowledges the necessity of an artistic mettle associated with the selfish principle of Mammon. Selflessness was the essence of the "poetical character" for Keats, who admitted that he was himself "not old enough or magnanimous enough to annihilate self" (*KL* 1:292). To curb one's magnanimity was to curb one's dissolution into the "unpoetical . . . no Identity" of the chameleon poet, and thereby to experience the metallic aftertaste of existence. W. J. Bate suggests that Keats's *Hyperion* poems "anticipate much that we associate with existentialism," and this casual association deserves closer analysis, since what Keats discovers in *Hyperion* is that existentialism's roots lie in a discourse where nausea plays a philosophical role, namely, the discourse of taste.[43]

The Keatsian poet who "lives in gusto" lives in world of consuming orality: he pounces upon, gorges, and digests beauty into essential verse. Everything in this restricted cycle of consumption circulates through the mouth, the portal through which one passes from appetite into expression, from leaden existence into aesthetic identity. But to be a chameleon poet feeding on air was rapidly becoming an impossibility for a starving poet. Having spent his annus mirabilis writing against the threat of hunger, Keats concludes within weeks (even days) of the above letter to Shelley: "The last two years taste like brass upon my Palate" (*KL* 2:312). The final inheritance of the chameleon poet who "lives in gusto" is nausea, and in *The Fall of Hyperion* Hyperion's nausea becomes the experience of the human speaker. In a world deprived of all hope of redemption, aesthetic or otherwise, all one needs is the will to go on, to move forward through randomly directed spurts, and in this the speaker of *The Fall of Hyperion* succeeds where the gods of *Hyperion* fail: he finds the will to drag himself toward inevitable doom. He seems to know the desperate truth that feeling nauseated (the "nauseous feel" of his own existence) is better than feeling nothing at all.[44]

Striving to Escape the Nausea

After witnessing the sickness numbing the all gods of *Hyperion,* including Apollo, who complains that "a melancholy numbs my limbs" (3.89), the speaker of *The Fall of Hyperion* considers numbness a condition to be struggled *against.* Unlike the drugged Coleridgean poet of "Kubla Khan," to which this poem has been compared, Keats's human speaker makes it clear that the substance he consumes at its outset is "No Asian poppy, nor elixir fine" (1.47). He seems determined to pull himself out of a numbed existence and into a condition of greater sensibility to pleasure and pain. In the spring of 1819, between the two *Hyperion*s, Keats described a numbed experience in which "pleasure has no show of enticement and pain no unbearable frown" (*KL* 2:78–79). In a letter to the George Keatses, which serves as the working draft for Keats's "Ode on Indolence," he versifies this same condition as follows: "Benumb'd my eyes; my pulse grew less and less / Pain had no sting, and pleasure's wreath no flower" (17–18). Like most of Keats's poetic personae, the speaker of *The Fall of Hyperion* does not experience "the pain alone; the joy alone; distinct" (1.174), and thus for him also, where pain has no sting pleasure's wreath has no flower. Donald Goellnicht points out that the botanist William Salisbury, with whom Keats studied in the spring of 1816, describes the aftereffects of opium as "a degree of nausea, a difficulty of respiration, lowness of the spirits, and a weak languid pulse."[45] Long before he ever sought refuge in the "cursed bottle of Opium," which Severn snatched from him three months before his death, Keats's own experience had familiarized him with the nauseating effects of this "Asian poppy" (*KL* 2:372). His speaker's attempt "to escape / The numbness" (1.127) in *The Fall of Hyperion* is an attempt to escape the nausea of an absurd, because aesthetically insensible, existence.

After a hallucinatory induction on the nature of dreams, he wakes up to what at first seems to be a Miltonic invitation to gorge. But upon closer inspection, the banquet he stumbles onto at the start of the poem turns out to be the remains of an already ravished feast:

> a feast of summer fruits,
> Which, nearer seen, seem'd refuse of a meal
> By angel tasted, or our mother Eve;
> For empty shells were scattered on the grass,
> And grape stalks but half bare, and remnants more. (1.29–33)

Keats heavily marked Milton's description of the meal in book 5 of *Paradise Lost* as well as Raphael's effusions upon the joys of angelic eating (*KPL* 40). The "empty shells" and "grape stalks" in the lines above seem directly descended from the "smooth rind, or bearded husk, or shell" that Eve gathers with unsparing hand (*PL* 5.342). Critics as diverse as Bate, Bloom, and Levinson have read this scene as an allegory of poetic belatedness, the remnants of an "apparently interrupted meal" left over from Milton. Yet instead of paradisiacal food, Keats's sickened speaker finds "refuse"; instead of remnant grapes, only picked-over "grape stalks."

Originally, Keats had turned to *Hyperion* and the epic struggle of the gods as a refuge from the sufferings of his brother Tom, whom he was nursing through the advanced stages of tuberculosis. Experience had taught him that vegetable food was commonly prescribed for the consumptive patient, and it is likely that he felt himself threatened by the disease the entire time he was working on *Hyperion*.[46] His medical training would have enabled him to predict that before long he too would be "under an interdict with respect to animal food [and] living upon pseudo victuals" (*KL* 2:271). By October 1819 he had in fact "left off animal food" (*KL* 2:225). The vegetable scraps (or "pseudo victuals") in the lines above seem hardly sufficient for a poet who wanted to gorge on the red-blooded beauty of life. He seems to face a fear that can be traced back to *Endymion,* where the hero's "fever parches up my tongue" (2.319); through "Ode on a Grecian Urn," whose represented passions mirror the poet's "parching tongue" (29); to *The Fall of Hyperion,* where even the fires are "fainting for sweet food" (1.233). Fever was thought to be an early sign of consumption, and it is a constant preoccupation in Keats's letters contemporaneous with the poem. Once he enters the epic world of *The Fall of Hyperion* as its starving first-person speaker, he has already become a mere "fever of [him]self" (1.169). He appears to be wasting away like the ailing knight of "La Belle Dame sans Merci," and immediately following the feast above he is warned that if he does not keep moving, his flesh "Will parch for lack of nutriment" (1.110).

Unlike the knight of Keats's ballad, however, this speaker seems determined to avoid giving into the nauseous taste of existence and to live through the allegory of taste defined by Keats. He digs into the refuse before him with "appetite / More yearning than on earth [he] ever felt" (1.38–39), gorging in the manner that is supposed to produce essential verse. Once he has eaten the vegetable scraps, he quaffs a "transparent juice" and proclaims: "That full draught is parent of my theme" (1.42–46). Keats had not forgotten the ad hominem attack on him in *Blackwood's Magazine* where "Z" (John Gibson

Lockhart), reviewing *Endymion* in August 1818, had gibed: "Whether Mr John had been sent home with a diuretic or composing draught to some patient far gone in the poetical mania, we have not heard. This much is certain, that he has caught the infection, and that thoroughly."[47] Whether we can associate Lockhart's "composing draught" with the "full draught" that prompts the composition of *The Fall of Hyperion,* its consumption is productive of verse and suited to the Keatsian purpose of allegorizing taste.

The marginal gloss containing Keats's allegory of taste in *Paradise Lost* embellishes the poet's ravenous pursuit of gusto by adding that "in no instance is this sort of perseverance more exemplified than in what may be called his *stationing or statu[a]ry:* He is not content with simple description, he must station" (*KPL* 142). Relics of the kind of statuary described in his sonnet "On Seeing the Elgin Marbles" (1817), the gods of *Hyperion* appear as "sculpture builded up upon the grave / Of their own power" (*Fall* 1.383–84). The first-person speaker of this early sonnet senses that he must die "Like a sick eagle looking at the sky," and by the time he reaches the diseased world of *The Fall of Hyperion,* the entire "eagle brood" (2.13) seem to suffer "an immortal sickness" (1.258). As the speaker looks into the goddess Moneta's mind, or "sullen entrails rich with ore" (1.274), he finds himself in a realm of poisoned stasis. This is the same valley of existential sickness that has trapped the other fallen gods, who reappear in the same tortured postures that they had held in *Hyperion.* The speaker himself succumbs to the statuesque numbness he had been striving to avoid, and he is left "gasping with despair / Of change" (1.398–99).

Eventually, one begins to wonder whether all this statuary, whether of metal or of marble, is not simply the reverse of a melting subjectivity as a response to the material obtuseness of existence. *Being and Nothingness* (1943) was a foundational text of French existentialism, and Christopher Ricks intuitively quotes from it in his discussion of Keatsian taste and distaste. In a section cited by Ricks, Sartre writes: "There is in the fact that we cannot grasp water a pitiless hardness which gives to it a secret sense of being *metal;* finally it is incompressible like steel."[48] As a defensive reaction against the slimy (for Sartre the repulsive sticky stuff of existence), the leaden figures of *Hyperion* are the obverse of a melting subjectivity. As we have seen, when Saturn awakes from his stupefied condition in *The Fall of Hyperion,* he moans that he is thawing. And like so many of Keats's dissolving personae, from Endymion to Lamia, Keats writes of himself on October 13, 1819: "I have a sensation at the present moment as though I was dissolving" (*KL* 2:223). This feeling continues through the following spring when he laments, "Feeding upon sham victuals and sitting by the fire will completely annul me. I have no need of an enchanted wax figure to duplicate me for I am melting in my proper person" (*KL* 2:286). Such liquefaction is poignantly registered in the bitter words of his own epitaph, "here lies one whose name was writ in water." In the end, the image of Keats as "a schoolboy . . . / With face and nose pressed to a sweet-shop window" (from Yeats's "Ego Dominus Tuus") is more apt than we may have acknowledged. Looking out with Yeats at the boy with face and nose pressed up against the sweetshop window, we confront the reality of what Levinson calls "the embarrassingly squashed nose."[49] This squashed nose (and face, since both are pressed against glass) is metonymic for a breakdown of form, a disintegration that plays itself out on the hungry body of the poet.

Ultimately both extremes, whether the subjective rigor mortis of poisonous metal or a dissolving subjectivity, represent defenses against an existentialist nausea. While the fallen Titans are too "clenched" in the concentration of selfhood, Apollo is too "magnanimous" to sustain being within the space of the poem. Just as Hyperion snuffs, and the human speaker of *The Fall of Hyperion* drinks a "transparent juice," Apollo imbibes a "bright elixir peerless" (3.129) that causes his limbs to become "celestial" or nonmaterial, and the poem dissolves. Readers have recognized in this "bright elixir" the nature of the *pharmakon,* an ambiguous Greek word meaning either a healing or poisonous substance, since many drugs can be deadly in higher doses. It is derived from Apollo himself as the original Pharmakeus, god of medicine, pestilence, and poetry.[50] When Keats's Apollo drinks the strange potion in canto 3 of *Hyperion,* he undergoes a transformation that is either beneficent, malevolent, or both: "Soon wild commotions shook him, and made flush / All the immortal fairness of his limbs," as he struggles like those who "with fierce convulse / Die into life" (3.124–30). Similarly, when Hyperion snuffs the "Savour of poisonous brass and metal sick," it acts as a kind of *pharmakon* that causes him to die into a life reduced to existence.[51]

Whereas Apollo dissolves into celestial ethereality ("no Identity") at the end of the first *Hyperion,* Hyperion is annulled at the end of the second. The incomplete second canto of *The Fall of Hyperion* is imported virtually un-changed from book 1 of *Hyperion,* and here too Hyperion's "ample palate takes / Savour of brass and metals sick" (2.32–33). Hyperion is still sitting, still snuffing the same repugnant medley of smells from before ("Blazing Hyperion on his orbed fire / Still sits, still snuffs the incense teeming up / From man to the Sun's God" [2.15–17]), though the line "Still sits, still snuffs" is now in the present tense — closer, if possible, to a condition of self-concentrated stasis. The poem's final words, "on he flared," deliver this "large limb'd" Titan in one apocalyptic blast from our view. Keats's aesthetic allegory of consuming and expressing beauty finally will not sustain the poet, whose end is registered in these two poetic extremes. In classical mythology, the two sun gods are not analogous, since Hyperion lacks Apollo's status as god of poetry, but in Keats's poem they are complementary figures. Both are transient occupants in an aesthetic allegory in which the greater on the lesser feeds evermore, and neither finally provides a viable paradigm of the "poetical character" for the hungry poet.

According to Keats, "Hyperion" was abandoned because the weight of Milton's language was too heavy to bear: "I have given up Hyperion," he told Reynolds, "there were too many Miltonic inversions in it"; and to the George Keatses he wrote: "I have but lately stood on my guard against Milton. Life to him would be death to me."[52] As a result of these pronouncements, we tend to read the meal in *The Fall of Hyperion* as a sickening oversaturation of poetic tradition. But Keats was becoming too ill to compose on epic proportions — to pounce, digest, and express beauty with gusto — and the Miltonic legacy was too heavy in ways extending past diction.[53] I am not the first to suspect that when *The Fall of Hyperion* was abandoned, "the reason may have been simply that the complex process it dramatized was being transferred from the poem to its author's literary biography."[54] As Robert Gittings remarks, "The last few months left to Keats, though barren of poetry, a time when he felt he had lost his vocation for ever, have nevertheless a living poetry of their own."[55] I do not intend (nor do I imagine does Gittings) this "living poetry" as a romanticization of dying from tuberculosis. Keats lived through the physical atrocities of the disease first with his mother, then with his brother, and he would not have endorsed the view that (in Susan Sontag's words) "It was glamorous to look sickly."[56] Rather, the "living poetry" of his final months is an extension of the "posthumous life" begun in *The Fall of Hyperion*, when the speaker wakes up nauseated from his leftover meal into an existence from which he has no hope of transcendence (*KL* 2:378).

Even among the highly mythologized Romantic poets, Keats is virtually unique in the fact that the details of his physical disintegration, the "ghastly wasting-away of his body and extremities" documented in painful detail in the journal letters of Severn, form an appendix (if not a more vital appendage) to his literary corpus. If not *The Fall of Hyperion*, then certainly Keats's poetic corpus can be said to conclude with Keats himself. Just as Milton's God expels all dregs from the tasteful economy of his cosmic ontology; just as Enlightenment taste philosophers expel impurities from the tasteful self; just as Wordsworth expels all rude residues from his transcendentally feeding mind; and just as all these things wind up in an unconscious abyss of materiality, Keats describes an embodied, late-Romantic aesthetic writ large in the starving figure of the poet. "Too intense a Contemplation is not the Business of Flesh and

Blood; it must by the necessary Course of Things, in a little Time, let go its Hold, and fall into *Matter*," as Swift's narrator remarks in *The Mechanical Operation of the Spirit;* "a perfect Moral to the Story of that Philosopher, who, while his Thoughts and Eyes were fixed upon the *Constellations,* found himself seduced by his *lower Parts* into a *Ditch*" (*SPW* 189–90). If intimations of spirit can be easily "reduced" to matter and physical process, the ditch where we all eventually wind up is the receptacle of our original metaphysical "fall into *Matter*."[57] Keats's epic allegorization of taste results in the awareness that the attempt to relish the world with gusto may provide no escape from the unidealizable ditch of existence.

8

The Gastronome and the Snob: George IV

*In a necessary follow-up to the Revolution, a turn-about put fortunes
into new hands and the mind of all these nouveaux riches turned especially toward purely animal pleasures . . . their emotions are nothing
more than sensations, and their desires, appetites. They are properly
served by being given in several pages, in the guise of good food, the
means of getting the best for their appetites and money.*
— *Alexandre Balthazar Laurent Grimod de la Reynière,*
Almanach des gourmands *(1803–12)*

This literary history of taste concludes with a cultural figure of Regency
England, George Augustus Frederick of Hanover, Prince of Wales and later
George IV, whose image proliferated in verbal and visual satire of the Roman-
tic era through the Victorian. George Cruikshank caricatured him as *The
Prince of Whales* in 1812, and Charles Lamb, picking up the cetacean image
("Not a fatter fish than he / Flounders round the polar sea") found George
to be fitter for classification by "Buffon, Banks, or sage Linnaeus" than the
more nuanced social categories of tasteful distinction.[1] In his biography of
George in *The Four Georges* (1860), Thackeray condemned the prince's intemperance in the spheres of food, wine, and women at a time when gourmands and their sartorial counterparts—dandies—were attempting to in-

stitute an aristocracy of taste over the hereditary aristocracy of breeding, based on a more knowing code of consumer discrimination: better food, better serving dishes, better neckties, and so on. The everyday pleasures of taste, smell, and touch with their culturally unsavory relation to the physical body had always been lower on the social hierarchy than the fine arts, catering to sight and hearing. In the nineteenth century these senses became increasingly identified with the materialist sphere of consumerism, principally through fashion and gastronomy.

Middle-class ideals of moderation had upstaged aristocratic excess, but conspicuous consumption of consumer goods had become a paradoxically legitimate terrain for the exercise of taste.[2] While the aesthetic impulse was upward, away from the body toward the pleasures of the mind, gastronomical "professors" of taste in the early nineteenth century educated the public on the best "means of getting the best for their appetites and money," as Alexandre Balthazar Laurent Grimod de la Reynière writes in the epigraph above, excerpted from his *Almanach des gourmands* (1803–12), the founding text of Romantic gastronomical literature.[3] Addison may have compared the neo-classical Man of Taste to a connoisseur of tea, but this was simply by way of analogy, since his Man of Taste was really a man of aesthetic distinction in the arts. The nineteenth-century connoisseur, by contrast, was not restricted to the pleasures of the imagination alone, for as taste was increasingly expressed through choices of consumerism, it expanded to encompass all the arts, including the culinary. As representations of George IV later in the nineteenth century suggest, consumer culture ultimately challenges the philosophical hierarchy of the senses, and even philosophy itself, through a self-conscious mode of expression that takes place through the consumer objects — food, clothes, china — that fill the pages of Victorian fiction.

Gillray's Voluptuary

George's reputation held him to be better versed in sensual gratification than in the more culturally elevated pleasures of aesthetic appreciation. Steven Parissien informs us that in the 1780s George's favorite cook, Louis Weltje, served as his "gambling associate, drinking companion, political advisor, picture agent, arbiter of taste and Brighton estate agent"; moreover, until 1787 the French chef Guillaume Gaubert, "no more qualified than Weltje, supervised the interior decoration at Carlton House."[4] George relied on his head cooks as arbiters of taste, and perhaps not surprisingly, by the mid-1780s when the prince had moved into Carlton House it boasted new kitchens, food cellars, larders, and (on the French model of separating *officers of cuisine* from *officers of the mouth,* responsible for sweets), a new custom-designed pastry scullery, coffee pantry, and confectionery.[5] Joanna Richardson imagines a typical breakfast "he gives in the gardens of Carlton House in the early summer of 1784 . . . moving round the marquees, where two hundred and fifty guests are enjoying 'the finest fruits of the season, confectioneries [*sic*], ices, creams, and ornamental designs.' "[6] George's mode of *ancien-régime,* conspicuous consumption struck many contemporaries as singularly distasteful, especially in the midst of wartime privation in the 1790s.

James Gillray's popular 1792 caricature, "A Voluptuary under the horrors of Digestion," depicts George as Prince of Wales sprawled across a chair in his new residence at Carlton House (figure 5). George's belly bulges out of his waistcoat and britches, as the focal point of Gillray's image, a spherical swelling that recurs in circular patterns throughout the image, threatening all rectilinear containment. Behind him, a heraldic coat of arms in the form of a crossed knife and fork illustrates the political double entendre "Ich Dien" (I serve), and a portrait of Luigi Cornaro (1475–1566), the author of *Discorsi sulla vita sobria* (a treatise on longevity that advocated abstemiousness), depicts the bishop downing a good-sized glass of wine. To George's right are remnants of a large-limbed roast and empty decanters of port, to his left an overflowing chamber pot atop unpaid bills from the butcher, baker, and poulterer. The bloody, barbarous joint before him on the table looks as if it has been torn rather than carved from the carcass and partly devoured—a forerunner to the licked bones dangling from his plate and the edge of the table. Conveniently nearby, venereal prescriptions, such as Velnos Vegetable Syrup and Leakes Pills, stand ready at hand to alleviate the upsets of his notorious sexual appetites. Although lavish scenes of feasting like these had always been a hallmark of aristocracy, they seemed out of place in the 1790s, a time of sugar boycotts, tea revolutions, and changing economic standards that made moderation synonymous with the middle-class ideal of taste.

As specters of hunger and extravagant consumption haunted the "civilized" world, the middle ranks (whose fortunes varied with the market and who were always a step away from starvation or overindulgence) were pointedly determined to stay middle. The regulating code of manners was one way to restrain extremities of appetite, and Thackeray recalls with scandalized horror Gillray's image of George disregarding all table etiquette and picking his teeth with a fork: "We remember, in one of those ancient Gillray portfolios, a print which used to cause a sort of terror in us youthful spectators, and in which the Prince of Wales . . . was represented as sitting alone in a magnificent hall after a voluptuous meal, and using a great steel fork in the guise of a toothpick. Fancy the first young gentleman living employing such a weapon in such a way! The most elegant Prince of Europe engaged with a two-pronged iron fork — the heir of Britannia with a *bident!*" (*WMP* 23:491). Here Thackeray gives voice to a segment of the population for whom such behavior suggests a return to savage barbarity verging on a snobbish indifference to cultural codes and practices of self-containment. Elias has shown how in the course of the civiliz-ing process the fork emerged as "the first authority in our decision between 'civilized' and 'uncivilized' behavior at table," insofar as it limited the role of the body in the social sphere of commensality: "The fork is nothing other than the embodiment of a specific standard of emotions and a specific level of revulsion."[7] When Gillray portrayed the prince lounging in a mood of post-prandial satisfaction and picking his teeth "with a *bident!*" or "two-pronged iron fork," this mundane gesture contained a wealth of symbolic significance.

Not introduced into England until the seventeenth century, the fork spread relatively slowly in the British world of dining, since it was considered "an effeminate piece of finery."[8] By the middle of the eighteenth century, however, its use was common if not de rigueur at table among members of the middle ranks; accordingly, it was regulated by rules of decorum. In 1737, *The Man of Manners* pronounced it "very uncivil to pick one's Teeth with the Knive or Fork, because it looks like a *Lyon's Inn* Lawyer at the end of his Dinner, in the long Vacation."[9] Because the Lyon's Inn was a club for young lawyers in training at the Inner Temple, the comparison does not say much for the polite-ness of the practice (especially during the relaxed atmosphere of the long vacation). Lord Chesterfield advised his son that "it is exceedingly rude . . . to pick your teeth before the dishes are removed."[10] By the nineteenth-century, etiquette guides would summarily advise: "Never be seen to pick your teeth."[11] Young Thackeray was in possession of the common knowledge that picking one's teeth with a knife or a fork was "exceedingly rude" when he viewed Gillray's image with "a specific level of revulsion." The idea was common knowledge in polite society. Gillray's Voluptuary displays an outmoded, *je ne sais quoi* attitude defined by an antipathy to rules, consciously flouting the code of etiquette developed carefully over the course of the civilizing process.[12]

Not only does George pick his teeth before the dishes have been removed — he does so with a fork, and he does not even use the correct fork in Gillray's image. The functional, two-pronged carving fork had remained relatively un-changed since antiquity, but the table fork progressed along with its users in the Century of Taste. Henry Petroski explains that "fashion and style dictated that tableware look different from kitchenware, and so since the seventeenth century the tines of table forks have been considerably shorter and thinner than those of carving forks."[13] The earliest form of the table fork had two straight, longish tongs on the model of the kitchen fork used for carving, though the shortcomings of this model soon became apparent to diners attempting to practice politeness. One and eventually two prongs were added, resulting in a more delicate instrument for carrying food elegantly to the mouth. By the early eighteenth century, four-tined forks were common in Europe, and by the end of the nineteenth century they had become standard table utensils in England. Already in the 1790s, Gillray would have been aware of the rules guiding the beau monde in which the two-pronged (primitive or barbaric) fork had been delegated to those responsible for the activities of carving and serving.[14] It is perhaps no wonder that the prince's behavior in Gillray's print should stick in viewers' minds like the two-pronged bident itself.

A companion to Gillray's portrait of the Prince of Wales as a Voluptuary was his popular, equally grotesque portrayal of the royal parents, George III and Queen Charlotte, as "Temperance enjoying a Frugal Meal" (1792). In a self-contradictory effort to model the bourgeois fashion for domesticity and temperance, George III takes his soft-boiled egg from a golden cup with the help of a golden spoon (figure 6). These table items reflect the golden fittings on the door and the ornate golden frames on the wall. Next to the table, an enormous gold pitcher contains "Aqua Regis," a paradoxical phrase for the plainest of drinks. Scattered nearby are standard manuals of household economy and treatises on vegetarian diet, including an anonymous "Essay on the Dearness of Provisions" and "Dr. Cheyne on the benefits of a Spare Diet."[15] From an opposite perspective to their son George, Gillray's royal symbols of "Temperance" are beyond the pale of tasteful selfhood.

In his 1848 *Book of Snobs*, Thackeray maintains that "Stinginess is snobbish" just as "Ostentation is snobbish" (*WMP* 14:108). George IV's ill-mannered ostentation struck Thackeray with a note of snobbishness, and this satiric portrayal of royal "Temperance" suggests snobbishness in the form of ostentatious stinginess. Against the backdrop of real hunger and starvation clouding these years, the self-dramatized display of privation by the overweight king and his hypocritical queen (who gorges on salad with a bident to match her son's) indicate a meanness that is tantamount to snobbery. Stinginess is, after all, merely ostentation of a different sort, a pretending to be what one is not, and these would-be frugal diners make a mockery of self-denial. By the turn of the century, to be tasteful was to be moderately middle-class, but to be *ostentatiously frugal,* as in these images of the Hanoverian dynasty by Gillray, was simply the opposite end of snobbery.

Given the ideological significance of diet to the concept of taste at this time, it is remarkable that George should have continued to adhere to an aristocratic ideal of connoisseurship associated with the French. Linda Colley has suggested that in the eighteenth century a certain emulation of foreign fashions was a way for British persons of taste to achieve social distinction at home, but "by the last quarter of the eighteenth century, this strategy was coming to be seen as decidedly imprudent . . . an expensive, degenerate and suspect failure of home-grown Protestant plainness."[16] From the fleur-de-lis décor of his residence at Carlton House to his hiring of the famous French chef Antonin Carême in 1815, George actively identified with French fashion. True, he joined the exclusive Beef Steak Society (known as the "Sublime Society of Beefsteaks"), founded in part as a project of English national identity; the club united such members as Byron's friend John Cam Hobhouse, the actor John Kemble, the satirist George Colman, and others under the banner "Beef and Liberty."[17] But by wavering between a taste for bullish portions of port, arrack-punch, and beefsteak and a taste for French haute cuisine, George wavered between two cultural ideals of *aristocratic* taste. That the modern Man of Taste must subjugate his appetites to middle-class ideals of moderation, tempered by manners, was a fact that the prince (unable to read the times like his more "Temperate" parents) somehow missed.

In a world of knowledgeable consumers, George found himself cast as no innately "knowing" neoclassical connoisseur, reliant upon the concept of *je ne sais quoi,* but as lazy and unwilling to work for his taste: a glutton rather than a gourmand. George's inaugural dinner was "probably the most splendid and the most expensive that ever was given" in England, feting roughly three thousand people at a two-hundred-foot banquet table, with a simulated river running down the middle and mossy banks along the side.[18] Hearing that the dinner had cost approximately £120,000, Shelley predicted that its "ludicrous magnificence" and "disgusting splendours" would not "be the last bauble which the nation must buy to amuse this overgrown bantling of Regency."[19] Byron's friend Moore, a onetime diner at Carlton House, also criticized George for his extravagance. In a parodic "Intercepted Letter" (1813) from the prince after his imprisonment of Leigh Hunt for slander, Moore wrote:

> The dinner, you know, was in gay celebration
> Of *my* brilliant triumph and H——nt's condemnation;
> A compliment too to his Lordship the J——e
> For his Speech to the J——y — and zounds! who would grudge
> Turtle-soup, though it came to five guineas a bowl,
> To reward such a loyal and complaisant soul?
> We were all in high gig — Roman Punch and Tokay
> Travell'd round, till our heads travell'd just the same way;
> And we car'd not for Juries nor Libels — no — damme! nor
> Ev'n for the threats of a last Sunday's Examiner![20]

Critics like Hunt complained that George went "from mistress to mistress, and from lavishment to lavishment," on the brink of his Regency, carousing and following an ideal of "good living" descended from ancient Roman banquets.[21] The modern era privileged quality over quantity, and the corresponding ability to make fine distinctions. George's drunken companions in Moore's parody are in "high gig" and behave in a manner that blunts the discriminating capacity necessary to exercise taste, symbolically as well as literally.

To discourse knowledgeably about one's gastronomical preferences was essential to a growing portion of the public, eager to prove its refinement through dining and the dictates of gastronomical Juries of Taste, though this English prince "car'd not for Juries nor Libels." The path to taste was now more than ever through the body, a democratizing vehicle that offered all who were willing to work for their taste an equal share of epistemological authority. George (in representation anyway) was not, and in the period of his Regency he was out of touch with the middle-class concept of taste as something to be acquired through education — or the financial power necessary to procure it in the form of restaurant guides, conduct books, etiquette instructors, and so forth. Culture had come to replace the auratic *je ne sais quoi* of Continental origins, and although George believed himself to be the princely epitome of taste, to many of his contemporaries he was an emblem of immoderate appetite surrounded by his own uncouth remains.

Georgian Gourmands

Elevating gourmandism to the status of the fine arts and establishing its legitimate link to aesthetic taste was a project of Romantic-era gastronomy. The French chef Antonin Carême, reputed to be the greatest chef of all time and the founder of modern haute cuisine, was brought by George IV to Brighton at a salary of £2,000 per annum.[22] By January 1817, he was preparing hundred-dish dinners for the prince and his guests at Brighton, introducing the small English resort town to cutting-edge European cuisine. The "King's Kitchen" at the Brighton Pavilion cost the British treasury £6,000 on trimmings alone, making it the most technologically advanced kitchen in Europe. Its elaborate confectionery contained three separate rooms devoted to the preparation of desserts and an additional two for the construction of pastries. From the ice of the adjacent ice room, drawn from a detached "ice-house," a steady flow of sorbets and ice cream passed through the alimentary architecture of the Brighton Pavilion to the Regent's ever-ready palate.[23]

George's saccharine extravagance may have been the envy of Europe, but to the British public it was a sign of gluttony, not gastronomical good taste. The paradox of this moment in the literary (and cultural) history of taste is that George's aristocratic appetites, to many the ostentatious oral indulgence of an overstuffed regent, helped to inform the concept of taste in the nineteenth-century Britain as a field of gastronomical pleasure. After Waterloo (1815), as the historian John Burnett writes, many of the greatest French chefs emigrated to England, lured by enormous salaries as "ornaments to the acquisitive society which industrialism had fostered"; as a result, nineteenth-century Britons, "who denounced gluttony almost as vehemently as they did immorality, had their palates educated, and came to be as fond of good food as they were of other sins of the flesh."[24] Food was fast becoming a fine art, and a public was being trained by self-appointed gastronomical Men of Taste in how to appreciate it.

The same year that Carême was concocting his hundred-dish dinners at Brighton for George and his companions, the British physician William Kitchiner published *Apicius Redevivus, or The Cooks Oracle; Actual Experiments Instituted in the Kitchen of a Physician* (1817). Adopting the French fashion of applying physiological knowledge and theory to cookery, Kitchiner approaches the preparation of food as both a science and an art, cooking as a medium for self-expression. As one society lady remarked of the book in 1822, "Neither Walter Scott nor Lord Byron have had so quick and profitable a sale."[25] Walter Scott himself, observing the "singular correspondence the Doctors name bears to the subject which he has rendered so interesting," remarked how far *The Cook's Oracle* surpassed the generic collection of recipes: "Somebody told me there was to be an edition in which all the fun was to be omitted. I hope that in that case the Doctor will do as Mr. Hardcastle is asked to do in She Stoops to Conquer — 'Knock out the brains and serve them up by themselves.'"[26] For Scott, Kitchiner's *Oracle* was a gastronomical work of literary merit. Its numerous subsequent editions, retitled *The Cook's Oracle, Containing Receipts for Plain Cookery, on the Most Economical Plan for Private Families,* were prefaced by an essay that pivots between cookbook and gastronomical treatise. Kitchiner was largely responsible for transporting French gastronomical tradition, as a philosophical and literary genre of writing about culture under the guise of food, into English.

The preface multiplied along with the number of editions, introducing the book as a compendium of empiricist experiments in taste. Each recipe, Kitchiner claimed, had been submitted to a " 'COMMITTEE OF TASTE,' (composed of thorough-bred GRANDS GOURMANDS of the first magnitude,)."[27] He models his concept of the "committee of taste" directly on Grimod de la Reynière's "Tasting Jury" (*Jury des Dégustateurs*) featured in his *Almanach des gourmands,* which also echoes the judiciary language of aesthetic taste on which the literary genre of gastronomy was based. To leave the cookbook and enter the world of gastronomical writing was to leave the kitchen and enter the dining room, a new public exhibition space for taste.[28] According to Kitchiner, his committee of trained gourmands "during their arduous progress of proving the respective Recipes . . . were so truly philosophically and disinterestedly regardless of the wear and tear of teeth and stomach, that their Labour — appeared a Pleasure to them."[29] The gastronomical consumer takes his appetite seriously in order to comprehend the finer shades or tones (neither metaphor will any longer serve) of his pleasure in a philosophical manner.

Just as the Man of Taste worked hard to distinguish specific qualities of beauty in order to pronounce exact judgments of taste, the gourmand now worked with equal devotion to distinguish among different flavors of food. No longer a barbarous glutton, the gastronomical epicure, an expert in "the important science of good-living" (as one British contemporary put it) grinds away disinterestedly, subordinating his body to the labor of taste.[30] The findings of Grimod's Tasting Jury, which included a number of prestigious members, were published serially in the *Almanach des gourmands* as the basis of a literary genre whose aesthetic approach to eating informs the modern restaurant review, restaurant guide, and culinary journalism generally (trade journals, gourmet magazines, newspaper columns, television shows, and so forth).[31] Like his British successors, including Kitchiner, Grimod insisted that an unprejudiced body empirically proved all judgments of taste elaborated in his work, individual as well as collective.

Gastronomical interest was less on the side of production than consumption, and Grimod set the terms for his British successors by announcing that "the Almanac of Gourmands is not a cookbook; our obligation is to try to stimulate our readers' appetites; it is up to artists alone to satisfy them."[32] This French father of gastronomy may not have been the most voracious eater of the Romantic period, but this was intentional, as he was one of its most expressive. His persona combined, in Rebecca Spang's words, "the olfactorily and gustatorily gifted gourmand, and the literate, narrative-building narrator."[33] Readers knew they were witnessing the remaking of aesthetic taste explicitly as a gustatory phenomenon: culinary artistry was to be appreciated philosophically, and a culinary public was being created and trained in the judgment of oral and olfactory sensation. Just as Addison and Steele, for example, had trained readers in the appreciation of literary beauties, the Romantic gourmand considered it his "civilizing mission" to be a leader in matters of taste.[34] His task was to train a public in how to appreciate the "Pleasures of the Table," which are more than "the actual and direct sensation of satisfying a need," according to Grimod's more famous successor Brillat-

Savarin. "The pleasures of the table are a reflective sensation which is born from the various circumstances of place, time, things, and people who make up the surroundings of the meal" (*PT* 182). At the turn of the century, cookery was professionalized as an art through the developing restaurant industry, and gastronomers worked hard to professionalize the public as expert consumers of food.[35]

The restaurant review emerged from the genre of the dramatic review, and the world of the Romantic gourmand was theatrical in orientation. As Spang explains, Grimod "evoked a world where restaurateurs and pastry-chefs were the equivalent of theater entrepreneurs and playwrights, and where one candymaker charged admission simply to look at his new bonbons."[36] Gastronomers themselves were aware of the relation between gastronomy, as "the great art of the palate" (*le grand art de la gueule*), and postrevolutionary consumerism. As restaurants became cultural exhibition spaces in the years following the French Revolution in France, and later in the nineteenth century in England, gastronomical Men of Taste materialized as conspicuous consumers. Gastronomy transformed the urban topography of France and England into a spatial relation between flavors. In this newly scrambled gastronomical geography, the logic of streets and neighborhoods gave way to the map or *carte* of the gourmand, philosophically following his nose and regulating his movements by olfactory sensation. To Romantic-period gastronomes, *cartes* were maps as well as menus, and an "alimentary topography" replaced sociopolitical boundaries with culinary divisions.[37]

Gastronomers recognized that more goes into the making of a good meal than food itself, and judgments of taste were reflective pleasures founded on epistemological verifiability and what constitutes correct behavior, menu composition, methods of service, sequence of courses, and techniques of service — as Milton put it, "Taste after taste, upheld with kindliest change." Much as Kitchiner submitted his recipes to a Committee of Taste, Grimod organized his *Jury des Dégustateurs* from a group of trained gourmands, who met weekly to pass judgment on the dishes (or *légitimations*) before them (figure 7). Individual taste objects were discrete samples of food, labeled *légitimations* (a term borrowed from diplomacy) after their ability to legitimate the culinary artist in the eyes of a discriminating public. According to Grimod, "These legitimations are tasted in a large mechanism [*un grand appareil*] and with rigorous fairness; opinions are gathered according to appetites: the whole trial is recorded; and it is when the results are in that the contestants [*prétendans*] get honorable mention in *l'Almanach des gourmands*."[38] For the first time in the history of taste, the most seemingly subjective part of the judging anatomy — the tastebuds clustered on the tongue and palate, whose operations are chemical and which vary from mouth to mouth — must be held accountable to the same universal standards as music, poetry, and other expressions of beauty.

With an emphasis on objectivity and juridical process, gastronomical experiments of taste legitimate not only the cook, I would suggest, but also the critic as a modern-day Man of Taste. Who is to say there is no disputing in matters of taste? Because the Tasting Jury operated in private, its decisions could not be ascribed to any single individual: they asked to be taken as the universal standard of a group of ideal critics, Hume's fantasy come true. Mental taste was confounded with gustatory taste, and the pronouncements of the Tasting Jury came to replace the "joint verdict" of ideal critics, which for Hume had defined the standard of taste. Aesthetic taste involved a political dimension as a social force of community, and gastronomical writers now considered the dinner table (in Grimod's words) to be "the pivot of all political, literary, financial, and business matters."[39] In 1834 a British follower of Grimod who styled himself "Dick Humelbergius Secundus," after the annotator of the famous Roman cook Apicius, observed "that the table is the only chain which connects every branch of society."[40] Accordingly, for Romantic-era gourmands like Grimod, "the result of the changes of *gourmandise* is much more important to the happiness of man in society than that of social, administrative, or judiciary changes."[41] Even more than other categories of social change, *gourmandise* places power directly in the hands — or mouths — of the discriminating consumer.

The first full-length gastronomical work of note in English is by the pseudonymous Launcelot Sturgeon, *Essays, Moral, Philosophical, and Stomachical, on the Important Science of Good-Living* (1822), which describes the ideal gourmand knowingly as an aesthetic Man of Taste.[42] When Sturgeon lists the qualities necessary for the epicurean critic, he sounds much like Hume in "Of the Standard of Taste." Hume's five things necessary for the ideal critic are: "Strong sense, united to delicate sentiment, improved by practice, perfected by comparison, and cleared of all prejudice" (*EMP* 241). For the gourmand who comes into his own during the Romantic period as a food connoisseur, these translate into (1) "a capacious stomach"; (2) "an insatiate appetite"; (3) "a delicate susceptibility in the organs of degustation, which enables him to appreciate the true relish of each ingredient in the most compound ragoût, and to detect the slightest aberration of the cook; added to" (4) "a profound acquaintance with the rules of art in all the most approved schools of cookery, and" (5) "an enlightened judgment on their several merits, matured by long and sedulous experience." According to Sturgeon, the stomach worked in tandem with the palate, and it is "the happy combination of both these enviable qualities that constitutes that truly estimable character, the real epicure."[43] Once gastronomy had emigrated from the Continent during the English Regency, the gourmand united the hearty appetite of the British beefeater with the delicacy of the French gourmet.

The title page of Sturgeon's *Philosophical, and Stomachical* essays identifies its author as a "Fellow of the Beef-Steak Club, and an Honorary member of several Foreign Pic Nics, &c. &c. &c.," much as the original 1826 title page of Brillat-Savarin's *Physiology of Taste* would identify its author as a "Professor" and "Member of Numerous Scholarly Societies." These gastronomical accreditations were in turn based on more "serious" culinary treatises, such as Fredrick Accum's *Treatise on Adulterations of Food* (1820), which credited the writer as a "Lecturer on Practical Chemistry, Mineralogy, and on Chemistry applied to the Arts and Manufactures; Member of the Royal Irish Academy; Fellow of the Linnaean Society; Member of the Royal Academy of Sciences, and of the Royal Society of Arts of Berlin, &c. &c." in the manner of the philosophical treatise. As a licensed English epicure, "Sturgeon" boasts professional qualifications that suggest a lifetime's labor devoted to attainment in the gastronomical arts. His "gastronomic tour on the Continent" and acquaintance with "that very erudite work, the '*Almanach des Gourmands*'" yields one of the most original attempts in English to "stimulate the powers of discriminating appetites" in a moral and philosophical, as well as comical, manner.[44]

Following Enlightenment taste tradition, gastronomers found that the slightest anatomical deviation of the tasting organs can cause a judgment of taste to go awry. The genuine epicure, with an educated palate and correct assemblage of qualifications, was consequently a rare breed, according to Sturgeon: "few men are able to do equal justice to a dinner — '*Ab ovo usque ad mala*' — from the soup to the coffee; that demands a universality of taste, and a profundity of judgment, which fall to the lot of only some favoured individuals. Such gifted beings do, however, exist."[45] Such rhetoric again echoes Hume, who insists that wherever true critics are to be found, one "must acknowledge a true and decisive standard to exist somewhere, to wit, real existence and matter of fact" (*EMP* 242). Just as the Enlightenment Man of Taste proves an ability to discern particular qualities of beauty, the gourmand must practice his art of judgment and acquire "a profound acquaintance with the rules of art" better to discern individual taste flavors. Sturgeon himself relates an anecdote in which Hume, having been complimented on his epicureanism, pronounced himself "only a glutton!" The distinction is central to nineteenth-century gastronomical writing, as we have seen, and Sturgeon enters his "most solemn protest against the indiscriminate application of the terms *Epicurism* and *Gluttony;* which are but too commonly applied synonymously, with a degree of ignorance, or of malignity, worthy only of the grossness of mere beef-eaters, or the envy of weak appetites." The aspiring Romantic gourmand emulates the elite members of the Tasting Jury in devoting his "labours" to refining his palate.[46]

Rather than seeking tasteful status through the disinterested attitude, those who do not take their eating seriously enough were chastised by gastronomical writers for their lack of interest — in Brillat-Savarin's words, their "disgraceful indifference" (*PT* 153). The most famous of all gastronomical essays is his *Physiology of Taste; or, Meditations on Transcendental Gastronomy* (1825), in which he counsels his readers: "Work hard, Excellencies. Preach, for the good of your science; digest, in your own peculiar interests; and if, in the course of your labors, you happen to make some important discovery, be good enough to share it with this, the humblest of your servants!" (*PT* 440). One no longer needed to match the wealth of the aristocrat to qualify as a connoisseur. The rapid burgeoning of the restaurant industry permitted anyone with the correct amount of cash to enjoy the "pleasures of the table" like a prince (if not an English Regent): "If he has fifteen or twenty francs to spend," writes Brillat-Savarin, "and if he can sit down at the table of a first class restaurateur, he is as well off as if he dined with a prince, or more so, for the feast at his command is quite as splendid, and since he can order any dish he wishes, he is not bothered by personal considerations or scruples" (*PT* 331).[47] Brillat-Savarin's *Physiology of Taste* was written during the 1820s when the word *gastronomy* was on everyone's tongue in Paris and when gastronomical "professors" of taste were expected to work with great zeal. It rapidly eclipsed Grimod's aristocratic *Almanach des gourmands,* and one reason may be its author's more representative status as middle-class Man of Taste.

The middle-class road of the gastronomical Man of Taste intentionally dismissed attention from the extremities of appetite — hunger and luxurious overindulgence — as unworthy of philosophical attention, much as had the eighteenth-century discourse of aesthetics. In the tongue-in-cheek style of this gastronomical, table-talky genre, Brillat-Savarin claimed that "lexicographers, no matter how knowing otherwise, are not numbered among those agreeable scholars who can munch pleasurably at a partridge wing *au suprême* and then top it off, little finger quirked, with a glass of Lafitte or Clos Vougeot" (*PT* 147). No mindless glutton, the Romantic gourmand was a "scholar," a self-dubbed "professor," who through years of hard work and application fashioned himself an extremely refined palate. The English Regency leader, by contrast, whose enormous shadow extended from the 1780s through the 1830s, failed to recognize the period he symbolically hovered over as one in which the abstract, aristocratic ideal of the *je ne sais quoi* was giving way to a more mundane rendering of the term in which lack of knowing must be taken at face value. The aristocracy and the "the aristocracy of culture" (to borrow Pierre Bourdieu's phrase) were no longer one, and as a result, George IV came to embody in his own corpulent frame the "disgraceful indifference" of the snob.

Books of Snobs

There was a connection between gourmands and dandies as modern Men of Taste at this time. The gourmand treated food with philosophical consequence, and the "traditional dandy," as Regina Gagnier writes, "was the first to make dress and fashion the basis of a philosophy, of the only philosophy, in fact, that was consistent with modern, materialist life."[48] Broadly defined, dandies of nineteenth-century England were "opposed to business pursuits or habits, ostentatiously even refusing to wear a watch, and spurning all domestic burdens," as Leonore Davidoff and Catherine Hall explain, "the antithesis of domesticated masculinity dedicated to business."[49] The Regency Man of Taste sought to express refinement through fashion as well as food, the commodified language of clothes and conduct, but unlike the gourmand, who at least recognized the need to work hard for his taste, the dandy was an aristocratic figure who denied his own status as a worker and corresponding member of a wider mass of consumers.

Critics have noticed the portrait of George IV in *Vanity Fair,* Thackeray's epic satire of Regency England, based on what he considered to be "the Regent's unfitness to occupy the great post of first dandy of the empire."[50] For many contemporaries, he was pure sartorial polish; at one point, he was reputed to have gone through seventy-two waistcoats in a span of two months. Thackeray complains in *The Four Georges* (1860) that he can find nothing of substance beneath these superficial layers: "I try and take him to pieces, and find silk stockings, padding, stays, a coat with frogs and a fur collar, a star and blue ribbon, a pocket-handkerchief prodigiously scented, one of Truefitt's best nutty brown wigs reeking with oil, a set of teeth and a huge black stock, underwaistcoats, more underwaistcoats, and then nothing" (*WMP* 23:107–08). In *Vanity Fair,* he introduces his fictional George as the obese bon vivant Jos Sedley, a dandified man in boots: "A very stout, puffy man, in buckskins and Hessian boots, with several immense neckcloths, that rose almost to his nose, with a red-striped waistcoat and an apple green coat with steel buttons almost as large as crown pieces (it was the morning costume of a dandy or blood of those days)" (*WMP* 1:26). In the symbolic visual language of the period, George IV was frequently associated with boots, often "jack-boots" or above-the-knee cavalry boots that stood for military ostentation without the substance to back it up. Biographers like to describe how George "designed shoe buckles and lavishly frogged surtouts for himself," as "he would one day delight in devising new uniforms for his army."[51] Thackeray's disgust with him comes to a searing focus on this very buckle: "A sweet invention! lovely and useful as the Prince on whose foot it sparkled" (*WMP* 23:113). The irony, of course, is that the buckle is *not* useful. It does nothing but shine.

George sought the advice of other Regency dandies, such as Sir Lumley Skeffington, who designed his own clothes and accoutrements at the rate of £800 per annum. Gillray also caricatured "Skiffy," along with his friend Montague Matthews, as quite literally all polish: a pair of highly polished boots (figure 8). The concept of polish, as it descends from Shaftesbury, is available in theory to all members of society. Everyone who "takes particular care to turn his eye from everything which is gaudy, luscious and of a false taste" can obtain social polish, according to Shaftesbury (*C* 151). Enlightenment taste theory was an emulation model underwritten by a commitment to an ideal of human perfectibility. Like other aesthetic taste philosophers, Shaftesbury held that "in the very nature of things there must of necessity be the foundation of a right and a wrong taste, as well in respect of inward characters and features as of outward person, behaviour, and action" (*C* 150). Self-making subjects in civil society found it their social duty to mimic la crème de la crème, or what Shaftesbury calls "mankind of the better sort" (*C* 162). What made this duty feasible was the belief in a self-evident standard, maintained by actually embodied persons of taste. But in a nineteenth-century cultural milieu in which inward character rarely matched "outward person," it was not so easy to determine where good taste was to be found.

Consumer capitalism allowed anyone with enough cash to express "taste" in commodified form through acts of conspicuous consumption accompanied by ceremonial display. Joseph Litvak has argued that as class barriers implicit in the distinguishing project of taste became blurred through the influence of capital, which enables more fluid social mobility, gender lines acquired heightened significance as markers of sophistication and taste. His showcase example is the snobbish Jos Sedley, who, he claims, reveals Thackeray's "own anxious awareness of sophistication's homosexualizing potential . . . his effeminate double, the fat dandy who represents not just naïveté but, far worse, a naïve travesty of sophistication itself."[52] Thackeray's narrator in *Vanity Fair* informs us that Jos "was lazy, peevish, and a *bon-vivant;* the appearance of a lady frightened him beyond measure," adding that "He was as vain as a girl" (*WMP* 1:31–32). Like his historical prototype (George IV), he "took the hugest pains to adorn his big person, and passed many hours daily in that occupation . . . his toilet-table was covered with as many pomatums and essences as ever were employed by an old beauty: he had tried, in order to give himself a waist, every girth, stay, and waistband then invented" (*WMP* 1:31–32). Unlike the gastronome or epicure, who made the transition to a middle-class conception of the tasteful consumer, the dandy remained one step to the side of the "masculine" convention of the Man of Taste.[53]

Like Jos, George was prone to accumulating "superabundant fat" (*WMP* 1:31), and by eighteen he was spending the exorbitant sum of £10,000 annually on clothes. Parissien reports that by the time he was king, he "was wearing a 'Bastille of whalebone' to encase his burgeoning body, which weighed as much as twenty stone. In 1824 his corset was made to fit a waist of fifty inches; by 1830 the Duke of Gloucester was comparing the king's body to 'a feather bed.'"[54] At the end of his life, George was virtually immobile. Two months before he died, the Duke of Wellington described his breakfast as a meal more fit for Gulliver on Lilliput, or the ravenous giants of Rabelais: "A Pidgeon and Beef Steak Pye of which he eat two Pigeons and three Beefsteaks, Three parts of a Bottle of Mozelle, a Glass of Dry Champagne, two Glasses of Port [&] a Glass of Brandy!"[55] The fictional Jos ineffectively struggled with "every girth, stay, and waistband then invented," and the whalebone bulwark against George's blubber could not successfully compress *his* figure into an aesthetically acceptable form. The painter David Wilkie reputedly took three hours to "lace up all the bulgings and excrescencies" in George's clothing, trying to paint a sympathetic portrait of him at Windsor in the final year of his life (1830).[56] Robert Seymour's contemporaneous caricature of George as *The Great Joss and his Playthings* (1829) shows him enjoying the overwrought Far East fashions of the Brighton Pavilion—an image also fit for Jos Sedley, who adopts the India Mogul style of an East India Company collector from Boggley Wollah.

The ostentatious mania of consumerism, Thackeray complained in his *Book of Snobs*, alienated the "middle ranks" from their status as middling.[57] In a chapter on "Dinner-Giving Snobs," he rhetorically demands, "Why should Jones and I, who are in the middle rank, alter the modes of our being to assume an *éclat* which does not belong to us—to entertain our friends, who . . . are men of the middle rank too, who are not in the least deceived by our temporary splendour; and who play off exactly the same absurd trick upon us when they ask us to dine?" (*WMP* 14:113). Thackeray's Jones is a hearty, John Bullish figure with no patience for French-affiliated culinary ostentation. One may recall his brief appearance in *Vanity Fair*, when the narrator pauses to reflect on his description of the middle-class, hostess-in-the-making, Amelia Sedley: "I can see Jones at this minute (rather flushed with his joint of mutton and half-pint of wine), taking out his pencil and scoring under the words 'foolish, twaddling,' &c., and adding to them his own remark of '*quite true*'" (*WMP*

1:8–9). A fictional reflection of the first-person author of Thackeray's *Book of Snobs,* Jones finds the nineteenth-century dinner party, with its middle-class mentality of keeping up with the Joneses, downright snobbish.

Ostentation was the sign of the snob, and in the Victorian novel snobs abound. The term *snob* is of dubious origins, and lexicographers speculate that it derives from the word *cobbler,* or more broadly, craftsman qua person of the lower orders. The earliest recorded usage of the word is from the 1780s to indicate a "person belonging to the ordinary or lower classes of society; one having no pretensions to rank or gentility" (*OED*). By the early nineteenth century, "snob" was no longer a neutral term signifying rank but a synonym for vulgar: "One who has little or no breeding or good taste; a vulgar or ostentatious person" (*OED*). By the 1830s, it had come to mean one "who meanly or vulgarly admires and seeks to imitate, or associate with, those of superior rank or wealth; one who wishes to be regarded as a person of social importance" (*OED*). In the short span of the historical George's ostentatious career, then (the 1780s through the 1830s), the "snob" went from being a member of the lower classes to being a member of an aspirant middling class, or socially hyperconscious set of people who look up. By the twentieth century, "snob" acquired the connotation it carries today: "One who despises those who are considered inferior in rank, attainment, or taste" (*OED*). The paradox is that a term that originally meant a person of inferior rank flip-flops entirely to mean a person of superior rank, who looks down on those considered inferior. This semantic inversion is epitomized in the middle-class snob of the nineteenth-century novel, who pretends to a higher social status, or apes a more sophisticated taste, than he or she can economically afford.

As economic historians suggest, the middle-class ideal of moderation had given way by mid-century to a form of competitive expenditure in which "new values were demonstrated in terms of houses and furnishings, horses and carriages, the lavish employment of domestic servants, dress, and — not least — in terms of food."[58] The growth of entertaining marked British social life of this period, and people of the "middle ranks" began to host elaborate dinners for parties of half a dozen or more. These events often required the assistance of professional caterers, thereby bringing the restaurant (and the concept of the restaurant as a public exhibition space) into the home. Eighteenth-century culinary writers addressed an audience ideologically invested in moderation, a middle class keeping careful tabs on expenditure with no self-consciousness about doing so, but nineteenth-century cookery books appealed to the middle ranks attempting to climb the social ladder through the medium of consumption. Accordingly, as Stephen Mennell explains, cookery books now discussed "precisely those matters which were causes of concern and social anxiety to the aspiring middle classes — etiquette, table settings, the hierarchy of servants and how many of them were required."[59] The dinner party of early Victorian England thus became a paramount occasion for the public display of taste in conspicuously material terms.

A society hostess was expected to give a dinner party once or twice a week and a middle-class family once a month, events requiring enormous preparation, expenditure of energy, time (at least a whole day), and money. "In these years," as Burnett explains, "the choice of foods, their manner of preparation, order of service, and even the times of eating, all became matters of high social importance and class demarcation: in particular, the dinner-party became a prestige symbol which at once announced the taste, discrimination, and bank balance of the donor."[60] The middle-class dinner party demanded the best silver, china, and glass, and the traditional serving of the meal *à la française* (where many plates and courses were presented all at once) gave way to the more complicated dinner *à la Russe,* with courses following one upon the other. The new presentation style was a better technique to display tableware, and it involved more distinct boundaries between kinds of dishes and more ways of demarcating those boundaries (as in elite restaurants today where plates are presented never intended to be used).

Cookery books of the 1820s and 1830s still catered to a traditionally British taste for "plain cookery," but by the 1840s more elaborate recipe collections, such as that by the French émigré chef Alexis Soyer, *The Gastronomic Re-generator* (1846), which included two thousand elaborate dishes for upscale entertainment, had for the most part replaced them. In his preface to *The Cook's Oracle,* Kitchiner criticized "the multiplicity of dishes which luxury has made fashionable at the tables of the Great, the Wealthy — and the Ostentatious, who are, often, neither great nor wealthy."[61] We may translate these categories into the Great (aristocrats), the Wealthy (nouveaux riches), and the Ostentatious: middle-class "snobs" aspiring to status with the former two. Carême also advised in 1833 that it was "an error for those of lesser station to try to pattern their tables after the rich, crowding them with badly prepared food, badly served because of inexperienced help. Better to have a simple meal, well-prepared; and not to try to cover the bourgeois table with an imitation of the rich."[62] Despite such protestation, from the 1820s through the 1840s the sophistication factor of the dinner party only increased.

Charles Dickens captures this changing bourgeois aesthetic in *Our Mutual Friend* (1865) in two contrasting middle-class dinner parties, specifically those given early in the novel by the Veneerings and the Podsnaps. These families represent two distinctive modes of ostentation, as described by Thackeray in his 1848 *Book of Snobs.* The Veneerings are a financially successful middle-class couple, whose surname suggests them to be all polish or social veneer. Like George IV layered over with waistcoats, they are all superficies and no substance:

> Mr. and Mrs. Veneering were bran-new people in a bran-new house in a bran-new quarter of London. Everything about the Veneerings was spick and span new. All their furniture was new, all their friends were new, all their servants were new, their plate was new, their carriage was new, their harness was new, their horses were new, their pictures were new, they themselves were new, they were as newly married as was lawfully compatible with their having a bran-new baby, and if they had set up a great-grandfather, he would have come home in matting from the Pantechnicon, without a scratch upon him, French polished to the crown of his head.
>
> For, in the Veneering establishment, from the hall-chairs with the new coat of arms, to the grand pianoforte with the new action, and upstairs again to the new fire-escape, all things were in a state of high varnish and polish.[63]

The Veneerings' taste is not based upon ancestry but rather is acquired (or accumulated) in the form of commodities: objects valued principally for their exchangeability. Unlike the intrinsic value system based on use, which maintains the object's phenomenological integrity, the system of exchange value dictates that things are worth only what others say they are worth. "Appearance becomes just as important" in the world of the commodity, as the Marxist Wolfgang Haug notes, "and practically more so—than the commodity's being itself."[64] No longer valued for their aura of hereditary prestige, objects in the liquid world of capital must be fashionably replaced on a continual basis, turning consumerism into a compulsion, a drive for those seeking social status akin to the physical drives of appetite.[65] Andrew H. Miller has argued that in nineteenth-century fiction an "ability to consume, whether comestibles or more lasting commodities, is without limit and, finally, repellant; when objects of use enter into a system of exchange, need is lost amid the pulsations of desire."[66] As opposed to more idealized taste objects, commodities offered themselves up for a kind of consumption that was less a discretionary opportunity than a Darwinian act of survival in a social world of status.

Not only consumables are exchangeable in such a world. Consumers themselves at the middle-class dinner party find themselves as exchangeable as the dinner table itself. A regular dinner guest at "the Veneering establishment" is Twemlow, described as "an innocent piece of dinner-furniture." Twemlow is related to a lord and represents a certain amount of prestige to the Veneerings. "Mr. and Mrs. Veneering," therefore, when "arranging a dinner, habitually started with Twemlow, and then put leaves in him, or added guests to him.

Sometimes, the table consisted of Twemlow and half a dozen leaves; sometimes, of Twemlow and a dozen leaves. Sometimes, Twemlow was pulled out to his utmost extent of twenty leaves."[67] The table is an object Marx adopts at the outset of *Capital* as an analogy for the commodity; as such, Twemlow's stature expands or contracts with the number of guests who register his significance. Marx writes that the commodity is a thing "which through its qualities satisfies human needs of whatever kind. The nature of these needs, whether they arise, for example, from the stomach, or the imagination, makes no difference."[68] In the world of consumer capitalism, a craving for food and a craving for status are irrevocably scrambled up as appetites. The condition of possibility for aesthetic taste, disinterestedness, becomes less and less possible in this dizzying world of commodity consumption.

The snob is desperate for survival in this mercurial world made by capital, and the counterpart to the Veneerings' style of snobbishness is the ostentation of the Podsnaps. *Their* snobbish aesthetic takes place not at the surface level of polish, but at the weightier level of substance. The Podsnaps are also financially successful members of the Victorian middle class, but they manifest hostility to the very concept of polish. For them (as for Thackeray's Jones), such polish, or social veneer, translates into false aestheticization:

> Mr. Podsnap could tolerate taste in a mushroom man who stood in need of that sort of thing, but was far above it himself. Hideous solidity was the characteristic of the Podsnap plate. Everything was made to look as heavy as it could, and to take up as much room as possible. Everything said boastfully, "Here you have as much of me in my ugliness as if I were only lead; but I am so many ounces of precious metal worth so much an ounce; — wouldn't you like to melt me down?" A corpulent straddling epergne, blotched all over as if it had broken out in an eruption rather than been ornamented, delivered this address from an unsightly silver platform in the centre of the table. Four silver wine-coolers, each furnished with four staring heads, each head obtrusively carrying a big silver ring in each of its ears, conveyed the sentiment up and down the table, and handed it on to the pot-bellied silver salt-cellars. All the big silver spoons and forks widened the mouths of the company expressly for the purpose of thrusting the sentiment down their throats with every morsel they ate.[69]

The most telling object in the Veneering household is the expandable dinner table ("personified" as Twemlow), and here it is the "corpulent straddling epergne," a typically Victorian centerpiece made foremost for show, though it could also hold candles or edibles. Its very utility is exchangeable, losing itself in ornamentation, and in this respect the epergne is an emblem of Mr. Podsnap himself.[70] Symbolically looming over the overburdened table, with its pot-bellied saltshakers and silver plate, this enormous leaden epergne indicates a kind of wealth accrued through the Marine Insurance business that is as variable as the waves. Its gross materiality can be readily liquefied as capital, and this is its only appeal. In the Podsnap establishment, exchange value has become the only secure means to measure status, and commodities such as this resemble its inhabitants. Trapped in material form, they long to be released through what Marx labels "the miracle of this transubstantiation."[71] Whether as high-gloss furniture items or pot-bellied saltcellars that look like blobs of precious metal, these mid-nineteenth-century markers of taste serve as mere signs, not things-in-themselves imbued with intrinsic value.

These novelistic snapshots of the Veneerings and Podsnaps suggest that aesthetic taste is now expressed through a form of material consumption, which some, such as Thackeray, would find snobbish and hence distasteful. The *ancien régime* of taste based on the aristocratic *je ne sais quoi* of French neoclassicism, and adapted to the British discourse of taste by way of the connoisseur, transforms into its antithetical horizon: the benighted don't-know-don't-care philistinism of Victorian England. In the nineteenth-century aesthetic of snobbery, in other words, the auratic *je ne sais quoi* of the aesthetic connoisseur yields to the truly befuddled condition of the middle-class snob. Taste had always been an appropriate metaphor for a kind of subjective pleasure that does not submit to objective laws, and in the end these Dickensian snobs find that it cannot be packaged, exchanged, or bought. Taste is ever on the wing from middle-class consumers of the nineteenth-century novel, who cling to the language of the commodity as their best means of self-expression. In a sea of unbounded consumption, they not only do not know what genuinely counts as tasteful: they don't even know that they don't know. As a result, they adopt the only solution left, which is snobbery.

Notes

Chapter 1. Aesthetics and Appetite

1. The phrase "committee of taste" is used in the introduction to William Kitchiner's best-selling cookbook, *The Cook's Oracle, Containing Receipts for Plain Cookery, on the Most Economical Plan for Private Families; also The Art of Composing the Most Simple and Most Highly Finished Broths, Gravies, Soups, Sauces, Store Sauces, and Flavouring Essences; Pastry, Preserves, Puddings, Pickles, &c. containing also a Complete System of Cookery for Catholic Families*, 7th edition (London: Robert Cadell, 1831), 3. It is modeled on Alexandre Balthazar Laurent Grimod de la Reynière's "Tasting Jury" (*Jury des Dégustateurs*), from his *Almanach des gourmands*, published serially between 1803 and 1812 as the foundational text of gastronomy. This is a topic discussed in chapters 5 and 8 of this book and in my introduction to *Gusto: An Anthology of Nineteenth-Century Gastronomy from England and France* (New York: Routledge, forthcoming).

2. On taste as an evolution of European art criticism, particularly French neoclassicism, see Dabney Townsend, "Taste: Early History," *Encyclopedia of Aesthetics* (Oxford: Oxford University Press, 1998), 4:355–60; and Howard Caygill, *Art of Judgement* (Oxford: Basil Blackwell, 1989). For the role of moral-sense philosophy, particularly the works of Lord Shaftesbury, in founding modern aesthetics, see Jerome Stolnitz, "On the Significance of Lord Shaftesbury in Modern Aesthetic Theory," *Philosophical Quarterly* 11 (1961): 97–113; "On the Origins of 'Aesthetic Disinterestedness,'" *Journal of Aesthetics and Art Criticism* 10 (1961–62): 131–42; "Beauty: Some Stages in the History of an Idea," *Journal of the History of Ideas* 22 (1961): 185–204; and "The Aesthetic

Attitude in the Rise of Modern Aesthetics," *Journal of Aesthetics and Art Criticism* 36 (1977–78): 409–22. On Addison and Steele as founding fathers of modern (postclassical) aesthetics, see Monroe C. Beardsley, *Aesthetics from Classical Greece to the Present: A Short History* (New York: Macmillan, 1966).

3. This is Jürgen Habermas's phrase from "Excursus on Leveling the Genre Distinction between Philosophy and Literature," in *The Philosophical Discourse of Modernity*, trans. by Frederick Lawrence (Cambridge: Harvard University Press, 1987), 185–210 (201). On one hand, this can be taken as a weakness of language to capture reality as it is. Bernard Harrison comments that "The existence of literature is plainly something of a puzzle for Habermas, as it generally is and has generally been for the theoreticians in our midst. But he is clear, nevertheless, that it can have no role in constituting cultural or personal identity, or in forming the outlook and terms of association of societies"; "'White Mythology' Revisited: Derrida and His Critics on Reason and Rhetoric," *Critical Inquiry* 25 (Spring 1999): 505–34 (524). On the other hand, it can be interpreted positively as the semantic "power of metaphor to project and reveal a world." Paul Ricocur, *The Rule of Metaphor: Multi-disciplinary Studies of the Creation of Meaning in Language,* trans. by Robert Czerny with Kathleen McLaughlin and John Costello (Toronto: University of Toronto Press, 1975), 93. The debate over whether metaphor can have access to knowledge and other cognitive processes is one that dates back to classical times; cf. Donald Davidson, "What Metaphors Mean," *Critical Inquiry* 5:1 (1978): 31–47; and Jacques Derrida, "White Mythology: Metaphor in the Text of Philosophy," in *Margins of Philosophy,* trans. by Alan Bass (Chicago: University of Chicago Press, 1982), 209–71.

4. Following the work of Fernand Braudel, *Capitalism and Material Life, 1400–1800,* trans. by Miriam Kochan (New York: Harper and Row, 1967), historians have sought to identify the origins of modern consumer society and the nature of the relationship between culture and consumption. Braudel draws on Marcel Mauss ("it is not in production that society found its impetus; luxury is the great stimulus"); Gaston Bachelard ("the attainment of the superfluous causes a greater spiritual excitement than the attainment of necessities. Man is a creature of desire and not a creature of need"); Jacques Rueff ("production is the daughter of desire"); among others (123ff.). Grant McCracken provides a helpful review of related scholarship in *Culture and Consumption: New Approaches to the Symbolic Character of Consumer Goods and Activities* (Bloomington: Indiana University Press, 1990). A key text for locating the consumer revolution in late eighteenth-century England is Neil McKendrick, John Brewer, and J. H. Plumb, *The Birth of a Consumer Society: The Commercialization of Eighteenth-Century England* (London: Europa, 1982). By the Victorian era, production and consumption had become equivalent components of culture, according to Thomas Richards, *The Commodity Culture of Victorian England: Advertising and Spectacle, 1851–1914* (Stanford: Stanford University Press, 1990).

5. Touch in ancient Greek theories of cognition was often ranked between the "higher" senses of sight and hearing and the "lower" senses of taste and smell, though it was also occasionally relegated to the bottom of the hierarchy as the most limited means of perception (a subset of taste and smell). John I. Beare, *Greek Theories of Elementary Cognition from Alcmaeon to Aristotle* (Oxford: Clarendon Press, 1906), 180–201; cf. David Sum-

mers, *The Judgment of Sense: Renaissance Naturalism and the Rise of Aesthetics* (Cambridge: Cambridge University Press, 1987), 56ff.

6. Carolyn Korsmeyer, *Making Sense of Taste: Food and Philosophy* (Ithaca: Cornell University Press, 1999), 22.

7. John Locke, *An Essay Concerning Human Understanding* (Oxford: Clarendon Press, 1979), 108.

8. Ernst Cassirer, *The Philosophy of the Enlightenment,* trans. by Fritz C.A. Loelln and James P. Pettegrove (Princeton: Princeton University Press, 1951).

9. James Boswell, *The Journal of a Tour to the Hebrides with Samuel Johnson,* ed. by Ian McGowan (1785; Edinburgh: Cannongate Classics, 1996), 177n.

10. William Godwin, *An Enquiry Concerning Political Justice, and its Influence on General Virtue & Happiness,* 2 vols. (London: Printed for G. G. J. & J. Robinson, 1793), 2:386.

11. Peter Farb and George Armelagos, *Consuming Passions: The Anthropology of Eating* (Boston: Houghton Mifflin, 1980), 190.

12. "The eighteenth century *was* the century of taste, that is, of the theory of taste." George Dickie, *The Century of Taste: The Philosophical Odyssey of Taste in the Eighteenth Century* (New York: Oxford University Press, 1996), 3.

13. J. B. Bamborough, *The Little World of Man* (London: Longman, Green, 1952), 41.

14. Ibid., 42.

15. Thomas Hobbes, *Leviathan,* ed. by Richard E. Flathman and David Johnston (New York: W. W. Norton, 1997), 31.

16. Irwin Primer, "Mandeville and Shaftesbury: Some Facts and Problems," *Mandeville Studies: New Explorations in the Art and Thought of Dr. Bernard Mandeville* (The Hague: Martinus Nijhoff, 1975).

17. Terry Eagleton, *The Ideology of the Aesthetic* (Oxford: Blackwell, 1990), 43.

18. Norbert Elias, *The Civilizing Process: The History of Manners,* trans. by Edmund Jephcott, vol. 1. (New York: Urizen Books, 1978). Stephen Mennell applies Elias's work to the history of food in "On the Civilizing of Appetite," *Food and Culture: A Reader,* ed. by Carole Counihan and Penny Van Esterik (New York: Routledge, 1997): 315–37; and *All Manners of Food: Eating and Taste in England and France from the Middle Ages to the Present,* 2d ed. (Urbana: University of Illinois Press, 1996), esp. 26–39.

19. There have been various approaches by historians, sociologists, and cultural critics to define the segment of society labeled "middle class" or "middle classes," since this social tier need not be seen as a block, though "by the middle of the nineteenth century, these disparate elements [of the middle class] had been welded together into a powerful unified culture." Leonore Davidoff and Catherine Hall, *Family Fortunes: Men and Women of the English Middle Class, 1780–1850* (Chicago: University of Chicago Press, 1987), 23. While the income bands of the middle ranks could range from as low as £100 per annum to several thousand from 1780 to 1850, generally £200 to £300 per annum would suffice for the average family. John Burnett estimates that in the early nineteenth-century Britain, an income of £150 to £350 per annum would secure a family firmly within the middle class, or £250 per annum for a family with three children; *Plenty and Want, A Social History of Food in England from 1815 to the Present Day,* 3d ed. (London: Routledge, 1989), 74–77.

20. Lorna Weatherill, *Consumer Behaviour and Material Culture in Britain, 1660–1760* (London: Routledge, 1988), 13–14.

21. Lance Bertelson, *The Nonsense Club: Literature and Popular Culture, 1749–1764* (Oxford: Clarendon Press, 1986), 4.

22. Thomas Newcomb, *The Woman of Taste. Occasioned by a late poem, entitled The Man of Taste* (London, 1733), 16.

23. James Boswell, *Life of Johnson* (London: Oxford University Press, 1953), 756. Much has been said about the distastefulness of Johnson's table manners. "When at table," Boswell informs us, "he was totally absorbed in the business of the moment; his looks seemed rivetted to his plate; nor would he, unless when in very high company, say one word, or even pay the least attention to what was said by others, till he had satisfied his appetite, which was so fierce, and indulged with such intenseness, that while in the act of eating, the veins of his forehead swelled, and generally a strong perspiration was visible" (331). However, Johnson's friends attest that he considered himself an expert of polite conduct and would frequently criticize the etiquette of others. "It was amazing," says Frances Reynolds, "so dim-sighted as Dr Johnson was, how very observant he was of appearances in Dress, in behaviour, and even of the servants, how they waited at table, etc., *the more particularly so, seeming as he did to be stone-blind to his own* dress and behaviour"; quoted in Christopher Hibbert, *The Personal History of Samuel Johnson* (London: Longman, 1971), 197.

24. Boswell, *Life of Johnson*, 756.

25. Brillat-Savarin called this "disgraceful indifference" (*PT* 153).

26. Boswell, *Life of Johnson*, 756.

27. Samuel Johnson, *The Yale Edition of the Works of Samuel Johnson*, 16 vols., ed. by W. J. Bate and A. B. Strauss (New Haven: Yale University Press, 1958–), 5:384.

28. Boswell, *Life of Johnson*, 942, 332.

29. Peter Melville offers an astute reading of Kant's dinner party in " 'A Friendship of Taste': The Pragmatics of Eating Well in Kant's *Anthropology from a Pragmatic Point of View*," in *Cultures of Taste, Theories of Appetite: Eating Romanticism*, ed. by Timothy Morton (New York: Palgrave, 2003), 203–16.

30. Quoted from Arjun Appaduri in Warren Belasco, "Food Matters: Perspectives on an Emerging Field," in *Food Nations: Selling Taste in Consumer Societies*, ed. by Warren Belasco and Philip Scranton (New York: Routledge, 2002), 2–23 (2). For a detailed summary of this line of thinking from the nineteenth century, see Jack Goody, *Cooking, Cuisine and Class: A Study in Comparative Sociology* (Cambridge: Cambridge University Press, 1982), 10–39. Recent anthropological and sociological work, building on Claude Lévi-Strauss, Max Veblan, Norbert Elias, and Emile Durkheim, demonstrates "a preoccupation with food as a marker of difference, including such classic sociological variables as gender, age, class and ethnicity"; Pat Caplan, "Introduction," *Food, Health and Identity*, ed. by Pat Caplan (London and New York: Routledge, 1997), 1–31 (9). Mary Douglas argues that "we need to stop talking of food as something that people desire apart from social relations"; *Food in the Social Order: Studies of Food and Festivities in Three American Communities* (New York: Russell Sage, 1984), 36. See also Pierre Bourdieu, *Distinction: A Social Critique of the Judgement of Taste*, trans. by Richard Nice (Cambridge: Harvard University Press, 1984); and Marshall Sahlins, *Culture and Practical Reason* (Chicago: University of Chicago Press, 1976), 170–71ff.

31. Daniel Pool, *What Jane Austen Ate and Charles Dickens Knew: From Fox Hunting to Whist, the Facts of Daily Life in Nineteenth-Century England* (New York: Simon and Schuster, 1993), 72.

32. Between 1790 and 1812 food shortages drove up the price of meat and bread 100 percent and 167 percent, respectively; T. L. Richardson, "The Agricultural Labourer's Standard of Living in Kent, 1790–1840," in *The Making of the Modern British Diet,* ed. by Derek Oddy and Derek Miller (London: Croom Helm, 1976), 103–16 (106). Given the high proportion of the average laborer's budget that went toward bread, the doubling and almost tripling of costs had devastating effects.

33. Representations of the latter are acutely analyzed by Rebecca Spang, *The Invention of the Restaurant: Paris and Modern Gastronomic Culture* (Cambridge: Harvard University Press, 2000), 123–33.

34. *CCL* 2:388. Coleridge's friend Poole also experimented with cheaper ways of making bread from barley, beans, and potatoes; Rosemary Ashton, *The Life of Samuel Taylor Coleridge* (Oxford: Blackwell, 1996), 66. Michael Rosa explains the procedure for making bread from acorns in *On Acorns and Oak Trees and Other Useful Things for Food and Cultivation* (1802); quoted in Massimo Montanari, *The Culture of Food,* trans. by Carl Ipsen (Oxford: Blackwell, 1988), 132: a procedure that had been used in France during desperate times in 1672 and 1673 (Braudel, *Capitalism and Material Life,* 73).

35. Stanley Cavell, " 'Who Does the Wolf Love?': *Coriolanus* and the Interpretations of Politics," in *Shakespeare and the Question of Theory,* ed. by Patricia Parker and Geoffrey Hartman (New York: Methuen, 1985), 245–72 (269–70).

36. Galen's system of humoral physiology evolves from Empedocles's notion that all matter is composed of four elements; his important dietetic texts were *De alimentorum facultatibus, De sanitae tuenda,* and *De probis pravisque alimentarum succis.* For a recent study, see Mark Grant, *Galen on Food and Diet* (London: Routledge, 2000).

37. Ken Albala, *Eating Right in the Renaissance* (Berkeley: University of California Press, 2002), 84–104.

38. *PL* 8.622–29; also in *Samson Agonistes,* Milton laments the limited nature of human sense perception: "why was the sight / To such a tender ball as the eye confined? / So obvious and so easy to be quenched, / And not as feeling through all parts diffused, / That she might look at will through every pore?" (93–97).

39. John Hunter, *Observations on Certain Parts of the Animal Oeconomy* (London, 1786), 147–48.

40. Johann Friedrich Blumenbach, *The Institutions of Physiology,* trans. by John Elliotson, 2d ed. (Philadelphia: Benjamin Warner, 1817), 351.

41. Quoted in Daniel Cottom, "The Work of Art in the Age of Mechanical Digestion," *Representations* 66 (spring 1999): 52–74 (63); also see Richard D. Altick, *The Shows of London* (Cambridge: Harvard University Press, 1978), 66.

42. Cookery developed differently in Britain than in France. While British cooking evolved according to bourgeois ideals of economy by female housekeepers; French cooking was traditionally performed by male chefs for aristocratic consumers and retained an aura of prestige. Stephen Mennell discusses three areas of influence that may have contributed to these differences in British and French cuisine as they developed from the second half of the seventeenth century: (1) a Puritanism (and Protestantism more generally) that

denounced luxury and the pleasures of the flesh; (2) the role of the court, whose impact on haute cuisine lasted roughly a century and a half longer in France than in England; and (3) the greater stratification of town and country in France than in England, whose countryside and rural ways of life blurred power hierarchies among various social groups; he mainly discredits the first area of influence, however; *All Manners of Food,* 103 ff.

43. Korsmeyer, *Making Sense of Taste,* 30. Elizabeth Telfer pursues similar lines of thought in *Food for Thought: Philosophy and Food* (London: Routledge, 1996).

44. Samuel Foote, *Taste* and *The Orators,* ed. by Mary C. Murphy (Annapolis: United States Naval Academy, 1982), 4.

45. See also G. J. Barker-Benfield, *The Culture of Sensibility: Sex and Society in Eighteenth-Century Britain* (Chicago: University of Chicago Press, 1992), and Robert W. Jones, *Gender and the Formation of Taste in Eighteenth-Century Britain: The Analysis of Beauty* (Cambridge: Cambridge University Press, 1998).

46. *The Connoisseur. A Satire on the Modern Men of Taste* (London, 1735), 10.

47. As Deane W. Curtin argues, by "marginalizing the lives of women, manual laborers, and persons of color (those who have been defined as responsible for food), dominant persons also marginalize the aspects of their own lives that are 'ordinary' and 'bodily' "; "Introduction," *Cooking, Eating, Thinking: Transformative Philosophies of Food,* ed. by Deane W. Curtin and Lisa M. Heldke (Bloomington: Indiana University Press, 1992): 3–22 (4).

48. Quoted from Aristotle's *Nicomachean Ethics* in Summers, *The Judgment of Sense,* 57.

49. Summers discusses "the social distinction between mental and physical labor" in classical aesthetics; *Judgment of Sense,* 235.

50. Jocelyn Kolb argues that the development of the novel as a literary form made room for "low" topics, such as food, which traditionally did not belong in the higher province of art, in *The Ambiguity of Taste: Freedom and Food in European Romanticism* (Ann Arbor: University of Michigan Press, 1995). Other studies, such as Maggie Lane, *Jane Austen and Food* (London, Ohio: Hambledon Press, 1995), are conceived in this vein, though a literary history of taste originating in Milton reconfigures the parallelism of poetry/novel and taste/appetite.

51. Henry Fielding, *The History of Tom Jones,* ed. by R. P. C. Mutter (Harmondsworth: Penguin, 1966), 51.

52. For more on this topic, see Neil Vickers, "Coleridge's 'Abstruse Researches,' " in *Samuel Taylor Coleridge and the Sciences of Life,* ed. by Nicholas Roe (Oxford: Oxford University Press, 2001), 155–74 (171 ff.).

53. David Bromwich, *Hazlitt: The Mind of a Critic* (New York: Oxford University Press, 1983), 228.

54. Exemplary culinary uses of "gusto" occur in the preface to Robert May's *The Accomplisht Cook, or the Art and Mystery of Cookery* (London: Nathaniel Brooke, 1660) and Hannah Woolley's *The Cook's Guide; or, Rare Receipts for Cookery . . . Whereby Noble Persons and Others in their Hospitalities may be Gratified in their Gusto's* (London: Peter Dring, 1664).

55. James Engell, *The Creative Imagination: Enlightenment to Romanticism* (Cambridge, Mass.: Harvard University Press, 1981), 205.

56. Raymond Williams, "Taste," in *Keywords: A Vocabulary of Culture and Society* (New York: Oxford University Press, 1976), 264; Dabney Townsend, "Taste: Early History," *Encyclopedia of Aesthetics* (Oxford: Oxford University Press, 1998), 4:355–60 (356).

57. Baltasar Gracián y Morales, *The Oracle: A Manual of the Art of Discretion*, trans. by L. B. Walton (London: J. M. Dent, 1953), 97.

58. Hans-Georg Gadamer, *Truth and Method* (New York: Seabury Press, 1975), 33–34.

59. François-Marie de Voltaire, "Taste," in Diderot and d'Alembert, *Encyclopedia: Selections*, trans. by Nelly S. Hoyt and Thomas Cassirer (Indianapolis: Bobbs-Merrill, 1965), 336; "Ce sens, ce don de discerner nos alimens, a produit dans toutes les langues connues, la métaphore qui exprime par le mot *goût*, le sentiment des beautés & des défauts dans tous les arts: c'est un discernment prompt comme celui de la langue & du palais, & qui prévient comme lui la réflexion"; *Encyclopédie ou Dictionnaire Raisonné des Sciences des Arts et des Métiers*, vol. 7 (Günther Holzboog: Fredrich Frommann Verlag, 1966). The entry, appended to Montesquieu's entry on taste (which was abandoned with the latter's death), was translated into English and added to the first two editions of Gerard's *An Essay on Taste* (1759, 1764).

60. Remy G. Saisselin, *The Rule of Reason and the Ruses of the Heart: A Philosophical Dictionary of Classical French Criticism, Critics, and Aesthetic Issues* (Cleveland: Press of Case Western University, 1970); Luc Ferry, *Homo Aestheticus: The Invention of Taste in the Democratic Age*, trans. by Robert De Loaiza (Chicago: University of Chicago Press, 1993), 14.

61. Karen L. Edwards has recently argued, along similar lines, that "what Eve accepts from Satan is 'empirical science'"; *Milton and the Natural World: Science and Poetry in Paradise Lost* (Cambridge: Cambridge University Press, 1999), 31.

62. W. J. Bate, *From Classic to Romantic: Premises of Taste in Eighteenth-Century England* (New York: Harper and Row, 1946), 46.

63. E.g., Addison (*SPT* 2:587) and Burke (*PE* 61); Lucy Newlyn examines a number of examples in *Paradise Lost and the Romantic Reader* (Oxford: Clarendon Press, 1993).

64. Sir Joshua Reynolds, *Discourses on Art*, ed. by Robert R. Wark (New Haven: Yale University Press, 1997), 171.

65. As commercial society consolidated into capitalism during the Romantic era, all "uneconomic" rhythms, passions, and desires were expected to conform to "the methodical way of life of industrial capitalism"; E. P. Thompson, *The Making of the English Working Class* (New York: Vintage, 1966), 403.

66. Mark Storey opens his study of Byronic appetite by observing that the gap between Byron and Keats "was not as great as either poet would have wished, but it was sufficiently marked for both of them to chew at it in fascination." *Byron & the Eye of Appetite* (London: Macmillan, 1986), 1.

Chapter 2. Mortal Taste

1. Christopher Ricks, *Milton's Grand Style* (Oxford: Clarendon, 1963), 69.

2. Shaftesbury inquires: "Will it not be found . . . that what is beautiful is . . . true; and

what is at once both beautiful and true is, of consequence, agreeable and good?" (*C* 415); cf. *C* 124; and Hume: "The approbation of moral qualities most certainly is not deriv'd from reason, or any comparison of ideas; but proceeds entirely from a moral taste, and from certain sentiments of pleasure or disgust" (*THN* 581); cf. *EMP* 230–32; and Addison (*SPT* 3:566ff.).

3. Eating in medieval and early modern Europe was "an occasion for union with one's fellows and one's God, a commensality given particular intensity by the prototypical meal, the eucharist, which seemed to hover in the background of any banquet." Caroline Walker Bynum, *Holy Feast and Holy Fast: The Religious Significance of Food to Medieval Women* (Berkeley: University of California Press, 1987), 3. Mikhail Bakhtin argues that banquet scenes in Rabelais provide images of the "open, biting, rending, chewing mouth" as a synecdoche for the early modern body, a grotesque if comic entity transgressing limits of self and world: "Man's encounter with the world in the act of eating is joyful, triumphant; he triumphs over the world, devours it without being devoured himself." Mikhail Mikhailovich Bakhtin, *Rabelais and His World,* trans. by Hélène Iswolsky (Bloomington: Indiana University Press, 1984), 281. Bakhtin's optimistic reading of Renaissance orality has invited substantial critique, though it remains a reference point for thinking through the politics of pleasure in early modern culture. Cf. Peter Stallybrass and Allon White, *The Politics and Poetics of Transgression* (Ithaca: Cornell University Press, 1986); and Leah S. Marcus, *The Politics of Mirth: Jonson, Herrick, Milton, Marvell, and the Defense of Old Holiday Pastimes* (Chicago: University of Chicago Press, 1986), 24–63. On Ben Jonson's digestive imagery, see Bruce Boehrer, *The Fury of Men's Gullets: Ben Jonson and the Digestive Canal* (Philadelphia: University of Pennsylvania Press, 1997). To the best of my knowledge, a comprehensive study of the topic of eating in Shakespeare has yet to be written.

4. The seminal account of the bourgeois public sphere, by Jürgen Habermas, places its origins in the major structural changes to society of the 1690s; *The Structural Transformation of the Public Sphere: An Inquiry into a Category of Bourgeois Society,* trans. by Thomas Burger (Cambridge, Mass.: MIT Press, 1989). On Milton's role in the public sphere see, e.g., Sharon Achinstein, *Milton and the Revolutionary Reader* (Princeton: Princeton University Press, 1994); Annabel Patterson, *Early Modern Liberalism* (Cambridge: Cambridge University Press, 1997); David Norbrook, *Writing the English Republic: Poetry, Rhetoric, and Politics, 1627–1660* (Cambridge: Cambridge University Press, 1999). Cf. Howard Caygill, who argues that the British "theory of taste . . . stemmed from the realignment of state and civil society prepared in the revolutions of the seventeenth century," *Art of Judgement* (Oxford: Basil Blackwell, 1989), 100; and Luc Ferry, who traces what he takes to be the central issue of aesthetic theory (whether individual preference can be reconciled to a universal standard) to the mid-1660s and the simultaneous "invention" of notions of taste (individual preference) and modern democracy (the state as a consensus among individuals).

5. Regina M. Schwartz, *Remembering and Repeating: On Milton's Theology and Poetics* (Chicago: University of Chicago Press, 1993), 15.

6. "[Man] was to be condemned both for trusting Satan and for not trusting God; he was faithless, ungrateful, disobedient, greedy, uxorious; she, negligent of her husband's welfare; both of them committed theft, robbery with violence, murder against their

children (i.e. the whole human race); each was sacrilegious and deceitful, cunningly aspiring to divinity although thoroughly unworthy of it, proud and arrogant" (*YP* 6:383–84).

7. James Patrick McHenry, "A Milton Herbal," *Milton Quarterly* 30 (1996): 45–115 (53).

8. Edwards, *Milton and the Natural World*, 143–53.

9. Robert Applebaum, "Eve and Adam's 'Apple': Horticulture, Taste, and the Flesh of the Forbidden Fruit in *Paradise Lost*," *Milton Quarterly* 36 (2002): 221–39 (223).

10. William Kerrigan, *The Sacred Complex: On the Psychogenesis of "Paradise Lost"* (Cambridge, Mass.: Harvard University Press, 1983), 204.

11. Arkady Plotnitsky, *Reconfigurations: Critical Theory and General Economy* (Gainesville: University Press of Florida, 1993), 71.

12. Albala, *Eating Right in the Renaissance*, 219.

13. Georges Bataille, *The Accursed Share: An Essay on General Economy* (New York: Zone, 1991); cf. "The Notion of Expenditure," in *Visions of Excess: Selected Writings, 1927–1939*, ed. by Allan Stoekl, trans. by Alan Stoekl with Carl R. Lovitt and Donald M. Leslie Jr. (Minneapolis: University of Minnesota Press, 1985); and Jacques Derrida, "From Restricted to General Economy: A Hegelianism without Reserve," in *Writing and Difference*, trans. by Alan Bass (Chicago: University of Chicago Press, 1978), 251–77.

14. Bataille, *Visions of Excess*, 119–21.

15. Michele Richman, *Reading Georges Bataille* (Baltimore: Johns Hopkins University Press, 1982), 148.

16. Jacques Derrida, "Economimesis," trans. by R. Klein, *Diacritics* 11:2 (1982): 3–25 (16).

17. Deborah Kuller Shuger, *The Renaissance Bible: Scholarship, Sacrifice, Subjectivity* (Berkeley: University of California Press, 1994), 163.

18. Derrida, "Economimesis," 11.

19. The tradition of reading *De Doctrina Christiana* (first published in 1825) as a gloss on *Paradise Lost* begins with Maurice Kelly's *This Great Argument* (1941), though the relation between poetry and treatise has been an important concern in Milton scholarship since 1991, when William B. Hunter challenged Milton's authorship of the treatise. After several years of articles and rebuttals, a committee report by Gordon Campbell, Thomas N. Corns, John K. Hale, David J. Holmes, and Fiona J. Tweedie appeared in *Milton Quarterly*, affirming Milton's authorship but cautioning: "The relationship of *de doctrina Christiana* to the Milton oeuvre must remain uncertain, since in the case of a work of revision that has halted before completion we cannot know what other changes, especially what deletions of doctrines to which he did not subscribe, Milton would have made in completing his task." "The Provenance of *De Doctrina Christiana*," *Milton Quarterly* 31:3 (1997): 67–110 (110). For Hunter's full-length argument, see *Visitation Unimplor'd: Milton and the Authorship of De Doctrina Christiana* (Pittsburgh: Duquesne University Press, 1998).

20. Milton's last antiprelatical tract, *Of True Religion, Haeresie, Schism, Toleration, and What Best Means May be Us'd against the Growth of Popery* (1673), expresses tolerance toward Arians, Socinians, and other Protestant sects but none toward Catholics.

21. Maggie Kilgour, *From Communion to Cannibalism: An Anatomy of Metaphors of Incorporation* (Princeton: Princeton University Press, 1990).

22. Critical concern with Milton's monism can be traced to Dennis Saurat's *Milton: Man and Thinker* (1925), though its widespread acceptance is owing to J. H. Adamson's "Milton and the Creation," *Journal of English and Germanic Philology* 61 (1962): 756–78, which made it possible to understand Milton's monism in a way that does not presume a material, hence esoteric, God. Adamson points out that Milton carefully avoids attributing corporeality to God; the substance of God contains a "bodily force," but not necessarily a body (*YP* 6:309). For a critical overview of the topic, see Stephen M. Fallon, *Milton Among the Philosophers: Poetry and Materialism in Seventeenth-Century England* (Ithaca: Cornell University Press, 1991), 4–6.

23. Werner Hamacher, *Pleroma: Reading in Hegel*, trans. by Nicholas Walker and Simon Jarvis (Stanford: Stanford University Press, 1998), 191. Hamacher refers specifically to Hegel's critique of the Catholic sacrament, though these are an extension of the metaphysical qualms of Milton.

24. Adamson, "Milton and the Creation," 756–67.

25. John Guillory, *Poetic Authority: Spenser, Milton, and Literary History* (New York: Columbia University Press, 1983), 113.

26. J. Martin Evans also notices that "Metaphorically, at least, the 'Infernal Pit'" (1.657) is a sewer." *Milton's Imperial Epic: Paradise Lost and the Discourse of Colonialism* (Ithaca: Cornell University Press, 1996), 33–34; his concern is the imperial geography of seventeenth-century England, which viewed colonists as "England's excrements." Cf. Don Parry Norford, who reads Milton's cosmology as a system in which "God is the head or reason, Chaos the belly or womb, and Hell the bowels"; "The Devouring Father in *Paradise Lost*," *Hebrew University Studies in Literature* 8:1 (spring 1980): 98–126.

27. A. S. P. Woodhouse, "Notes on Milton's Views on the Creation: The Initial Phases," *Philological Quarterly* 28:1 (1949): 211–36 (229n.).

28. John P. Rumrich, "Milton's God and the Matter of Chaos," *PMLA* 110:5 (1995): 1035–46 (1045n.).

29. John Milton, *The Works of John Milton*, ed. by F. A. Patterson, 21 vols. (New York: Columbia University Press, 1931–38), 15:22–23.

30. John Rogers, *The Matter of Revolution: Science, Poetry, and Politics in the Age of Milton* (Ithaca: Cornell University Press, 1996), 130–43.

31. Kerrigan, *The Sacred Complex*, 202–5.

32. Quoted from Macrobius's *Commentary on the Dream of Scipio* in William B. Hunter, "Milton's Arianism Reconsidered," *Harvard Theological Review* 52:1 (1959), 18.

33. Quoted in Sigmund Freud's *Civilization and Its Discontents* in *The Freud Reader*, ed. by Peter Gay (New York: W. W. Norton, 1989), 755.

34. John E. Parish, "Milton and the Well-Fed Angel," *English Miscellany* 18 (1967): 87–109; John F. Huntley, "Gourmet Cooking and the Vision of Paradise in *Paradise Lost*," *Xavier University Studies* 8:2 (1969): 44–54; Marshall Grossman, "Milton's 'Transubstantiate': Interpreting the Sacrament in *Paradise Lost*," *Milton Quarterly* 16:2 (May 1982): 42–47; Anthony Low, "Angels and Food in *Paradise Lost*," *Milton Studies* 1

(1969): 135–45; Jack Goldman, "Perspectives of Raphael's Meal in *Paradise Lost,* Book V," *Milton Quarterly* 11:2 (1977): 31–37.

35. Albala, *Eating Right in the Renaissance,* 64.

36. Nigel Smith, "Enthusiasm and Enlightenment: Of Food, Filth, and Slavery," in *The Country and the City Revisited: England and the Politics of Culture, 1550–1850,* ed. by Gerald Maclean, Donna Landry, and Joseph P. Ward (Cambridge: Cambridge University Press, 1999), 106–18 (111).

37. C. S. Lewis, *A Preface to "Paradise Lost"* (London: Oxford University Press, 1942), 106.

38. William Riley Parker, *Milton: A Biography,* ed. by Gordon Campbell, 2d ed. 2 vols. (Oxford: Clarendon Press, 1966), 1:584.

39. Quoted from Milton's maid, Elizabeth Fisher, in David Masson, *The Life of John Milton: Narrated in Connexion with the Political, Ecclesiastical, and Literary History of His Time,* 7 vols. (reprint of 1877–96 ed. by Macmillan; Gloucester, Mass.: Peter Smith, 1965), 6:728.

40. Leigh Hunt, *Leigh Hunt's Literary Criticism,* ed. by Lawrence Huston Houtchens and Carolyn Washburn Houtchens (New York: Columbia University Press, 1956), 557.

41. Quoted in *The Romantics on Milton,* ed. by Joseph Wittreich (Cleveland: Case Western University Press, 1970), 106.

42. Edmund Spenser, *The Faerie Queene,* ed. by Thomas P. Roche Jr. and C. Patrick O'Donnell Jr. (London: Penguin, 1978), 44.

43. Cf. Spenser's Errour: "Halfe like a serpent horribly displaide, / But th' other halfe did womans shape retaine" (*Faerie Queene,* 1.1.14).

44. Seth Lerer, "An Art of the Emetic: Thomas Wilson and the Rhetoric of Parliament," *Studies in Philology* 98 (2001): 158–83 (159).

45. In William Friedkin's 1973 horror film, Blair's satanically possessed character spits out foul, fragmented language with projectile vomit.

46. Borrowing Milton's parody of Satanic emission, Charles Lamb uses it to "damn" an unreceptive audience: "Mercy on us that God should give his favorite children *men,* mouths to speak with . . . and that they should turn them into mouths of adders, bears, wolves, hyenas, and whistle like tempests and emit breath thro' them like distillations of aspic poison . . . — *Blind Mouths!* as Milton somewhere calls them"; *LM* 2:273; cf. *WCL* 1:88.

47. Quoted from Aubrey's *Lives* (first pub. 1813) in *The Early Lives of Milton,* ed. by Helen Darbishire (London: Constable, 1932), 1023; this interpretation is also suggested by Parker, *Milton: A Biography,* 1:162.

48. Harold Bloom points out that in the Hebrew Bible "Satan" is not a proper name; in the book of Job he is called *ha-Satan* ("the Satan"), which means something like "blocking agent." *Omens of Millennium: The Gnosis of Angels, Dreams, and Resurrection* (London: Fourth Estate, 1997), 67.

49. Rumrich, "Milton's God," 1039.

50. William B. Hunter, "The Double Set of Temptations in *Paradise Regained,*" *Milton Studies* 14 (1980): 183–93 (183). For a further articulation of this structural problematic, see Northrop Frye, "Revolt in the Desert," in *The Return of Eden* (Toronto: University of Toronto Press, 1965), 135–36.

51. On *Paradise Regained* as a series of mounting temptations see, e.g., Barbara Kiefer Lewalski, *Milton's Brief Epic: The Genre, Meaning, and Art of Paradise Regained* (Providence: Brown University Press, 1966); and Elizabeth Marie Pope, *Paradise Regained: The Tradition and the Poem* (Baltimore: Johns Hopkins University Press, 1947). The randomness of the temptations is usually considered Stanley Fish's argument: "one cannot say that this or that moment is crucial, because every moment is crucial (every moment offers an opportunity to be either faithful or idolatrous)." "Things and Actions Indifferent: The Temptation of Plot in *Paradise Regained*," in *Critical Essays on John Milton*, ed. by Christopher Kendrick (New York: G. K. Hall, 1995), 85. However, Alan Fisher argues to similar effect in an article that appeared slightly before Fish's, namely, "Why Is *Paradise Regained* So Cold?" *Milton Studies* 14 (1980): 195–217.

52. Hunter, "Double Set of Temptations," 191.

53. Deuteronomy 8:3; *The New Oxford Annotated Bible*, ed. by Bruce M. Metzger and Roland E. Murphy (New York: Oxford University Press, 1994); unless otherwise indicated, all further references are to this edition, quoted within the text.

54. In *Paradise Lost*, God declares: "This day I have begot whom I declare / My only Son" (*PL* 5.603–4), and in *Christian Doctrine* Milton speaks directly of "the bizarre and senseless idea that the Son, although personally and numerically distinct, was nevertheless essentially one with the Father. . . . It would have been a waste of time for God to thunder forth so repeatedly that first commandment which said that he was the one and only God, if it could nevertheless be maintained that another God existed as well, who ought himself to be thought of as the only God" (*YP* 6:212). One of the central "heresies" of this treatise is its denial of the doctrine of equality between Father and Son, though like the nature of "matter" the Son is a complex issue in Milton scholarship, perhaps the most complicated. Focal points in the critical debate include Maurice Kelley, *This Great Argument: A Study of Milton's De Doctrina Christiana as a Gloss upon Paradise Lost* (Gloucester, Mass.: Peter Smith, 1962), 84–106; Hunter, "Milton's Arianism Reconsidered"; as well as Adamson's and Patrides's works in *Bright Essence*. Michael Bauman provides a detailed reassessment in *Milton's Arianism* (Frankfurt: Peter Lang, 1986), and John P. Rumrich discusses its significance in twentieth-century reception history in "Milton's Arianism: Why It Matters," in *Milton and Heresy*, ed. by Stephen B. Dobranski and John P. Rumrich (Cambridge: Cambridge University Press, 1998), 75–92.

55. Technically, Milton does not use the term *cannibalism*, which did not exist in Latin; rather, he refers to a Cyclops' feast when discussing the Catholic sacrament of transubstantiation: "quae coenam Dominicam in coenam prope dixerem cyclopeam converterunt," which Sumner renders similarly to Carey as "a banquet of cannibals." *Works*, 15:196–97.

56. Gregory W. Bredbeck, *Sodomy and Interpretation: Marlowe to Milton* (Ithaca: Cornell University Press, 1991).

57. Lewalski, *Milton's Brief Epic*, 202.

58. Lee Sheridan Cox, "Food-Word Imagery in *Paradise Regained*," *ELH* 28:3 (1961): 225–43.

59. Albala, *Eating Right in the Renaissance*, 197–214.

60. Hunter, "Double Set of Temptations," 184.

61. William Shakespeare, *The Tempest*, 5.1.123–25; *The Riverside Shakespeare* (Boston: Houghton Mifflin, 1974).

62. Sidney W. Mintz, *Sweetness and Power: The Place of Sugar in Modern History* (New York: Viking, 1985), 74–96.

63. Albala, *Eating Right in the Renaissance*, 212.

64. "Enter Ariel, like a harpy; claps his wings upon the table; and with a quaint device the banquet vanishes." *The Tempest* 3.3.52–53.

65. *The Poetical Works of Christopher Smart*, ed. by Marcus Walsh and Katrina Williamson, 6 vols. (Oxford: Clarendon Press, 1983), 2:341. For a catalogue "Of the Bibliophagi or Book-eaters," and "Of Book-Drinkers," see Holbrook Jackson, *The Anatomy of Bibliomania* (London: Sonsino Press, 1930), 187–212, 213–16, respectively.

66. Fisher, "Why Is *Paradise Regained* So Cold?" 199.

67. Fish, "Things and Actions Indifferent," 87.

68. Fisher, "Why Is *Paradise Regained* So Cold?" 211.

69. Jacques Derrida, *Of Grammatology*, trans. by Gayatri C. Spivak (Baltimore: Johns Hopkins University Press, 1976), 144–45.

70. James Nohrnberg, "'Paradise Regained' by One Greater Man: Milton's Wisdom Epic as a 'Fable of Identity,'" in *Centre and Labyrinth: Essays in Honour of Northrop Frye*, ed. by Eleanor Cook et al. (Toronto: University of Toronto Press, 1983), 83–114 (88); Kilgour, *From Communion to Cannibalism*, 137.

71. Just as the epistemological element of *sapere* was important to Milton, it was important to taste theorists in the century following him. Shaftesbury asserts that "there must of necessity be the foundation of a right and wrong taste" (*C* 150), Hume speaks of an "erroneous" taste (*EMP* 241); Burke of an "absurd and ridiculous" taste (*PE* 4); and Kant of "an erroneous judgement of taste" (*CJ* 57). Cf. Reynolds, 141; and Alexander Gerard, *An Essay on Taste*, fac. reprod. of 3d ed. (1798), ed. by Walter J. Hippel Jr. (Gainesville: Scholars' Facsimiles and Reprints, 1963), 121.

72. Louis Althusser, "Ideology and Ideological State Apparatuses (Notes toward an Investigation)," in *Lenin and Philosophy and Other Essays*, trans. by Ben Brewster (London: New Left Books, 1971), 127–86 (171); this quotation is fully italicized in the original.

73. Hugh Blair, "Lecture XLIV," in *Lectures on Rhetoric and Belles Lettres*, 8th American ed. from the last Edinburgh ed. (New York: L. and F. Lockwood, 1819), 452.

Chapter 3. The Century of Taste

1. George Colman and Bonnell Thornton, "On Taste," in *The Connoisseur. By Mr. Town, Critic and Censor-General*, 2d ed., 4 vols. (London: R. Baldwin, 1757): 4:121–27 (121). A witty successor to Addison and Steele's *Spectator* (1711–14), *The Connoisseur* first appeared on January 31, 1754, and continued weekly through 140 issues until September 30, 1756.

2. Lance Bertelsen, *The Nonsense Club: Literature and Popular Culture, 1749–1764* (Oxford, Clarendon Press, 1986), 45.

3. Roy Porter, "Consumption: Disease of the Consumer Society?" in *Consumption and the World of Goods*, ed. by John Brewer and Roy Porter (London: Routledge, 1993), 58–81 (60).

4. Anthony Ashley Cooper, third earl of Shaftesbury, *The Life, Unpublished Letters, and Philosophical Regiment of Anthony, Earl of Shaftesbury*, ed. by Benjamin Rand

(London: Swan Sonnenschein; New York: Macmillan, 1900), 256. The notebooks, arranged topically, offer a glimpse into Shaftesbury's inner life between 1698 and 1704, though Rand eliminates dates. Lawrence E. Klein finds in the notebooks and Shaftesbury's other writings a conflict between philosophical idealism and "the existential reality of an individual"; *Shaftesbury and the Culture of Politeness: Moral Discourse and Cultural Politics in Early Eighteenth-Century England* (Cambridge: Cambridge University Press, 1994), 71.

5. Little is known about Mandeville's life, but his Latin dissertation and early medical writings, including *Bernardi a Mandeville de Medicina Oratio Scholastica* (Rotterdam, 1685); *Disputatio Philosophica de Brutorum Operationibus* (Leyden, 1789); and *Disputatio Medica Inauguralis de Chyosi Vitiata* (Leyden, 1791), indicate that his specific medical training was in digestive and nerve disorders, or "Hypochondriack and Hysterick Diseases," all attributed to poor digestion. Helpful on the *Treatise* are Hector Monro, *The Ambivalence of Bernard Mandeville* (Oxford: Clarendon Press, 1975), 48–74; and Richard I. Cook, *Bernard Mandeville* (New York: Twayne, 1974), 60–76.

6. Jonathan Swift satirizes English physicians who try to cure all bodily ills through evacuation: "Their Fundamental is, that all Diseases arise from *Repletion;* from whence they conclude, that a great *Evacuation* of the Body is necessary, either through the natural Passage, or upwards at the Mouth. . . . For Nature (as the Physicians alledge) having intended the superior anterior Orifice only for the *Intromission* of Solids and Liquids, and the inferior Posterior for Ejection; these Artists ingeniously considering that in all Diseases Nature is forced out of her Seat; therefore to replace her in it, the Body must be treated in a Manner directly contrary, by interchanging the Use of each Orifice; forcing Solids and Liquids in at the *Anus,* and making Evacuations at the Mouth." *Gulliver's Travels: An Authoritative Text,* ed. by Robert A. Greenberg, 2d ed. (New York: W. W. Norton, 1970), 220–21.

7. Albala, *Eating Right in the Renaissance,* 141.

8. Francis Bacon, *The Essayes or Counsels, Civill and Morall,* ed. by Michael Kiernan (Oxford: Clarendon Press, 2000), 153.

9. Cf. Martha Woodmansee, *The Author, Art, and the Market: Rereading the History of Aesthetics* (New York: Columbia University Press, 1994); Jon P. Klancher, *The Making of English Reading Audiences, 1790–1832* (Madison: University of Wisconsin Press, 1987).

10. Francis Jeffrey, "Review of *Essays on the Nature and Principles of Taste* by Archibald Alison," *Edinburgh Review* 35 (1811): 1–46 (44).

11. Colman and Thornton, *The Connoisseur,* 4:123–24.

12. James Engell, "The Source, and End, and Test of Art: Hume's Critique," in *Johnson and His Age,* ed. by James Engell (Cambridge: Harvard University Press, 1984), 233–53 (237); cf. his "Non Disputandum: Hume's Critique of Criticism," in *Forming the Critical Mind: Dryden to Coleridge* (Cambridge, Mass.: Harvard University Press, 1989), 106.

13. As Clement Hawes explains, "the figure of the bodily, excremental hack" represents a style of literary production that was "seen as grotesquely material in its determinations," against an older model of the Ancients who were thought to provide more spiritual food. *Mania and Literary Style: The Rhetoric of Enthusiasm from the Ranters to Christopher Smart* (New York: Cambridge University Press, 1996), 109.

14. For classical theories of smell, see Beare, *Greek Theories of Elementary Cognition,* 131–59; cf. John Baillie, who claimed that *"Taste, Smell,* nor *Touch* convey nothing that is Great and Exalted"; *An Essay on the Sublime* (1747), ed. by Samuel Holt Monk (Los Angeles: Augustan Reprint Society, 1953), 41; and Burke, who also trivialized the role that smell and taste could play in aesthetic experience: *"Smells,* and *Tastes,* have some share too, in ideas of greatness; but it is a small one, weak in its nature, and confined in its operations . . . no smells or tastes can produce a grand sensation, except excessive bitters, and intolerable stenches" (*PE* 85).

15. Alain Corbin, *The Foul and the Fragrant: Odor and the French Social Imagination* (Cambridge, Mass.: Harvard University Press, 1986), 14–15.

16. Cf. Dominique La Porte, *History of Shit,* trans. by Nadia Benabid and Rodolphe el-Khoury (Cambridge, Mass.: MIT Press, 1993).

17. Swift feels compelled to distinguish himself from Shaftesbury, the idealist philosopher, in an apology added to the fifth edition of *A Tale of a Tub,* complaining that readers have *"pronounced another Book to have been the Work of the same Hand with this* [Shaftesbury's *A Letter on Enthusiasm*]; *which the Author directly affirms to be a thorough mistake; he having yet never so much as read that Discourse"* (*SPW* 1:3).

18. Ronald Paulson, *The Beautiful, Novel, and Strange: Aesthetics and Heterodoxy* (Baltimore: Johns Hopkins University Press, 1996), 28.

19. Ibid., 6.

20. Gerard, *An Essay on Taste,* 217.

21. Bamborough, *The Little World of Man,* 54.

22. E. M. W. Tillyard, *The Elizabethan World Picture* (London: Chatto and Windus, 1952), 64–65.

23. Some of Hume's primary examples are taken from *Paradise Lost*; in a highly resonant moment of the essay, he conjures Milton to contradict the maxim that there can be no disputing about tastes: "Whoever would assert an equality of genius and elegance between OGILBY and MILTON, or BUNYAN and ADDISON, would be thought to defend no less an extravagance, than if he had maintained a mole-hill to be as high as TENERIFFE, or a pond as extensive as the ocean" (*EMP* 230–31); in *Paradise Lost* Satan looms as tall as Teneriffe, his stature reaching the sky (*PL* 4.985–87). With the perspective of hindsight (and given Hume's skepticism, perhaps from his own perspective too), the binary of Bunyan and Addison deconstructs the first, but the name Milton is usually strong enough to override potential confusion.

24. Kerrigan, *The Sacred Complex,* 204.

25. Immanuel Kant, letter to Marcus Herz, August 20, 1777, in *Philosophical Correspondence 1759–99,* trans. by Arnulf Zweig (Chicago: University of Chicago Press, 1987), 88; cf. Paul Youngquist on Kant's physiological aesthetics: "De Quincey's Crazy Body," *PMLA* 114 (1999): 346–58.

26. For more on Coleridge's digestive travails, see Paul Youngquist, "Romantic Dietetics! or, Eating Your Way to a New You!" in Morton, ed., *Cultures of Taste,* 237–55; and Martin Wallen, *City of Health, Fields of Disease: Revolutions in the Poetry, Medicine, and Philosophy of Romanticism* (Aldershot, U.K.: Ashgate, 2004).

27. From "Lecture XXII," in Blair, *Lectures on Rhetoric and Belles Lettres,* 18.

28. Although Descartes considered animals to be machines in his 1637 *Discourse on*

Method, he made an exception for humans, whose will exerted itself through the pineal gland. In 1748, his student Julien de La Mettrie did away with this final exception: "Let us then conclude boldly that man is a machine, and that in the whole universe there is but a single substance differently modified." Julien Offray de La Mettrie, *Man a Machine,* trans. by Gertrude C. Bussey and M. W. Calkins (Chicago: Open Court, 1912), 148. Thomas S. Hall helpfully discusses La Mettrie's work in *Ideas of Life and Matter: Studies in the History of General Physiology 600 B.C.–1900 A.D.,* 2 vols. (Chicago: University of Chicago Press, 1969), 1:351–408; 2:5–118.

29. "Want of taste is very common in fevers, owing frequently to the dryness or scurf of the tongue, or external organ of that sense, rather than to any injury of the nerves of taste." Erasmus Darwin, *Zoonomia; or, the Laws of Organic Life,* 2 vols. (London: J. Johnson, 1794), 2:145. Cf. Hume's *Treatise on Human Nature,* which suggests that discrepancies in judgments of taste "depend upon several circumstances. Upon the different situations of our health: a man in a malady feels a disagreeable taste in meats, which before pleased him the most. Upon the different complexions and constitutions of men: that seems bitter to one, which is sweet to another" (*THN* 226).

30. Korsmeyer, *Making Sense of Taste,* 53.

31. On Hume's alteration of the story, see James Shelley, "Hume's Double Standard of Taste," *Journal of Aesthetics and Art Criticism* 52:4 (1994): 437–45; and Steven Sverdlik, "Hume's Key and Aesthetic Rationality," *Journal of Aesthetics and Art Criticism* 45:1 (1986): 69–76. Roger A. Shiner proposes that the confusion in how precisely Hume intends the analogy to work is due to a mistaken causal interpretation according to which one can identify certain gustatory defects (iron, leather) in a taste object but cannot pronounce, or positively identify, its taste properties; by contrast, it should be possible to identify certain positive aesthetic properties in an object, and this distinction gets lost in the analogy to bodily taste. "Hume and the Causal Theory of Taste," *Journal of Aesthetics and Art Criticism* 54:3 (1996): 237–49 (240).

32. Voltaire echoes the idea in Diderot and d'Alembert's *Encyclopedia* when he remarks that "intellectual and artistic taste resembles sensual taste: just as the gourmet immediately perceives and recognizes a mixture of two liqueurs, so the man of taste, the connoisseur, will discern in a rapid glance any mixture of styles" (337).

33. Quoted in Harold Osborne, *Aesthetics and Art Theory* (New York: E. P. Dutton, 1970), 162.

34. On Hume's debt to Hutcheson, see Peter Kivy, "Breaking the Circle," *British Journal of Aesthetics* 7 (1967): 57–66; cf. Norman Kemp Smith, *The Philosophy of David Hume* (London: Macmillan, 1964); and Dabney Townsend, *Hume's Aesthetic Theory: Taste and Sentiment* (London: Routledge, 2001).

35. Thomas Reid, *Philosophical Works,* ed. by Sir William Hamilton, 2 vols. (Hildesheim: Georg Olms Verlag, 1983), 490. Roger D. Gallie discusses Reid's analogy between external and internal taste senses in *Thomas Reid: Ethics, Aesthetics and the Anatomy of the Self* (Dordrecht and Boston: Kluwer, 1998), 145–60.

36. John Gilbert Cooper, "Essays on Taste," from *Letters Concerning Taste,* 3d ed. (1757), ed. by Ralph Cohen (Los Angeles: University of California Press, 1951), 6–7.

37. Archibald Alison, *Essays on Nature and Principles of Taste;* from the Edinburgh edition of 1814 (Boston: Cummings and Hilliard, 1812), iii, 103.

38. On ancient Greek theories of the taste sense, see Beare, *Greek Theories of Elementary Cognition*, 160–79.

39. J. F. Blumenbach, *A Manual of Comparative Anatomy,* trans. by William Lawrence, 2d ed., ed. by William Coulson (London: Printed for W. Simpkin and R. Marshall, 1827), 264.

40. Nehemiah Grew, *The Comparative Anatomy of Stomachs and Guts Begun. Being Several Lectures Read before the Royal Society in the Year, 1676* (London: W. Rawlins, 1681), 216.

41. Jeffrey Wieand, "Hume's Two Standards of Taste," *Philosophical Quarterly* 34 (1984): 129–42 (135).

42. Burke discovers the foundation of sublime experience in the fluids, and Mandeville explains that fear is "a Defect in the Principle of the *Fluids,* as other Deformities are faults of the *Solids*" (*FB* 1:212).

43. Elsewhere, he classes them together: "Thirst considered nakedly as animal sensation has nothing sublime in it nor has Hunger, or the sexual appetite or any other animal appetites." This comment is scrawled in the margins of Coleridge's copy of Richard Payne Knight's *An Analytical Inquiry into the Principles of Taste,* 3d ed. (London: Printed for T. Payne and J. White, 1806), 93; owned by the Huntington Library. A note in it from N. B. Cuthbert to Edna A. Shearer of April 10, 1836, supposes these pencil annotations to be in "Wordsworth's vile hand."

44. Leo Damrosch, *Fictions of Reality in the Age of Hume and Johnson* (Madison: University of Wisconsin Press, 1989), 181.

45. Tom Furniss explicitly reads Burke's *Reflections* in the light of his *Philosophical Enquiry* as a politicized aesthetics in *Edmund Burke's Aesthetic Ideology: Language, Gender, and Political Economy in Revolution* (Cambridge: Cambridge University Press, 1993).

46. Bamborough, *The Little World of Man,* 67. As Laurence Sterne remarks, "Why the most natural actions of a man's life should be called his Non-Naturals, — is another question." *The Life and Opinions of Tristram Shandy, Gentleman,* ed. by Graham Petrie (Harmondsworth: Penguin, 1967), 97–98.

47. Bamborough, *The Little World of Man,* 119.

48. Alexander Pope, *Essay on Man,* 2.129–30; in *Poetical Works,* ed. by Herbert David (London: Oxford University Press, 1966), 253–54.

49. Hutcheson's 1725 title page reads: *An Inquiry into the Original of our Ideas of Beauty and Virtue; in Two Treatises. In which the Principles of the late Earl of Shaftesbury are Explain'd and Defended, against the Author of the Fable of the Bees;* facsimile edition by Bernhard Fabian (Hildesheim: Georg Olms, 1971). Emily Michael and Fred S. Michael discuss how Hutcheson's opposition to Mandeville became a virtual obsession in "Hutcheson's Account of Beauty as a Response to Mandeville," *History of European Ideas* 12:5 (1990): 655–68.

50. Patrick Francis McKee, "An Anatomy of Power: The Early Works of Bernard Mandeville." Unpublished diss. (Glasgow Caledonian University, May 1991), 309.

51. Cf. Kant, "The beautiful alone is that which appertains to taste" (*AN*144).

52. Edmund Burke, *The Writings and Speeches of Edmund Burke,* Paul Langford, gen. ed., 9 vols., (Oxford: Clarendon Press: 1981–91), 9:245. R. B. McDowell notes: "It was

reported in an English newspaper that after the fall of Tuileries a man was seen drinking the blood of a Swiss guard and that the hearts of Swiss guards were eaten by some of the people (*St. James's Chronicle,* 21 August 1792). Two years later, *The Times* (1 January 1794) stated that it had been suggested in France that blood should be drunk at public festivals, and undoubtedly Danton, in a vehement oration, declaimed: 'what does it matter to be called a blood drinker — well! drink the blood of the enemies of humanity' (*Moniteur,* 13 March 1793). The story that Mlle. de Sombreuil (*c.* 1767–1823) drank a glass of blood during the September massacres to save her father does not seem to have appeared in print until 1800" (9:245n.).

53. Peter Stallybrass and Allon White, *Politics and Poetics of Transgression* (Ithaca: Cornell University Press, 1986), 27–79.

54. Daniel Isaac Eaton, *Politics for the People: or, a Salmagundy for Swine; Consisting of the choicest Viands, contributed by the Cooks of the present Day, and Of the highest flavoured Delicacies, composed by the Caterers of former Ages,* 2 vols. (London: Printed for D. I. Eaton, at the Cock and Hog-Trough, 1794); his original epigraph read: "Thy magic Rod, audacious Burke, / Could metamorphize Man to Pork, / And quench the Spark divine; / But Eaton's Wonder-working Wand, / By scattering Knowledge through the Land, / Is making Men of Swine."

55. Republished by Leigh Hunt on August 30, 1818, in *The Examiner,* ed. by Yasuo Deguchi, 15 vols. (London: William Pickering, 1996), 11:548.

56. T. L. Richardson reports that between 1793 and 1812 food and drink constituted 67.7 percent of the average English laborer's household expenditure and that bread alone rose from 48 percent to 74.2 percent of that figure; *Making of the Modern British Diet,* 105. Wartime scarcities and inflation pushed up the price of bread by 167 percent between 1793 and 1812, and from the 1790s virtually no laborer's family ate fresh meat: "Almost all families, however careful, had a budget deficit, which was only made up by poaching, stealing, debt, or parish relief." John Burnett, *Plenty and Want: A Social History of Food in England from 1815 to the Present Day,* 3d ed. (London: Routledge, 1989), 22; in short, the "first half of nineteenth century was miserably hungry for many laborers. . . . This was a population existing on the edge of starvation"; Burnett, *Plenty and Want,* 22, 35.

57. The situation had its counterpart in France, as explicated by Steven L. Kaplan in *Bread, Politics, and Political Economy in the Reign of Louis XV,* 2 vols. (The Hague: Martinus Nijhoff, 1976).

58. By 1790 most English people had turned from coarser cereals to wheat, and in 1795 wheat constituted 95 percent of the nation's bread. Burnett, *Plenty and Want,* 4; E. P. Thompson, *The Making of the English Working Class* (New York: Vintage, 1966), 315.

59. Thompson, *The Making of the English Working Class,* 314–15.

60. Quoted in Burnett, *Plenty and Want,* 10. Arthur Young wrote between 1776 and 1779: "If anyone doubts the comparative plenty, which attends the board of a poor native of England and Ireland, let him attend to their meals; the sparingness with which our labourer eats his bread and cheese is well known; mark the Irishman's potatoe bowl placed on the floor, the whole family upon their hams around it, devouring a quantity almost incredible, the beggar seating himself to it with a hearty welcome, the pig taking

his share as readily as the wife, the cocks, hens, turkies, geese, the cur, the cat, and perhaps the cow — and all partaking of the same dish." Quoted in Redcliffe N. Salaman, *The History and Social Influence of the Potato* (Cambridge: Cambridge University Press, 1949), 261.

61. Hannah More, "The Way to Plenty; or The Second Part of Tom White," in *Cheap Repository*, no. 12 (Philadelphia: B. and J. Johnson, 1800), 13. Samantha Webb brought these pamphlets to my attention in "An Eighteenth-Century Martha Stewart: Recipes and the Politics of Cooking in Hannah More's Cheap Repository Tracts," North American Society for the Study of Romanticism Conference (Arizona, September 2000).

62. Thompson, *The Making of the English Working Class,* 318; Carole Shammas records that as grain prices rose in the second half of the eighteenth century, dietary change reflected an "increasing reliance on appetite appeasers such as tobacco, caffeine drinks, and sugar." *The Pre-industrial Consumer in England and America* (Oxford: Clarendon Press, 1990), 147. Charlotte Sussman suggests that "the new availability of these luxury goods may have stimulated both consumption, as a wider group of people were able to purchase such comforts, and industrial production, as the working classes slowed their intake of beer and ale, which were more nutritious than sugared tea, but had been less conducive to regulated, supervised labor." *Consuming Anxieties: Consumer Protest, Gender, and British Slavery, 1713–1833* (Stanford: Stanford University Press, 2000), 30.

63. More, "Way to Plenty," 13.

64. Cf. note 59 above. The vocabulary of "luxury" and "necessity" has never been sufficient to understand the meaning of consumption. Weatherill, *Consumer Behaviour and Material Culture,* 15–16, and Colin Campbell, *The Romantic Ethic and the Spirit of Modern Consumerism* (Oxford: Basil Blackwell, 1987), 58–60, among others, discuss the relativism of these terms. On "The Roast Beef of Old England" as "the artisan's pride and the aspiration of the labourer," see Thompson, *The Making of the English Working Class,* 315. For Henry Fielding on roast beef ("When mighty roast beef was the Englishman's food, / It enobled our hearts, and enriched our blood, / Our soldiers were brave, and our courtiers were good. / Oh the roast beef of England, / And old England's roast beef!"), see *The Grub-Street Opera,* ed. by L. J. Morrissy (Edinburgh: Oliver and Boyd, 1973), 69; and William Hogarth, *O the Roast Beef of Old England* (1748).

65. Although the precise figures are in dispute, economists calculate that between 1793 and 1812 meat fell from roughly a quarter to 6 percent of total food consumption in Britain. Burnett, *Plenty and Want,* 22.

66. Mary Douglas and Baron Isherwood, *The World of Goods* (New York: Basic Books, 1979), 56.

67. "Eating from plates, using knives, forks and spoons became the norm in aristocratic circles from the end of the seventeenth century, and had spread soon after to the urban middle classes"; Eszter Kisbán, "Food Habits in Change; The Example of Europe," in *Food in Change: Eating Habits from the Middle Ages to the Present Day,* ed. by Alexander Fenton and Eszter Kisbán (Edinburgh: John Donald and National Museums of Scotland, 1986), 8.

68. See my introduction to *Gusto* forthcoming from Routledge.

Chapter 4. Digesting Wordsworth

1. In *Biographia Literaria* Coleridge also discusses the imagination as an assimilative power, applying the physiology of digestion to the creative mind at work; M. H. Abrams, *The Mirror and the Lamp: Romantic Theory and the Critical Tradition* (London: Oxford University Press, 1953), 169.

2. Geoffrey Hartman, *Wordsworth's Poetry, 1787–1814* (New Haven: Yale University Press, 1964), 189.

3. The phrase "wordsworthian egotistical sublime" is Keats's from a letter to Richard Woodhouse of October 27, 1818, though Hazlitt frequently made use of the concept too: "An intense intellectual egotism swallows up everything" (*HCW* 4:113); cf. "On the Living Poets," where he suggests that Wordsworth's "egotism is in some respects a madness" (*HCW* 5:163).

4. Charles Cuthbert Southey, ed., *The Life and Correspondence of Robert Southey*, 6 vols. (London: Longman, Brown, Green, and Longmans, 1849–50), 1:63; cf. Alan Richardson, *British Romanticism and the Science of the Mind* (Cambridge, Mass.: Cambridge University Press, 2001), xiii.

5. Frank A. Geldard, *The Human Senses* (New York: John Wiley; London: Chapman and Hill, 1953), 270; Richard Chenevix, "Cookery," *Edinburgh Review* (March 1821): 43–62 (45).

6. In *Civilization and Its Discontents,* Freud compares the mind as a psychic entity to present-day Rome as a site of archaeological complexity "in which nothing that has once come into existence will have passed away and all the earlier phases of development continue to exist alongside the latest one," making excavation a challenging, ongoing process; *The Freud Reader*, 726.

7. Theresa M. Kelley, *Wordsworth's Revisionary Aesthetics* (Cambridge: Cambridge University Press, 1988), 10.

8. I intend this term, coined from *poesis* (meaning creative production) by Nikolas Luhmann, as it is used by Tilottama Rajan in "(In)digestible Material: Illness and Dialectic in Hegel's *The Philosophy of Nature*," in Morton, ed., *Cultures of Taste*, 217–36 (224).

9. The five-book *Prelude* of 1804 is a scholarly reconstruction for which no fair copy exists. Critical discussion of the Snowdon revisions from 1804 and 1805 has focused on the "analogy passage," which Wordsworth excised from the five-book *Prelude* and which originally followed the ascent of Snowdon with a series of analogies for the sublime experience. A reading text of the analogy passage is appended to the Norton *Prelude* (496–99) and included in *WU*, lines 197–204. Revisions to the Snowdon episode, stemming from this passage, continued from 1805 through 1839, but because they are external to Wordsworth's "mind that feeds," they are not considered here. See Joseph F. Kishel, "The 'Analogy Passage' from Wordsworth's Five-Book *Prelude*," *Studies in Romanticism* 18 (1979): 273–85; and Richard Schell, "Wordsworth's Revisions of the Ascent of Snowdon," *Philological Quarterly* 54:3 (1975): 592–603.

10. Jonathan Wordsworth, *William Wordsworth: The Borders of Vision* (Oxford: Clarendon Press, 1982), 324–25.

11. As Wordsworth was revising the Snowdon passage, he experienced digestive trib-

ulations of Miltonic proportions, which he associated with his own creative activity (*LEY* 1:453); Reed mentions related episodes in *TBP* 1:8.

12. Herbert Lindenberger, *On Wordsworth's Prelude* (Princeton: Princeton University Press, 1963), 52.

13. Hamacher, *Pleroma,* 259.

14. Alan Liu, *Wordsworth: The Sense of History* (Stanford: Stanford University Press, 1989), 515.

15. Rajan, "(In)digestible Material," 218.

16. G. W. F. Hegel, *Phenomenology of Spirit,* trans. by A. V. Miller (Oxford: Oxford University Press, 1977), 492.

17. Rajan, "(In)digestible Material," 12.

18. Ibid.

19. Friedrich Nietzsche, *On the Genealogy of Morals,* trans. by Walter Kaufmann and R. J. Hollingdale (New York: Vintage, 1969), 23.

20. E. D. Hirsch assumes no direct influence of Schelling on Wordsworth, but he notes their simultaneous development of a similar *Weltanschauung* in *Wordsworth and Schelling: A Typological Study of Romanticism* (New Haven: Yale University Press, 1960).

21. F. W. J. Schelling, *Idealism and the Endgame of Theory: Three Essays by F. W. J. Schelling,* trans. by Thomas Pfau (Albany: SUNY Press, 1994), 207.

22. Ibid., 207–8.

23. Ibid., 236.

24. Ibid., 206–7.

25. Julia Kristeva, *Powers of Horror: An Essay on Abjection* (New York: Columbia University Press, 1982), 3.

26. I refer to vol. 5 of *The Poetical Works of William Wordsworth,* ed. by Ernest de Selincourt and Helen Darbishire (Oxford: Clarendon Press, 1949).

27. Joshua Wilner, *Feeding on Infinity: Readings in the Romantic Rhetoric of Internalization* (Baltimore: Johns Hopkins University Press, 2000).

28. According to Reed, the C-stage reading text is unreliable, since the transcription, prepared by John Carter, was not carefully reviewed by Wordsworth (*TBP* 1:5–10).

29. David Haney suggests that the above C-stage revision "reflects the later poet's preoccupation with the clearly prioritized relation between sound and sight"; " 'Rents and Openings in the Ideal World': Eye and Ear in Wordsworth," *Studies in Romanticism* 36:2 (1997): 173–99 (184).

30. For more on this topic, see Paul Youngquist, "Lyrical Bodies: Wordsworth's Physiological Aesthetics," *European Romantic Review* 10:2 (1999): 152–61.

31. Quoted from Raleigh's *History of the World* in Tillyard, *The Elizabethan World Picture,* 85.

32. Wordsworth annotated and read this book (which belonged to Coleridge) "with great care" in November 1801. Duncan Wu, *Wordsworth's Reading, 1800–1815* (Cambridge, Mass.: Cambridge University Press, 1995), 167.

33. Robert Burton, *Anatomy of Melancholy: What it is, With all the Kinds, Causes, Symptomes, Prognostickes, & Seuerall Cures of it . . . philosophically, medicinally, Historically Opened & Cut up by Democritus Junior,* 8th ed., ed. by A. H. Bell (London: G. Bell and Sons, 1926), 176. On Wordsworth's reading of this, see Wu, *Wordsworth's Reading,* 38.

34. Wordsworth's first response to the projected railway scheme took the form of a sonnet, "On the Projected Kendal and Windermere Railway," published in the *Morning Post* on October 12, 1844. On December 11, it was followed by the first of two polemical essays on the same topic. The second essay, published on December 21, concludes with a second sonnet, "Proud were ye, Mountains, when, in times of old." In January 1845 Wordsworth reprinted the sonnets and letters as a pamphlet, which he distributed to influential persons.

35. Wilfrid Hindle, *The Morning Post, 1772–1937: Portrait of a Newspaper* (London: Routledge, 1937), 165–66.

36. Peter T. Newby, "Literature and the Fashioning of Taste," in *Humanistic Geography and Literature: Essays on the Experience of Place,* ed. by Douglas C. D. Pocock (London: Croom Helm, 1981), 134.

37. Tim Fulford, *Landscape, Liberty and Authority: Poetry, Criticism and Politics from Thomson to Wordsworth* (Cambridge: Cambridge University Press, 1996), 127.

38. John Ruskin, *The Works of John Ruskin,* ed. by E. T. Cook and Alexander Wedderburn, 39 vols. (London: George Allen, 1908), 34:141; on this second railway scheme, projected to extend to Wordsworth's residence at Rydal and Ambleside, see Jonathan Bate, *Romantic Ecology: Wordsworth and the Environmental Tradition* (London and New York: Routledge, 1991), 62–84; Stephen Gill, *Wordsworth and the Victorians* (Oxford: Clarendon Press, 1998), 148–60; and Ian Ousby, *The Englishman's England: Taste, Travel, and the Rise of Tourism* (Cambridge: Cambridge University Press, 1990), 191–92.

39. Ruskin, *The Works,* 34:139.

40. Quoted in Henry Crabb Robinson, *Diary, Reminiscences, and Correspondence of Henry Crabb Robinson,* ed. by Thomas Sadler, 3d ed., 2 vols. (London: Macmillan, 1872), 2:264.

41. Raymond Williams, *Keywords: A Vocabulary of Culture and Society* (New York: Oxford University Press, 1976), 266.

42. Wordsworth's "Select Views" was written as an introduction to John Wilkinson's picturesque etchings of the Lake District, the original version of his *Guide to the Lakes.* A decade later, Wordsworth detached his text from Wilkinson and appended it as a "Topographical Description of the Country of the Lakes in the North of England" to his 1820 *River Duddon* volume.

43. Matthew Brennan, *Wordsworth, Turner, and Romantic Landscape: A Study of the Traditions of the Picturesque and the Sublime* (Columbia, S.C.: Camden House, 1987), 23.

44. Uvedale Price, *An Essay on the Picturesque, as Compared with the Sublime and the Beautiful; and, on the Use of Studying Pictures, for the Purpose of Improving Real Landscape* (London: Printed for J. Robson, 1796), 105.

45. William Gilpin, *Observations, Relative Chiefly to Picturesque Beauty, Made in the Year 1772, on Several Parts of England; particularly the Mountains, and Lakes of Cumberland, and Westmoreland,* 2 vols. (London: Printed for R. Blamire, 1786), 1:xxvi; cf. Wu, *Wordsworth's Reading,* 93.

46. Gilpin, *Observations,* 1:xxviii–xxix; xxxi–xxxii.

47. Wordsworth modeled his *Guide to the Lakes* on Thomas West's *Guide,* which promoted the landscape glass as a convenient device to subdue nature to the constraints

of material portraiture. "Where the objects are great and near," West writes, "it removes them to a due distance, and shews them in the soft colours of nature, and in the most regular perspective the eye can perceive, or science demonstrate." Thomas West, *A Guide to the Lakes in Cumberland, Westmorland and Lancashire,* 3d ed. (London: Printed for B. Law et al., 1784), 12.

48. Charles Dickens, *Great Expectations,* ed. by Charlotte Mitchell (1860–61; Harmondsworth: Penguin, 1996), 409.

49. Thomas Gray, *The Works of Thomas Gray in Prose and Verse,* ed. by Edmund Grosse, 4 vols. (London: Macmillan, 1884), 1:260. Because the landscape glass had to be held in reverse, over the shoulder, Gray's thousand-pound picture cost him a painful fall. Like the modern pocket camera of roughly the same size, the glass was "perhaps the best and most convenient substitute for a camera obscura." West, *Guide,* 198n.

50. Price, *An Essay on the Picturesque,* 100.

51. Neil Hertz, *The End of the Line: Essays on Psychoanalysis and the Sublime* (New York: Columbia University Press, 1985), 60. Cf. Frances Ferguson, who observes that in the experience of Kantian sublimity landscape replaces the human body as the ideal image or "picture of the human soul": "This is to say that the landscape does not so much replace portraiture as become it." *Solitude and the Sublime: Romanticism and the Aesthetics of Individuation* (New York: Routledge, 1992), 28.

52. Brennan, *Wordsworth, Turner, and Romantic Landscape,* 73. Although not explicitly, Mark Edmundson also reads the Simplon Pass episode as Wordsworth's foremost example of the positive sublime. *Towards Reading Freud: Self-Creation in Milton, Wordsworth, Emerson, and Sigmund Freud* (Princeton: Princeton University Press, 1990), 102–14.

53. Christoph Bode writes that "the very fact that Wordsworth discards a whole 'natural' or ahistorical aesthetics and now embraces a historical, dynamic concept of *acquired taste* indicates that something of supreme importance is at stake here." "Putting the Lake District on the (Mental) Map: William Wordsworth's *Guide to the Lakes,*" *Journal for the Study of British Cultures* 4:1–2 (1997): 95–111 (107). James Mulvihill claims that their "thesis, that taste is culturally constructed, is pretty far-reaching and flies in the face of the 1800 'Preface''s essentialism." "Consuming Nature: Wordsworth and the Kendal and Windermere Railway Controversy," *Modern Language Quarterly* 56:3 (1995): 305–26 (313).

54. Ousby, *The Englishman's England,* 180.

55. Quoted in Crabb Robinson, *Diary, Reminiscences, and Correspondence,* 264.

56. His founding of the Lake District Defence Society was a driving force behind the British National Trust, the Lake District National Park, and the national park system in America.

57. For more on this, see Christopher Rovee, *Imagining the Gallery: The Social Body of British Romanticism* (Stanford: Stanford University Press, forthcoming).

Chapter 5. Lamb's Low-Urban Taste

1. The term *gastronomy* first appeared as the title of Joseph Berchoux's 1801 poem "*La Gastronomie, ou l'Homme des champs à table,*" and it was rapidly adopted throughout

France and England to indicate the art and science of delicate eating. The pioneers of gastronomical writing, Alexandre-Balthazar-Laurent Grimod de la Reynière (1758–1838) and Jean-Anthelme Brillat-Savarin (1755–1826), were French, but there was no separating French culinary art from English, and British gastronomical writing imitated French models from the outset of the nineteenth century.

2. The phrase "day of horrors" is from Lamb's letter to Coleridge of October 3, 1796 (*LM* 1:48); the tragedy was never explicitly mentioned by Lamb again in writing after this letter. Details of this terrible event are common knowledge within the limited sphere of Lamb scholarship, but they may be useful to recall here. An excerpt from an account of it published in the *Morning Chronicle* on September 26 reads: "while the family were preparing for dinner, the young lady seized a case knife laying on the table, and in a menacing manner pursued a little girl, her apprentice, round the room; on the eager calls of her helpless infirm mother to forbear, she renounced her first object, and with loud shrieks approached her parent. The child by her cries quickly brought up the landlord of the house, but too late — the dreadful scene presented to him the mother lifeless, pierced to the heart, on a chair, her daughter yet wildly standing over her with the fatal knife, and the venerable old man, her father, weeping by her side, himself bleeding at the forehead from the effects of a severe blow he received from one of the forks she had been madly hurling about the room" (*LM* 1:45n.).

3. Friedrich von Schiller, *Naïve and Sentimental Poetry and On the Sublime,* trans. by Julias A. Elias (New York: Frederick Ungar, 1966).

4. The title of Robert D. Frank's *Don't Call Me Gentle Charles!: An Essay on Lamb's Essays of Elia* (Corvallis: Oregon State University Press, 1976) suggests this.

5. Algernon Charles Swinburne, *Miscellanies* (London: Chatto and Windus, 1886), 194–95.

6. After Lamb's epistolary outburst, Coleridge canceled the phrase "My gentle-hearted CHARLES!" in his copy of Southey's *Annual Anthology,* but this was a virtually unknown concession since all later printings of the poem retained it (*CCW* 12.1:95). James Engell discusses the repetition in "Imagining into Nature: This Lime-Tree Bower My Prison," in *Coleridge, Keats, and the Imagination: Romanticism and Adam's Dream,* ed. by J. Robert Barth, S.J., and John L. Mahoney (Columbia: University of Missouri Press, 1990), 81–96 (91–92) and provides a helpful critical history of the poem.

7. On the East India Company and the tea trade, see P. Mathias, "The British Tea Trade in the Nineteenth Century," in Oddy and Miller, eds., *The Making of the Modern British Diet,* 91–100; cf. Patrick Tuck, ed., *The East India Company: 1600–1858,* 6 vols. (London and New York: Routledge, 1998); esp. vol. 2: *Problems of Empire: Britain and India, 1757–1818.* Statistical accounts of tea and sugar from 1840 to 1853 are provided by Alexander Russel, "Consumption of Food in the United Kingdom," *Edinburgh Review* 99 (1854): 581–632.

8. G. N. Johnstone, "The Growth of the Sugar Trade and Refining Industry," in Oddy and Miller, eds., *The Making of the Modern British Diet,* 58–64; J. R. McCulloch offers a comprehensive account of the growth of the sugar industry in "East and West India Sugar," *Edinburgh Review* 38 (1823): 209–25, a review of James Cropper's *Letters addressed to William Wilberforce, M.P. Recommending the Cultivation of Sugar in our Dominions in the East Indies, as the natural and certain means of effecting the total and*

general Abolition of the Slave Trade (Liverpool, 1822); Thomas Fletcher's *Letters in Vindication of the Rights of the British West India Colonists, in answer to Mr Cropper's Letters* (Liverpool, 1822); *East and West India Sugar, or a Refutation of the Claims of the West India Colonists to a Protecting Duty on East India Sugar* (London, 1823); and *On Protection to West India Sugar* (London, 1823).

9. Quoted in Michael Scrivener, ed., *Poetry and Reform: Periodical Verse from the English Democratic Press, 1792–1824* (Detroit: Wayne State University Press, 1992), 47–48.

10. There is a growing critical literature on the cultural, political, and historical significance of sugar: Sidney W. Mintz, *Sweetness and Power: The Place of Sugar in Modern History* (New York: Viking, 1985); also his *Tasting Food, Tasting Freedom: Excursions into Eating, Culture, and the Past* (Boston: Beacon Press, 1996), chapters 4 and 5; Keith Albert Sandiford, *The Cultural Politics of Sugar: Caribbean Slavery and Narratives of Colonialism* (Cambridge: Cambridge University Press, 2000); and "Vertices and Horizons with Sugar: A Tropology of Colonial Power," *The Eighteenth Century* 42:2 (2001): 142–60; Timothy Morton, "Blood Sugar," *Romanticism and Colonialism: Writing and Empire, 1780–1830*, ed. by Tim Fulford and Peter J. Kitson (Cambridge, Mass.: Cambridge University Press, 1998) 87–107; repr. as chapter 4 of *The Poetics of Spice: Romantic Consumerism and the Exotic* (Cambridge: Cambridge University Press, 2000); Tim Fulford, "The Fruits of Romanticism in the Empire: The Taste of Paradise," in Morton, ed., *Cultures of Taste/Theories of Appetite*, 41–58; Charlotte Sussman, *Consuming Anxieties: Consumer Protest, Gender, and British Slavery, 1713–1833* (Stanford: Stanford University Press, 2000), 110–29.

11. Karl Marx, *Capital: A Critique of Political Economy*, trans. by Ben Fowkes (New York: Vintage, 1977), 1:166. For Coleridge's lectures, see *CCW* 1:231–59; cf. Robert Southey, *Poems* (Bristol and London: Printed by N. Biggs for Joseph Cottle, Bristol, and G. G. and J. Robinson, London, 1797–1799), 29–43 (32).

12. "If food is treated as a code, the messages it encodes will be found in the pattern of social relations being expressed." Mary Douglas, "Deciphering a Meal," *Daedalus: Journal of the American Academy of Arts and Sciences* (1972): 61–81 (61).

13. *A Vindication of Natural Diet* first appeared in 1813 as an extended footnote to *Queen Mab* and then as a pamphlet; its pirated 1821 editions sold briskly in England and America in the 1820s through the 1840s, popularizing Shelley's radical views about diet.

14. Timothy Morton, "The Pulses of the Body: Romantic Vegetarianism and Its Cultural Contexts," *1650–1850: Ideas Aesthetics, and Inquiries in the Early Modern Era*, ed. by Kevin L. Cope (New York: AMS Press, 1998), 31–87 (58). Cf. his *Shelley and the Revolution in Taste: The Body and the Natural World* (New York: Cambridge University Press, 1994). The term *vegetarian* did not exist in English before 1842 and was not current until The British Vegetarian Society was formed in September 1847.

15. Thomas Manning, *The Letters of Thomas Manning to Charles Lamb* (New York: Harper, 1926), 40.

16. Cf. Coleridge's "Frost at Midnight" (1798), which compares life in the "populous village" of "sea, and hill, and wood" to the speaker's childhood experience "in the great city, pent 'mid cloisters dim" (11–12; 51).

17. For a typical Bill of Fare, from the Lord Mayor's Dinner at Guildhall, November 10, 1828, see the pseudonymous British gastronomer Dick Humelbergius Secundus, *Apician Morsels; or, Tales of the Table, Kitchen, and Larder: With Reflections on the Dietic Productions of Early Writers; on The Customs of the Romans in Eating and Drinking; on Table Ceremonies, and Rules of Conviviality and Good Breeding; with Select Epicurean Precepts, Gourmand Maxims and Medicines, &c. &c.* (London: Whittaker, Treacer, 1834), 212–15; portions of this text are imported wholesale from other sources.

18. An average of fifty-two thousand suckling pigs were consumed per year in London in the eighteenth century. William Maitland, *The History of London,* 2 vols. (London: Printed by S. Richardson, 1739), 2:758.

19. Fred V. Randel, *The World of Elia: Charles Lamb's Essayistic Romanticism* (Port Washington, N.Y.: Kennikat Press, 1975), 120.

20. Barry Cornwall (Bryan Waller Procter), *Charles Lamb: A Memoir* (Boston: Roberts, 1866), 237–38.

21. Lucy Newlyn, "Lamb, Lloyd, London: A Perspective on Book Seven of *The Prelude,*" *Charles Lamb Bulletin* 47/48 (1984): 169–87 (172).

22. Lamb's friends insisted that "much of the pose of Lamb as a *bon viveur* was pure humour, and that as a matter of fact he was a moderate eater and drinker, and very little in the way of liquor affected him." William Carew Hazlitt, *The Lambs: Their Lives, Their Friends, and Their Correspondence* (London: Elkin Mathews; New York: Charles Scribner's Sons, 1897), 40. Indeed, at thirty-nine Lamb weighed approximately 129.5 lbs. "in boots." Bonnie Woodbery, "Lamb's 'Confessions of a Drunkard' in Context," *Charles Lamb Bulletin* 90 (1995): 94–100 (94).

23. Benjamin Robert Haydon, *The Autobiography and Memoirs of Benjamin Robert Haydon (1786–1846),* ed. by Tom Taylor, 2 vols. (New York: Harcourt Brace, 1926), 1:253. Cf. the chronicle of Shelley's eccentric eating habits in Thomas Jefferson Hogg, *The Life of Percy Shelley* (London: Routledge, 1906), 86–87; 177; 448–52.

24. Plutarch, *Moralia,* trans. by Harold Cherniss and William C. Helmbold, 15 vols. (Cambridge, Mass.: Harvard University Press, 1957), 12:551.

25. Cf. *A Vegetable System of Diet,* SP 94; and Joseph Ritson, *An Essay on Abstinence from Animal Food, as a Moral Duty* (London: Richard Phillips, 1802): "The animals that subsist on vegetables have all of them blunt teeth, as the horse, the ox, the sheep, and the hare; but the teeth of animals naturally carnivorous are sharp, as those of the cat, the dog, the wolf and the fox" (41).

26. "The compileër himself, induce'd to serious reflection, by the perusal of Mandeville's Fable of the bees, in the year 1772, being the 19th year of his age, [desisted from animal food, and] has ever since, to the revisal of this sheet, firmly adhere'd to a milk and vegetable diet, having at least, never tasteëd, dureing the whole course of those thirty years, a morsel of flesh, fish, or fowl, or any thing to his knowledge prepare'd in or with those substanceës or any extract thereof, unless . . . in eating egs, which, however, deprives no animal of life, though it may prevent some from comeing into the world to be murder'd and devour'd by others." Ritson, *An Essay on Abstinence from Animal Food,* 201. Ritson's iconoclastic spelling is part of a radical reform effort that included, along with diet, atheism, political revolution, and language. Joseph Haslewood, *Some Account*

of the Publications of the Late Joseph Ritson, Esq. (London: Printed for Robert Trip-hook, 1824), 29.

27. Harriet Ritvo, *The Animal Estate: The English and Other Creatures in the Victorian Age* (Cambridge, Mass.: Harvard University Press, 1987), 28–29. Here one can presumably regard lion and tiger as alternate versions of "big wild cat."

28. Alexander Pope, *Essay on Man*, 1.83–84; in *Poetical Works*, ed. by Herbert David (London: Oxford University Press, 1966), 243. Shelley, *Queen Mab*, 8.212–13 (*SPP* 62–63). By contrast, in a prelapsarian state, the lion frolicked with the lamb. In Milton's version of Paradise, as in Isaiah 11, "the Lion ramp'd, and in his Paw / Dandl'd the Kid; Bears, Tygres, Ounces, Pards, / Gambol'd before them" (*PL* 4.343–45). With reference to these lines, Mandeville asks, "What was it, the Lion fed upon; what Sustenance had all these Beasts of Prey, in Paradise?" (*FB* 2:234). Cf. Pope (*Essay on Man*, 3.148, 152–53) and Shelley's apocalyptic vision in *Queen Mab*: "The lion now forgets to thirst for blood: / There might you see him sporting in the sun / Beside the dreadless kid; his claws are sheathed, / His teeth are harmless, custom's force has made / His nature as the nature of a lamb" (8.124–28).

29. "Auguries of Innocence," 23–24 (*CPB*, 490). See also David Perkins, "Animal Rights and 'Auguries of Innocence,'" *Blake: An Illustrated Quarterly* 33:1 (1999): 4–11.

30. John Frank Newton, *The Return to Nature, or A Defence of the Vegetable Regimen; with some Account of an Experiment Made During the Last three or four Years in the Author's Family* (London: T. Cadell and W. Davies, 1811), 104. Newton presided over a vegetarian salon at which Shelley was a frequent guest in the early 1800s, and his work underwrites Shelley's *Vindication of Natural Diet*. James Turner, *Reckoning with the Beast: Animals, Pain, and Humanity in the Victorian Mind* (Baltimore: Johns Hopkins University Press, 1980), 17.

31. George Cheyne, *The English Malady: or, A Treatise of Nervous Diseases of all Kinds as Spleen, Vapours, Lowness of Spirits, Hypochonriacal, and Histerical Distempers, &c.* (London: G. Strahan and J. Leake, 1733), 163.

32. Erasmus Jones, *The Man of Manners; or Plebian Polished*, reprint of the 3d London edition, 1737 (Sandy Hook, Conn.: Hendrickson Group, 1993), 9.

33. Elias, *The Civilizing Process*, 120. From the vegetarian perspective, this process was responsible for obscuring the atrocities that made possible an animal diet. Thus, John Oswald: "On the carcass we feed, without remorse, because the dying struggles of the butchered creature are secluded from our sight; because his cries pierce not our ear; because his agonizing shrieks sink not into our soul." Oswald, *The Cry of Nature; or, An Appeal to Mercy and to Justice on Behalf of the Persecuted Animals* (1792; Lewiston, Queenston, and Lampeter: Edwin Mellen Press, 2000), 25.

34. *The Habits of Good Society: A Handbook of Etiquette for Ladies and Gentlemen* (London: James Hogg, 1859), 314.

35. Colman, *The Connoisseur*, 1:153.

36. Newton, *The Return to Nature*, 62–63.

37. The vegetarian Oswald remarks, "the ungracious task of shedding the tide of life, for the gluttony of our table, has, in every country, been committed to the lowest class of men; and their profession is, in every country, an object of abhorrence"; *The Cry of*

Nature, 25. On the myth that butchers due to their hardened natures were disqualified from jury service, which prevailed from the seventeenth century through the 1790s, see Kaye, who notes that Swift and Locke accepted the erroneous belief (*FB* 175n.); Keith Thomas adds Rousseau, Henry Homes, and Thomas Young in *Man and the Natural World: Changing Attitudes in England, 1500–1800* (London: Penguin, 1983), 297, 40n.

38. Henry Brougham, "Review of *An Essay on Abstinence from Animal Food*," *Edinburgh Review* 2:3 (1803): 128–36 (134); the attribution of authorship is from *The Wellesley Index to Victorian Periodicals, 1824–1900*, ed. by Walter E. Houghton, 5 vols. (Toronto: University of Toronto Press, 1966), 1:432. (The title of this index is misleading, since it contains listings for the *Edinburgh Review* from 1802.)

39. Ritson, *An Essay on Abstinence from Animal Food*, 124.

40. Even Captain James Cook, when determined to give a positive eyewitness account of the existence of cannibalism in his second voyage to the South Seas (1772–1775), describes the cooking and the eating but not the taste of human flesh. *The Explorations of Captain James Cook in the Pacific as told by Selections of His Own Journals, 1768–1799*, ed. by A. Grenfell Price (New York: Dover, 1971), 145.

41. Newton quotes Gibbon on this proverbially bloodthirsty race, whose animals "are slaughtered by the same hand from which they are accustomed to receive their daily food; and the bleeding limbs are served, with very little preparation, on the table of their unfeeling murderer." *The Return to Nature*, 35.

42. Lamb claimed that it was Manning who gave him the idea for "Roast Pig" (*LM* 2:95; *LL* 2:373); on Manning's travels in China and status as the first Englishman to reach Tibet, see Reginald Watters, "Thomas Manning (1772–1840): 'An Interesting man, but nothing more,'" *Charles Lamb Bulletin* 33 (1981): 10–17.

43. William Lambe, *Water and Vegetable Diet in Consumption, Scrofula, Cancer, Asthma, and other Chronic Diseases* (New York: Fowlers and Wells, 1850), 131. The book was first published as *Additional Reports on the Effects of a Peculiar Regimen in Cases of Cancer, Scrofula, Consumption, Asthma, and other Chronic Diseases* (1815).

44. On the cultural context of drinking in the Romantic era, see Anya Taylor, *Bacchus in Romantic England: Writers and Drink, 1780–1830* (New York: St. Martins Press, 1999); her third chapter treats Lamb's "The Confessions of a Drunkard" and *John Woodvil*.

45. *SP* 89; Lambe, *Water and Vegetable Diet*, 133.

46. Thomas Trotter, *An Essay Medical, Philosophical, and Chemical on Drunkenness and its Effects on the Human Body*, ed. by Roy Porter (1802; London and New York: Routledge, 1988), 163. Trotter's *Essay* went into several editions (1807, 1810, 1812) prior to when Lamb's "Drunkard" appeared.

47. Inflaming the passions was tantamount to chilling one's sensibility, and Trotter relates the story of a drunkard who cut off his fingers in a fit of intoxication, without any recollection of the event. Ibid., 51.

48. Vegetarian writers also rely upon physiology and comparative anatomy to make the case against drinking; e.g., Lambe points out that unless one bends over and drinks like a quadruped from a pool—an awkward endeavor due to the construction of the human mouth and the positioning of the nose—one must construct a mechanism to hold the liquid. "Nature seems therefore fully to have done her part toward keeping men from

the use of liquids. And doubtless on a diet of fruits and recent vegetables there would be no thirst, and no necessity for the use of liquids"; *Water and Vegetable Diet,* 140.

49. Quoted from Thomas Tryon (1634–1704), one of the few authors who remained in Lamb's dissipated book collection after Mary Lamb's death, in Smith, "Enthusiasm and Enlightenment," 111.

50. He claims an impatience for all "indigestible trifles," "impalpable to the palate" (*WCL* 2:263), and directs his appetites, thinly veiled as tastes, at everything from cards ("[Whist] was a long meal; not, like quadrille, a feast of snatches" [*WCL* 2:33]); to plays ("I felt all . . . 'Was nourished, I could not tell how' " [2:100]); to puns ("we love to see a wag *taste* his own joke"; "W. had no relish of a joke" [2:253, 89]); to "books, those spiritual repasts" ("he will make one hearty meal on your viands, if he can give no account of the platter after it" [2:91, 26]); to the food that permeates his essays. He renders the moral theodicy of Pope ("Whatever is, is RIGHT") as "Whatever is, is to me a matter of taste or distaste; or when once it becomes indifferent, it begins to be disrelishing" (*WCL* 2:58), a term that descends to Lamb from book 10 of *Paradise Lost,* where the fallen angels writhe their jaws upon bitter ashes, "With hatefulest disrelish" (*PL* 10.567–70); anything that does not stimulate Elia's taste is as meaningless as that false fruit. Pope's refrain occurs three times in his *Essay on Man:* "Whatever is, is RIGHT" (1.294); "Whatever IS, is RIGHT" (4.145); "WHATEVER IS, IS RIGHT" (4.394).

51. "This wil, doubtless, be particularly disgusting to the humane Engleish reader, for whom similar crueltys, or others at least equally shocking are committed" [Ritson's note and spelling; see note 26 above]; *An Essay on Abstinence from Animal Food,* 93–94. Shelley claims that by this point in history stamping pregnant sows to death and roasting suckling pigs alive had gone out of practice (*SP* 94).

52. For Claude Lévi-Strauss, "empirical categories — such as the categories of the raw and the cooked, the fresh and the decayed, the moistened and the burned" stand in for more abstract notions of nature and culture; *The Raw and the Cooked,* trans. by John and Doreen Weightman (Chicago: University of Chicago Press, 1969), 1.

53. *SP* 94; cf. *SP* 84 and *CWL* 1:122. The belief was widely held; Rousseau claims that man cannot eat raw meat, though his dubious anthropology makes an exception for Eskimos: "With the possible single exception of the Eskimos . . . even savages grill their meats." Jean-Jacques Rousseau, *The First and Second Discourses together with the Replies to Critics and Essay on the Origin of Language,* ed. by Victor Gourevitch (New York: Harper and Row, 1990), 268.

54. Quoted from Menon's *La Cuisinière bourgeoise* (1746) in Mennell, *All Manners of Food,* 83.

55. William Kitchiner, *The Art of Invigorating and Prolonging Life, by Food, Clothes, Air, Exercise, Wine, Sleep, &c.* (London: Hurst, Robinson, 1822), 27.

56. Ritson, *An Essay on Abstinence from Animal Food,* 104. For Taylor's translation see *Porphyry on Abstinence from Animal Food,* trans. by Thomas Taylor, ed. by Esme Wynne-Tyson (London: Centaur Press, 1965), 165–66.

57. Kitchiner, *Cook's Oracle,* 168. Elia's "Amicus Redivivus" (1823) likely plays on Kitchiner's original title, *Apicius Redivivus* (after the Roman chef, Apicius).

58. Manning, *The Letters,* 122–23.

59. Lamb took Wordsworth to Bartholomew fair in September 1802 (*LM* 2:66), and

his portrayal of the annual pig roast as an occasion for low-urban taste contrasts the Lake poet's vision of it in the hellish booths of book 7 of *The Prelude*.

60. James White, *Falstaff's Letters* (London: B. Robson, 1877), xiii–iv. Leigh Hunt discusses their collaboration in *The Autobiography of Leigh Hunt*, 2 vols., ed. by Roger Ingpen (Westminster: Archibald Constable, 1903), 62–63.

61. *The Medusa; or Penny Politician* 3:1 (1819): 17–20 (19).

62. Cf. Byron to Thomas Moore on April 9, 1814: "the other day I nearly killed myself with a collar of brawn, which I swallowed for supper, and *in*digested for I don't know how long; — but that is by the by. All this gourmandize was in honour of Lent; for I am forbidden meat all the rest of the year, — but it is strictly enjoined me during your solemn fast" (*BLJ* 4:92). From the viewpoint of Romantic dietetics, the traditional view that gusto "does not belong in the higher provinces of literary art, because it is too sensual a quality" misinterprets aesthetic experience redefined as low-urban taste; Robert Ready, "Hazlitt: In and Out of 'Gusto,' " *Studies in English Literature, 1500–1900* 14:4 (1974): 531–46 (540).

63. Thomas Taylor, *A Vindication of the Rights of Brutes* (1792), ed. by Louise Schutz Boas (Gainesville, Fla.: Scholars' Facsimiles, 1966), 18–19. The increase in "sympathy" for animals can be attributed, among other things, to developments in comparative anatomy, which found the higher animals to resemble humans; urbanization and a growing distance from agriculture; a growing sense of refinement that militated against such cruelties as bull-baiting; and the increase of pets across classes. David Perkins, "Religion and Animal Rights in the Romantic Era," in *The Fountain Light: Studies in Romanticism and Religion,* ed. by J. Robert Barth (New York: Fordham University Press, 2002), 1–21; cf. Hilda Kean, *Animal Rights: Political and Social Change in Britain since 1800* (London: Reaktion Books, 1998), 23–25; Thomas, *Man and the Natural World,* 36–192; Turner, *Reckoning with the Beast,* 1–38.

64. John Lamb's pamphlet addressed the primary opponent of the first animal rights bill to be proposed in the British parliament, Burke's disciple and minister of war in Pitt's government, William Windham. Thomas Erskine's "Act to prevent malicious and wanton Cruelty to Animals," proposed on May 15, 1809, to the House of Lords, was defeated in the House of Commons due to Windham's effective, if contorted, argumentation: he claimed that just as the animal abuses of hunting, angling, and horse racing provided entertainment for the upper classes, the bloody sport of bull-baiting (the chief objection of Erskine's bill) provided harmless entertainment for the "industrious labourers" of England. *Journals of the House of Lords,* (London: HMSO), 47:255. For Erskine's bill against animal abuse, see Hansard, *Parliamentary Debates,* series 1, vol. 3 (1809): 388–90 (90); Erskine's *Speech of Lord Erskine in the House of Peers on the Second Reading of the Bill for Preventing Malicious and Wanton Cruelty to Animals* (London: Richard Phillips, 1909) was published by Richard Phillips (1767–1840), a vegetarian and publisher of Ritson's *Essay on the Abstinence from Animal Flesh* as well as a radical republican imprisoned for printing Paine's *The Rights of Man* in 1793. On the debate between Erskine and Windham, see Christine Kenyon-Jones, *Kindred Brutes: Animals in Romantic-Period Writing* (Aldershot: Ashgate, 2001), 79–99.

65. Plutarch, *Moralia,* 12:547–51.

66. Mary Wollstonecraft, *A Vindication of the Rights of Woman,* 2d ed., ed. by Carol H. Poston (New York: W. W. Norton, 1988), 10.

67. Marcus Wood, *Blind Memory: Visual Representations of Slavery in England and America, 1780–1865* (New York: Routledge, 2000).

68. "All we do is *roast* beef and so we take in the full strength of the animal in a cultural and yet undiluted form. Meanwhile, the French are notorious for adding complicated sauces to their food . . . the French are absurdly effeminate." Keith Tester, *Animals and Society: The Humanity of Animal Rights* (London: Routledge, 1991), 144.

69. Quoted from Eneas Sweetland Dallas, *Kettner's Book of the Table* (1877; London: Centaur Press, 1968), 5.

70. For the claim that "Roast Pig" was the "best-known" of the *Elia* essays in Lamb's lifetime, I rely on the expertise of Winifred F. Courtney, *Young Charles Lamb, 1775–1802* (New York: New York University Press, 1982), 317.

71. Stallybrass and White, *The Politics and Poetics of Transgression*, 47.

72. Marvin Harris, *Cows, Pigs, Wars, and Witches: The Riddle of Culture* (New York: Vintage, 1978), 28–50.

73. Quoted in Michael Scrivener, ed., *Poetry and Reform*, 62. "A Fellow Grunter" thanks Spence for "supplying us with good wholesome Food; on which I hope we shall long continue to feast ourselves, in spite of those who would wish to . . . starve us to death in 'the sty of Taxation.' "

74. "Of their flesh you shall not eat, and their carcasses you shall not touch; they are unclean to you" (Leviticus 11:8); in Mark (5:9–13), Jesus expels unclean spirits from Legion, driving them off a cliff as a herd of swine.

75. Lamb's "On the Custom of Hissing at the Theaters, with Some Account of a Club of Damned Authors" (1811) fantasizes about forming a club with other damned authors and eating the hissers in a retributory meal: "on our feast-nights we cut up a goose, an animal typical of the *popular voice,* to the deities of Candour and Patient Hearing. A zealous member of the society once proposed that we should revive the obsolete luxury of viper-broth; but the stomachs of some of the company rising at the proposition, we lost the benefit of that highly salutary and *antidotal dish*" (*WCL* 1:91); cf. Lamb's letter to Manning of February 26, 1818 (*LM* 2:272–73).

76. E .V. Lucas, *The Life of Charles Lamb,* 2 vols., 3d ed. (London: Methuen, 1906), 1:278; a current rhyme preempted Lamb's resolution: " 'Brighton is a pretty street, / Worthing is much taken: / If you can't get any other meat, / There's Hogsflesh and Bacon.'"

77. Gerald Monsman, *Confessions of a Prosaic Dreamer: Charles Lamb's Art of Autobiography* (Durham: Duke University Press, 1984), 83.

78. Charles Lamb, *Essays of Elia, to which are Added Letters, and Rosamund, a Tale* (Paris: Baudry's European Library, 1835), xi.

79. Sigmund Freud, "The Economic Problem in Masochism" (1924), in *General Psychological Theory: Papers on Metapsychology,* ed. by Philip Rieff (New York: Colier Books, 1963), 193.

80. Seamus Perry, "Charles Lamb and the Cost of Seriousness," *Charles Lamb Bulletin* 83 (1993): 78–89 (86).

81. Hunt, *Autobiography,* 2:54.

82. Sigmund Freud, *The Complete Psychological Works,* trans. by James Strachey with Anna Freud, vol. 14 (London: Hogarth Press, 1957), 257–58.

83. From the 1835 Paris edition of *Essays of Elia* (note 78), iii.

84. Freud, *Psychological Works,* 246.

85. Burton, *Anatomy of Melancholy,* 250.

86. Bamborough, *The Little World of Man,* 68.

87. Quoted from Edward Topsell's *The History of Four-footed Beastes* (1607) in David Perkins, "Cowper's Hares," *Eighteenth-Century Life* (1996): 57–69 (60); cf. Henry Tegner, *Wild Hares* (London: John Baker, 1969), 22–23.

88. Perkins, "Cowper's Hares," 62.

89. George Ewart Evans and David Thomson, *The Leaping Hare* (London: Faber and Faber, 1972), 91.

90. Jane Aaron, *A Double Singleness: Gender and the Writings of Charles and Mary Lamb* (Oxford: Clarendon Press, 1991), 10–13.

Chapter 6. Taste Outraged

1. There has been skepticism about Trelawny's sensational accounts of Byron's life; see William St. Clair, *Trelawny: The Incurable Romancer* (New York: Vanguard Press, 1977); David Crane, *Lord Byron's Jackal: The Life of Edward John Trelawny* (London: HarperCollins, 1998).

2. Benjamin Robert Haydon, *The Diary of Benjamin Robert Haydon,* ed. by Willard Bissell Pope, 5 vols. (Cambridge, Mass.: Harvard University Press, 1960), 2:317.

3. M. K. Joseph, *Byron the Poet* (London: Gollancz, 1964), 228. Byron treats his appetite directly in *BLJ* 1:113–33; 2:131; 3:212ff.; 8:165; 9:180; the critical response includes *The Ambiguity of Taste,* 55–114; Jane Stabler, "Byron's World of Zest," in Morton, ed., *Cultures of Taste,* 141–60. Carol Shiner Wilson, "Stuffing the Verdant Goose: Culinary Esthetics in *Don Juan,*" *Mosaic* 24:3–4 (1991): 33–52; Peter W. Graham, "The Order and Disorder of Eating in Byron's *Don Juan,*" in *Disorderly Eaters: Texts in Self-Empowerment,* ed. by Lilian R. Furst and Peter W. Graham (University Park: Pennsylvania State University Press, 1992): 113–123; Arthur Crisp, "Ambivalence towards Fatness and Its Origins," *British Medical Journal* 7123 (December 20–27, 1997), 1697–703; and Wilma Paterson, *Lord Byron's Relish: The Regency Cookery Book* (Glasgow: Dog and Bone, 1990). This latter, whose medical analysis of anorexia nervosa is quite thin, is worth consulting for its recipes, menus, and table arrangements of the banquet scene in canto 15 of *Don Juan.*

4. But in 1858 Trelawny scandalized readers by claiming that Byron had not one, but two deformed feet and that both of his legs were shriveled from the knee down. According to Trelawny, only well-crafted footwear, an upper body kept in shape by riding and swimming, and an acquired talent for moving in calculated rapid spurts in public could have disguised the emasculating disability for so long. St. Clair assesses the veracity of this report in his *Trelawny,* 218–19n.

5. On the nineteenth-century discourse of vampirism in relation to consumer capitalism, see C. Richard King, "The (Mis)uses of Cannibalism in Contemporary Cultural Critique," *Diacritics* 30:1 (2000): 106–23.

6. The two influential works I have in mind are Sigmund Freud, *Civilization and Its Discontents,* trans. by James Strachey (New York: W. W. Norton, 1961); and Michel Foucault, *The History of Sexuality,* trans. by Robert Hurley (New York: Pantheon Books,

1978). Elsewhere, Freud sums up the kernel of his social theory: "At bottom society's motive is economic; since it has not means enough to support life for its members without work on their part, it must see to it that the number of these members is restricted and their energies directed away from sexual activities on to their work"; *A General Introduction to Psychoanalysis*, trans. by Joan Riviere (Garden City, N.Y.: Garden City Publishing, 1943), 273. Cf. "The Most Prevalent Form of Degradation in Erotic Life," where he argues that "the grandest cultural achievements . . . are brought to birth by ever greater sublimation of the components of the sexual instinct"; *Collected Papers*, vol. 4, trans. by Joan Riviere (London: Psychoanalytical Library, 1934), 203–16 (216).

7. Davidoff and Hall report that with the growth of capital society: "Sexuality, regarded as one of the most irrational forces, was relegated to the inner core of marriage and sexual play became the ultimate antithesis of rational work"; *Family Fortunes*, 26–27. The idea also informs Albert O. Hirschman's *The Passions and the Interests: Political Arguments for Capitalism before Its Triumph* (Princeton: Princeton University Press, 1977).

8. See chapter 3, note 52.

9. Peter J. Kitson, " 'The Eucharist of Hell'; or, Eating People is Right: Romantic Representations of Cannibalism," *Romanticism on the Net* 17 (2000): http://users.ox.ac.uk/~scato385/17cannibalism.html.

10. The authors were aware of the strained political tensions surrounding the disaster, and in their expanded book-length account (pub. November 1817; trans. 1818), J. B. Henri Savigny and Alexander Corréard claim that "the critical situation of our country also mingled with our grief; and certainly, of all the afflictions we experienced, this was not the least. . . . Several of us regretted not having fallen in the defence of France"; *Narrative of a Voyage to Senegal in 1816 Undertaken by Order of the French Government, Comprising an Account of the Shipwreck of the Medusa, the Sufferings of the Crew and the Various Occurrences on Board the Raft, in the Desert of Zaara, at St. Louis, and at the Camp of Daccard*, ed. by John Philips (Marlboro, Vt.: Marlboro Press, 1986), 62–63.

11. Ibid., 53.

12. Unlike survival cannibalism, ritual cannibalism "is never just about eating but is primarily a medium for nongustatory messages — messages having to do with the maintenance, regeneration, and, in some cases, the foundation of the cultural order." Peggy Reeves Sanday, *Divine Hunger: Cannibalism as a Cultural System* (Cambridge: Cambridge University Press, 1986), 3. William Arens initiated a tidal wave of scholarly debate by proposing that ritual cannibalism is nothing more than a myth invented by Western anthropologists for the purpose of affirming cultural differentiation (and hence their own discipline) in *The Man-Eating Myth* (1979). Peter Hulme provides a concise sketch of this in his introduction to *Cannibalism and the Colonial World*, ed. by Francis Barker, Peter Hulme, and Margaret Iverson (Cambridge: Cambridge University Press, 1998), 6–10. Although it carries greater cultural significance, ritual cannibalism has only been accessed through representation. Thus, Diego Alvarez Chanca, who sailed with Columbus on his second voyage to the Caribbean in 1493, records finding five human bones but no actual cannibals, nevertheless concluding "that the islands were those of the *Caribe*, which are inhabited by people who eat human flesh"; quoted in *Wild Majesty: Encounters with*

Caribs from Columbus to the Present Day, ed. by Peter Hulme and Neil L. Whitehead (Oxford: Clarendon Press, 1992), 32.

13. Savigny and Corréard, *Narrative of a Voyage to Senegal,* 52–53; "Mais il fallait un moyen extrême pour soutenir notre malheureuse existence: nous frémissons d'horreur en nous voyant obligés de retracer celui que nous mîmes en usage; nous sentons notre plume s'échapper de nos mains; un froid mortel glace tous nos membres et nos cheveux se hérissent sur nos fronts. Lecteurs! nous vous en supplions, ne faites pas retomber sur des hommes déjà trop accablés de tous leurs maux, le sentiment d'indignation qui va peut-être s'élever en vous; plaignez-les bien plutôt, et versez quelques larmes de pitié sur leur déplorable sort." Alexandre Corréard and Jean Baptiste Henri Savigny, *Relation complète du naufrage de la frégate la Méduse, faisant partie de l'expédition du Sénégal en 1816* (Paris: Jean de Bonnot, 1968), 85.

14. John M'Leod, *Narrative of Voyage, in His Majesty's Late Ship Alceste, and the Yellow Sea, along the Coast of Corea, and through its numerous Undiscovered Islands, to the Island of Lewchew; with an Account of Her Shipwreck in the Straits of Gaspar* (London: John Murray, 1817), 224–25. He notes: "Truth requires it to be stated, and it may naturally be supposed, that, among so many, one or two progging sort of people might be observed, who had no disinclination to a little more than their just allowance; but the general feeling was much too manly and fine to admit of contamination."

15. M'Leod, *Narrative of Voyage,* 224–25.

16. *The Shipwreck of the Alceste, an English Frigate, in the Straits of Gaspar; also, the Shipwreck of the Medusa, a French Frigate, on the Coast of Africa, with Observations and Reflections Thereon* (Dublin: Printed by C. Bentham, 1820), 73.

17. W. T. Moncrieff, *Shipwreck of the Medusa; or, The Fatal Raft! A Drama, in Three Acts* (London: Thomas Richardson, 1830), 31.

18. *The Shipwreck of the Alceste,* vi.

19. Thomas Robert Malthus, *An Essay on the Principle of Population; or a View of Its Past and Present Effects on Human Happiness,* 7th ed. (Fairfield, N.J.: August M. Kelley, 1986), 22.

20. Richard Chenevix, "Review of *Voyage of H.M. Ship Alceste along the Coast of Corea, to the island of Lewchew; with an Account of her subsequent Shipwreck,* by John Mc'Leod, 2d ed. (London: J. Murray, 1818) and *Naufrage de la Fregate la Méduse . . .* by Alexandre Corréard and J. B. Henri Savigny, 2d ed. (Paris, 1818)," in *Edinburgh Review* 30 (1818): 388–406 (403–04).

21. Savigny and Corréard, *Narrative of a Voyage to Senegal,* 49.

22. Malthus, *An Essay on the Principle of Population,* 29; Savigny and Corréard, *Narrative of a Voyage to Senegal,* 53.

23. "Remarks on *Don Juan,*" *Blackwood's Edinburgh Magazine* 5 (1819): 512–22 (522).

24. Percy Bysshe Shelley, letter (567) to Byron of May 26, 1820, *The Letters of Percy Bysshe Shelley,* ed. by Frederick L. Jones, 2 vols. (Oxford: Clarendon Press, 1964), 2:198.

25. In his effort to capture the most dramatic moment of the *Medusa* shipwreck to depict, Géricault passed through a number of stages, including (1) the nighttime mutiny of the sailors on the raft; (2) the rescue of the survivors; (3) the cannibalism; (4) the hailing of the rescue boat *Argus;* and (5) the sighting of the rescue boat, which he ultimately

chose for the painting; Lorenz Eitner, *Géricault's Raft of the Medusa* (New York: Phaidon, 1972), 23.

26. After viewing Géricault's painting in June 1820, the critic from the *Globe* remarked, "there is one figure of an old man, who still retains at his feet the dead body of his son, that is full of appalling expression. It is the very countenance of Ugolino's despair, which Reynolds portrayed with an effect finely forcible indeed, though without the haughty distinction." Quoted in Eitner, *Géricault's Raft of the Medusa*, 64. Cf. Sir Joshua Reynolds's *Ugolino and His Children in Dungeon* (1771).

27. Quoted in Andrew Rutherford, *Byron: The Critical Heritage* (New York: Barnes and Noble, 1970), 175.

28. Critics have sought to reconcile Byron, satire, and Romanticism; see Robert F. Gleckner, *Byron and the Ruins of Paradise* (Baltimore: Johns Hopkins University Press, 1967), 332ff.; and his "From Selfish Spleen to Equanimity: Byron's Satires," *Studies in Romanticism* 18:2 (1979): 173–205; Frederick L. Beaty, *Byron the Satirist* (DeKalb, Ill.: Northern Illinois University Press, 1985); Alvin B. Kernan, *The Plot of Satire* (New Haven: Yale University Press, 1965). On the broader context of Romantic satire, see Gary Dyer, *British Satire and the Politics of Style: 1789–1832* (Cambridge: Cambridge University Press, 1997), and Steven E. Jones, *Satire and Romanticism* (London: Macmillan, 2000); neither, however, treats Lamb. On the related genre of Romantic irony (in which the dialectic of satire and romance synthesize), see Anne K. Mellor, *English Romantic Irony* (Cambridge, Mass.: Harvard University Press, 1980); and Frederick Garber, *Self, Text, and Romantic Irony: The Example of Byron* (Princeton: Princeton University Press, 1988).

29. Harold Bloom, "Introduction," *Modern Critical Views: George Gordon, Lord Byron*, ed. by Harold Bloom (New York: Chelsea House, 1986), 21. Kitson also notes the civility of this act in "The Eucharist of Hell," 15–17.

30. Claude Rawson keenly summarizes the different levels of satire at work in "A Modest Proposal" in *Critical Approaches to Teaching Swift*, ed. by Peter J. Schakel (New York: AMS Press, 1992), 187–202.

31. There is an enormous sociological, historical, and economic literature devoted to capitalism and its chronological parameters. Mica Nava provides a helpful summary in "Consumerism and its Contradictions," *Cultural Studies* 2 (1987): 204–10. Much social criticism emanating from Marx considers consumer society a distinctive form of advanced capitalism, which consolidated in the years 1780 to 1850. Others argue that capitalism develops out of consumer society, e.g., Chandra Mukerji, *From Graven Images: Patterns of Modern Materialism* (New York: Columbia University Press, 1983); Carole Shammas, *The Pre-industrial Consumer in England and America* (Oxford: Clarendon Press, 1990); Lorna Weatherill, *Consumer Behaviour and Material Culture in Britain, 1660–1760* (London: Routledge, 1988). We can distinguish between the cash society of early modern capitalism (dating to the increased availability of goods through colonialist exploration) and the industrial capitalism developed in late eighteenth-century England.

32. Edward Trelawny, *Recollections of the Last Days of Shelley and Byron*, ed. by Edward Dowden (London: Henry Frowde, 1906), 31.

33. Christine Kenyon-Jones also notes that "the assurance of a clear moral stance here

is deceptive, and many of the clauses which seem most definite are in fact tentative or can be read as deliberately provocative about meat-eating and vegetarianism"; *Kindred Brutes: Animals in Romantic-Period Writing* (Aldershot: Ashgate, 2001), 124; see also her " 'Man is a Carnivorous Production': Byron and the Anthropology of Food," in *Prism(s)* 6 (1988): 42–58.

34. Leslie A. Marchand, *Byron: A Biography*, 2 vols. (New York: Alfred A. Knopf, 1957), 1:116, 160–61, 286–87.

35. John Byron, *The Narrative of the Honourable John Byron, Containing an Account of the Great Distresses Suffered by Himself and His Companions on the Coast of Patagonia, from the Year 1740, till their Arrival in England, 1746* (London: S. Baker, G. Leigh, and T. Davies, 1768), 47, 30.

36. James Cook, *The Explorations of Captain James Cook in the Pacific as Told by Selections of His Own Journals, 1768–1799*, ed. by A. Grenfell Price (New York: Dover, 1971), 145. *The Silence of the Lambs* (1990), directed by Jonathan Demme and starring Anthony Hopkins as Hannibal Lecter, does not actually show Lecter eat human liver with fava beans, but we witness enough of his elegant-repulsive dining habits to imagine it when it is mentioned.

37. Milton's Latin in *De Doctrina Christiana* has been alternately translated as "cannibal feast" and "banquet of cannibals" (*YP* 6:554; *Works* 15:196), though Milton himself, to avoid the anachronism of the colonial term *cannibal* (which did not exist in Latin) renders the sacrament of communion a banquet of Cyclops: "quae coenam Dominicam in coenam prope dixerem cyclopeam convertunt." *Works* 15:196–97. Cf. chapter 2, note 55.

38. "Review of *Naufrage de la Frégate La Méduse, faisant partie de l'Expédition du Sénegal, en 1816*," *Quarterly Review* 18 (1818): 168–76 (173). Cf. "Voyant que cette affreuse nourriture avait relevé les forces de ceux qui l'avaient employée, on proposa de la faire sécher pour la rendre un peu plus supportable au goût." Corréard and Savigny, *Relation Complète*, 87.

39. Savigny and Corréard, *Narrative of a Voyage to Senegal*, 53.

40. Sigmund Freud, *Totem and Taboo: Some Points of Agreement between the Mental Lives of Savages and Neurotics*, ed. by James Strachey (New York: W. W. Norton, 1989), 176.

41. The cultural equivalence between cannibalism and incest is discussed by Claude Lévi-Strauss, *The Savage Mind* (Chicago: University of Chicago Press, 1966), 105–06.

42. A similar paradigm is discussed by Eve Kosofsky Sedgwick, *Between Men: English Literature and Male Homosocial Desire* (New York: Columbia University Press, 1985).

43. See Philip W. Martin, *Byron: A Poet Before His Public* (London: Cambridge University Press, 1982), 210–13.

44. Jerome Christensen, *Lord Byron's Strength: Romantic Writing and Commercial Society* (Baltimore: Johns Hopkins University Press, 1993), 245. For Christensen, Byron sees the fate of his poetry in Julia's letter.

45. George Gordon, Lord Byron, *Autographs Once in the Possession of the Countess Guiccioli: Don Juan, Cantos I–V*, ed. by Alice Levine and Jerome J. McGann; *Facsimiles of Manuscripts in the Pierpont Morgan Library*, 4 vols.; in *Manuscripts of the Younger Romantics*, Donald H. Reiman, gen. ed., 11 vols. (New York: Garland, 1985), 2:127.

46. As Herbert Marcuse writes, all oral and libidinal cravings, which exist in-themselves for the sake of their own pleasure, are "tabooed as perversions, sublimated, or transformed into subsidiaries of procreative sexuality"; *Eros and Civilization: A Philosophical Inquiry into Freud* (Boston: Beacon Press, 1966), 40–41.

47. Freud, *Civilization and Its Discontents,* 50–51.

48. Moncrieff, *Shipwreck of the Medusa,* 34.

49. The OED derives this meaning of Nancy from "Nancy Dawson," defined as "a sailor's dance or song; a nancy-boy," in use from the mid-eighteenth (1766) through the end of the nineteenth century. The point at which Nancy Dawson evolves from a sailor's dance into an effeminate male or homosexual is unclear; its last entry, dated 1890, is from a dictionary of slang that defines it as "a name for a molly, an effeminate youth, apathetic, &c." Cf. Leigh W. Rutledge, who traces the "nancy" or "nancy boy" to nineteenth-century English slang for buttocks. *The New Gay Book of Lists* (Boston: Alyson Publications, 1996), 59–60. I am grateful to Jolene Hubbs for her research on this matter.

50. Delacroix had been obsessed with Géricault's painting in 1819, for which he modeled as the figure spread-eagle and face-down in the front of the raft. His original sketch for *Le Naufrage de Don Juan* (1841) was faithful to Géricault's sublimity ("C'est quelche chose de sublime"), though the final version swerves with Byron into the satiric. Eugène Delacroix, *Journal de Eugène Delacroix*, ed. by Paul Flat and René Piot (Paris: E. Plon Nourrit, 1893), 2:251. Cf. Alain Daguerre de Hureaux, *Delacroix* (Paris: Hazan, 1993), 144.

51. Karl Marx, *Capital: A Critique of Political Economy,* trans. by Ben Fowkes, intro. by Ernest Mandel, 3 vols. (London: Penguin, 1990), 1:342.

52. Sussman, *Consuming Anxieties,* 16.

53. William Fox, *An Address to the People of Great Britain, on the Propriety of Abstaining from West India Sugar and Rum,* 25th ed. (London: M. Gurney, 1792), 2.

54. Robert Southey, *Thalaba the Destroyer* (1801 repr.; Oxford: Woodstock Books, 1991), 8.103–23n.

55. Polidori's narrative was a version of a story Byron had begun at Villa Diodati on June 17, 1816, and in this respect some confusion was inevitable. To distance himself from *The Vampyre,* Byron asked Murray to publish his fragmentary vampire tale in the periodical press, such as the *Edinburgh Magazine, Wilson's,* or *Blackwood's,* along with an explanatory note, though Murray appended it to *Mazeppa* (1819), much to the author's chagrin (*BLJ* 6:126). Polidori claimed authorship of the *New Monthly* vampire in a letter to the *Courier* of 5 May 1819, but as Judith Barbour points out, he "only tightened the links of association with Byron, by advertising his composition as a completion of a 'ghost story' begun by Byron in 1816"; "Dr. John William Polidori, Author of *The Vampyre,*" in *Imagining Romanticism: Essays on English and Australian Romanticisms,* ed. by Deirdre Coleman and Peter Otto (West Cornwall, Conn.: Locust Hill Press, 1992), 91.

56. John Polidori, *The Vampyre; a Tale* (1819 repr.; Oxford: Woodstock Books, 1990), 27.

57. Patricia L. Skarda, "Vampirism and Plagiarism: Byron's Influence and Polidori's Practice," *Studies in Romanticism* 28 (1989): 249–69 (250).

58. On the literary vampire tradition, see Ken Gelder, *Reading the Vampire* (London:

Routledge, 1994); James B. Twitchell, *The Living Dead: A Study of the Vampire in Romantic Literature* (Durham, N.C.: Duke University Press, 1981); Brian J. Frost, *The Monster with a Thousand Faces: Guises of the Vampire in Myth and Literature* (Bowling Green, Ohio: Bowling Green State University Press, 1989). On vampire tradition, the most exhaustive study is Montague Summers, *The Vampire: His Kith and Kin* (London: K. Paul, Trench, Trubner, 1928); but also see Anthony Masters, *The Natural History of the Vampire* (New York: G. P. Putnam, 1972), and Gabriel Ronay, *The Truth About Dracula* (New York: Stein and Day, 1972).

59. "Remarks on *Don Juan*," *Blackwood's*, 513.

60. *KC* 2:134; "Remarks on *Don Juan*," *Blackwood's*, 522.

61. William Hazlitt, *The Spirit of the Age* (1825 repr.; Oxford: Woodstock Books, 1989), 167.

62. Jonathan David Gross, " 'One half what I should say': Byron's Gay Narrator in *Don Juan*," *European Romantic Review* 9:3 (1998): 323–50 (332); he notes that Lionel Trilling and Harold Bloom discuss the Byronic persona as "fundamentally homosexual," and that Jerome Christensen and Andrew Elfenbein, among others, connect his sexual identity to vice. Cf. Susan Wolfson " 'Their She Condition': Cross-Dressing and the Politics of Gender in *Don Juan*," *ELH* 54:3 (fall 1987): 585–617 (585).

63. Gary Dyer, "Thieves, Boxers, Sodomites, Poets: Being Flash to Byron's *Don Juan*," *PMLA* 116:3 (2001): 562–78 (567).

64. Byron's letter to Murray on April 16, 1819, bears out the potential interminability of the poem: "You shall have enough of *Juan* for I'll make 50 cantos" (*BLJ* 6:105).

65. Bram Stoker, *Dracula*, ed. by Maurice Hindle (London: Penguin, 1993), 55.

66. Christopher Craft, " 'Kiss Me with Those Red Lips': Gender and Inversion in *Dracula*," *Representations* 8 (fall 1984): 107–33.

67. Barbara Belford discusses Stoker's fascination with the actor Henry Irving in *Bram Stoker: A Biography of the Author of Dracula* (New York: Knopf, 1996). One of Irving's best-loved possessions was a Circassian dagger once owned by Byron. Bram Stoker, *Personal Reminiscences of Henry Irving*, 2 vols. (London: William Heinemann, 1906), 2:92–111, 90.

68. On the Byrons' mutually unhappy marriage, see Leslie A. Marchand, *Byron: A Biography*, 3 vols. (New York: Knopf, 1957), 2:507–91. (The portrait of Donna Inez in canto 1 was thought to be modeled on Lady Byron.)

69. "Review of *Sardanapalus, a Tragedy. The Two Foscari, a Tragedy. Cain, a Mystery*," *Edinburgh Review* 36 (1822): 413–52 (452). Cf. Wilner, who observes that the Eucharistic confusion of wine and human blood in the shipwreck scene (where the survivors quaff "a draught from the fast-flowing veins" of Pedrillo) bespeaks a morality that is "a matter of dietary code"; *Feeding on Infinity*, 83.

70. From stanza 137 of *Don Juan: With a Biographical Account of Lord Byron and His Family; Anecdotes of his Lordship's Travels and Residence in Greece, at Geneva &c. Canto III* (London: William Wright, 1819); 67.

71. Ghislaine McDayter, "Conjuring Byron: Byromania, Literary Commodification, and the Birth of Celebrity," in *Byromania*, ed. by Francis Wilson (New York: St. Martin's Press, 1999), 43–62 (54). Like Christensen, she finds that the commodification of the Byronic voice and persona caused Byron a deep anxiety about the fate of his literary corpus.

72. The "Extract of a Letter, Containing an Account of Lord Byron's Residence in the Island of Mitylene" has been attributed to John Mitford, who was hired as a hack writer by Henry Colburn, editor of the *New Monthly Magazine,* to provide sensational material about Byron to accompany *The Vampyre: Notes and Queries.* 3d ser. vol. 7 (March 1865): 201. For Byron's complaints on the memoir, see *BLJ* 6:125, 131–32; 139–40.

73. Thomas Medwin, *Conversations of Lord Byron: Noted During a Residence with his Lordship at Pisa, in the Years 1821 and 1822* (London: Henry Colburn, 1824), 120.

74. George Gordon, Lord Byron, "Augustus Darvell: A Fragment of a Ghost Story (1816)," in *The Complete Miscellaneous Prose,* ed. by Andrew Nicholson (Oxford: Clarendon Press, 1991), 59.

75. Louis Crompton, *Byron and Greek Love: Homophobia and Nineteenth-Century England* (Berkeley: University of California Press, 1985).

76. Crompton, *Byron and Greek Love,* 5.

77. Quoted in Polidori, *The Vampyre,* 83.

78. Joseph Conrad, *Heart of Darkness and Other Tales,* ed. by Cedric Watts (Oxford: Oxford University Press, 1990), 135.

79. Ibid., 224–34; 232. It is worth noting (as per note 12 above) that Conrad's ritual cannibals are never actually shown eating human flesh; on their route up-river with the narrator, Marlow, the people referred to as cannibals survive on rotting rhinoceros meat.

80. H. G. Wells, *The Time Machine* (New York: Dover, 1995), 3, 26.

81. Robert Louis Stevenson, *The Strange Case of Dr Jekyll and Mr Hyde,* ed. by Martin A. Danahay (Peterborough, Ontario: Broadview, 1999), 49, 83–84.

82. Nicholas Roe discusses this letter as a response to Burke in *John Keats and the Culture of Dissent* (Oxford: Clarendon Press, 1997), 155–59.

Chapter 7. Keats's Nausea

1. Elizabeth Bishop, letter to Robert Lowell, March 30, 1959; *One Art: Letters, Selected and Edited,* ed. by Robert Giroux (New York: Farrar Straus Giroux, 1994), 372.

2. Quoted in G. M. Matthews, *Keats: The Critical Heritage* (London: Routledge and Kegan Paul, 1971), 35.

3. This portrait of Keats occurs in "Ego Dominus Tuus." *Yeats's Poems,* ed. by A. Norman Jeffares (Dublin: Gill and Macmillan, 1989), 266.

4. Lionel Trilling, *The Opposing Self* (New York: Viking, 1955), 17.

5. The phrase is from the final stanza of Keats's "Ode on Melancholy" (*KCP* 284). Even Keats's friends, such as Charles Cowden Clarke, identified as his "civil creed," "A thing of beauty is a joy for ever." Charles Cowden Clarke and Mary Cowden Clarke, *Recollections of Writers* (New York: Charles Scribner's, 1878), 146. David Masson observed in 1861 that this is "one of the most startling and significant sayings ever uttered by a man respecting himself." Quoted in Matthews, *The Critical Heritage,* 374. Since then, critics have challenged the absolutism of the binary between the aesthetic and the political, e.g., Roe, *John Keats and the Culture of Dissent;* and David Bromwich, "Keats's Politics," in *A Choice of Inheritance: Self and Community from Edmund Burke to Robert Frost* (Cambridge, Mass.: Harvard University Press, 1989), 92–105.

6. Engell, *Creative Imagination,* 204.

7. Reynolds, *Discourses on Art,* 43.

8. Cf. "What the imagination seizes as Beauty must be truth" (*KL* 1:184).

9. Coleridge defines allegory in *The Statesman's Manual* (1816) as an inferior literary device compared to the symbol—a false "picture-language which is itself nothing but an abstraction from objects of the senses" (*CCW* 6:30–31). This elevation of symbol over allegory has been productive of critical debate, beginning with Paul de Man's claim that Coleridge privileges "a mere reflection of a more original unity that does not exist in the material world," and hence the symbol as a vehicle of ideology. *Blindness and Insight: Essays in the Rhetoric of Contemporary Criticism,* 2d ed., intro. by Wlad Godzich (Minneapolis: University of Minnesota Press, 1983), 192. For a helpful analysis of the issues at stake in the symbol-allegory distinction, see Thomas McFarland, "Involute and Symbol in the Romantic Imagination," in *Coleridge, Keats, and the Imagination: Romanticism and Adam's Dream,* ed. by J. Robert Barth and John L. Mahoney (Columbia: University of Missouri Press, 1990), 29–57.

10. Walter Jackson Bate, *John Keats* (Cambridge, Mass.: Harvard University Press, 1963), 309.

11. Fredrick Accum, *Culinary Chemistry, Exhibiting the Scientific Principles of Cookery, with Concise Instructions for Preparing Good and Wholesome Pickles, Vinegar, Conserves, Fruit Jellies, Marmalades, and Various Other Alimentary Substances Employed in Domestic Economy, with Observations on the Chemical Constitution and Nutritive Qualities of Different Kinds of Food* (London: R. Ackermann, 1821), 17–18.

12. Leon Waldoff, *Keats and the Silent Work of Imagination* (Urbana: University of Illinois Press, 1985), 152.

13. David Perkins, *The Quest for Permanence: The Symbolism of Wordsworth, Shelley, and Keats* (Cambridge, Mass.: Harvard University Press, 1959), 216. He notes that "The poetry of Keats is everywhere invested with an eager appetite for a full, vivid, and concrete experiencing" and that "these images are usually associated with eating or drinking" (205–6).

14. Helen Vendler, *The Odes of John Keats* (Cambridge, Mass.: Harvard University Press, 1983), 180, 159.

15. Marjorie Levinson, *Keats's Life of Allegory: The Origins of a Style* (Oxford: Basil Blackwell, 1988), 77–78.

16. Harold Bloom, *The Visionary Company: A Reading of English Romantic Poetry,* 2d ed. (Ithaca: Cornell University Press, 1971), 385.

17. Bate, *John Keats,* 480.

18. As we have seen, Porphyry was a locus classicus for vegetarian writing of the Romantic era, and given that Keats refers in his letters to vegetable food as "pseudo victuals" (*KL* 2:271), a type of food unable to sustain any poor wight with "Real hunger," one may wonder about Keats's naming of Porphyro in "The Eve of St. Agnes." Timothy Morton discusses its thirtieth stanza as replete with luxurious or supplemental food in *The Poetics of Spice: Romantic Consumerism and the Exotic* (Cambridge: Cambridge University Press, 2000), 109–70.

19. Hobbes, *Leviathan,* 33. Oneration here means burdening or filling.

20. Ibid., 56. Without Hobbes's "powerful precedent, one may say with little hesitation that the criticism of . . . Addison, and others who made notable contributions to a psychology of effect would have been different"; Clarence DeWitt Thorpe, *The Aesthetic*

Theory of Thomas Hobbes; with Special Reference to his Contribution to the Psychological Approach in English Literary Criticism (Ann Arbor: University of Michigan Press, 1940), 149.

21. Levinson, *Keats's Life of Allegory,* 52–53.

22. Stuart M. Sperry, *Keats the Poet* (Princeton: Princeton University Press, 1994), 192.

23. Ibid., 192–93.

24. Andrew Bennett, *Keats, Narrative, and Audience: The Posthumous Life of Writing* (Cambridge: Cambridge University Press, 1994), 149.

25. John Keats, *Anatomical and Physiological Note Book,* ed. by Maurice Buxton Forman (New York: Haskell House, 1970), 55.

26. Geldard, *The Human Senses,* 300.

27. John Hunter, *Essays and Observations on Natural History, Anatomy, Physiology, Psychology, and Geology,* ed. by Richard Owen, 2 vols. (London: John van Voorst, 1861), 1:179.

28. Johann Gaspar Spurzheim, *Phrenology; or the Doctrine of the Mental Phenomenon* (Philadelphia: J. B. Lippincott, 1908), 300.

29. Harold Bloom, *Poetry and Repression: Revisionism from Blake to Stevens* (New Haven and London: Yale University Press, 1976), 123.

30. Blumenbach, *Institutions of Physiology,* 240.

31. This view is confirmed today: "To stimulate the sense of smell materials must be airborne and in a finely divided state." Geldard, *The Human Senses,* 271.

32. Spurzheim, *Phrenology,* 301.

33. Freud is thinking along the same lines when he writes that "the coprophilic elements in the instinct have proved incompatible with our aesthetic ideas, probably since the time when man developed an upright posture and so removed his organ of smell from the ground." Sigmund Freud, "The Most Prevalent Form of Degradation in Erotic Life," trans. by Joan Riviere, in *Collected Papers* (London: International Psycho-Analytical Library, 1934), 4:215.

34. Derrida, "Economimesis," 22.

35. John Keats, *Manuscript Poems in the British Library: Facsimiles of the Hyperion Holograph and George Keats's Notebook of Holographs and Transcripts,* ed. by Jack Stillinger (New York: Garland, 1988), 13.

36. Jonathan Bate, "Keats's Two *Hyperions* and the Problem of Milton," *Romantic Revisions,* ed. by Robert and Keith Hanley (Cambridge: Cambridge University Press, 1992), 321–38 (328).

37. Aileen Ward, *John Keats: The Making of a Poet* (New York: Farrar, Straus and Giroux, 1986), 134, 427–28; Robert Gittings, *John Keats* (London: Heinemann, 1968), 155–58, 446–50; Douglas Bush, *John Keats: His Life and Writings* (New York: Macmillan, 1966), 62–64. For a brief history of the debate see Donald C. Goellnicht, *The Poet-Physician: Keats and Medical Science* (Pittsburgh: University of Pittsburgh Press, 1984), 201–3.

38. John Hunter, *Treatise on Venereal Disease,* ed. by George Gisborne Babington (Philadelphia: Haswell, Barrington, and Haswell, 1839), 19.

39. Hermione de Almeida, *Romantic Medicine and John Keats* (New York: Oxford University Press, 1991), 152.

40. Hunter, *Treatise on Venereal Disease,* 294, 289.

41. Etymologically, "absurd" (from the Latin *surdus*, "deaf") suggests its own lineage in the philosophical discourse of taste: as an orifice of aesthetic perception, the ear registers the absurd object as tasteless. Existentialism adopts the term for its subgenre of absurdism.

42. De Almeida, *Romantic Medicine and John Keats,* 167. Here I intend no disrespect; the confusion works productively in the other direction as well.

43. W. J. Bate, *John Keats,* 591.

44. Cf. Keats's dying letter to his friend Charles Brown: "I wish for death every day and night to deliver me from these pains, and then I wish death away, for death would destroy even those pains which are better than nothing" (*KL* 2:345–46). Severn describes Keats's final days as painfully existentialist: "this noble fellow lying on the bed — is dying in horror — no kind of hope smoothing down his suffering — no philosophy — no religion to support him — yet with all the most knawing [*sic*] desire for it — yet without the possibility of receiving it" (*KL* 2:368).

45. Goellnicht, *Poet-Physician,* 226.

46. Biographers from the time of Leigh Hunt agree that Keats felt himself to be suffering from tuberculosis several years before his death: "Keats had felt that his disease was mortal, two or three years before he died." *The Autobiography of Leigh Hunt with Reminiscences of Friends and Contemporaries, and with Thornton Hunt's Introduction and Postscript,* ed. by Roger Ingpen, 2d ed., 2 vols. (Westminster: Archibald Constable, 1903), 2:46. Indeed, one discerns throughout the early poetry ("On Seeing the Elgin Marbles," "Sleep and Poetry") indications that this is so.

47. Quoted in Matthews, *The Critical Heritage,* 98.

48. Jean-Paul Sartre, *Being and Nothingness: A Phenomenological Essay on Ontology,* trans. by Hazel E. Barnes (New York: Washington Square Press, 1956), 775; also quoted in Christopher Ricks, *Keats and Embarrassment* (Oxford: Clarendon Press, 1974), 139.

49. Levinson, *Keats's Life of Allegory,* 89n.

50. Plato's *Phaedrus* hinges on the indeterminacy of *pharmakon* as both "remedy" and "poison." Jacques Derrida, *Dissemination,* trans. and intro. by Barbara Johnson (Chicago: University of Chicago Press, 1981), 65–171. Cf. Levinson, *Keats's Life of Allegory,* 210–11; and De Almeida, *Romantic Medicine and John Keats,* 146–74.

51. For a fuller explication of what it means for Keats to "die into life," see my "The Monster in the Rainbow: Keats and the Science of Life," *PMLA* 117:3 (2002), 433–48.

52. Letter to J. H. Reynolds, 21 September 1819 (*KL* 2:167); letter to the George Keatses, 24 September 1819 (*KL* 2:212).

53. Keats explains his trouble with *Hyperion* (by which he means the two *Hyperion*s) as a belated struggle with Milton; on September 21, 1819: "I have given up Hyperion — there were too many Miltonic inversions in it — Miltonic verse cannot be written but in an artful or rather artist's humour. I wish to give myself up to other sensations" (*KL* 2:167); and to George and Georgiana Keats on September 24, 1819: "I have but lately stood on my guard against Milton. Life to him would be death to me. Miltonic verse cannot be written but i[n] the vein of art — I wish to devote myself to another sensation" (*KL* 2:212).

54. Irene H. Chayes, "Dreamer, Poet, and Poem in *The Fall of Hyperion,*" *Philological Quarterly* 46:4 (1967): 499–515 (515).

55. Gittings, *John Keats,* 410.

56. Susan Sontag, *Illness as Metaphor* (New York: Vintage, 1979), 28.

57. For more on this "ditch" as it recurs in Beckett, see my "The Endgame of Taste: Keats, Sartre, Beckett," *Romanticism on the Net* 24 (2001), 29 paras. http://users.ox.ac .uk/~scato385/articles.html, repr. in *Cultures of Taste,* ed. Morton, 183–201.

Chapter 8. The Gastronome and the Snob

1. Charles Lamb, "The Triumph of the Whale" (1812), in *The Examiner,* 15 vols. (London: William Pickering, 1996), 5:173.

2. We inherit the phrase "conspicuous consumption" from Thorstein Veblen, *The Theory of the Leisure Class: An Economic Study of Institutions* (New York, Macmillan, 1912), 68–101.

3. Grimod's *Almanach des gourmands* has not received the attention it deserves because it has been rarely reprinted, never reedited in its entirety, and never (except in bits) translated into English. Michael Garval finds that "Grimod has been undeservedly overshadowed, indeed nearly eclipsed by his successor, and in many ways imitator, Jean-Anthelme Brillat-Savarin," whose *Physiology of Taste* has been in print since its first publication in 1826; "Grimod de la Reynière's *Almanach des gourmands:* Exploring the Gastronomic New World of Postrevolutionary France," in *French Food: On the Table, on the Page, and in French Culture,* ed. by Lawrence R. Schehr and Allen S. Weiss (New York: Routledge, 2001), 51–70 (52). I have used Garval's translation in the epigraph above, as I do in my anthology, *Gusto.* The original reads: "Le bouleversement opéré dans les fortunes, par une suite nécessaire de la Révolution, les ayant mises dans de nouvelles mains, et l'espirit de la plupart de ces riches d'un jour se tournant sur-tout vers les jouissances purement animales . . . leurs sentiments ne sont plus que des sensations, et leurs désirs que des appétits; c'est donc les servir convenablement que de leur donner, en quelques pages, les moyens de tirer, sous le rapport de la bonne chère, le meilleur parti possible et de leurs penchants et de leurs écus." Grimod de la Reynière, *Almanach des Gourmands, ou Calendrier Nutrif, servant de Guide dans les Moyens Du Faire Exce Excellente Chère* (Paris: Maradan, 1803), i–ii.

4. Steven Parissien, *George IV: The Grand Entertainment* (London: John Murray, 2001), 167.

5. Joanna Richardson, *George the Magnificent: A Portrait of King George IV* (New York: Harcourt, Brace and World, 1966), 21. The Prince of Wales acquired Carlton House in 1783, engaging Henry Holland to supervise extensive "Improvements," which were in progress for much of his tenancy. Carlton House was pulled down in 1827.

6. Joanna Richardson, *George the Magnificent,* 23.

7. Elias, *The Civilizing Process,* 126–27.

8. John Beckmann, *A History of Inventions, Discoveries, and Origins,* trans. by William Johnston, 4th ed. (Amsterdam: B. M. Israël, 1974), 407–14 (413n.).

9. Jones, *Man of Manners,* 9.

10. Lord Chesterfield, *Principles of Politeness, and of Knowing the World; Methodified and digested under distinct headings and additions by John Trusler* (Boston: Booksellers, 1794), 55.

11. *The Illustrated Manners Book; A Manual of Good Behaviour and Polite Accom-*

plishments (New York: Leland Clay, 1855), 135. The examples are many; e.g, "It is a vulgar habit to pick your teeth when in company, and especially at meals, and in the presence of ladies"; *Book of Politeness* (Philadelphia: Fisher and Brothers, 1851), 13.

12. For more on the *je ne sais quoi* aesthetic, see W. J. Bate, *From Classic to Romantic* (New York: Harper and Row, 1961), 44.

13. Henry Petroski, *The Evolution of Useful Things* (New York: Knopf, 1992), 10.

14. A comprehensive cultural history of the fork is Petroski's "How the Fork Got Its Tines" (3–21); but also see James Cross Giblin, *From Hand to Mouth: Or, How We Invented Knives, Forks, Spoons, and Chopsticks and the Table Manners to Go with Them* (New York: Thomas Y. Crowell, 1987), 45–54. Reay Tannahill, *Food in History* (New York: Stein and Day, 1973), 227–30; Francis Sellon White, *A History of Inventions and Discoveries* (London: C. and J. Rivington, 1827), 296–97; and Humelbergius, *Apician Morsels,* 141–49; the chapter entitled "A Short Dissertation on the Origin of Dentiscalps, or Toothpicks."

15. These books are intended as emblems of cultural attitudes, but the first is probably a reference to the Scottish clergyman Adam Dickson's *An Essay on the Causes of the Present High Price of Provisions* (1773); or Joseph Wimpey's *An Essay on the Present High Price of Provisions* (1772). The second is a reference to the extremely overweight Scottish physician George Cheyne (1671–1743), who advocated dietary temperance in *An Essay of Health and Long Life* (1724), an idea also contained in his *The English Malady* (1733) and *An Essay on Regimen* (1740).

16. Linda Colley, *Britons: Forging the Nation, 1707–1837* (New Haven: Yale University Press, 1992), 166.

17. The Roast Beef Society, founded in 1735 by John Rich, machinist and harlequin of the Covent Garden Theatre, lasted 132 years. For seventy years, the society met at the Covent Garden Theatre; it moved to the Bedford Coffee House in 1808, and to the posh Beef-steak Rooms of the Lyceum Tavern in 1809; see Walter Arnold, *The Life and Death of the Sublime Society of Beef Steaks* (London: Bradbury, Evans, 1871). On George's membership, see Wilson Braddyll to Robert Gray or Colonel McMahon, letter 1520 in *The Correspondence of George, Prince of Wales, 1770–1812,* 4 vols., ed. by A. Aspinall, D. Litt (New York: Oxford University Press, 1967), 4:113.

18. Sir Samuel Romilly, *Memoirs of the Life of Sir Samuel Romilly,* 3 vols. (1840), 2:403. Romilly contrasts the feast to "the misery of the starving weavers of Lancashire and Glasgow" and claims that a reason given for the "great expense" of the dinner was "that it might give employment to the manufacturers," since "it was desired that the dresses of all the guests should be of British manufacture." As a result of such inventions as spinning and weaving machines and steam engines, there was widespread unemployment, which, combined with disastrous agricultural failures between 1809 and 1814, caused depressions in these basic industries in 1816, 1826 to 1827, 1841 to 1843, and 1848 to 1849. Burnett, *Plenty and Want,* 23, 35, 41.

19. Shelley, *Letters,* 1:110.

20. Thomas Moore, *Intercepted Letters; or, the Two-penny Post-bag.* From the 8th London edition (Baltimore: F. J. Coale et al., 1813), 25–26.

21. *The Reflector; a Quarterly Magazine,* 2:3 (1811): 1–13 (5).

22. Insofar as his work and writings provided a *theory* of food as a fine art, Carême was

one of the founders of modern gastronomy. Previous chefs placed value principally on their skill of execution, but Carême stressed the creative power of inventiveness in the culinary arts. Food experts suggest that he initiated and oversaw a transition from *ancienne cuisine,* with an emphasis on craftsmanship and skill in combination, to modern cuisine, which values originality and culinary genius. Philip Hyman, "Culina Mutata: Carême and *l'ancienne cuisine,*" in Schehr and Weiss, eds., *French Food,* 71–89 (71).

23. Parissien, *George IV,* 168.

24. Burnett, *Plenty and Want,* 83.

25. *The Remains of the Late Mrs. Richard Trench, Being Selections from her Journals, Letters, and other Papers,* edited by her son, 2d ed. (London: Parker, Son, and Bourn, 1862), 471.

26. *The Letters of Sir Walter Scott,* 12 vols., ed. by H. J. C. Grierson (London: Constable, 1934), 7:80–81.

27. Kitchiner, *Cook's Oracle,* 3.

28. As Joanne Finkelstein argues, "as foodstuffs and the manner of their consumption become symbols of social differentiation and individual preference, dining out has become a commodity reflective of desires other than those of immediate physical gratification"; *Dining Out: A Sociology of Modern Manners* (Cambridge, Mass.: Polity Press, 1989), 27.

29. Kitchiner, *Cook's Oracle,* 3–4.

30. Launcelot Sturgeon, *Essays, Moral, Philosophical, and Stomachical, on the Important Science of Good-Living,* 2d ed. (London: G. and W. B. Whittaker, 1823); first published in 1822. The book was owned if not written by Charles Lamb. At Edward Moxon's sale of Lamb's library in 1858, Lamb's copy of the 1823 edition was bought by his friend Captain Francis Jackson (of Red House, Mare Street, Hackney) and later came into the hands of his grandson, the eccentric bachelor Richard Charles Jackson, who lived alone among eight thousand books and who catalogued this one as number 133 of "The Lamb Collection of Books." In this copy, owned by Pennsylvania State University, Jackson writes: "It is surmised that this book is from the pen of Charles Lamb—my father told me that my grandfather would say that our immortal Charles was author of two or three other works, for which he had paid the cost of publication." Others attribute the book to William Beckford.

31. For more on Grimod's Tasting Jury, see Giles Macdonough, *A Palate in Revolution: Grimod de la Reynière and the Almanach des Gourmands* (London: Robin Clark, 1987), esp. 66–70. Priscilla Parkhurst Ferguson outlines five cultural conditions that factored into the aestheticization of food in "A Cultural Field in the Making: Gastronomy in Nineteenth-Century France," in Schehr and Weiss, eds., *French Food,* 5–50. Early examples of the restaurant guide include Honoré Blanc, *Le Guide des dîneurs de Paris* (The Paris Diner's Guide, 1815) and Georges Auguste Escoffier, *London at Table: How, When, and Where to Dine and Order a Dinner, and Where to Avoid Dining* (1851).

32. Grimod, *Almanach,* 5:7–8, qtd. in Garval, "Grimod de la Reynière's *Almanach des gourmands,*" 56.

33. Spang, *Invention of the Restaurant,* 165.

34. Garval, "Grimod de la Reynière's *Almanach des gourmands,*" 55.

35. The Revolution in Paris enabled the emergence of a cookery profession catering to

a dining public as "chefs moved from aristocratic hotels to public restaurants while dressmakers and tailors who had once served noble patrons now opened public shops . . . it was public consumption rather than private consumption that directed the work of the producers of luxury goods." McCracken, *Culture and Consumption*, 23; cf. Garval, "Grimod de la Reynière's *Almanach des gourmands*," 51. The restaurant can be distinguished from the eighteenth-century inn, where one ate what one was served. A closer English approximation to the French restaurant was the London tavern of the late eighteenth century, where men went to drink wine (as opposed to ale houses in which beer was sold) and chose from a fairly extensive list of English fare and French dishes. The larger London taverns by the end of the eighteenth century had become fashionable places much praised by Dr. Johnson to dine; Boswell, *Life of Johnson*, 694. But they still did not approach the culinary ambitions of the early French restaurants. Beauvillier's first great restaurant, opened in 1782 or 1786, was La Grande Taverne de Londres; see Mennell, *All Manners of Food*, 137–38, and Amy B. Trubek, *Haute Cuisine: How the French Invented the Culinary Profession* (Philadelphia: University of Pennsylvania Press, 2000), 36ff.

36. Spang, *The Invention of the Restaurant*, 150; Grimod's restaurant review is based on the drama review, and my copy of Grimod is, strangely, bound into some pages from an Italian opera.

37. The phrase is from Spang, who discusses the first *carte gastronomique* to appear in print in 1808; *Invention of the Restaurant*, 167.

38. Grimod, *Almanach*, 2:xv–xvii; qtd. in Garval, "Grimod de la Reynière's *Almanach des gourmands*," 66. Cf. Spang, *The Invention of the Restaurant*, 165, who suggests that the Tasting Jury may have been a fiction.

39. Grimod, *Almanach*, 8:61; qtd. in Garval, "Grimod de la Reynière's *Almanach des gourmands*," 55.

40. Humelbergius, *Apician Morsels*, 177.

41. Grimod, *Almanach*, 7:31; qtd. in Garval, "Grimod de la Reynière's *Almanach des gourmands*," 53.

42. See my chapter on Sturgeon in *Gusto*, forthcoming.

43. Sturgeon, *Essays*, 3–4.

44. Ibid., 9–10.

45. Ibid., 5–6. On the Roman origins of *Ab ovo usque ad mala*, see Kitchiner, *Cook's Oracle*, 28.

46. Sturgeon, *Essays*, 2–3, 6.

47. As Trubek writes, this may be "the most important innovation of the restaurant and the à la carte menus: an individual, regardless of social class, has the chance to eat like a king"; *Haute Cuisine*, 37. Unlike the wealthy Parisian Grimod, Brillat-Savarin was a self-made lawyer from the provincial town of Belley and a successful bourgeois financier of the French Restoration; see Giles MacDonough, *Brillat-Savarin: The Judge and His Stomach* (London: John Murray, 1992).

48. Regenia Gagnier, *Idylls of the Marketplace: Oscar Wilde and the Victorian Public* (Stanford: Stanford University Press, 1986), 139.

49. Davidoff and Hall, *Family Fortunes*, 21.

50. John P. Frazee, "George IV and Jos Sedley in *Vanity Fair*," *English Language Notes* 19:2 (1981): 122–28 (123).

51. Joanna Richardson, *George the Magnificent,* 49.

52. Joseph Litvak, *Strange Gourmets: Sophistication, Theory, and the Novel* (Durham: Duke University Press, 1997), 56. The new aristocracy of taste was cultured rather than hereditary, based on a more "knowing" mode of consumption, and Jos Sedley strikes certain readers as an embodiment of consumer capitalism. Christoph Lindner, for example, reads "this gourmand's complete inability to control, limit or even inhibit the compulsion to consume" as a symbol for nineteenth-century commodity culture, which "profiles the psychology of a compulsive consumer of material goods"; *Fictions of Commodity Culture: From the Victorian to the Postmodern* (Burlington, Vt.: Ashgate Press, 2003), 51.

53. As George Walden writes, "Dandyism in its essence is not a homosexual condition. The confusion however is natural. Homosexuals can be and frequently are dandies, but their sexuality is an adjunct, rather than at the centre, of the dandy's creed"; *Who Is a Dandy?* (London: Gibson Square Books, 2002), 45.

54. Parissien, *George IV,* 171.

55. Arthur Wellesley Wellington, letter of April 10, 1830; *Wellington and His Friends: Letters of the First Duke of Wellington to the Rt. Hon. Charles and Mrs. Arbuthnot, the Earl and Countess of Wilton, Princess Lieven, and Miss Burdett-Coutts,* ed. by the seventh Duke of Wellington (London: Macmillan, 1965), 90; George IV died on June 26, 1830.

56. Quoted in Parissien, *George IV,* 171.

57. Most economic and social historians remark that nineteenth-century England was "a period of conspicuous expenditure and social imitation such as had never been seen before," as "landed gentry, formerly the sole exemplars of taste and fashion, now found that position being challenged by the 'new rich'; anxious to demonstrate that humble origins did not imply a lack of culture and refinement." Burnett, *Plenty and Want,* 66. McCracken similarly argues that there was no "consumer boom" in nineteenth-century Britain, because by this time consumerism had installed itself as the organizing structure of social life; individuals now found themselves increasingly reliant on the symbolic language of goods "to accommodate themselves to a perilous and liquid world"; *Culture and Consumption,* 22, 29.

58. Burnett, *Plenty and Want,* 66–67.

59. Mennell, *All Manners of Food,* 213.

60. Burnett, *Plenty and Want,* 67 (and following) provides details upon which I rely in this paragraph.

61. Kitchiner, *Cook's Oracle,* 32.

62. Quoted in Mennell, *All Manners of Food,* 145.

63. Charles Dickens, *Our Mutual Friend,* ed. by Adrian Poole (New York: Penguin, 1997), 17.

64. Wolfgang Fritz Haug, *Critique of Commodity Aesthetics: Appearance, Sexuality, and Advertising in Capitalist Society,* trans. by Robert Bock (Cambridge, Mass.: Polity Press, 1971), 16.

65. Consumer goods valued principally for exchange value "helped to conceal the status origins of their owners and to this extent encouraged mobility." McCracken, *Culture and Consumption,* 21.

66. Andrew H. Miller, *Novels Behind Glass: Commodity Culture and Victorian Narrative* (Cambridge: Cambridge University Press, 1995), 25.

67. Dickens, *Our Mutual Friend,* 17.

68. Marx, *Capital,* 1:163–64, 125.

69. Dickens, *Our Mutual Friend,* 135.

70. On Victorian taste associated with "the ugly, the ornate, and the inorganic," see Jerome Hamilton Buckley, *The Victorian Temper: A Study in Literary Culture* (Cambridge, Mass.: Harvard University Press, 1969), 142.

71. Marx, *Capital,* 2:208.

Index

9 780300 172249